A SCIENTIST'S AND ENGINEER'S GUIDE TO WORKSTATIONS AND SUPERCOMPUTERS

A SCIENTIST'S AND ENGINEER'S GUIDE TO WORKSTATIONS AND SUPERCOMPUTERS

Coping with Unix™, RISC, vectors, and programming

RUBIN H. LANDAU
Department of Physics
Oregon State University
Corvallis, Oregon

PAUL J. FINK, JR.
Thinking Machines Corporation
Cambridge, Massachusetts

A Wiley-Interscience Publication
JOHN WILEY & SONS, INC.
New York · Chichester · Brisbane · Toronto · Singapore

Copyright ©1993 by John Wiley & Sons, Inc.

Library of Congress Cataloging in Publication Data:

Landau, Rubin H.
A scientist's and engineer's guide to workstations and
supercomputers: coping with Unix, RISC, Vectors, and programming/
Rubin H. Landau, Paul J. Fink, Jr.
      p. cm.
      Includes index.
      ISBN 0-471-53271-1 (paper)
      1. Microcomputer workstations. 2. Supercomputers. 3. Computer
software. I. Fink, Paul J., 1954- . II. Title.
QA76.5.L3224 1992
004'.0245–dc20   92-19556

*To scientists, engineers, and students who need and
love to use computers to get their work done;
especially our cohorts Guangliang, Jeff, and Milt*

CONTENTS

CHAPTER 3   **WORKSTATION SETUP AND USE 47**

CHAPTER 4   **COMPUTER-COMPUTER INTERACTIONS 77**

II   TOOLS

CHAPTER 10   **UNIX TOOLS AND TIPS 225**

III TECHNIQUES FOR POWER USERS

CHAPTER 14 PARALLEL COMPUTING 325

PREFACE

Okay, so now you have read the title page and covers to this book and you are asking yourself, "What are a couple of physicists doing writing a book about computers?" You are not alone; we, too, have knocked that one around many times over the last three years. As we see it, the answer is that the computer systems and techniques discussed in this book are our tools of trade, and while we may not care about these tools for their own sake as much as a computer scientist, we have a vested interest in using them to advance science and engineering. In other words, we are writing this book to help increase the creativity, productivity, and effectiveness of people who do technical computing on workstations, supercomputers, or both. We think it's mandatory to incorporate this new technology and knowledge into all areas of science and engineering in order to meet the *Grand Challenges* of the 1990s.

In many ways, the question of tools is fundamental because tools not only influence the work we do, but increasingly define that work, as well as our identity as scientists. Indeed, many Nobel prizes in science are awarded for developing and applying new tools. Our interest in new tools is not just because they are new and fashionable; we personally find profound enjoyment in doing real-world science with computing tools, are fascinated by their use as intellectual levers for our creative work, and just can't help talking about them (or, in this case, writing about them).

One of us (PJF) developed and supported Unix systems at the University of Minnesota, Oregon State University, and the IBM T. J. Watson Research Center, as well as conducted thesis research in computational physics. The other one of us has been doing theoretical nuclear and particle physics research using computers for the last 25 years (the last decade on Unix machines) and helped develop and teaches a computational physics course at Oregon State University. We became convinced of the need for this sort of book as a consequence of our work and travels. We found ourselves continually in contact with students and colleagues who wanted to know what we knew about computing scientifically within a Unix working environment.

To be honest, this book is somewhat of a *Coping Guide* because we all know there is no such thing as a free lunch. Even though Unix may not truly challenge your intelligence, you must exert effort and thought to make use of all its power and flexibility. In common with the Alaskan Malemute, it is an intelligent and powerful animal which knows its own mind and is best handled by an owner with at least equal intelligence; but, not unlike the Irish Water Spaniel, once you have had one, you will have no other.

Because we started working on this book before workstations were popular, we had to convince our publisher of the need for it as well as the notion that, in the future, much technical computing would be conducted on networked workstations and supercomputers (our style of working). As our writing project concludes, there are workstations surrounding us. We also have a greater appreciation of how little can be done in one book. We see much more clearly the widespread need for entire courses of study in computational science, including computer science, mathematics, science, and engineering.

Although this book should be useful to a beginner, it is not a Unix manual. Instead, our goal is to present a guide for coping with the complexities of accomplishing an entire scientific computing project from start to finish predominantly under a Unix operating system. More specifically, we aim to assist technical people in writing and organizing files and programs, as well as running, debugging, and visualizing the results of scientific programs. Our philosophy is one of simplicity and survival: don't try to master every aspect of every available command and utility, but first learn the minimum that you need to get your work done and then pick up more as you become familiar with the tools. In keeping with this philosophy, we think it important not to be a computational bigot who can live with only one system (or version of Unix), detesting all others to the extent that he or she loses effectiveness or composure when having to deal with them. We try to show how to make use of widely available tools to help get your work done, even if it means working on more than one computer or computer system.

A book such as this could be used as a text for a one-term introductory class on scientific computing using Unix. If the course includes laboratory work (programming of RISC, vector, and parallel computers with visualization), we suspect the students would find a second term useful. Alternatively, for an audience familiar with scientific computing in general, this book could be used in a several-day workshop or tutorial or as a reference. For those of you who already know Unix, we think this book will acquaint you with some new or different techniques and computing environments, as well as serving as a reference for available tools and their options.

We try throughout to provide examples and tutorials to lead the reader-and-terminal duo from simple, and then more complex, exercises. One format we use is a computer dialog that looks like this:

```
System says.  User commands.                    Our comments.
```

The first field, in monospaced font, is the computer speaking. The second field, in **bold monospaced font**, is the user commanding. The last field, in small font, is for cryptic comments by the authors. Here is an example:

```
gnuplot>  plot "data.graph"                    Plot data in file data.graph.
```

We have tried to avoid the temptation to tell the reader everything there is to know about every command or application because this is an approach which often makes computer manuals opaque. Instead, we present examples and concise tables of definitions or options, and then refer the reader to the man pages on the computer for more details (on the theory that it's easier to find something when you know what you're looking for).

We use a second format throughout the book for definitions. A sample is:

<u>**OPTIONS**</u>

-align *name*   Align COMMON *name* on page boundaries.

-c   Compile and make `.o` files, do not link.

You see that there is an underlined title line in capitals, the item to be defined is in **bold print** on the left, and the definition on the right. When there is a word the user should supply as an option, we write that word in *italics*.

The third format we use is a box to encapsulate fragments of code:

```
/* Sample C Program Fragment with includes */     Search /usr/include.
# include <stdlib.h>                               Search user's library.
# include "mylibe.h"
```

The code is in `monospaced font on the left` and our comments are in small font on the right.

When examining the sample command and code fragments given in this book, please be aware that sometimes we fought a losing battle with the margins. In some cases this meant leaving out spaces whose inclusion would have increased clarity; in other cases it meant using variable names which were too truncated to be self-explanatory; and in yet other cases it meant continuing the command to the next line. As a consequence, you will sometimes see the backslash character \ at the end of a line, which acts as a continuation character for Unix commands and C code, or a number in column 6 for Fortran code. In general we advise you the user to keep the command or code on one line.

We have organized this book into three parts. Part I is *Getting Started*, Part II, *Tools*, and Part III is *Techniques for Power Users*. This is based on our experience with workstations: all the great features of the machine are worthless until you get the system working just right for you. Particularly if you have to personally manage and customize your workstation, or do not have a consultant to help you, you will probably want to plan to spend extra time in Part I. If you are just learning Unix, then Chapters 2, *Getting Friendly with Unix*, and 10, *Unix Tools*, serve as a Unix manual. If you need to transfer programs to or from your computer, then you will probably find Chapter 4, *Computer–Computer Interactions*, helpful. If your workstation has the X Window System, we think you'll find that working your way through Chapter 5, *Looking Through X Windows*, will be enjoyable, fruitful, and much less painful than the official X manuals.

In Part II we get down to the business of tools: graphical and visualization applications, the Fortran and C compilers and their options, and associated Unix tools. As is also true for the other parts of the book, we try to not limit ourselves to one version of Unix or one manufacturer's machine. (We have tried out the commands on every computer we could get our networked hands on: Suns, IBMs, HPs, DECs, Crays, IBM/3090s, IBM/ES9000's, PCs, Macintoshes, and obsolete Ridges.) When differences occur, such as in the more specific compiler options, we note those which are machine specific. We suspect even the experienced user will find something of use in Part II—although it will also be accessible to the novice who has read Part I.

The material in Part III, *Techniques for Power Users*, is something all computational scientists may find interesting. Chapter 11, *Scientific Programming Hints*, is more properly the subject for a semester- or year-long course than just one chapter. For this reason we call it *Hints* hoping that the reader has studied the subject thoroughly. For those of you who like to know how the computer works before turning it on, Chapter 12, *RISC and Supercomputer Architectures*, might be a good beginning for you because it describes just that. In line with the operational nature of this book, we have decided to put these intellectual concerns off until later in the book when they become essential in the programming of RISC workstations and supercomputers. Appropriately, then, Part III ends with discussions of programming vector and parallel supercomputers. Even if you are not going to be doing that type of programming, we think you'll find the chapters interesting because they help explain what this type of computing is all about.

Appendix A gives a number of *dot files*, that is, files we have found useful in customizing Unix and making it more friendly to a working scientist. If you want to use these files, you can also find them on the floppy disk included with this book. (It is a DOS floppy and so you may want to read Chapter 4 to see how to read it into your system, and then read the README file on the floppy for directions and table of contents.) The floppy also contains a number of the small programs and data files discussed in the book. Appendices B and C give sample Fortran runs tuned specifically to RISC, vector, and parallel computers. In Appendix D we provide a glossary of terms which you may find handy throughout the book, and after that, our References grouped by subject.

Just as the only bug-free program is a dead one, we are bound to have erred in this book. We anticipate the need to receive and convey information between authors and readers. For that purpose, we have set up an electronic mail account guide where we can be reached. There will also be an updated floppy accessible via anonymous **ftp** in the directory /pub/guide.

guide@physics.orst.edu	Mail address.
physics.orst.edu	Account for anonymous **ftp**.
128.193.96.01	Equivalent anonymous **ftp** account.

You should be able to **ftp** into physics and find information about the book in pub/guide. (Examples of anonymous **ftp** are given in Chapter 4.)

This book was written by us in LaTeX. We created a Wiley style-file for this purpose, and it is included on the floppy and in the files available via anonymous **ftp**. Bob Hilbert, the production editor at Wiley Interscience, supervised the final page makeup. The figures were prepared on an IBM RS/6000 workstation with *idraw* and *xwd*, or from the specific graphical packages under discussion. A script for our use of *xwd* is also included on the floppy. The manuscript was written on computers including Ridge 32, IBM RT, IBM RS, Sun Sparcstation, Macintosh (512, Plus, and SE), Panasonic laptop DOS, and Toshiba laptop DOS. The chapters were transferred among these machines and across the country on a nearly daily basis. We used appropriate editors for each machine, including *vi, Emacs, QED*, and *WordPerfect*.

We compiled this book, when there was nothing quite like it, to help us and our friends and colleagues. We are proud of our creation and hope it contributes to the development of computational science. Nevertheless, the basic material we have assembled is predominantly the fruits of other people's labors, and consequently we are deeply indebted to those who have created the materials and to those who put us in contact with it and taught us how to use it. It is our particular pleasure to acknowledge the help and materials of Angelo Rossi, Guangliang He, Milton Sagen, Jeff Schnick, Henri Jansen, Tim Mefford, Greg Merkel, Viktor Decyk, and the students who sat through our classes in computational physics and Unix.

We wish to acknowledge financial and equipment support from the U.S. Department of Energy, the IBM Corporation, and Oregon State University, and the hospitality of many people at IBM Research and the National Institute for Nuclear Theory, Seattle. We are particularly grateful to Angelo Rossi, Jordan Becker, Linda Emtman, and Don Abbott for their assistance and good will. Without them the book may not have been written. A special thanks to members of the Marineland and Farm projects at T. J. Watson especially Barry Appelman, Marc Donner, Steve Hiemlich, Scott Kennedy, Bill Moran, and Jacob Parnas. Thanks also goes to the staff at Wiley-Interscience for their encouragement, support, and wisdom. In particular, it has been our pleasure to work with Maria Taylor, Bob Hilbert, Greg Franklin, Maggie Irwin, Lisa Hockstein, and Kate Roach.

Finally, we wish to express our gratitude to our wives, Jan and Anita. They have been a constant source of friendship, understanding, and support during the writing of this book—even while being shamefully neglected themselves. Any assistance in proofreading was service beyond the call of marital duty—but offered, and accepted, lovingly.

RUBIN H. LANDAU

Corvallis, Oregon

PAUL J. FINK JR

Carmel, New York

This above all, —to thine own self be true;
And it must follow, as the night the day,
Thou canst not then be false to any man.
Farewell: my blessing season this in thee!

—Shakespeare, *Hamlet* I.III

A SCIENTIST'S AND ENGINEER'S GUIDE TO WORKSTATIONS AND SUPERCOMPUTERS

PART I

GETTING STARTED

## CHAPTER 1

INTRODUCTION

... Then at the balance let's be mute,
we never can adjust it;
What's done we partly may compute,
But know not what's resisted.

—Robert Burns

1.1   The Nature of Computational Science

Computational science is a developing field in which computers help solve problems whose difficulty or complexity places them beyond analytic solution or human endurance. Sometimes the computer serves as a super calculating machine, sometimes as a laboratory for numerical simulation of complex systems, sometimes as a lever for our intellectual abilities, and optimally as all of the above. In computational science, we explore the unknown with the aim of understanding and investigating nature, mathematical models, and mathematics at depths greater than otherwise possible.

Computational science's real interest is science, and the aim of this book is to help scientists and engineers compute. Computational scientists stand in contradistinction to "computer scientists," who study computing for its own intrinsic interest and who develop the hardware and software tools computational scientists use. This difference is not just semantic or academic. Our interest is in actually doing research and development in science and engineering, and our values, prejudices, tools, organizations, goals, and measures of success reflect that interest. As an example of the difference between the two, a procedure which a computational scientist may consider reliable, self explanatory, and easy to port to laboratories throughout the world may appear awkward and inelegant to a computer scientist.

Computational science draws together people from many disciplines via a commonality of technique, approach, and philosophy. You must know a good deal from many areas in order to be successful. But since the same tools are used for many problems in different fields, you are not limited to one specialty area. So a study of computational science helps broaden horizons—an exception to the stifling subspecialization found in so much of science.

Traditionally, science is divided into experimental and theoretical approaches; computational science requires the skills of both and contributes to both. Transforming a theory into an algorithm requires significant theoretical insight, detailed physical and mathematical understanding, and mastery of the art of programming. The actual debugging, testing, and organization of scientific codes is much like experiment. Throughout the entire process, the synthesis of numbers into generalizations, predictions, and conclusions requires the insight and intuition common to both experimental and theoretical science. As visualization techniques advance, computational science enters into and uses psychology and art; this too makes good science because it reveals the beauty contained within our theoretical picture of nature and permits us to use the well-developed visual processing capabilities of our brains to better see our discipline.

How Computational Scientists Do It

A computational scientist uses computers in a number of distinct ways, with new ways not necessarily eliminating old ones.

- Classically in science and engineering, a problem was formulated and solved as much as possible analytically, and then the computer was used to determine numerical solutions to some equations or to evaluate some hideously complicated functions. In many cases, computing was considered a minor part of the project with little, if any, discussion of technique or error.

- Now a computational scientist formulates and plans the solution of a problem with the computer and program libraries as active collaborators. Use is made of past analytic and numerical advances during all stages of work. And, as the need arises, new analytic and numeric studies are undertaken.

- In a different, yet now also classical approach, computers play a key role from the start by *simulating* the laws of nature. In these programs, the computer responds to input data as might a natural system to different initial conditions. Examples are the computer tracing of rays through an optical system and the numerical generation of random numbers to simulate the radioactive decay of nuclei.

- A modern use of computers is to perform symbolic manipulations as one might analytically. Programs such as *Mathematica, Maple, Macsyma,* and *Reduce* make such extensions possible.

- One of the most pleasing uses of computers is to *visualize* the results of calculations in a graphical or pictorial form. This may encompass two- and three-dimensional plots, color shading, geometric modeling, and animation. Visualization assists the debugging process, the development of physical and mathematical intuition, and the enjoyment of your work. We discuss it in Part III of this book.

- Finally, many applications developed for business uses with personal computers have value in computational science as well. For example, a numerical *spreadsheet* is a helpful way to analyze data as well as the results of calculations, and *hypertext* is a true advance in storing various types of information which may well replace the lab notebook and the research paper.

When you consider all the things a computational scientist may want to do or may be doing, it makes computational science a hard field for us to define. It is, nevertheless, a challenging and rewarding one in which to work. Even while first learning how to use computers as part of your science, you will be rewarded for your hours of hack work at a keyboard and screen by finding yourself understanding nature or devices at a level previously encountered only after years of research. And throughout your career, you will savor the pleasures of discovery and creativity right before your eyes.

In this book we try to assist your work in computational science by helping you learn to create a work environment which blends many useful computer applications. High-performance scientific computing is not one thing, but rather a balance of hardware, software, numerics, science, visualization, and operating system. While bundles of this sort have been available for business users from major manufacturers like DEC, IBM, and HP, they have not previously been available for scientists and engineers. As we hope to show, Unix and its associated use of TCP/IP for communications, the X Windows System for interfaces, and newly-improved graphical packages can provide you with the needed transparent, multiple-windowed working environment. By taking advantage of some of the Unix tools to help you prepare good and portable codes, you finish off the package and attain a useful, fun and effective work environment.

1.2   How Computers Do It

During your regular coping with computers, you'll want to keep in mind that computers do exactly as they are told. They are incredibly error free, but they must be told everything they have to do. This means that when you run a program, there should be no mystery to the results; the computer did just what you told it to do, and you can figure out what it did just by reading the program. Of course, the program may be so complicated and have so many logical paths that you may not have the endurance to figure it out in detail. But if you can maintain the attitude that you are in control, no matter how illusionary, you'll usually be able to figure out at least what path the computer took.

Life is not simple for computers. The instructions it understands are in a *basic machine language* which tells the hardware to do things like move a number stored in some memory location to another location, or do some simple, binary arithmetic.[1] Hardly any computational scientist really talks to the computer in its machine language. We interact with our computers through a program known as a *shell* and by writing our programs in a *high level language*. Eventually these commands or programs all get translated to the basic machine language.

A *shell*, or *the command line interpreter*, is a set of medium level commands or small programs, run by a computer. While every general-purpose computer will have some type of shell, usually each computer system has its own set of commands which constitute its shell. It is the shell's job to run various programs—the compilers, linkage editors, utilities—as well as the users' programs. There can be different types of shells on a single computer, or multiple copies of the same shell running at the same time for different users. It is useful to think of these shells as the outer layers of the computer's *operating system*. The nucleus of the operating system is called, appropriately, the *kernel*. The user does not usually interact directly with the kernel.

---

[1] The *BASIC* programming language should not be confused with *basic machine language*.

The operating system is the group of instructions used by the computer to communicate with users and devices, to store and read data, and to execute programs. The operating system itself is just a bunch of programs which tell the computer what to do. It views you, other devices, and programs as input data for it to process; in many ways it is the indispensable office manager. While all this may seem unnecessarily complicated, its purpose is to make life easier for you by letting the computer do much of the nitty-gritty work so you can think higher level thoughts and communicate with the computer in something closer to your normal, everyday language. Operating systems have names like *Unix, VMS, MVS, DOS*, and *COS*.

For the purposes of this book, we will be assuming that you are using a *compiled* high level language like *Fortran, C,* or *Pascal*, in contrast to an *interpreted* one like *Basic*. In a compiled language, the computer translates an entire subprogram into basic machine instructions all at one time. In an interpretive language, the translation is done one statement at a time. We prefer compiled languages since they lead to more efficient programs, permit the use of vast libraries of subprograms, and tend to be more portable because they are less machine dependent.

When you submit a program to your computer in a high level language, the computer runs a *compiler* to process it. The compiler is another program that treats your program as a foreign language and uses a built-in dictionary and set of rules to translate it into basic machine language.[2] As you can imagine, the final set of instructions are quite detailed and long, and the compiler may make several passes through your program to decipher your logic and do an optimal job at translating it. The translated statements form an *object code*, and when *linked together* with other needed subprograms, form a *load module*. A load module is a complete set of machine language instructions which can be *loaded* into the computer's memory and followed by the computer. At last!

1.3   History of Workstations and Supercomputers

Computers have been changing so quickly in terms of speed and capability that any specific details we give regarding their speeds and memories are bound to become obsolete in a period of years or even months. As indicated in Table 1.1, computer technology has changed so rapidly that we have actually passed through several paradigms in the last three decades. In fact, we are still somewhat awestruck at seeing workstations on the desks of scientists and engineers that are more powerful than the computers used by universities for computational science when the authors were in graduate school. However, therein lies a challenge—to maintain a level of scientific creativity and advancement commensurate with the ever-growing power of these new computers. One of our aims in writing this book is to help scientific users meet that challenge.

In the dark ages of the late 1960s, laboratory and university computing was often done on a central, *mainframe* computer. Typically, users submitted their *jobs* to the *batch queue* by literally submitting a deck of IBM punchcards held together by rubber bands or stuffed into a box. The decks and printed output came back in a matter of hours or days. The user often found he or she had mispunched a character, had to punch new cards, and begin the laborious process of running the program again. By the early 1970s, *time sharing* and *remote job entry* stations became available, and it was possible to electronically edit and

---

[2]If you feel yourself getting lost in jargon, there are definitions in the *Glossary* to help you find your way.

Table 1.1: Four Paradigms of Computing (from Tesler (1991))

	Batch	Time Sharing	Desktop	Network
Decade:	1960s	1970s	1980s	1990s
Integration:	Medium	Large	Very large	Ultra
Location:	Computer building	Terminal room	Desktop	Mobile
Users:	Experts	Specialists	Individuals	Groups
User status:	Subservient	Dependent	Independent	Free
Data:	Alpha–numeric	Text, vector	Fonts, graphs	Script, voice
Language:	Cobol, Fortran	PL1, BASIC	Pascal, C	Object oriented
Objective:	Calculate	Access	Present	Communicate
User activity:	Punch & submit	Remember & type	See & point	Ask & tell
Operation:	Process	Edit	Layout	Orchestrate
Application :	Custom	Standard	Generic	Components

submit jobs. Sometimes, if you worked when no one else was around, you could feel the excitement of the computer's immediate response—as if you had something personal and special going on between just you and it.

The increased access permitted by this advancing technology tended to overload the available computing resource. It became nearly impossible to get work done on a weekday afternoon (mid-afternoon brown-out). A solution found in the mid-1970s was the *minicomputer*, typified by the DEC *VAX*. This was a respectable computing machine which was inexpensive enough for a department or group to purchase and *distribute* throughout an institution. By providing computing resources without overwhelming hourly charges these minicomputers led to a revolutionary increase in computer use. *Personal* or *micro* computers were also becoming popular, but with only limited use for scientific computation. At the same time, *supercomputers* with their high speeds, vector processing, large memories, and large storage capacities were being manufactured. But their access was limited.

Enter Unix

By the mid-1980s, two advances changed the computing picture: workstations and networks. The development of the *workstation* (or *mini mainframe*, or *supermicro*) provided the power of the VAX at a price which small groups or individuals could afford. As a break from the proprietary operating systems of the time, all workstations employed versions of *Unix*.

Accompanying this increase in available computing power, *graphical user interfaces* (GUI) and relatively high resolution video displays were developed (although they were not as good as those available on video games and on personal computers, both of which had entered the consumer electronics marketplace). The graphical development for workstations, on the one hand, congealed around *The X Window System* developed at MIT, and, on the other hand, extended itself to specialized *graphical workstations*. The graphical workstations had the capacity to render three-dimensional pictures of molecules, surfaces, and the like. They symbolized the change in computing from just number crunching to visualizations, that is, producing output our brains could readily see and understand.

The *Unix* operating system was originally developed by AT&T's Bell Laboratories for internal purposes, in particular, for easy development of computer systems. It has proven to be of major importance for computational science. If your computer runs Unix, you have a high capability to connect your computer to hardware (such as terminals, printers, plotters, disks, and so forth) made by other companies. Freeing users from the tyranny of one manufacturer completely revolutionized computing and gave users with limited means the opportunity to create an environment suited to their needs, but flexible enough to accommodate changes in technology. In addition, once a user learned how to compute on one Unix workstation, transporting programs and knowledge to other workstations became straightforward. In fact, by the mid-1980s, the value of the *universality* of Unix was recognized to a point where manufacturers of mainframes and supercomputers were making them available with Unix operating systems (yet hiding the fact and respecting the copyright by using names like *UNICOS* and *ULTRIX*).

The second major advance that changed the computing picture of the 1980s was the development of computer networks. Unix became the platform for much of the early work in computer–computer communications and network development. Unix was available on many machines and it was being distributed as source code to universities who then could modify and extend it. Unix became synonymous with *distributed computing* and helped make the 1980s a decade in which central, mainframe computing lost importance to the concept that said "the network is the computer." Rather than having isolated *compute servers*, Unix made possible a sharing (whether intended or not) of printers, tape drives, hard disks, and central processing unit (CPU) cycles. Users could sit at one machine and use the resources of others as if all were local. While the workstations of the 1980s were considerably less powerful than their mainframe cousins, they assumed an important place in computational science because of their ability to share resources, to provide unlimited distributed computing time, and to grow or change incrementally.

Once machines started communicating efficiently, it was not long before users were also communicating. Networks to send mail, talk, and exchange files became popular. Initially this was based on the simple modem–to–modem protocol uucp, but soon changed to TCP/IP. This *usenet* grew to a point where large parts of North America, Europe, Australia, and Japan were interconnected. In North America, this network was free to most users, and when combined with the ethic of the free exchange of ideas, led to a policy of sharing programs and help which is firmly entrenched in the Unix world. In a personal and practical sense, this permitted a lowly undergraduate in the cosmic ray lab at the University of Minnesota to put questions on the network which were answered by a Unix expert from Berkeley or to find Pace Willisson's *ispell* program on almost every Unix implementation (which is nice, since spelling is still not this author's strong point).

Thanks to the foresight and support of the federal funding agencies in North America and Europe, the mid-1980s also brought supercomputing to the masses. The number of supercomputer centers increased (they became somewhat of a status symbol for any self-respecting university) and free, high-speed networks which connected these centers to many universities and laboratories were established. Accordingly, we now are at the stage where a workstation is used to write and debug a program, a supercomputer is used for the *production runs* or to mass produce output for visualization, and the workstation is used again to examine the output. This process becomes even simpler if the supercomputer is operating under a Unix system, because you can just open a window on the terminal connected to the supercomputer and use essentially the same commands and procedures as you use on your workstation.

At the time we write this book, the boundary between the power of personal computer and workstation, and between workstation and supercomputer, is becoming blurred. While this is not a bad thing, we must admit some sadness at seeing the advance of technology without a commensurate advance in meeting the scientific grand challenges. We see the time rapidly approaching when there will be a desktop supercomputer on most scientists' and engineers' desks with not enough knowing how to write programs for it.

Initials; Their Machines and Advocates

As mentioned previously, an *operating system* is a group of programs used by a computer to communicate with people and devices and to execute programs. The Unix operating system permits many users to be "on" the computer at one time (*multiuser*), as well as permitting any one user to run many jobs apparently all at one time (*multitasking*). Unix is an incredibly complete set of small utility programs (a veritable, virtual *tool box*) from which very complicated and powerful tasks can be constructed. While it takes some learning to be able to use these commands, they do give an isolated workstation user a wealth of standard tools previously available only at larger central computing facilities.

Two major versions of Unix have evolved: *System V*, AT&T's own version, and *BSD*, Berkeley Standard Unix, a modification made at the University of California, Berkeley. The Unix system itself is usually written in C, a portable, high level programming language, and then compiled.[3]

Many computer manufacturers install Unix on their computers but use a different name (usually ending in *x*). There are, for example, AUX, ULTRIX, AIX, and UNICOS. To differing extents, modern Unix systems are combinations of System V and BSD, although the Unix on most university computer science department machines tends to be BSD. As we write this book, there are efforts being made to standardize and unify the various flavors of Unix. So far this has led to a host of new two-letter-plus-x acronyms and much confusion. Virtually all Unix implementations support either the BSD or System V command sets or both. Once you become familiar with both (and they are very similar), you should be able to work on any Unix system. We have, in fact, tried out most of the commands and programs in this book on several systems and will try to give alternative formulations (or maybe just warnings) when things differ.

The differences among Unix's can be real and really frustrating, but the similarities far outweigh the differences. A scientist's or engineer's interests are served best by being able to work with different Unix's. Because much modern computing is done over networks connecting a number of machines, it is likely that a number of Unix's will be connected together, and you may actually end up working with a number of Unix's all at one time! As we indicate in Chapter 3, *Workstation Setup and Use*, with just a little work it is possible to customize your working environment so that it looks the same under different Unix's; anyway, confusion is the first step towards understanding.

---

[3] Do not confuse C *language* with the Unix command line interpreter, C *shell*. While the similarity in names is confusing, it is a small price to pay for a good pun.

1.4   Programming

Even with a perfect set of physical laws, a perfect algorithm, and a perfect computer, there still remains the challenge of *programming*.[4] We view programming as a written art which blends elements of science, mathematics, and computer science into a set of instructions in order for the computer to accomplish a scientific goal (say, generating the cross section for the scattering of an electron from a krypton atom). Sooner or later, if you try to do something new or different enough, you will have to write your own programs. As computational scientists who place a high value on collaboration with other people, as well as making contributions to the development of science and engineering, we think the *aims* of programming are programs which:

- Give the correct answers.

- Are simple and easy to read, making the action of each part clear and easy to analyze.

- Documents themselves so that the programmer and others understand what the programs are doing.

- Are easy to use.

- Are easy and safe to modify for different computers or systems.

- Can be passed on to others to use and further develop.

Chapter 11's *Scientific Programming Hints* strive to convert these aims into code. Before you get lost in other details or decide to skip that chapter, let us stress that the lack of program readability leads to credibility problems and the stifling of creativity for computational science. It is in our own interests to follow some of the developments of computer science and write clearer programs. After all, ours is a creative and realistic field which makes our programs complicated and ever evolving. The program is the ultimate documentation of a computational science project.

Is Fortran for the Birds?

> *I think conventional languages are for the birds. They're really low-level languages. They're just extensions of the von Neumann computer, and they keep our noses pressed in the dirt of dealing with individual words and computing addresses, and doing all kinds of silly things like that, things that we've picked up from programming for computers; we've built them into programming languages; we've built them into FORTRAN; we've built them into PL/I; we've built them into almost every language. The only languages that broke free from that are LISP and APL, and in my opinion they haven't gone far enough.*
>
> —John Backus, *co-author of Fortran.*[5]

Until recently, Fortran was the standard choice for most scientific applications. It was portable and reliable, most computer systems support Fortran with well-tested and optimized compilers, and it was the only language available on supercomputers. Although

---

[4]An algorithm is a set of rules for getting the mathematics done.
[5]Wexelblat (1981).

excellent for teaching how to program in a structured manner, Pascal seemed too restrictive for scientific applications.

With the rise of the Unix operating system written in C, the C language has become very popular. It is being applied to an ever increasing number of scientific problems, and sometimes is the only scientific language taught by computer science departments. On the one hand, C is powerful since it allows for a lot of programming freedom. On the other hand, it is easy to misuse C. It demands good programming practices and it is more difficult to write scientific code in C than in Fortran, at least for a beginning programmer. At present, much parallel programming is done in a version of C, and some supercomputers support C (although the compilers are not yet very efficient, and subprogram libraries are not yet available on a number of them). Applications in C^{++}, with its stronger emphasis on object-oriented programming, are still few in number.

As you can see, this book is written in English (or at least our best shot at it). Now, some of us do not particularly care for English or find it easy to use, and if it became our turn, we might try to write a new language that was easier to use. Yet as witnessed by our great works of literature, English more than suffices as a language, and we suspect our shortcomings in usage are probably due more to our weaknesses than to those of the language.

Fortran is much the same, but it is in some ways better. There are many important programs and subroutines written in Fortran, it is the standard throughout the world, and it is used on the largest supercomputers as well as on many personal computers. Many computer scientists do not care for its old fashioned structure, and so will teach only C. When we do use Fortran, we inherit many sophisticated programs and libraries which make it is easier for us to get on with our business of doing and applying science. Furthermore, the enhancements present in *Fortran 90* come a long way towards adding the needed structure and constructs for modern parallel programming.

In Chapter 11's *Scientific Programming Hints* we discuss ways to make your programming adhere to modern practices. In Chapters 12–14 we discuss modern extensions to Fortran and C which make them applicable to computers with advanced *vector, pipelined,* and *parallel* architectures. In all cases, we will stick with Fortran and C as our working languages even though most of what we have to say would work just as well with other compiled languages.

1.5 How Computers Really Do It

Representing Numbers

Computers can be made powerful, but they remain finite. A consequence of this is that a number is stored in a finite amount of space, and so in general the representation of a number in a computer's memory is an approximation! To understand more fully what we mean, remember that the digits 0, and 1 are the microscopic units of memory. It is no great surprise, then, that all numbers are ultimately represented in *binary* form. Correspondingly, if an integer is represented with the N bits, $n_1 n_2 ... n_N$, each bit n_i is either 0 or 1, there are only 2^N integers that can be so represented. Since the sign of the integer is represented by the first bit ($0 \Rightarrow +$), this leaves the remaining $N - 1$ bits to represent *integers* in the range $[0, 2^{N-1}]$. Thus, we already see a limitation.

Long strings of 0's and 1's are fine for computers, but they are rather boring and hard for us to remember. Usually binary strings are converted to the *octal, decimal,* or *hexadecimal* number system before results are communicated to people. Octal and hexadecimal numbers are nice since the conversion loses no precision, even though our decimal rules of arithmetic do not work with them. Converting to our old friend the decimal numbers does makes the numbers easier for us to work with, but also decreases the precision.

A description of a particular computer system will normally state the number of bits used to store a number (also called *word length*). Since big numbers tend to scare people, this word length is often expressed in *bytes* (abbreviated "B") where

$$1\,\text{byte} = 8\,\text{bits} \tag{1.1}$$

Conventionally, storage size is measured in bytes B or kilobytes KB. Be careful. Not everyone means the same thing by a thousand:

$$1\,\text{K} \equiv 1\,\text{KB} = 2^{10}\,\text{bytes} = 1024\,\text{bytes} \tag{1.2}$$

This is often (and confusingly) compensated for when memory size is stated, for example:

$$512\,\text{K} = 2^{19}\,\text{bytes} = 524,288\,\text{bytes} \times 1\text{K}/1024\,\text{bytes} \tag{1.3}$$

Conveniently, 1 byte is also the amount of memory needed to store a single character like "a" or "b." This leads to a typical typed page requiring 2000–5000 bytes = 2–5 KB (the smaller number if there are displayed equations).

The memory chips in some of the older personal computers used 8-bit words. This means the maximum integer is $2^7 = 128$ (7 since one bit is used for the sign). Trying to store a number larger than possible (*overflow*) was common on these machines, sometimes accompanied by an informative error message and sometimes not. At present, most workstation level computers use at least 32 bits for an integer, which means the maximum integer is $2^{31} \simeq 2 \times 10^9$. While at first this may seem a large range, it really isn't compared to the range of sizes encountered in the physical world (the ratio of the size of the universe to the size of a proton is approximately 10^{41}).

Representing real numbers on computers is done in two ways, *fixed point* or *floating point*, notation. In fixed point notation the number x is represented as

$$x_{fix} = \text{sign} \times \left(\alpha_n 2^n + \alpha_{n-1} 2^{n-1} + \dots + \alpha_0 2^0 + \dots + \alpha_{-m} 2^{-m}\right) \tag{1.4}$$

That is, one bit is used to store the sign (1: negative, 0: positive), and the remaining $N-1$ bits are used to store the α_i's ($n + m = N - 2$). The particular values for N, m, and n are machine dependent. The advantage of this representation is that you can count on all fixed point numbers to have the same absolute error 2^{-m-1} [the term left off the right hand end of (1.4)]. The corresponding disadvantage is that *small* numbers (those for which the first string of α's are zeros) have large *relative* error. Since in the real world relative errors tend to be more important than absolute ones, fixed point numbers are used mainly in special applications (like bookkeeping). Your scientific work will be mainly with floating point numbers. For a typical 32-bit machine, the integers of 4 byte length are in the range

$$-2147483648 : 2147483647 \tag{1.5}$$

In floating point notation the number x is represented as

$$x_{float} = (-1)^s \times \text{mantissa} \times 2^{\text{expfld - bias}} \tag{1.6}$$

Here the mantissa contains the significant figures of the number and s is the sign bit. Just as introducing a sign bit guarantees that the mantissa is always positive, so introducing the bias guarantees that the number stored as the exponent field expfld in (1.6) is always positive (the actual number's exponent can of course be negative).

The use of bias is rather indirect. For example, a single-precision 32-bit word may use 8 bits for the exponent in (1.6) and represent it as an integer. This 8-bit integer "exponent" has a range $[0, 255]$. Numbers with actual negative exponents are represented by a bias equal to 127, a fixed number for a given machine. Consequently, the exponent has the range $[-127, 128]$ even though the value stored for the "exponent" in (1.6) is a positive number. Of the remaining bits, one is used for the sign, and 23 for the mantissa. *Single precision numbers (4 bytes) thus have about 6–7 decimal places of precision* (1 part in 2^{23}) and have magnitudes in the range

$$1.175494 \times 10^{-38} \ : \ 3.402824 \times 10^{38} \tag{1.7}$$

The mantissa of a floating number is represented in memory in the form

$$\text{mantissa} = m_1 \times 2^{-1} + m_2 \times 2^{-2} + ... + m_{23} \times 2^{-23} \tag{1.8}$$

with just the m_i's stored—similar to (1.4). As an example, the number 0.5 is stored as

```
0     0111 1111     1000 0000 0000 0000 0000 000
```

indicating that the bias is $0111\ 1111_2 = 127_{10}$.

In order to have the same relative precision for all floating point numbers, it is standard to choose the value of the exponent, that is, *normalize* the number, such that the leftmost bit is unity, $m_1 = 1$. Once this convention is adopted, this leading bit does not even have to be stored and the computer need only recall that there is a *phantom bit*. During the processing of numbers in a calculation, the first bit of the mantissa of an intermediate result may become zero, but this will be corrected before the final number is stored.

The largest possible floating point number for a 32-bit machine

```
0     1111 1111     1111 1111 1111 1111 1111 111
```

has 1's for all its bits (except sign) and adds up to $2^{128} = 3.4 \times 10^{38}$. The smallest possible floating point number

```
0     0000 0000     1000 0000 0000 0000 0000 000
```

has 0's for almost all its bits and adds up to $2^{-128} = 2.9 \times 10^{-39}$. As built in by the use of bias, the smallest number possible to store is indeed the inverse of the largest.

If you write a program requesting *double-precision*, 64-bit (8-byte) words will be used in place of the 32-bit (4-byte) words. With 11 bits used for the exponent and 52 for the mantissa, double-precision numbers thus have about 16 decimal places of precision (1 part in 2^{52}) and have magnitudes in the range

$$2.225074 \times 10^{-308} \ : \ 1.799693 \times 10^{308} \tag{1.9}$$

In our experience, serious scientific calculations almost always require double precision (64 bit words) sooner or later. And if you need double precision in one part of your calculation, you probably need it all over—and that includes double-precision library routines.

Machine Precision

A consequence of this memorization scheme for numbers is that they can be recalled with only a limited precision. While the exact precision depends on the computer, for 32-bit word machines, *single precision* is usually 6–7 decimal places, while double precision is 15–16 places.[6] To see how this *machine precision* affects calculations, consider the simple addition of two 32-bit words:

$$7 + 1.0 \times 10^{-7} =? \tag{1.10}$$

The computer fetches these numbers from memory and stores the bit patterns:

$$7 = 0 \; 10000010 \; 1110 \; 0000 \; 0000 \; 0000 \; 0000 \; 000 \tag{1.11}$$
$$10^{-7} = 0 \; 01100000 \; 1101 \; 0110 \; 1011 \; 1111 \; 1001 \; 010 \tag{1.12}$$

in *working registers* (pieces of fast-responding memory). Since the exponents are different, it would be incorrect to add the mantissas. So the exponent of the smaller number is made larger while progressively decreasing the mantissa by *shifting bits* to the right (inserting 0's) until both numbers have the same exponent:

$$10^{-7} = 0 \; 01100001 \; 0110 \; 1011 \; 0101 \; 1111 \; 1100101 \; (0)$$
$$= 0 \; 01100010 \; 0011 \; 0101 \; 1010 \; 1111 \; 1110010 \; (10) \tag{1.13}$$

...

$$10^{-7} = 0 \; 10000010 \; 0000 \; 0000 \; 0000 \; 0000 \; 0000 \; 000 \; (0001101....)$$
$$\Rightarrow 7 + 1.0 \times 10^{-7} = 7 \tag{1.14}$$

Since there is no more room left to store the last digits, they are lost, and after all this hard work the addition just gives 7. As we have said, a 32-bit computer only stores 6–7 decimal places and in effect ignores the 10^{-7}.

The preceding loss of precision is categorized by defining the *machine precision* ϵ_m as the maximum positive number which, on the computer, can be added to the number stored as 1 without changing the number stored as 1

$$1_c + \epsilon_m = 1_c \tag{1.15}$$

(the subscript c is reminder that this is the number stored in the computer's memory). Likewise, x_c, the computer's representation of x, and the actual number x are related by

$$x_c = x(1 + \epsilon), \quad |\epsilon| \le \epsilon_m$$

In a typical case for single precision, if x is larger than 2^{128} an *overflow* occurs, and if x is smaller than 2^{-128} an *underflow* occurs; in these cases x_c may end up being a machine-dependent pattern, or "NAN" (not a number), or unpredictable.

Since the only difference between the representation of a positive and negative number on the computer is the *sign bit* of 1 for negative numbers, similar considerations hold for negative numbers.

---

[6]Some of the symbolic manipulation programs can store numbers with "infinite precision." This clearly indicates a word size which increases in length as the requisite precision increases.

Exercises for Your Machine

Although we have yet to get to programming and running Unix commands, here are some exercises to help those readers who are ready to explore their system. If you cannot yet write the programs needed for these exercises, you can read them through as a summary of the preceding points, and plan to come back to them later.

1. Write a program to determine the underflow and overflow limits of your computer system. A sample pseudocode is

```
under = 1.
over = 1.
  begin do
  do N times
   under = under/2.
   over = over x 2.
   write out:  number of time, under, over
  end do
```

You may need to increase the number N if your initial choice does not lead to underflow and overflow.

(a) Check where and how under- and overflow occur for single-precision, floating point numbers.

(b) Check where and how under- and overflow occur for double-precision, floating point numbers.

(c) Check where and how under and overflow occur for integers.

2. Write a program to determine the machine precision of your computer system. A sample pseudocode is:

```
eps = 1.
  begin do
   do N times
   eps = eps/2.
   one = 1.  + eps                    Make smaller.
   write out:  number of time, one, eps
  end do
```

(a) Check the precision for single-precision, floating point numbers.

(b) Check the precision for double-precision, floating point numbers.

CHAPTER 2

GETTING FRIENDLY WITH UNIX

It is our repeated and avowed agreement *not* to write another Unix manual. By reviewing some of the Unix features we find useful and essential in our work, we hope we have assembled in this chapter an eclectic mini manual which does not waste your time by telling you more than you need to know. Feel free to skip through this chapter or just use it for reference if you feel you know it already; please feel compelled to study a real Unix manual if you do not know it at all.

Our convention is to write in **bold type** commands which you give Unix, to have the computer's response or file names in `monospaced type`, and to have key words or jargon (you may need to look up their meaning) in *italics*. Unfortunately the responses and error messages Unix produces often differ from implementation to implementation. In our examples we use generic BSD and System V commands and responses.

2.1 Logging In

The Naming of Cats is a difficult matter,
It isn't just one of your holiday games;
You may think at first I'm as mad as a hatter
When I tell you, a cat must have THREE DIFFERENT NAMES.

—T. S. Eliot

To use the workstation, you must first *login*. To do so, you must have (at the minimum) a *login name* by which the computer and other users will know you as well as a *password* which you should keep to yourself. In fact, since the password protects your work and the entire system from unauthorized and careless users, and since it is relatively easy for other users (all throughout the networked world no less!) to move through Unix systems, you should carefully guard your password.

In addition to your login name, the system will also assign you a *user ID number* and a *group ID number*. The user ID is a number which has a unique correspondence to your login name and which the system uses to keep tabs on you. When personal information is printed, such as in response to **ls -l** or **ps** commands, the system matches the user ID to the login name and prints out the login name. The group ID is a higher level identification shared among users which automatically permits (or forbids) a number of users permission to read and write the same files.

Essentially all Unix commands require you to end or activate them by hitting the key labeled **Enter** (or **Return** or **Carriage return** or **[ret]**). If you make a mistake keying in your command, you can correct it with the **Backspace** key if you have not yet entered in **[ret]**. You can often abort the running command with **control-c, ctrl-c** or **^c** or **[Del]**.

After you have given the computer your login name and password, there is a short delay while the computer validates your account. It then responds by introducing itself, telling you if you have *mail*, possibly asking you to identify the type of *terminal* you are on, and setting off a chain of actions as commanded by a file labeled **.login** or **.profile** (see Appendix A, *Sample Dot Files*).[1] Finally, with a typically verbose Unix response, the computer presents you with a *prompt* as its way of saying, "my wish is your command."

The prompt you see depends upon the Unix *shell* you are using. By "shell," we mean that part of Unix which interprets the user's commands. The three standard choices are the *Borne shell*, with program name *sh*; the *C shell* called *csh*; and the *Korn shell*, called *ksh*. The Borne shell came from System V and has fewer features than the others. BSD added the *csh* with useful features such as job control, the ability to reenter and edit past commands, and the ability to define your own commands via **alias**. The Korn shell is a newer offering from AT&T which extends the Borne shell and adds many of the features of the C shell.

If the prompt **%** appears, it means you are using (or in) the C shell, *csh*. If the prompt **$** appears, it means you are using the Borne or Korn shell. The **#** prompt is usually reserved for use by the all-knowing, all-powerful, system administrator, known as *superuser* or *root*. If you see it appear on your terminal and you are not acting as the system administrator, you should exit or logout before serious harm is done (seriously).

If a more personal and revealing prompt appears (like your name or your computer's name), it means the *.cshrc* (for csh) or *.profile* (for ksh or sh) file has been so set. You can select your shell by using the change shell commands **csh, sh** or **ksh**.

Logging Off

Before we continue we should mention how to quit your workstation. The command **logout** will log you off the system. The command **exit** also works; it terminates the shell you are using and may be used to close **xterm** windows and in other situations where **logout** will not work. A **ctrl-d** may also act like exit, but because it is easy to confuse terminating normal input with **ctrl-d**, this feature is generally turned off.

2.2   Unix Commands, Generalities

We will use the typical Unix syntax for documenting commands and their options. The command and arguments presented in **bold type** are entered verbatim. File name(s)

---

[1]Unix must know what type of terminal you are using in order for applications such as full screen editors to work. It is to your benefit to tell Unix if it asks. If you are on a PC, most terminal programs emulate a Digital VT100 so you should respond with **vt100**. If you are using X Windows, you should answer **xterm**.

and user-supplied options are represented by terms such as *name* or *file*, with three dots signifying that more than one name may be given. The letter n refers to an integer option. Arguments enclosed in brackets [ ] are optional. A | separating arguments means "or":

```
command [ -a | -b ] file name ...
```

Unfortunately, Unix commands do not have a universal syntax (this probably reflects its heritage from and the organization of university research). In general, Unix commands are entered as:

```
command -option(s) filename(s)
```

The command is always the first word. The options modifying what the command does are usually one letter each and can be juxtaposed (grouped) into any order (as a test of the user's creativity in forming nonsense words). If the command operates on a file or several files, the filename(s) are given last.

This option syntax for commands is almost universal within Unix, but not quite. A few commands take options without the preceding dash while some commands accept dashes but do not require them. Some commands require a dash for each option separately, instead of permitting you to juxtapose several options after one dash. To check a command's syntax, refer to your local manual pages (possibly with the man command); or you can be experimental and try the command out on some temporary file you don't mind messing up a bit.

The following rules apply to all Unix commands and systems:

- Commands cannot be abbreviated (how can you with the few letters you have to begin with).

- Unix distinguishes between uppercase and lowercase letters for both commands and filenames. So the commands who, Who, and WHO are all different. Since standard Unix commands are lower case, who is the standard version.

- Unix shells use *wild-card characters* that allow you to select files without typing the complete name(s) of files. The two most useful *wild-card characters* are * and ?. The * is used to match any number of characters and the ? is used to match single characters. For example,

```
data?.out    matches files   data1.out, data2.out
  *.out      matches         data1.out, data2.out, data12.out
```

- Unlike *MS-DOS*, the dot . has no special meaning in Unix. A file name can have one or more dots, so it is perfectly okay to have files named prog.f or prog.old.f. To Unix, . is just another character. There are, however, conventions for naming files depending on the type of code contained in the file.[2] Here are some of these conventions (we discuss them further in Chapter 8, *Using Unix with Fortran and C*):

---

[2]The term *code* is a carryover from the good old days when "real men" programmed in machine code; now programmers compose source *code* in any level language.

FILE NAMES

file.f	Source or Fortran "code" for Fortran programs.
file.c	Source or C code for C programs.
file.o	Object code for Fortran or C programs.
file.tex	Text file for TEX or LATEX document.
file.dvi	Device independent output of TEX, LATEX.
file.Z	*Compressed* file (must **expand** to read).
s.file	Source code control system (SCCS) file form.
file.a	Archived object files, a *library*.
Makefile	Script file used by **make** to build programs.
file.tar	Files stored in archived (**tar**) form.
file.doc	Documentation file.
README	Documentation about local subdirectory.
src	Directory of source files.
bin	Directory of commands.

Control-Key Commands

Unix has several *control-key commands*, that is, commands you enter by holding down the control key **ctrl** while simultaneously striking a second key. For example, you can backspace by holding down the **control** key and **h** key at the same time; this is denoted as **ctrl-h**, or in some documents as **^h**. These commands are important and powerful, yet also can be confusing and file annihilating, so be careful! For example, using **ctrl-h** and **ctrl-u** hardly ever do too much harm, yet locking up your terminal with **ctrl-s** or signing off the computer with **ctrl-d** hardly ever leads to smiles.

CONTROL CHARACTER COMMANDS

^h	Backspace.
^d	End text input, EOF for **mail, write**
	(also acts as **logout** command).
^w	Delete last word typed.
^u	Delete (undo) last line typed.
^r	Repeat last line typed.
^s	Stop the screen from scrolling
	(sometimes takes a while to be effective).
^q	Unlock terminal screen, continue scrolling.
^c	Interrupt running program ([Del] in System V).
^z	Suspend running program (**fg** to resume).

2.3   Sample File to Input, area.f

We give here and on the floppy the listing for a program area.f (it's Fortran but that doesn't matter). We suggest you enter this program into a file called area.f on your computer, and then use this file to try out the Unix tools and editors. It is small, you can always get it back if it gets ruined, and you can even compile and run it (discussed further in Chapter 8 on *Using Fortran and C with Unix*).

```
        PROGRAM area
c area of circle, r input from terminal
        DOUBLE PRECISION pi, r, A
c     Best value of pi for IEEE floating point
        pi = 3.14159265358979323846
c read r from standard input (terminal)
        Write(*, *) 'specify radius, e.g. 1.0 '
        Read (*, *)  r
        A = pi * r**2
c     write area onto terminal screen
        Write(*, 10) 'radius r =', r, ' A =', A
 10     Format(a20, f10.5, a15, f12.7)
        STOP 'area'
        END
```

2.4   Specific Unix Commands

This section lists common Unix commands according to how they're used. We give them here as a reference with the promise that we will discuss most of them within the context of their use later on in the book. If you find it hard to wait, we suggest you set up some temporary or play files, and try these commands out with them as you read. More information will be found in the **man** pages on your system, other parts of this book, or a real Unix manual.

FILE MANIPULATION COMMANDS

mv *fold fnew*	Copy *fold* to *fnew*, remove *fold* (i.e. rename), files can be in different directories.
rm *fold*	Remove (delete) *fold*.
rm -rf *directory*	Remove *directory* and everything in it.
cp *fold fnew*	Copy *fold* to *fnew*, destroy previous *fnew*.
cat *fileA > fileB*	Copy *fileA* to *fileB*.
cat *fileA >> fileB*	Append *fileA* to end of *fileB* (add to end).
ls	List files in present directory.
ls -l	A long list of files.

PRINT COMMANDS

lpr *file*	Print *file* on line printer under BSD.
lp *fname*	Print *file* on line printer under System V.
lpq	Return status of jobs in print queue (BSD).
lpstat	Return status of jobs in print queue (System V).

VIEW COMMANDS

cat *file*	Print *file* on screen (or as directed by >, >>).
more *file*	Print *file*, one screenful at a time.
view *file*	Use the vi editor for viewing a file.
head *file*	Print first 10 lines of *file*.
tail *file*	Print *file*'s last 10 lines on screen.

COMPILING

cc *file.c*	Compile C source code in *file.c*.
f77 *file.f*	Compile Fortran 77 source code in *file.f*.
pc *file.p*	Compile Pascal source code in *file.p*.
as *file.s*	Assemble program in *file.s*.
ld *file.o*	Load, link, program in *file.o*.
lint *file.c*	Check C program in *file.c*.

DEBUGGING

sdb *prog*	Run debugger on executable *prog*.
dbx *prog*	Run debugger on executable *prog*.
adb *prog*	Run debugger on executable *prog*.

EXECUTING

batch *prog*	Run *prog* in batch queue (sequential **bg**).
at *prog*	Run *prog* at a later time.
ps -a	Return name and process ID's of all current processes.
ps -fu *user*	Returns list of processes owned by *user* (V).
kill -9 *pid*	Cancel job number *pid* (known from **ps**).

JOB CONTROL

ctrl-z	Stop active foreground job.
bg	Place stopped foreground job into background.
fg *job #*	Place background job into foreground.
jobs	Return names and job no. of suspended jobs.

SEARCH, COMPARE

diff *file1 file2*	List lines in *file2* differing from *file1*.
file *fname*	List *fname*'s type (ASCII, text, directory, object).
grep *pat fname*	Print lines in file *fname* containing pattern *pat*.
sort *fname*	Sort lines of *fname* based on options.
spell *fname*	Check *fname* for spelling errors, (programs such as **ispell** corrects them).

MISCELLANEOUS

wc *fname*	Count number of "words" in *fname*.
who (w)	List current users.
who am i (whoami)	Return my login name (useful when changing, machines, users, or spouses).
chmod *code file*	Change file's mode via esoteric code.

2.5   Setting Up Files and Directories

To use Unix commands wisely it is helpful to understand some basic concepts of how information is stored and jobs are processed on a computer. A basic fact of computing life is *all resources are finite*. Since Unix does a good job at sharing resources among simultaneous or sporadic users and tasks, it is all too easy to think of your computer as limitless. This is patently wrong since even the most powerful system can be slowed to a crawl by poor usage or overload.

Information in an operating systems such as Unix is stored in *files* which basically are just a series of characters or bytes. A file can contain any type of computer-readable information or data, and thus may be a letter you are writing, the output of a program, or a command which Unix will recognize. For example, this chapter is stored in a file called `2.tex`. As you enter programs or data into the computer, they first get written into the computer's temporary (or fast) memory and then, if so commanded, are stored in files on the computer's "hard disk" (hard compared to "floppy" diskettes). The spinning hard disk is "permanent" memory, at least until it wears out after some years of use.

The files you key ("type") in are called *text* or *ASCII files* because they contain human readable "text" stored in the American National Standards Code for Information Interchange. There are also *binary files* and *object files* containing information which is not readable by humans but meaningful to the computer (beware, if you develop an interest in reading these files). The *programs* you actually *run* on the computer are binary or *executable* files; binary since the instructions are written with just 0's and 1's and executable since these instructions can be loaded directly into the computer's memory and then directly obeyed. While you may now be curious enough to look at some binary files, do not do it with a *text editor* since editors are meant for reading text and may get quite confused when faced with a binary file.[3]

Directories

A system with many users will have hundreds or thousands of files, some useful, a few valuable. To organize and protect these files, Unix lets you group them into *directories*. Directories are like hanging file folders in a filing cabinet with each directory containing a number of files, as well as other directories (*subdirectories*). Accordingly, when you *open* (or *change to*) a directory, you gain access to all files and subdirectories contained in that directory.

As discussed further in Chapter 3, *The Project Directory Approach*, we have found it to be a good idea to use directories as separate work spaces for the many interesting projects and necessary administrative tasks facing hard-working scientists, engineers, and students. You may then *edit, compile*, and *run* programs within one directory without affecting files in other directories (although you can still access other directories).

The ability of Unix to have directories within directories makes it *hierarchical*. As an example, in Figure 2.1 is a schematic of a typical Unix file system. Note that all files or directories are below (or in) the topmost or *root* directory denoted by the " / " symbol.

---

[3]Likewise, electronic mail systems may well become uncooperative or unreliable when given binary files to deliver since the mailer can't read it well enough to break it up into small packages.

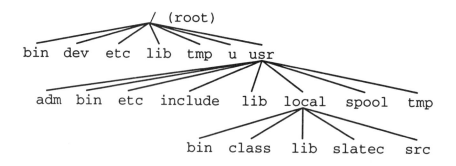

Figure 2.1: Unix file system tree.

The usr and local directories are expanded, showing how (sub-) directories are further organized within directories. Notice, too, that while the names bin, etc, and lib are used more than once, each is unique since each resides within a different parent directory (each has a unique full name). Since root (/) is the root of all directories, the full path name begins there. For example, the three lib's have the full path names

       /lib   /usr/lib   /usr/local/lib

Here the name begins at the root directory /, and after that shows the path through all the directories to get to each lib. This notation is somewhat confusing at first, since each directory name is also separated by a /, but these later /'s are just separators; don't blame us, we're just the bearers of bad news who also must bear bad notation.

The Unix file system tree can be quite confusing even to experienced users, probably because the human mind believes there must really be some logic in such a complicated construct. At one time there may have been a clear rationale for which files were placed in various directories and subdirectories, the proliferation of new commands, the addition of commercial software, and the fusion of System V and BSD Unix have left the branches in the tree rather tangled with few general rules.

The term usr is an abbreviation for *user service routines*, while the directory /u is where the users' home directories are kept. The directories bin, etc, and lib under / contain the basic programs and files needed for the system to *boot* and run, while the directories under usr contain programs and files that are for the users. Often this same arrangement is duplicated under /usr/local where programs are installed by the local system administrator. In the bin (binary) directory are stored executable programs, while the lib (library) directory contains object files used by other programs as well as the libraries used by compilers to create executable programs. The etc directory is basically everything else, and, in particular, the system and user configuration files as well as the password file passwd.

If you want to know who your real friends are, or at least fellow users, you can look at the users' directories in /u or /users. The home directories of your fellow users and their login names will be there. In fact, unless a user makes an extra effort to be private, you can probably go snooping through their file system. Be careful: *it is unethical and sometimes illegal to read, copy, or modify someone else's files or to use a system on which you are not an authorized user.*

Fortunately, a user seldom needs to know the location of the file containing a particular command since the shell will automatically search through a list of directories to find the file containing the command entered. The actual list is kept in a *shell variable*, or *environment variable*, called PATH (which is identical to the PATH variable used in MS-DOS). The PATH is defined differently for different shells, so you may need to consult the examples given in Chapter 3 on *A Word about Your* PATH. Or, better yet, develop a positive attitude and go exploring and experimenting.

If you must find the location of a command, there are some tools to help you. The command **whereis** will try to locate a command, while the command **which** will show you which of several possibly different programs with the same name will be executed. These commands are shell and system dependent and may not be on all systems. There also is the standard Unix utility **find** which will recursively search the file system tree for a file; however, its thoroughness may make it appear incredibly slow on some machines.

2.6   Your Home Directory

When you *login*, that is, log in, the computer starts up a program called a *shell* just for you and then does housekeeping by placing you into your *home directory*. Your *home directory* file system is the top of your workspace, and, if you so desire, you can keep all other users out of it. While you may use this workspace any way you wish, in Chapter 3, *Workstation Setup and Use*, we illustrate the making of subdirectories that keep your work (and play) separate and organized. Just as it is a poor practice to throw all your papers into one pile on your desk, it is also poor practice to do all your work in your home directory.

Like Eliot's cats, your Unix home directory can be called by at least three names. You can call it $HOME, or ~, or explicitly, /u/rubin. You can refer to the home directory of another user, paul, as ~paul. (Note: the ~ forms are actually C and Korn shell variations.)

A user's *home directory* often contains some files beginning with a "." which help customize Unix programs to just the way the user likes them. (Since files beginning with "." are not normally visible with the list command **ls**, you must say **ls -a** to see them.) At some point when you execute certain commands or run certain programs, these programs look for the dot files and then read them to determine your preferences. The dot files' formats and uses are described in the documentation for each program or command, and samples may be found in Chapter 3, *Workstation Setup and Use*, in Chapter 5, *Looking through X Windows*, in Appendix A, *Sample Dot Files*, and on the floppy. Some of the more common and useful ones are:

csh DOT FILES

.cshrc	Personalization for C shell.
.login	Commands to execute upon *login*, set environment.
.logout	Commands to execute upon *logout*, clean-up time.

sh, ksh DOT FILES

.profile	Personalization for sh and ksh, similar to .login.
.kshrc	Personalization for Korn shell, similar to .cshrc.
.envfile	Another name for .kshrc.

X WINDOWS DOT FILES

.Xdefaults	Setup characteristics of *X Windows*.
.mwmrc	Setup for *Motif Window Manager*.

EDITORS' DOT FILES

.emacs	Setup characteristics of *Emacs* editor.
.exrc	Setup characteristics of *vi* editor.

MAIL DOT FILES

.mailrc	Commands to set up the standard Unix mail command.
.mh_profile	Set behavior of **mh** mail handler.
.mh_alias:	Set aliases for **mh** mail handler.

UNIX DOT FILES

..	Unix's symbol for directory above present one.
.	Unix's symbol for present directory.

Working with Directories

Here are some commands for working with directories which you should try out on your terminal as you read about them:

DIRECTORY COMMANDS

mkdir *dirname*	Create new directory `dirname`.
rmdir *dirname*	Remove empty directory `dirname`.
cd *dirname*	Change to directory `dirname`.
cd	Change to home directory.
cd ..	Change directory to one level above
cd .	Change to current directory (this does nothing).
ls *dirname*	List files and directories in `dirname`, default: ..
ls -CF	List distinguishing directories, programs, and files.
pwd	Print working directory's name, i.e., where I am.

Using Directories

Here is an example in which user bohr goes exploring and is careful to keep track of where he is and what is around him:

```
login: bohr          User bohr logs in.
Password:            Bohr enters password - you can't see it.
```

`Welcome to OSU's Comphy Mate`	See, Unix really is friendly!
`%  pwd`	Print working directory.
`/usr/bohr`	Ah, my home directory.
`%  ls`	List files and subdirectories.
`class homefire.burn letters`	
`%  cd class`	Move to subdirectory `class`.
`%  ls -CF`	Coded listing.
`mybin/ plot* hw`	A directory (/), executable (*),
	& plain files.
`%  cd ..`	Move to preceding directory.
`%  pwd`	Tell me where I am!
`/u/bohr`	Ah, home again.
`%  cd ~bohr/class/mybin`	Go directly to subdirectory `mybin`.

Notice that the computer gives no response after changing directories. This is typical for many Unix commands; if they work properly, the computer simply returns the prompt. If not, you get an error message. At first, bohr moved forward in small steps, and later jumped around in really big steps by using the full path names. Big steps are quicker, but for beginners it is probably more comforting to move step by step, letting the computer tell you where you are at each step and what's there.[4] This is not so tedious if the `cd` and `ls` commands are combined, for example,

`%  cd; ls`	Move to home directory, list files.
`class homefire.burn letters`	The old files at home.
`%  cd class`	Move to class directory.
`%  ls`	List files.
`mybin plot hw`	Files in `class`.

To tell what's in a directory without going through the trouble of changing into it, just issue the `ls` command indicating the path leading to that directory from the present one. For example,

`%  ls /usr/local`	List contents of directory `usr/local`.
`bin class lib slatec src`	The contents.

Even if `local` is a file rather than a directory, listing it won't spill out its contents or do any harm. Unix will just tell you its name (the `ls -l` version tells you about the file). Now we list the contents of a directory two levels below `usr` (without visiting it):

`%  ls /usr/local/class`	List contents of class in `/usr/local`.
`exam.f`	
`%  ls -l /usr/local/class/exam.f`	Long listing of file exam.f.
`-rw-r--r-- 1 bohr 3784 Mar 2 18:57 src/asr/asr2.c`	

---

[4]As given in Appendix A on *Sample Dot Files* and the floppy, a useful alias for `cd` appends a `pwd` and a `ls` to it, in which case you will get a more informative response.

Making and Removing Directories

Before you can copy or move files into a directory, that directory must exist, and this means you or some super friend has made that directory with the command:

```
%  mkdir dirname
```
Make directory dirname.

And since she who giveth may also taketh,

```
%  rmdir dirname
```
Remove directory dirname.

These commands are fail safe; Unix won't let you remove a directory if there are any files in it, or let you make a directory with the a name which already exists.

As you can probably guess by now, the full path name may also be used to make a new directory (or remove an old one) anywhere in your workspace. So to make the directory lib, bohr could enter one of the following:

`%  mkdir /user/bohr/lib`	Make lib from anywhere.
`%  cp * /user/bohr/lib`	Copy all files to lib.
`%  ls /user/bohr/lib`	List files in directory.
`file1 file2 file3`	
`%  cd`	Go to bohr's own home directory.
`%  mkdir lib`	Make lib from bohr's home directory.
`mkdir:  src:  File exists`	**mkdir** returns an error message.
`%  rmdir /user/bohr/lib`	Remove lib from anywhere.
`rmdir:  src not empty`	Can only remove empty directory.

Copying and Removing Files

Unix tries to make life simple for you by having files follow the same naming conventions as directories. That means, though, that it is hard to tell files, directories, and commands apart, so, we use the **ls -l, ls -CF,** and file commands. The full path name for a file contains all the directories leading up to that file as well as the file name itself. For example, the full path name for the file exam.f, which bohr found above, is /usr/local/class/exam.f.

The basic commands for manipulating files are **cp, mv,** and **rm**. They are defined in § 2.4 and § 2.7. Here we give an example of their use with an undirected make work project undertaken by bohr; we suggest you try them on your terminal, too:

`%  cd`	Bohr changes to his home directory.
`%  pwd`	And checks where he is.
`/u/bohr`	Voilá, bohr's home directory.
`%  ls`	List files in this directory.
`%`	It's empty so we get the prompt back. [5]
`%  mkdir phys`	Bohr makes directory phys.

---

[5] Actually the home directory is not completely empty since there are file names beginning with a dot which are not shown.

```
%   cd phys                              Change into new directory.
%   ls                                   List files in working directory phys.
                                         Empty again.
%   cp /usr/local/class/exam.f  .        Copy exam.f via full path name
                                         directly to current directory, '.'
%   ls                                   Check what's there.
exam.f
%   mv exam.f myprog.f                   Rename exam.f to myprog.f.
%   ls
myprog.f
%   cat myprog.f                         List contents of myprog.f on screen.
line 1
line 2
...                                      And so forth.
%   rm myprog.f                          Bohr removes myprog.f.
%   ls
                                         Nothing is there.
```

Like a razor, the rm command is simple, quick, and irreversible; both require care.[6]

2.7 Alphabetized List of Unix Commands

This section contains an alphabetized list of common Unix commands which could be useful as a review and reference.

<u>**UNIX COMMANDS**</u>

^c	INTERRUPT program ([Del] in System V).
^d	END text input (also logoff).
^h	BACKSPACE.
^r	REPEAT last line typed (or !!).
^q	Unlock terminal screen.
^s	Stop the screen from scrolling.
^u	UNDO last line typed.
^w	Delete last WORD typed.
^z	SUSPEND a running program.
as *file.s*	Assemble program in *file.s*.
at *prog*	Run *prog* at a later time.
batch *prog*	Run *prog* in BATCH queue (sequential bg).
bg	Place stopped foreground job into BACKGROUND.
cat *fileA* > *fileB*	COPY *fileA* to *fileB*.
cat *fileA* >> *fileB*	APPEND *fileA* to end of *fileB* (add to end).
cat *file*	LIST *file* on screen (or where > or >> directs).
cc *file.c*	COMPILE C program in *file.c*.
cd *dirname*	CHANGE to *dirname*; default *home*, .. 1 up.
chmod *code file*	Change *file*'s access restrictions.

---

[6]Some users issue the command "mv file /tmp" to get rid of a file without really removing it, and then "cp /tmp/file ." to reclaim a file after removal.

UNIX COMMANDS

cp *oldfile newfile*	COPY *oldfile* to *newfile*.
dbx *prog*	Run DEBUGGER on executable *prog*.
diff *file1 file2*	List lines DIFFERING in *file1, file2*.
f77 *file.f*	Fortran 77 compile.
fg *job #*	Place background job into FOREGROUND.
file *fname*	Determine *fname*'s type.
grep *pat fname*	Look for *pat* in file *fname*.
head *file*	Print first 10 lines of *file*.
jobs	Return names and job # of suspended jobs.
kill -9 *pid #*	Cancel job with pid # (known from **ps**).
ld *file.o or file.a*	LOAD, LINK, program in *file.o, file.a*.
lint *file.c*	Check C program in *file.c*.
lp *fname*	Print *fname* on LINE PRINTER (System V).
lpq	Return status of jobs in print queue (BSD).
lpr *file*	Print *file* on LINE PRINTER (BSD).
lprm *numb*	Remove *numb* from print queue (BSD).
lpstat	Return status of jobs in print queue (System V).
ls	LIST files in present directory.
ls -l	A long list of files.
ls *dirname*	List files in *dirname*, default .,
	-1 long, -x list, -CF coded, -a invisibles.
mkdir *dirname*	Make directory *dirname*.
more *file*	List *file*, one screenful at a time.
mv *oldfile newfile*	MOVE *oldfile* to *newfile*, then remove *oldfile*.
pc *file.p*	Compile Pascal programs in *file.p*.
ps -a	Return name and process ID's of all current processes.
ps -fu *user*	List processes owned by *user* (System V).
pwd	Print working directory.
rm *oldfile*	REMOVE (erase) *oldfile*.
rm -rf *directory*	Remove directory and everything in it.
rmdir *dirname*	Remove directory *dirname*.
sort *fname*	SORT lines of *fname* based on options.
spell *fname*	Check *fname* for SPELLING.
tail *file*	Print *file*'s last 10 lines on screen.
view *file*	Use the vi editor for VIEWING a file.
wc *fname*	COUNT number of "words" in *fname*.
who (w)	List current users.
who am i (whoami)	Return my login name.

2.8   Viewing, Editing, and Printing Files

To do something creative, like writing and running your own program, you must be able
to view, edit, and print files. While viewing and printing is straightforward, editing can

be a challenge—if not a disaster—until the editors are mastered. (As hyperuser says: while you should not think of computers as disasters waiting to strike, you should do some work to avoid future unhappiness.) Practice, caution, and backups of your work are good ideas—especially at first on a new system.

In the latter part of this section we give a terse introduction to the *vi* editor, a "visual" editor available on most Unix systems. This is a powerful editor but is rather dated. If your system has an *Emacs* or an *nedit* editor, we recommend trying them first (*nedit* is friendlier but less powerful). While *Emacs* and *nedit* are not as universal as *vi*, they are easier, more modern, and more like the editors or word processors on personal computers. If you require more than a refresher, you may wish to refer to one of the texts listed in the Bibliography, or obtain tutorials with commands such as:

%	`learn vi`	Tutorial for vi .
%	`emacs tutorial`	Tutorial for Emacs.

More and View

In a previous example, the command **cat** was used to list a file on a terminal screen. A problem with **cat** is that the listing often flies by before you get a chance to read it. The programs **view** and **more** (or page **pg**) let you scroll through a file, one screenful at a time, and without the chance of changing it. The command **more** lets you step coarsely though a file (and on later versions step backwards as well). Both commands also do crude searches. The command **view** is a read-only version of the **vi** editor which actually uses **vi** for navigating through a file and performing searches. Its major drawback is that it cannot be used within a Unix *pipe* (we discuss pipes in a later section).

To use **more** or **view** to examine the file **fname**, enter:

%	`more fname`	To see more than file's name.
%	`view fname`	Read only vi editor.

An abridged list of **more** subcommands is given below, while commands to use with **view** are found in § 2.9 on **vi**. Most commands can be preceded by an integer argument to make them repeat. For example, `[ret]` moves down one line and `12[ret]` moves down 12 lines.

MORE COMMANDS

[space]	Forward one screen or number of lines given.
[ret]	Forward one line or number of lines given.
d (^d)	Scroll forward 11 lines.
q (Q)	EXIT from more.
f (^ f)	Skip FORWARD by screenful of text.
b (^ b)	Skip BACKWARDS by screenful of text.
'	Go to place where previous search started.
=	Display current line number.
/pattern	SEARCH for "pattern."
n	Search for next occurrence of previous "pattern."
!*cmd* (:!*cmd*)	Execute *cmd* in a user's shell.

MORE COMMANDS

v	Start up vi editor at current line.
h	HELP!
^l	REDRAW screen.
:n	Go to NEXT file.
:p	Go to PREVIOUS file.
:f	Show FILE name and line number.
.	REPEAT previous command.

Printing Files

Although we sometimes say a command "prints" out a message, most likely the output is appearing on a terminal screen and not on a piece of paper (where respectable printing belongs). There is still power and value in the printed word, and for this purpose a line or page printer is usually attached directly or through a network to your system.

BSD PRINT

lpr -P*printer file(s)*	Place *file(s)* in line printer queue.
lpq -P*printer*	List files in line printer queue.
lprm -P*printer job #*	CANCEL a printing job (get # from **lpq**).
lpc	Line printer control to enable printer.

SYSTEM V PRINT

lpstat	List printers, devices, files in queues.
lp -d*printer filename(s)*	Place *file(s)* in line printer queue.
cancel *job #*	CANCEL a printing job (get # from **lpstat**).
enable	ENABLE a printer (may have to be superuser).

BSD uses a system program **lpd**, a line printer daemon, to control printing to both local and remote printers. This makes the BSD printer commands superior at controlling print jobs on printers connected to remote machines. The **-P***printer* option allows the user to send, check status of, or remove a print job from any printer on the network. (Permission to use a printer is given by adding the user's machine name in the file /etc/host.lad on the remote machine which has the printer attached.) If the **-P** option is omitted, the job is sent to the printer defined in the environment variable **PRINTER** or, if **PRINTER** is not defined, to the default printer **lp**.

When you give the print command **lpr**, your print job is placed in the *printer queue*. If the printer is set and working properly, it will print out your job in turn. To check the status of your print job and to determine its *print job number*, use the **lpq** command. To stop a job from printing (say because you submitted the *Encyclopedia Britannica* by mistake, or because the printer is chewing up your output), try the command **lprm** or **cancel**, followed by your job number. Stopping a print job by turning off the power to the printer will certainly stop the printing, but it may *disable* the printer from further use by the system or confuse a (not so) smart printer or printer spool, or both. The printer can be enabled with the `lpc` or **enable** command, but it may take some system work to get the print spooler program working again.

As an example, here we see bohr finally getting his name in print:

```
%  cd class                          Change to directory class.
%  ls
prog.f                               One lonely Fortran program.
%  lpr prog.f                        Print prog.f on line printer.
%  lpq                               Tell me files being printed.
lp is ready and printing
Rank Owner Job Files Total Size
active fink 93 guide 367229 bytes
first bohr 94 prog.f 429 bytes
%  lprm 94                           Stop printing prog.f.
                                     The printer is busy so try elsewhere.
%  lpq -Pmath                        Check the math dept.'s printer.
no entries                           OK, it's idle.
%  lpr -Pmath prog.f                 Send the file to be printed.
math is ready and printing
Rank Owner Job Files Total Size
active bohr 86 prog.f 429 bytes      Ah, it's printing.
```

2.9 Editing with vi

The standard Unix text editor is **vi** is so called because it is "visually" oriented (at least compared to the line editors which the pioneers used on their teletypes while treading the Oregon Trail). The **vi** editor and its counterpart **view** display your file on your screen in a similar manner, with **vi** giving you the option of modifying the file in addition to looking at it. To edit an existing file, `filename`:

```
%  vi filename                       Edit filename with vi.
%  view filename                     Read filename with vi.
```

Note: if `filename` does not yet exist, this first command will create it.

The **vi** editor has *command* and *insert* modes. Command mode is the default (this differs from most PC programs), and in it you move the *pointer* or *cursor* around the file, delete text, and save your work. In *insert mode* you enter text into the file. The editor always begins in command mode and returns to it after executing an insert mode command successfully. To enter insert mode, you type insert commands like **i**, **o**, **I**, **O**, **cw**, **CW**; *to leave insert mode (return to command mode), hit the escape key (sometimes marked* **Esc**, *sometimes mapped onto ' [accent grave]).* If at some point you are not sure of your mode or what is happening or you just like to see flashes or hear bells, you can make it a practice to be sure and hit **esc**—it will hurt nothing.

Sometimes you realize you have made changes you don't want, or you think your original had something in it your changed version doesn't and you want to go back to the

vi MOVEMENT

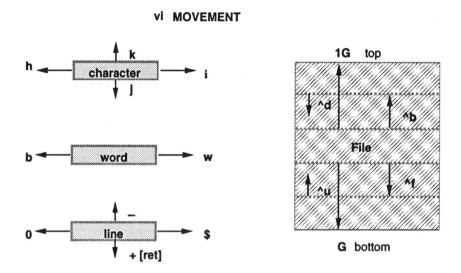

Figure 2.2: Movement commands in vi for different objects.

original. You undo the harm of your last command with **u**, or undo all changes on the present line with **U**. If you think you may have really messed up your file, you may want to **:q!**, that is, quit without rewriting the file. (You can write it to a temporary file with **:w temp** and then quit in case you think you may have done some good.)

vi Command Summary

vi MOVEMENT (Figure 2.2)

←↓↑→	Arrow keys to move cursor.
h j k l	Same as arrow keys above.
w	Move forward one WORD.
b	Move BACK one word.
e	Move to END of word.
^u	Scroll UP a partial screen.
^d	Scroll DOWN a partial screen.
^f	Scroll FORWARD a full screen (page down).
^b	Scroll BACKWARD a full screen (page up).
-	Move up one line.
[ret]	Return, move down one line.
0 (zero)	Move to BEGINNING of line.
$	Move to END of line.
G	Go to END of file.
n **G**	Go to line number *n*.

vi SEARCH

/*text* **[RET]**	SEARCH for *text*.
/ [RET]	CONTINUE search for previous *text*.
?*text*	Search backwards for *text*.

vi CHANGES

s	SUBSTITUTE for character.
S	SUBSTITUTE for line.
i *text* **[Esc]**	INSERT *text* before cursor.
cw *text* **[Esc]**	CHANGE word to *text*.
c3w *text* **[Esc]**	Change 3 words to *text*.
C *text* **[Esc]**	Change rest of line to *text*.
cc *text* **[Esc]**	Change line to *text*.
x	DELETE single character.
r *p*	REPLACE single character with *p*.
R *text* **[esc]**	Replace (type over) characters with *text*.
dw	DELETE word (**4dw** deletes 4 words).
dd	DELETE line (**3dd** deletes 3 lines).
D	DELETE from cursor to end of line.
u	UNDO last change (*remember this one*).
U	UNDO all changes to line (*don't forget this one*).
s	SUBSTITUTE character.
S	SUBSTITUTE lines.
J	JOIN lines.
a *text* **[Esc]**	ADD *text* after cursor.
A *text* **[Esc]**	ADD *text* to end of line.
I *text* **[Esc]**	INSERT *text* at start of line.
o *text* **[Esc]**	OPEN new line below with *text*.
O *text* **[Esc]:**	OPEN new line above with *text*.
esc, or '	END an **insert, replace** command.

vi SUBCOMMANDS

:w *fname*	WRITE (save) *fname* (default: to present file).
ZZ	EXIT the editor, saving all changes (same as **:wq**).
:q!	QUIT emphatically, do not save changes (! is your tool to insist; useful after messing up (also **:w temp**).
:e!	Edit again previous file, i.e., revert to last saved version.
:n	Edit NEXT file (after **vi file1 file2 ...**).
:f	Show current FILE name and cursor line number.

vi COPY and PASTE

Y [RET]	YANK (copy) current line.
yy [RET]	YANK (copy) current line.
yw	YANK (copy) next word.
p	PUT last thing yanked before cursor.
P	PUT last thing yanked after cursor.

2.10   Editing with Emacs

The editor *GNU Emacs* is "free" and we recommend it, especially for use with a mouse. If your system does not have Emacs, ask your system administrator to get it from someone or from "the network," that is, by anonymous ftp to `prep.ai.mit.edu`' (see Chapter 4 on *Computer–Computer Interactions*). Or you can support a good cause and "order the latest version of GNU Emacs and other GNU software on tape from the Free Software Foundation. The Foundation can supply industry standard 1/2 inch tapes, Exabyte tapes, and 1/4 inch cartridge tapes in several popular formats. The fee is around $200 per tape, varying slightly according to media type. For full information, phone the Foundation at (617) 876-3296." Note that the software itself is free, yet the fee is needed to support the distribution service and the development of more free software like *GNU Emacs*. Thus it is "free" in the distribution sense, that is, sometimes "users pay money for copies of GNU software, and sometimes they get copies at no charge. But regardless of how they got the software, they have the freedom to copy and change it."

In GNU's own words, it is "the GNU incarnation of the advanced, self documenting, customizable, extensible real-time display editor Emacs. (The "G" in "GNU" is not silent.)" Emacs is a *display* editor since it shows you what the file looks like (even as you are changing it). It is *real time* in that the display is updated as you enter commands—as well as your file if you have invoked *auto-save*. It is *advanced* since it contains features similar to those of word processors and PCs—which makes it particularly useful for manipulating computer and human languages. It is *self-documenting* since it contains a built-in help facility (just enter [Ctrl]-h = ^h) as well as a free manual. And finally, it is *customizable* and *extensible* in being able to modify and create commands to your liking. To help you get started, a sample .emacs file is given in Appendix A and on the floppy.

If your system has the Emacs editor, it probably also has the *GNU Emacs Manual* as part of the package. This is good because you can read more than the terse summary we give here to understand Emacs' general philosophy or to use some of its more advanced features. In addition, an excellent learning tool is the tutorial bundled as part of Emacs. To have it process you, even before you know what you are doing, give the commands:

```
%   emacs                              Get the editor going.
 ^h t                                  Help, tutorial.
```

To edit `filename` or create it if it does not exist:

```
%   emacs filename
```

In contrast to **vi**, Emacs is normally in the *insert* mode and is insensitive to the case of the commands. You can start entering or deleting text wherever the pointer is, and you can move the pointer with the arrow keys or the mouse. To change to *command* mode, you use the *control* key (sometimes labeled CNTRL, Ctrl, cntrl, or CTL) or the *meta* key (sometimes labeled Alt or EDIT). If there is no Meta, Alt, or Edit key, type [esc], release the escape key, and then type the character. Here, the *escape* key may be mapped to ' (accent grave) or something else on your system. (The Emacs manual and help commands use the notation c-x and m-x.)

Hints: Remember to practice with a scratch file and use the *undo* command ^x u to fix errors. If you have really messed up the file in the Emacs buffer, do NOT save it

(`^x^s`) as this replaces the original; instead, save it to a scratch file (`^x ^w temp`) or not at all. If Emacs seems "messed up" to you and you cannot get it back on track, try `^g` to make it return to a normal state. If that does not fix it, you can quit Emacs with `^x ^c`—but answer carefully the questions Emacs asks you if you do not want the disk file replaced (and remember to use `^h` for help).

Part of the attraction of Emacs is that you can view and edit several files simultaneously— or even different parts of the same file—and cut and paste among them. While this is not hard to do, we have found the Emacs terminology confusing at times, in part since it differs from the *vi* editor. For one thing, the display you see on the screen has at least three *windows*. The big window on top is where the text of your file is normally found, while the small windows below are the *mode line* and *echo line*. You can divide that big window into many smaller windows and then use them independently, activating a particular window by placing your cursor in it (or clicking your mouse).

Confusion arises from the fortunate fact that you do not really edit a file, but rather are editing a copy of the file in the computer's memory. The region of memory where Emacs stores the copy of your file is called a *buffer*, and every time you ask Emacs to *find* another file it copies it from the disk to *another* buffer (unless an unmodified copy of your disk file is already in one of its buffers). Accordingly, there may well be more files in the Emacs buffers than you are viewing in your window(s). Opening and closing the windows which look at these buffers has no effect on the buffers (although killing that buffer does), and likewise the modifications you make to the file in the buffer (to the buffer) have no effect on your disk file until you tell Emacs to *save* the buffer copy as a disk copy. This is the point where you should be very careful and don't do this if you are too tired or rushed.

Emacs Command Summary

emacs SPECIAL CHARACTERS

ˆx (c-x)	Press *control* key while typing x.
m-x (˜x)	A *meta-x*,
	press *Meta, Alt,* or *Option* while typing x.

emacs UNDO, HELP

ˆx u (ˆ_)	UNDO last command (repeatable).
ˆg	ABORT command in process.
ˆh	HELP.
ˆh t	Tutorial.
ˆh a *subject*	Help APROPOS *subject*.
[tab]	Emacs finish command, or give possibilities.
ˆxˆc	EXIT Emacs with queries.
ˆy	YANK back deleted text.
˜y	YANK back earlier deleted text.

emacs ENTERING FILES, EXITING

emacs *filename*	START Emacs *from Unix* with file *filename*.
emacs +*n filename*	START Emacs *from Unix* at line n of *filename*.
ˆx ˆf *filename*	FIND (open) file *filename*.
ˆx ˆf *dirname*	FIND and list directory *dirname*.
ˆx 4 ˆf *filename*	FIND (open) file *filename* in new window.
ˆxˆr *filename*	READ file *filename* to active buffer.
ˆx i [ret] *filename*	INSERT file *filename* into buffer.
ˆx ˆs	SAVE file from active window (buffer).
ˆx s	SAVE some file from inactive window (buffer).
ˆxˆw *filename*	WRITE active buffer into file *filename*.
ˆxˆc	EXIT Emacs with queries.

emacs BUFFERS .

ˆx ˆb	List BUFFERS,
	then 1 selects highlighted buffer.
ˆx b *buffername*	Switch to *buffername*.
ˆx 4 b *buffername*	Switch to *buffername* in separate window.
ˆx k	KILL active buffer.
ˆx ˆv	KILL active buffer, find alternative.
ˆx ˆc	QUIT Emacs.

emacs WINDOWS

ˆx 2	SPLIT display into 2 horizontal windows.
ˆx 5	SPLIT display into 2 vertical windows.
ˆx 1	Collapse display into ONE window.
ˆx 0	Kill (ZERO) inactive window.
ˆx o	Make OTHER window active.
ˆx p	Make PREVIOUS window active.
ˆx ˆ (caret)	Open active vertical window HIGHER.
ˆx }	Open active horizontal window WIDER.

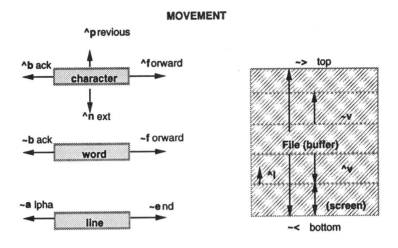

Figure 2.3: Emacs movement commands for differing objects.

emacs MOVEMENT (Figure 2.3)

ˆf	FORWARD a character.
ˆb	BACKWARD a character.
ˆn	NEXT line.
ˆp	PREVIOUS line.
˜f	FORWARD a word.
˜b	BACKWARD a word.
ˆa	Beginning (ALPHA) of line.
ˆe	END of line.
˜a	Beginning (ALPHA) of sentence.
˜n	Beginning of (NEW) paragraph.
˜p	End of PARAGRAPH.
˜99 ˆl	LINE 99.
˜99	Enter 99 as ARGUMENT.
˜x goto-line [ret] 99	LINE 99.
˜x goto-char [ret] x	CHARACTER x.
˜< (meta <)	BEGINNING of file.
˜>	END of file.
ˆv	FORWARD 1 screenful.
˜v	BACKWARD 1 screenful.
ˆ ˜v	Forward in inactive window.
ˆl (el)	RECENTER (cursor on same character).
˜l (el)	Change next word to LOWERCASE.
˜ what-line	Show what line cursor is on.
ˆ =	Show cursor position.

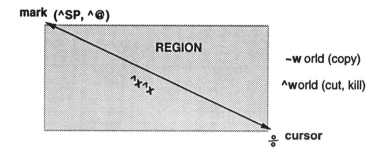

Figure 2.4: Emacs "region" definition and commands.

emacs MARKS and REGION (Figure 2.4)

^[space] (^@)	Set MARK at cursor.
cursor	REGION = mark - cursor position (new).
^x ^x	EXCHANGE mark and cursor (i.e. check region).
^w	Cut (KILL) region (WORLD) to clipboard.
~w	COPY region (WORLD) to clipboard; no delete.
^x [Tab]	Indent region.

emacs SEARCH AND REPLACE

^s *word*	Incremental SEARCH forward for *word*; end with [esc] or click, continue with `^s`.
^s	Continue SEARCH forward.
^r	REVERSE search.
[esc]	End search (or some other commands).
[bs]	Move back in search.
^r *word*	REVERSE search for *word*.
^s	Continue search forward.
~x occur [ret] *expression*	List all OCCURRENCES of *expression*, cursor on line in occur-buffer, `^c ^c` to find.
~x search-forward **[ret]** *word* **[ret]**	Non-incremental SEARCH.
~x replace-string **[ret]** *old* **[ret]** *new*	REPLACE ALL *old* with *new*.
~%	Synonym for **~x** `query-replace`.
~x query-replace [ret] *old* **[ret]** *new*	REPLACE after QUERY *old* with *new*, Emacs asks.
y, n, [esc], ,	Your replies: yes, no, quit, yes+stop (= ,).

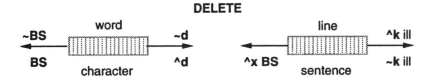

Figure 2.5: Emacs deletion commands for differing objects.

emacs DELETION AND KILLING (Figure 2.5)

[bs]	DELETE character BEFORE (left of) cursor.
^d	DELETE character AFTER cursor.
~[bs]	DELETE word BEFORE cursor.
~d	DELETE word AFTER cursor.
^k	KILL & store from cursor to end of line.
~k	KILL to end of sentence.
^w	CUT & store region (WORLD) to clipboard.
~w	COPY region (WORLD) to clipboard; no delete.

emacs CUT AND PASTE

^k	KILL & store from cursor to end of LINE.
~k	KILL to end of SENTENCE; stored on clipboard.
^w	Cut (KILL) region (WORLD); stored on clipboard.
~w	COPY region (WORLD) to clipboard.
~ ^w	Append kill to previous kill on clipboard.
^y	Paste (YANK) text of last kill (from clipboard).
~y	Paste (YANK) text of PREVIOUS kill.

emacs WORD PROCESSING

~q	FILL paragraph containing cursor.
~g	FILL region (mark - cursor).
~1 ~q	Fill and right JUSTIFY paragraph.
^o (oh)	OPEN a blank line here.
^x ^o	DELETE multiple OPEN (blank) lines.
~u	UPPERCASE next word.
~l	LOWERCASE next word.
~c	CAPITALIZE next word.
^x ^u	UPPERCASE region.
^x ^l	LOWERCASE region.
^t	TRANSPOSE letters.
~t	TRANSPOSE words.
^x [tab]	INDENT region.
~$	SPELLcheck last word.
~x spell-buffer	SPELLcheck buffer.
~x spell-region	SPELLcheck region.

X-Mouse Functions, Emacs

Emacs mouse functions are great time savers, and once you have learned to use them, your workstation will perform almost as well as a personal computer.

emacs MOUSE BUTTONS

left	SELECT window, SET MARK at mouse.
^middle	CUT (kill) text between cursor and mouse, also copies to clipboard.
[shift]+middle	COPY text between cursor and mouse to clipboard.
middle	Move cursor to mouse position, PASTE clipboard.
[shift]+R	Move cursor to mouse position, PASTE clipboard.
^[shift]+R	SELECT window, CLOSE other windows.
^R	SPLIT window into two windows.

Modes

The modes in Emacs act as both a formatting tool for a particular language as well as an environment in which to execute that language within Emacs.

emacs MODES

˜x *text* **[ret]**	Text.
˜x *latex* **[ret]**	LATEX.
˜x *tex-mode* **[ret]**	TEX.
˜x *fortran* **[ret]**	Fortran.
˜x *c-mode* **[ret]**	C language.
˜x *lisp-mode* **[ret]**	Lisp.
˜x *nroff* **[ret]**	Nroff.
˜x *auto-fill* **[ret]**	Auto-fill.
˜x *outline* **[ret]**	Outline.
˜x *overwrite* **[ret]**	Overwrite (repeat to toggle).

emacs TEX SUBCOMMANDS

"	Insert proper open/close quotes in TEXmode.
˜x validate-Tex	Finds unmatched braces {} and $.
˜{	Insert pair of braces with cursor in middle (Tex).
˜}	Move to right of }, used after above.

2.11   Redirecting I/O and Piping

While each Unix command has a *standard input* and *standard output* associated with it, the system is actually quite flexible and you can (or can at least try to) make any file or device serve as input or output. This not only frees you from having to type in the input for your program from your terminal and read its output on a screen but also permits you to study a problem at some depth by using and saving various input and output files. Further, you can really get organized and arrange your programs such that different kinds of input data are read from differing *devices* (aka *units* or *tapes*) and then store these files in appropriate places. You may find that as your programs get more powerful, they require more and more complicated input just to control what they do. Yet, you may also find that it is nearly impossible to type in a complicated sequence of control characters without errors (and subsequent disasters). Consequently, editing a master input file and then making only small changes in it is a great time saver and disaster avoider.

Unix's flexible input and output includes *redirection* and *piping*. This system saves you time and file space and can speed up the computation by permitting the computer to look ahead and plan ahead for the work it must do. Most Unix commands get their input from *standard input*, usually the terminal, and send their output to *standard output*, also usually the terminal. Redirection and piping allow you to tell a command to read its input from some file and write its output to some other file. Piping allows you to tell a *command* to read its input from another *command's* output or even to read its input from the output of a string of several commands without explicitly writing intermediate files. (Unfortunately, not every command gets its input from standard input or sends its output to standard output; in these cases Unix cannot redirect or pipe.)

Redirection

To **redirect input** for a Unix command from a file instead of the terminal, enter the command as:

%	`command < infile`	Take input from file infile.
%	`command` *arguments* `< infile`	Take input from file infile.

Here `infile` is the file from which the command gets its input, and the command's options and arguments are placed *before* redirection.

To **redirect output** generated by a Unix command to a file rather than the terminal, enter the command as:

%	`command > outfile`	Place output in file outfile.
%	`command` *arguments* `> outfile`	Place output in file outfile.

Here `outfile` is the file to which the command sends its output.

Consider the `grep` command. It is used to search a file for a string and write all lines that contain that string to the standard output device. For example,

%	`grep FORMAT *.f`	Search all .f files for word FORMAT.

will search all files with the suffix .f for the character string (word) **FORMAT** and will fill up your terminal screen in a flash with the file names and lines containing **FORMAT**. Or, you can place the screenfuls of output in the file **matches** with redirection

%	`grep FORMAT *.f >matches`	Search, puts finds in matches.

Piping

Piping takes a command's output and transports it (pipes it) to the input of another command:

```
%   command1 | command2
```
                                        Pipe command 1's output to 2's input.

Note that the | symbol is usually found on the far right side of the keyboard and sometimes has a small space in its middle. A common way to use piping is with the **more** command; this permits the examination of a command's output one screenful at a time. For example,

```
%   grep FORMAT myprog.f | more
%   ls -l | more
```
Locate "FORMAT," pipe finds to **more**.
Pipe long list of files to **more**.

These commands cause the output of **grep** and **ls** to go to **more**, which then lists it one screenful at a time. Interestingly enough, while **grep** is finding the lines in **myprog** containing the word FORMAT, its output is feeding into **more**'s input, and simultaneously **more**'s output is going to its output—which in this case is your terminal—possibly before the original command has been completed.

    Piping along a string of commands is also possible. For example,

```
%   myprog | grep alpha | more
```
                              $1 \rightarrow 2 \rightarrow 3.$

Here the program **myprog** sends its output to **grep**, which in turn separates out all occurrences of the string alpha and then sends its output to **more** so we can view it on our terminal screen in less than a flash.

Combining I/O Redirection and Piping

Combining piping, I/O redirection, and program execution provides a general technique for performing complex operations by putting together simple commands. Since programming languages run under Unix, your home-grown program which reads and writes to your terminal can easily be converted to one which reads and writes to files instead (this is how serious computational scientists do it).

    Suppose you are fed up and wish to change **myprog** from prompting you for input from your terminal to reading its input from a file **infile**. You do this with:

```
%   myprog < infile
```
                                    Execute myprog, input file infile.

If you want to examine the output from **myprog** in a civilized manner via **more**, you would combine these tricks,

```
%   myprog < infile | more
```
                              Input from **infile**, output to **more**.

If you still find you're wading through too much output, you can have Unix search through your program's output for, say, the specific string uninitialized with:

```
%   myprog < input-file | grep uninitialized | more
```

Redirecting Error Messages

All Unix commands can have their input and output redirected. Our examples have shown commands using standard input and output. Commands that use *standard error output* require additional attention. A notable example is the C compiler's output which goes to standard error. For example, if you enter the command

```
%  cc myprog.c | more                   This fails.
```

the output will appear on the screen rather than going through **more**. To redirect both standard error output and standard output when using the C shell, add an ampersand (**&**) after the vertical bar **|**:

```
%  cc myprog.c |& more                   Pipe both stderr and stdout in csh.
```

Similarly, if you want to send **cc**'s output to the file `err.file`, place an ampersand after the right arrow >:

```
%  cc myprog.c >& err.file              Redirecting stderr in csh.
```

When using the Korn or Born shells you may redirect standard error and standard output separately. The standard error is labeled **2** and standard output is labeled **1**. The phrase **2>&1** says to direct standard error into the same path as standard output. To pipe both standard error and standard output when using the Korn shell,

```
$  cc myprog.c 2>&1 | more              Pipe both stderr and stdout in ksh.
```

The same trick works when redirecting into a file:

```
$  cc myprog.c 2>&1 > err.file          Redirecting stderr in ksh.
```

If you want to direct the standard output and standard error to different locations, it becomes complicated in the C shell:

```
%  (cc myprog.c > output) >& err.file   Stderr & stdout to different files.
```

Here we have directed standard output to the file `output`. While it looks like we have also redirected both the standard output and the standard error to the file `err.file` because the standard output already has been redirected, we just get the standard error in the error file. In the Korn shell the redirection is simpler since we may direct standard output and standard error separately:

```
$  cc myprog.c 2> err.file > output     Redirecting stderr in ksh.
```

## CHAPTER 3

WORKSTATION SETUP AND USE

All beginnings are hard.

—Chaim Potok, *In The Beginning*

House keeping—that's what this chapter's about: how do you first get your workstation going and properly set up, how do you keep its various systems performing well, and how do you read and write tapes and floppy disks? Before we even try to talk about that, however, we introduce the various pieces that make up your workstation. Not only is it more fun to watch the game when you know the players' names, but it also may be useful to examine our recommended pieces if you are thinking of purchasing or upgrading a workstation.

3.1   The Unix Workstation's Components

It's hard to get the best use out of a tool (such as an automobile) without understanding how it works. With that observation in mind, we attempt here to define the various pieces of a workstation as well as give some of their general speed and size requirements.[1] The workstation is a computer small enough in size and cost to be used by a small group or an individual in a work location yet powerful enough for large-scale scientific and engineering applications. Typically the workstation employs a Unix operating system and has good graphics capability.

Although the specific speeds, sizes, and components of various workstations are constantly changing, the basic ideas should remain the same. Listing the minimum configuration needed to run Unix well, however, is not a clear-cut matter, since it depends on what the system will be used for and what performance will be expected from it (analogous to the engine requirements of an automobile). Users with "hot" systems generally cannot imagine enduring the pain of living with anything less, yet acquiring even a minimal configuration is a great advance for those with inadequate systems. In an additional analogy to

---

[1] A similar—but somewhat higher level—discussion for supercomputers occurs in Chapter 12, *RISC and Supercomputer Architectures*.

automobile, how fast a CPU or how large a block of memory you purchase will often be determined more by your budget and ego than by the requirements of the software. Even if you try to be Spartan, the new components introduced every year as optional luxury items often become required in the future. So you may well end up buying them but at a time when they have become less expensive.

CPU The central processing unit (CPU) combined with the floating point unit (FPU) is the brains of the workstation. The CPU's speed is determined by its design and, somewhat independently, by its *clock speed*, that is, the time it takes the computer to execute the simplest instruction. The relative speeds of two machine with the same CPU is the ratio of their clock speeds.

The collection of programs known as Unix has grown a lot in power and extent in recent years. This growth, combined with the wide use of CPU-intensive graphics displays and their associated use of the X Window System, means that a Unix workstation requires a fast processor.[2] It is easy to benchmark a particular numerical program to see exactly how long it takes a certain machine to turn out the right answer. It is harder, however, to determine ahead of time what the *response time* of your computer will be in an actual working situation when there are a number of users, a number of programs running in the background, and so forth. Since user productivity is significantly affected by this response time,this is an important consideration.[3]

Let's say your usage includes a good number of X applications, *X terminals*, graphics packages, symbolic manipulation users, and CAD/CAM users. You may find the response time of the system, and thus its usability and everyone's productivity, increase greatly as you move to a faster machine or a network of machines.

RAM The random access memory (RAM) is the computer's electronic storage. It is so named because each bit of it can be accessed directly, that is, "randomly," in contrast to the more sequential access of tapes and disks. Typically a commercial Unix system requires 4–8 megabytes (MB) of memory to simply run the base system. It is relatively easy to determine the memory requirement of any major programs which your workstation will run. Just read it from the compiler map. Apart from large numerical codes, X Windows tends to be the largest consumer of memory. Consequently, unless you really prefer a lean, and slow, lifestyle, consider 16 MB the minimum RAM for a Unix workstation running X Windows. If there will be heavy graphics use or intensive use by several people, the memory requirements increase. A single-user workstation with 32 MB of RAM is not uncommon.

Hard Disk Memory It seems that no matter how large or fast a hard disk you purchase, after a few months of use it appears to have become too small and too slow. Unix keeps a record of what's on the the hard disk(s) by first dividing the hard disks into *logical units* called *file systems* and then treating each file system as an independent unit. Therefore, several file systems may reside on a single, physical hard disk. Conversely, with a feature called *volume groups* under AIX and OSF/1, several physical disks may be grouped together to make a file system larger than any single

---

[2] The X Window System, known as X to its friends, is discussed in some detail in Chapter 5, *Looking through X Windows*.

[3] Doherty & Pope (1986).

disk. All Unix implementations are limited to 2 gigabytes (GB) maximum for any file or file system.[4] As CPU speeds and the scope of computations have increased, this limit has become a hardship for some users and may well be changed in the future.

Hard disks are rated by size and average access speed. The size is usually stated in megabytes for an unformatted disk. You can expect a 15- to 20% decrease after formatting. The smallest (PC) Unix systems require a minimum of 100–150 MB, while a workstation Unix may well require 300 MB minimum. While a 600 MB hard disk is adequate for scientific work, it is not uncommon to see systems with more than 1GB of disk space.

The access speed for a hard disk is the average time it takes the disk to move its "heads" to a place where it can read or write your data. Currently slow drives, such as found on laptops, have access times of 50 milliseconds or more, while fast workstation drives have access times of 15 milliseconds or less.

Console Terminals can be simple serial ones capable of displaying text only or graphical ones capable of displaying both text and pictures at high speeds and in colors.[5] The console is the communications center of the system while booting, the bulletin board for error and informational memos during operation, and should be the place where the system administrator works during system maintenance. From a systems point of view, workstations don't require a graphics display but do require a "console" as a device to handle text information. Depending upon the workstation, this could be a simple serial terminal or a small monochrome display.

Terminals Terminals previously denoted text-only displays connected to a computer by a serial (RS232) line. Now many ASCII terminals have been replaced by PCs running terminal emulation software and, increasingly, by X terminals.

System Bus A bus is a communication channel (bunch of wires) used for transmitting information quickly among parts of a computer. The system bus is the data channel between the CPU and the *adapters*. The adapters are boards containing the electronics for activities such as networking and graphics. Unless you have some special need for particular high speed I/O adapters, the size and speed of the system bus should not be a concern of yours.

SCSI Bus The SCSI or "scuzzy" bus has become the most popular standard for attaching hard disks and tape drives to workstations. The SCSI standards require each device on the bus to have its own intelligent controller so that the device and workstation can talk to each other in a high level language. This makes it possible to just plug in a new hard disk from a third-party vendor (not the computer manufacturer), reboot the system in the installation mode, and have it all work. To make sure things aren't so easy as to become boring, there now are several SCSI standards. The orignal SCSI, now called SCSI I, has a slow maximum data transmission rate of 2–5 MB/s. The new standard SCSI II corrects some deficiencies in the original protocol and boosts the bus speed up to 10 MB/s. Other standards, such as "Fast SCSI," have speeds greater than 10 MB/s.

---

[4]The exception is UNICOS on Cray computers.

[5]Some characteristics of graphical displays are discussed in Chapter 6 on *Introduction to Graphics and Visualization*.

Another attraction of SCSI is that it allows users to add hard disks or tape drives which are external to their workstations. This means the user can just plug a cable into a port on the backside without having to handle the "guts" of the computer. The external device resides in its own case with its own power supply and can be repaired or replaced with minimal disturbance to the system (and since drives are mechanical, they will break down regularly). While this may suggest to you that you need a computer with many ports on the back, that is not necessarily true since additional SCSI devices can be connected to the extra port usually located on a SCSI device. Having a number of such devices connected to each other with cable loops is called a *daisy chain*. At present, seven devices are the maximum number which can be controlled by a single SCSI bus.

Network Adapter A network connects one computer with another or, more commonly now, one local network of computers with many other networks. For the vast majority of workstation users, "network" means *ethernet,* a high speed local area network (LAN) composed of specific cable technology and communications protocols (TCP/IP). The worldwide interconnection of ethernets is called *internet*. Ethernets are serial networks which run at 10 MHz and so can transmit approximately 10 MBs of data per second (that is, their bandwidth is approximately ten floppies per second). IBM's *token ring* networks run at 4 or 16 MHz, while the common fiber optics network FDDI runs at 100 MHz.

Although ethernets are fast compared to PC networks like Appletalk, they can transmit only one message at a time, a so-called *packet*. The packet contains the data to be transmitted as well as the address of the destination and a return address. As the number of machines on a network increases, the fact that they all must share this 1 MB bandwidth means that the effective bandwidth for any one computer is decreased since it may have to wait while another machine's packet gets delivered. These packet *collisions* do not become much of a performance problem until there are many machines on the same network or until the network is used heavily for activities such as Network File System (NFS). If the traffic does become a problem, it may be a good idea to break the network up into subnets joined by *routers* or *bridges* .

The physical characteristic of your workstation's ethernet is either "thin ethernet" or "thick ethernet." Both carry the same electrical signals, yet do so on different size coaxial cables and with different connectors. The thin ethernet cables are lightweight, 75-ohm coaxial cables that get looped from one machine to the next. With thick ethernet, a 15-ohm cable connects the computer to a *transceiver* box which is securely fastened to a thick coaxial cable. The advantage of thin ethernet is lower cost and ease of cable hookup. The disadvantage is that if any one connection to a machine is broken, the entire network is down. Further, thin ethernet supports fewer connections and can be extended a shorter distance (185 m and 30 nodes for thin ethernet and 500 m and 100 nodes for thick ethernet). Commonly, a local group's ethernet may be thin while a department's ethernet may be thick.

Tape Drives Magnetic tapes provide mass storage. Along with floppy disks, they are used to back up programs and data, to exchange programs and data, and to receive updates of presently running software. It is always just a matter of time before any hard disk fails ("crashes"), so the need for backup should be attended to. Magnetic storage devices have also increased in size and speed. The standard for many years had been the 1/4-inch cartridge tape capable of holding some 60–150 MB of data. These are being replaced by 8-mm tape drives using inexpensive standard video tapes and capable of holding over 2 GB of data. There are also drives employing data compression to double the effective storage on a tape. By eliminating unneeded repetitions or space, compression is a good way to get something for nothing. But it does not always give the expected increase, since binary files do not compress as much as text files and since already compressed data files do not compress at all.

3.2 Starting Your Workstation

There are usually so many documents telling you how to properly set up every little part of your workstation that you probably have not read them. Rather than even attempt to summarize those documents, we give you here some general points to keep in mind. To start, we need to state something which is so obvious it may not appear in any technical manual: if you want to get your work done in a finite amount of time, you must have all pieces for your workstation connected together and working, and it should be working with consistent, up-to-date hardware and software.[6] If this is not the situation you find upon first sitting down to work at your workstation, it is probably best to talk about it with someone whose responsibility it is to manage your system (experienced friends can help too, but they may have limited patience and free time).

When starting up your system for the first time, logon as `root` and set `root`'s password with the `passwd` command. If `root` already has a password and you forgot it or never knew it, you may be out of luck. If a former manager cannot tell you the password, you may need to "boot" your system (read it into memory from disk) using the system maintenance or installation diskettes or tape. Alternatively, you can "break into" the system by interrupting the boot process at the correct time. As vendors strive to make Unix more secure, these methods become less available and you may be forced to use the sure method of reloading your machine completely with the manufacturer's supplied Unix. In this latter case, you probably do need help (otherwise you would not be reading this chapter).

When setting up your workstation, you should change the *passwords* on all accounts that the Unix vendor may have supplied with the system. This is for your security if your machine will be on a network or otherwise open to the public. There will be "hackers" who know the passwords of these accounts. Be careful not to eliminate accounts as there are a number of standard accounts that must exist in order for the system to manage ownership and to access files. It is wise, therefore, to make sure that all of these accounts have nonstandard passwords (for example are not words appearing in a dictionary) or are "locked" so they cannot be logged into.

If you are both learning Unix and configuring your system (about like doing brain surgery while first learning biology), you may want to keep things simple by not launching the windowing environment (which we assume is *the X Window System*). In fact, it is a good idea to close down X Windows, sign on as root, and load from the console whenever you install a new program as part of your Unix system. Messages and important questions may appear on the console, and the windowing environment may hide the console from view. If your terminal is not the console, you will need to check the console periodically.

---

[6]Consistent means that if a piece of soft or hard "ware" is upgraded, the other "wares" may not work right unless they too have been upgraded.

Alternatively, when using X Windows you may give the `xterm -C` command to start a separate window in which console messages appear (see Chapter 5 for more details).

If you encounter problems with which none of your friends are able to help, you may find a solution by writing to one of the electronic bulletin boards or mailing to a support group. Many computer manufactures and software vendors have employees that regularly (but possibly unofficially) read the electronic news groups and are willing to help users with problems. Electronic mail has become the standard method for reporting problems to both vendors and local support groups.

Electronic mail is a great way to get help, but it will be of no use if the problem with your system makes mail inoperative. Even if your system comes with "on-line" documentation which can be read on your terminal, it is still important to have printed copies of the more basic manuals and of the phone numbers of your maintenance staff. Put them in a readily accessible system notebook for the occasions when your system is down or having troubles. It is also a good idea to print copies of any system files you modify in the course of configuring your system and place them in the system notebook. For example, keep a list of *file systems*, their sizes, and the IP addresses of the computers whose names you enter into your system (these terms will be explained soon).

3.3   Shutting Down and Booting Up

Stopping Unix

Unix machines should go through a shutdown procedure before they are powered down or rebooted. There are a number of reasons for this. One is that many background processes need to be properly terminated so they can remove *locks* from files or update logs. An even more important reason is that Unix keeps up the *inode table*, that is, a table of file names and their locations on the disks. A copy of the table is always in memory while Unix is running, and before shutting off the inode table must be written out to disk. This operation is called a *sync* and is done automatically every 30–60 seconds. If the machine is powered down without "syncing," Unix may loose track of some files. This could lead to an unpleasant situation for system and user when the system is powered up again. Specifically, while blocks of disk space may be allocated for files, there will be no listing in the inode table of where to put them. Alternatively, there may be a listing in the inode table giving the file names, but not the information needed to allocate blocks to the files. In either case you have a "corrupted" file system, and you may need to use `fsck` (described soon) to fix it.

In case we have not been clear enough, we repeat:

Do not just turn off the power to your workstation when you are done working.

In fact, it is best to leave the power on all the time, unless you will be gone for extended periods or if safety, severe storms, or power irregularities are a consideration. A reason not to power down is that there may be jobs or programs waiting to run at night when they will affect other jobs the least, or other machines may try to deliver mail to your machine at anytime, or your machine may be part of a network which relies on your computer for service. And of course, if other users are sharing your facilities, they will be excluded (and probably turned off to you) if you power down.

To properly shut the system down, you must have superuser (root) authority and issue the **shutdown** command. The options and form of the shutdown command vary. On BSD or Sun machines, issuing **shutdown now** sends a warning to every user logged into the machine and then shuts the system down. In contrast, on System V and AIX machines, this is done by issuing **shutdown**. All versions allow you to specify a future time for the shutdown, as well as warn users currently logged on that the system is about to go down. The warning gets repeated at more frequent intervals as shutdown time approaches.

On System V the shutdown procedure is something like this:

```
login:  root                            Sign on as root at the console.
#  shutdown                             Enter the shutdown command.
Broadcast Message from root (ttyp00) on ns99
The system will be shut down in 60 seconds.
Please log off now.                     And then it repeats.
Do you want to continue?  (y or n):  y
Shutdown Complete                       Wait for this before turning off.
```

Restarting Your Workstation

You must bootup your workstation (load the system into memory from disk) after a system crash, a hopelessly confused communication network, a power failure, a shutdown period, or making certain modifications to the system. While the system is booting up, it's a good idea to check what's being written to the console and note any numbers on the machine's light-emitting diode display—if there is one. While this may not be an exciting way to spend five to ten minutes, it is something of a tutorial on the contents of your system and can help you locate the cause of problems when they do occur (and help you feel less foolish when you describe your troubles to that experienced friend). During boot up, the computer may ask you to enter the date, the time, and whether you want the system to check the correctness of its own file system. Do not just ignore these requests because you are anxious to get on with it; having the correct date is important in order for you and the system to keep track of which are new and which are old files, and having the system find and then correct errors in its file system with **fcsk** can prevent catastrophic problems later.

Checking the File Systems: fcsk

One of the first tasks that Unix performs when rebooting is a check of the hard disks to see if they were corrupted (usually the result of a rude shutdown).[7] The checking program is invoked with the command **fsck**. Each file system on the disk, beginning with the root file system, is checked separately. If problems are found in the root file system, the problem will be corrected and a message to that effect will appear on the screen. At this point either the system will reboot itself or it will prompt you to reboot it. You have little choice in the matter since the system will not run with a corrupted root file system. If errors are found in other file systems, the system will also ask you what to do. The questions are rather cryptic and we find it hard to believe that anyone but a Unix guru will understand what's

---

[7]AIX and OSF/1 skip the **fcsk** checks since these Unix systems use a different and safer method of updating the inode tables.

being asked. A sample **fsck** session is:

```
/dev/root
Fast File System:  Volume:
** Phase 1 - Check Blocks and Sizes
** Phase 2 - Check Pathnames
** Phase 3 - Check Connectivity
** Phase 4 - Check Reference Counts
** Phase 5 - Check Free List Bitmap
7378 files 194278 blocks 3974 free
```

Above, the system was fine; below there are problems:

```
/dev/usr
Fast File System:  Volume:
** Phase 1 - Check Blocks and Sizes
POSSIBLE FILE SIZE ERROR I=7233
** Phase 2 - Check Pathnames
** Phase 3 - Check Connectivity
** Phase 4 - Check Reference Counts
UNREF FILE I=4612 OWNER=root MODE=20000
SIZE=0 MTIME=Nov 18 06:26:47 1991
CLEAR? y                              Answering yes may remove files.
```

By dint of this last question, users may feel they are in a "Catch 22" situation. If they answer **yes** to **fsck**'s questions, they will have noncorrupted files, but some files may get lost. If they answer **no**, the existing files will remain unusable since they are corrupted. Actually, things are not that bad since **fcsk** places the mangled files or their remnants in the special directory lost+foundat the top of every file system, and you may be able to recover some lost data.

Unless the disk drive has experienced physical damage, as may occur after a voltage spike or a scratched disk, none of your old data files should be affected by the **fsck** recovery. Those new files you were working on at the time of the crash, as well as files that were open for reading or writing will be affected. While this situation may seem unpalatable, the only realistic option is to hope you have a good backup and let **fsck** repair the file system.

3.4   The Project Directory Approach

A useful aspect of Unix is the directory and subdirectory structures it permits. When combined with the **-CF** options to the **ls** command (to distinguish files, directories and executables), it lets you keep your projects separate, organized, and manifestly accessible to both you and others. *We suggest you give a separate directory to each project* you work on as well as to letters, subroutine libraries, and your own personalized commands. Then divide each major directory into subdirectories for data, input, output, source codes (src), object codes, etc. For example, peeking into loren's home directory we find:

```
% cd /u/loren                    Change to home directory.
% pwd                            Print name of working directory.
/u/loren                         Ah, home sweet home.
% ls -Fx                         List file Names in columns with codes.
Mail/  bin/  book/  comphy/
letters/ mbox       papers/    proton/
```

We see a directory `Mail` for saving outgoing mail, a file `mbox` for saving incoming mail, a directory `bin` where loren saves his personalized commands, a directory `book` where this book is being written, directories `comphy` and `proton` containing research projects on computational physics and proton scattering, respectively, directory `letters` containing correspondence, and a directory `papers`. Looking into the directory `papers` we see sub-directories, each containing manuscripts:

```
% cd papers                      Change to directory papers.
% pwd                            Check that I'm there.
/u/loren/papers                  Unix assuages loren's anguish.
% ls -Fx                         List files here!
carbon/ kaon/ pbar/ pole/        (Publish or perish, you know.)
% ls -Fx kaon                    List contents of kaon.
kn.aux kn.dvi kn.log kn.tex      LaTeX files for paper.
```

In loren's home directory we also find `proton`, a typical directory for a Fortran computing project:

```
% cd                             Change to home directory.
% cd proton                      Go to subdirectory from home.
% pwd                            Check where I am?
/u/loren/proton                  In subdirectory. Good.
% ls -Fx                         List what's here.
LPOTp*    README   data/   in/   Executable (*), file, directories (/).
out/    plots/  subs/
```

In this directory loren has placed notes in the file README describing what LPOTp does, how to use it, and what changes were made recently. LPOTp is an executable file (as denoted by the *). Related data files are in `data`, input files for running LPOTp are in `in`, object files in `obj`, output files in `out`, plot files in `plot`, and Fortran subroutines in `subs`.[8]

These few cases should give you ideas for organizing your projects in the way that is best for you. In particular, you may also find it effective to keep each level simple enough so you can quickly see what's there, to standardize your notation and organization throughout *all* your directories, and to leave notes in README files. You may be able to live well enough in your own mess, but if you want your work to be valuable to others as well, then they need to be able to find it and use it.

---

[8]This organization may make more sense after Chapter 8 on *Using Fortran and C with Unix.*

3.5 Personalizing Unix

While Unix (or your neighbor's dog) may not seem all that friendly at first, in a short time you will probably come around to appreciating its utility—if not its companionship. For example, Unix lets you customize commands for your own particular needs as well as choose how the system responds to just you. Furthermore, since Unix treats files, directories, hardware devices, and software all pretty much the same (as if they were files), you can connect terminals, printers, tape drives, etc., to your system without having to take a course in system programming, or look around for an expert.

Unix as a language has many elements. The *shell*, its outermost layer, interprets your commands as you interact with the system. Part of the power of Unix is that you can write your own shell or choose from a variety of available ones, all similar enough to still classify as Unix, yet different enough to confuse the unwary. The popular shells include the *C shell* (**csh**), the *Borne shell* (**sh**), and the *Korn shell* (**ksh**).

As a practicing scientist or engineer you may well have to work on a number of computers, many with different Unix. This should not be a problem—especially if you maintain somewhat of an experimental attitude and just keep trying some variation of the command you want the computer to obey. Eventually you may even make all environments very similar and equally friendly by setting up *aliases* in your .cshrc and .kshrc files.[9] We must admit, however, to having otherwise dear colleagues for whom the change to Unix or from one Unix to another was an emotion–laden, if not outright traumatic experience. To help avoid stress, we give you some information to help you get started.

Environmental Variables

Environmental variables are used to customize the behavior of programs and to pass information to them. In general, users do not set environmental variables from the command line, but rather have them set in their .profile or .cshrc files (examples of which are in Appendix A). In trying to install, write, or run some new programs, you may need to modify your environmental variables from the command line, and so we show you how to do that in the examples.

Environmental variables differ from the related *shell variables* in that the former are passed along to *all* programs that execute, whereas shell variables are passed only to the shell or shell scripts (programs written in the shell's own language) in which they are defined. Shell variables with which you may be or become familiar include **PATH** and **TERM**. Others include **TEXINPUTS**, which tells the programs **tex** and **latex** where to find input files on your system, and **MANPATH**, which tells the **man** command where to find **man** pages.

To view a particular environmental variable, you issue the **printenv** command with the variable name as the argument. To view all of your environmental variables, you use **printenv** with no arguments:

```
printenv SHELL                          Your default shell.
/bin/ksh
$  printenv                             An SCO Unix example of
```

---

[9]This use of the C and K shells can be quite a time saver. Sample .cshrc and .kshrc files with aliases are given in Appendix A, *Sample Dot Files*, and on the floppy.

```
_=/bin/printenv                          all variables.
HZ=60
VISUAL=vi
PATH=/bin:/usr/bin:/etc:/usr/dbin:/usr/ldbin
LOGNAME=root
MAIL=/usr/spool/mail/root
MERGE_SPCL_MSG=Open Desktop DOS
II_SYSTEM=/usr
SHELL=/bin/sh
HOME=/
TERM=xterm
PWD=/usr/man
TZ=EST5EDT
```

To change or set an environmental variable you use the **export** command. In **sh** or **ksh** you use an = sign, but not in **csh**:

```
$ date                                   We will change the behavior of date.
Fri Nov 22 17:56:14 EST 1991             We get Eastern US time.
$ TZ=CST6CDT                             Set Time Zone to cental time.
$ export TZ                              We must export it to take effect.
$ date
Fri Nov 22 16:56:25 CST 1991             Now we get central time.
$ export TZ=CST6CDT                      Set and export in one step.
csh$ setenv TZ CST6CDT                   csh version, note no "=."
```

Setting Terminal Characteristics

In contrast to proprietary systems like DEC's VMS or IBM's VM, Unix was written so that users may use terminals from any vendor. That being the case, for Unix to properly format output to your screen, the system must know your terminal's characteristic quirks. You tell Unix what kind of terminal you are using by setting the *environmental variable* **TERM** to a name corresponding to your terminal type. If the setting is improper, you may see:

```
% vi .cshrc                              Let's edit the .cshrc file.
Unknown terminal type - all I have is 'dumb' [Using open mode]
```

With an incorrectly set terminal, editors and listing commands will act incorrectly. For example, editors may have problems adding new lines, and pagers may not scroll properly.

To set your terminal type, you set the environmental variable **TERM**. In **sh** or **ksh** this is done with **export**, in **csh** with **setenv** :

```
% echo $TERM                             Tell me present terminal setting.
dumb                                     Don't take this personally.
ksh$ export TERM=ansi                    A popular generic terminal.
csh% setenv TERM ansi                    A popular generic terminal (csh).
```

TERMINAL TYPES

ansi	Popular generic type based on vt100; a good choice if you don't know better.
vt100	Actually a DEC terminal adopted as generic.
xterm	An X Window System terminal.
dumb	System default for unknown terminal.
unknown	Another default for unknown terminal.

More specific terminal characteristics are reported and set with the **stty** command. There are BSD and POSIX versions:

```
% stty
speed 9600 baud; evenp hupcl clocal
brkint -inpck -istrip icrnl -ixany
% stty everything
% Ctrl-J stty sane Ctrl-J
```
No options, show characteristics.
The characteristics.

Display everything, **-a** for System V.
Reset terminal after being messed up.

Once you have the terminal characteristics which you like and which work for you, you can put them in your `.login` file and not worry about it again. To learn more about **stty** and its options, refer to the **man** pages.

Abbreviations with Aliases

You may find after a while that you are giving the same series of commands over and over, and if that seems like needless repetition, it is. One approach, described in Chapter 10, *Unix Tools*, uses "job control" to repeat previous commands. The approach described here uses "aliases" which let you create nicknames for commands or change the name of a command to something you became familiar with in a previous existence (such as **del** and **dir**). Like environmental variables, aliases are defined in the `.cshrc` or `.kshrc` file in your home directory. For example, if you find yourself frequently typing **ls -Fas**, you can set up the alias **dir** for this command:

```
$ alias dir='ls -Fas'
% alias dir 'ls -Fas'
```
In Korn shell.
In C shell.

After the system's login procedure reads all your . (dot) files, typing **dir** acts exactly as if you had typed **ls -Fas**.

To determine the definition of a command, use **alias** with no definition:

```
% alias dir
dir=ls -Fas
% alias
j       (jobs -l)
l       (ls -F)
ll      (ls -lC)
ls      (ls -F)
```
Check the alias for dir.
Unix reveals your secret.
See all aliases.

Note that when we got tricky and gave the **alias** command with no argument, the shell interpreted that as a question and told us all the aliases we had already defined.

You can also *move* command arguments in **csh** and thus make it possible to string several commands together in a single alias. A sample use of this procedure is to combine **cd** and **ls** into a single command which tells you where you are as soon as you get there. To move the arguments of the **cd** command in the alias definition, use \!* . This is a special variable meaning "all the arguments given to the command":

```
alias cd 'cd\!*;ls -CF'          Combination cd and list.
```

Note the escape character before ! keeps the shell from thinking ! is a command.

A Word about Your PATH

Unix searches for commands by following what you have defined to be your **PATH** and executing the first command matching the string of characters you entered. So by defining your path appropriately, you may choose among different versions of the same command. For example, many implementations of Unix place programs written by the native user population into the directory /usr/local/bin. Often these programs are enhanced versions of standard Unix commands particularly suited to the local population (or so they think). Let's say someone at your site installs the GNU **egrep** into /usr/local/bin and you wish to use it rather than the standard **egrep**. To do so, simply make sure that /usr/local/bin is in your **PATH** before /usr/bin (where the standard **egrep** is kept).

Redefining your path to get one command right, say, **/usr/local/bin/egrep**, may cause problems when using a different command, say, **diff3**. Specifically, if one of your local buddies has installed a buggy version of **diff3** in **/usr/local/bin**, it, too, will get called. To get to the standard **diff3**, you would have to issue the command **/usr/bin/diff3** or define an alias for **diff3** that calls **/usr/bin/diff3**.

The order of your path is also important when it comes to programs that you create. Often the default behavior is to place the current directory last in your path. There is a security reason for doing this, but it sometimes has an undesirable side effect. For example, a new user writes a short program and calls it **test**. After compiling, the user tries to run the program by entering the command **test**. The command is accepted but produces no output, so the user assumes the program is buggy. What has happened is that the system's command **test** comes first in the path, so it is run and not the user's program. More than one user has been frustrated by this very example.

One solution to being overruled this way is to tell the shell to use the program in the current directory. You do this by adding a ./ to the front of the name of the program in the local directory. In our example the command would be ./test. This is cumbersome. A better solution is to ignore the advice of your local system administrator and place the current directory at the head of your **PATH**. This is what we do in the sample dot files in Appendix A where you'll find:

PATH=.:$HOME/bin:$PATH	In .profile for Korn shell.
export PATH	In .profile for Korn shell.
set path = (. $home/bin $path)	In .login for C shell.

3.6   Managing Disk Space

Just Give Me Some Room

Although current disk drives afford each user ample storage for ordinary needs, disk space is always finite. Ever-increasing file size and number decrease the total disk space available, and this leads to systemwide slowdown and eventual failure (and probably trouble at the worst possible time). To avoid system constipation, Unix provides tools to monitor and help eliminate unneeded storage. These tools include the du and df commands, which tell you how much space you're using (discussed soon), the *piping* utility, which reduces the need for intermediate files, and a hierarchical file system, which makes it easy to organize your files and avoid duplication.

An obvious but often ignored way to use disk space efficiently is to delete all files you don't need and to do it before the system administrator or the system does it for you (he/she will probably delete some you need as well). Accordingly, we recommend that you make it a habit to give scratch files manifestly temporary names like temp1, temp2, ... so you can remove them on a regular basis without much concern. Automated cleanup programs as well as many system administrators consider core files, a.out files, and sometimes even *.o files to be disposable if disk space gets short. Files in /tmp can also be removed by any user and are often removed by the system when it is rebooted.

Unix's hierarchical file system is one of its strengths. You can utilize this strength by placing your files in directories based on the project you are working on and by having subdirectories within each directory so that there is no more than a small screenful of files in any one directory. Improving your organization and decreasing the number of files you must think about, also decreases disk storage since you won't be afraid to delete a file when you know what's in it. (This is part of the "project" approach described earlier.)

If you want to keep files indefinitely, copy them to a floppy or a backup tape or *download* them to a microcomputer, and put them on one of its removable disks. That way you'll also have a copy when the system crashes (they all do eventually). As discussed later in this chapter and in Chapter 4, the floppies from a standard PC are also a convenient way to transport and exchange files.

Disk Usage, Is There Room?

Although you may know there is lots of room left on the hard disk, it is not unusual to run out of space on one of the disk's file systems or partitions, in which case an error message like

```
NO SPACE ON DEV 0,1
```

will appear on the console, and your program or command may fail with no further ado.[10] Likewise, if one of your programs produces an error message when it tries to write a file and you just know you never had that trouble before, it may well be that you have run out of disk space rather than into a programming error. You determine your personal disk usage, as well as that of the entire system, with the commands du and df.

---

[10]Beware, appearing on the console may mean being hidden behind X Windows, in which case you must switch between the console and X Windows to see the message. If the console is a separate terminal, you may have to look elsewhere.

Disk Free: df

The **df** command reports the amount of "disk free" for each file system. Use it to check how much space is left in your home directory as well as in system directories like /tmp and /. The Unix systems derived from BSD give a nice looking **df** report showing the file system size, the amount used (in both kilobytes and percentage), and the amount available. The Unix systems derived from System V give a cruder **df** report showing the amount available in the file system in blocks of 512-byte size.[11] With the **-t** option, **df** shows the total number of blocks as well:

```
sysV$  df -t                         System V disk free command.
/       (/dev/root        ):    3912 blocks     17789 i-nodes
                   total:  201402 blocks     25168 i-nodes
bsd%   df                            BSD disk free command.
Filesystem        kbytes     used    avail capacity   Mounted on
/dev/sd0a          15671     7612     6491     54%     /
/dev/sd0g         143119   120980     7827     94%     /usr
/dev/sd0e          30655     2494    25095      9%     /var
/dev/sd0d          10207     1784     7402     19%     /tmp
```

Disk Usage: du

The **du** command reports the "disk usage." Use it to show the total size of all files in the named directory and for all directories below it. That is, you use **df** to see if you have a problem and then **du** to see who is causing it:

```
$  ls                                List files and directories.
bin docs lib runs samples src
$  du src                            Show the usage of directory src.
432     src/kp                       The directory kp uses 432 disk blocks.
444     src/kabs                     444 in kabs.
356     src/dslac
392     src/apftn64
264     src/vkabs/test
116     src/vkabs/IBM
1124    src/vkabs                    This is the usage for  vkabs including
                                     the subdirectories test and IBM.
116     src/detmat
752     src/bs
3620    src                          This is the usage for all files
                                     and directories under src.
```

As we see, the size of each directory under src is listed by default. These listings can get to be quite long at times, in which case the **-s** option is handy to get a summary:

---

[11]Disk blocks are often 512 bytes, but they may also be 1 kilobyte. The way to tell is to read the manual for your system or experiment.

```
$  du -s src runs bin lib docs        Give me a summary of usage.
3620     src
19420    runs
160      bin
404      lib
24       docs
%  du | sort -rn                       Give me an ordered list of usage.
%  du -s * | sort -rn                  Give an ordered list of summed usage.
```

File Compression

A good way to conserve disk space is to *compress* files using the **compress, gzip,** or **pack** commands. All shrink files by replacing repeated characters by symbols. Text files compress the most, often by 50–75%. These methods are safe and are a good way to reduce the disk space taken up by seldom-used files. You expand files with the **uncompress, gunzip,** or **unpack** commands.

3.7 Managing the System

Among other things, Unix system management is somewhat of a black art best left to those so inclined. While Unix vendors are creating interfaces which respond to the need for friendlier system management tools, as a consequence of its power and vitality, Unix is still a complicated and ever-changing system. There are several books discussing systems management listed in the Bibliography, and we won't try to summarize them here. Instead, we'll look at a few commands which check the health of your system and make sensible reports. You probably should use these commands regularly since they are the Unix equivalent of checking the oil in your car. Even if you are not having problems, running these commands is a way to teach yourself the normal state of your machine and of discovering problems in the making. Furthermore, we suggest keeping print outs of the system's response to these commands in the system notebook for reference.

Processes: ps

You run a **ps** command with options to check that all system processes were successfully started. The specific processes vary from system to system, but a standard list should include: **init, cron, syslogd, getty, inetd, biod,** and **nsfd.** For example, here is a somewhat abbreviated sample:

```
$  ps -ef                             Full report on processes
   UID    PID  PPID   C   STIME    TTY  TIME CMD
root      1      0    0   Oct 04     -  130:49 /etc/init
root   2039      1    0   Oct 04     -  33:26 /etc/syncd 60
root   3321      1    0   Oct 04     -  1:57 /usr/lib/errdemon
root   3709   5941    0   Oct 04     -  0:00 /usr/lpd/lpd
root   4206      1    0   Oct 04        49:13 /etc/cron
tim    5567  26302    0   Feb 22  pts/1  0:07 /bin/ksh
```

```
root    6974  5941   0   Oct 04              1:51 /etc/syslogd
root    7233  5941   0   Oct 04          -   0:12 /usr/lib/sendmail
root    7492  5941   0   Oct 04          -   0:00 /usr/etc/portmap
root    7751  5941   0   Oct 04          - 11:43 /etc/inetd
ghe     9434  4825   0 01:19:38  pts/5    0:00 -ksh
lu     10007 18140   0 12:29:19  pts/16   0:00 vi t2b.pot
root   12390     1   0   Oct 04          -   4:28 /usr/etc/nfsd 8
root   12647  5941   0   Oct 04          -   0:00 /usr/etc/rpc.mountd
root   12905  5941   0   Oct 04          -   0:00 /usr/etc/rpc.statd
root   13163  5941   0   Oct 04          -   0:00 /usr/etc/rpc.lockd
loren   9462 28395   8 14:30:04  pts/10   0:00 /bin/ps -af -ef
```

You may also use the **ps** command to find processes that should be removed. As an example, it is common to find processes that users have stopped, perhaps by using **Ctrl-z**, and then forgotten. There may also be processes that should have been killed, such as a program that was running when a window was killed or a numerical program stuck in a loop, but are still running and still consuming system resources. You remove these processes by reading the *pid* number from the listing and then issuing the kill command:

```
$   kill pid                          Kill process.
$   kill -9 9462                      A severe kill of loren's process.
```

Job Statistics: vmstat

The command **vmstat** produces information about virtual memory, CPU usage, and disk usage. This is useful for determining if your system is properly configured and if your programs are paging extensively. The command **vmstat** takes two arguments, one for how long to wait between reports and the second for how many reports to write out before quitting:

`%   vmstat 1 8`   Write a report every second for 5 seconds.

procs		memory		page						faults			cpu			
r	b	avm	fre	re	pi	po	fr	sr	cy	in	sy	cs	us	sy	id	wa
1	0	4680	365	0	0	0	1	3	0	123	102	75	0	2	97	1
1	0	4680	364	0	0	0	0	0	0	121	86	67	0	3	76	21
1	0	4680	364	0	0	0	0	0	0	114	70	28	1	0	99	0
1	0	4680	364	0	0	0	0	0	0	123	70	32	2	0	98	0
1	0	4680	364	0	0	0	0	0	0	114	74	28	1	0	99	0
1	0	4680	364	0	0	0	0	0	0	113	84	67	0	21	69	10
1	0	4680	364	0	0	0	0	0	0	127	78	56	8	9	82	1
1	0	4680	364	0	0	0	0	0	0	119	91	71	0	3	86	11

The actual form of the output may vary somewhat from this, and again you should issue the **man vmstat** command to get the details for your system.

To help understand this output, we examine some of the fields. The first two columns under `procs` show the number of processes on the system. Column `r` shows "runable" or active processes, while column b shows "blocked" processes awaiting a resource such as input/output. The avm column under memory denotes *active virtual memory*, that is, memory which resides on the slow, hard disk and not in the fast electronics.[12] The number in the avm column is the number of pages, usually of 4 MB size, being used by that process. This is a good indication of how much memory your system is using; if this number is significantly larger that the size of RAM in your computer, then the system may be spending too much time reading data onto and back from the hard disk (*paging*). In these cases performance could be increased by adding more RAM. The fre column under memory in the listing is the number of pages, again of 4 MB size, of RAM that is unused. This is, however, an unreliable measure of free memory since the table of free pages is not updated until the system needs more pages.

The page columns in the **vmstat** listing tracks the paging activity of the system. This is a specific measure of how virtual memory is being used by your system. The "page in" and "page out" subcolumns, pi and po, tell how many pages of virtual memory are being read in from disk or written out to disk. While some paging activity is normal during program startup, if there is such extensive enough use of virtual memory as to make pi and po nonzero for extended periods of time, then the system has too little RAM to satisfy the needs of all programs during these periods.

The columns in the **vmstat** listing under cpu indicate how the CPU is spending its time. The numbers are the percentages of CPU time for the past interval spent on: us "user time," that is, doing things like running calculations, manipulating data, and drawing graphics and the normal activities of user programs; sy "system time," that is, kernel activities such as input/output; id "idle time," that is, something we all wish we had more of; wa "wait time," that is, the time spent waiting on a device to be ready, usually for input/output. A system well matched with its CPU should spend most of its time in users' work since they are the ones paying the bills. While programs containing lots of I/O can push the system time up, in normal use it should be low, say below 33%, even when the system is transferring large files.

It is illuminating to start **vmstat** before submitting a large, numerically intensive program and then redirect **vmstat**'s output into a file you can study later. As you observe the reports issued by **vmstat** every few seconds, you should be able to see how well the system preformed while running your program and possibly spot problems like excessive paging or input/output.

I/O Statistics: iostat

The command **iostat** is a useful complement to **vmstat**. Unfortunately, **iostat** is not found on as many Unix systems as **vmstat**. As the name implies, **iostat** tells you the status of input and output on your workstation, namely, how your hard disks and I/O (tty) ports are performing. Like **vmstat**, the arguments of **iostat** are the frequency of reporting and the total time for all reports. This report is for a workstation with three hard disks, xd0, sd0, and sd1. The columns under tty report the number of characters written in and out. The columns under each disk report bps, the number of blocks written per second to that disk; the number of transfers per second, tps; and the time in milliseconds for an average seek from that disk, msps.

---

[12]Virtual memory is discussed in some detail in Chapter 13 on *Programming RISC and Vector Machines.*

```
%  iostat 1 5                          Write a report every second for 5 seconds.
      tty          xd0           sd0            sd1            cpu
tin tout bps tps msps  bps tps msps  bps tps msps  us ni sy id
  0   16  13   2 10.4    4   1  0.0    2   0  0.0    3  0  5 92
  0   77   0   0  0.0    0   0  0.0  123  23  0.0    1  0 28 71
  0   77   0   0  0.0    0   0  0.0  132  22  0.0    1  0 32 67
  0   79   0   0  0.0    0   0  0.0  150  37  0.0    3  0 38 59
  0   78   1   1  9.5    0   0  0.0  127  32  0.0    4  0 30 66
```

You will notice that the cpu usage is reported on the extreme right. While the "wait time" is not available on the listing produced by this Sun system, the column ni reports the amount of time spent running low priority, that is, "niced," programs.

Disk Space: df and du

Part of system management is making sure there is enough disk space for the users and the system. If disk space gets too low, Unix will fail and will often do so in a rather perplexing and possibly ugly way (like bouncing mail or scrambling files). As described already in § 3.6, the df command reports the amount of "disk free" for each file system, while the du command reports the "disk usage." You correspondingly use df to see if you have a problem and then du to see who is causing it.

Active File Systems: mount

The command mount, with no options, shows what file systems are mounted, that is, which are available. This is often used to determine if an NFS (Networked File System) is available and to assist system maintenance.

Open Files: fuser

The command fuser lists which "users" or processes have "files" open. This is useful if you want to replace or remove a file or unmount a file system without making enemies of fellow users. For example,

```
%  fuser -u data.in              Is someone using data.in?
data.in:   21064(hank)           Yes hank is, the process is 21064.
```

Beware, fuser will not show if a user is editing a file since the editor copies the file to a buffer before editing.

3.8   Managing Networked Computing

According to the computing paradigms of Chapter 1, we are seeing and will continue to see more and more computing done over networks. For users on workstations this may mean receiving and sending mail, attending conferences with colleagues and common interest groups, transferring files between machines, running commands and programs on remote machines, and producing output or receiving input from afar. And so, here are some Unix tools to help in the setting up and looking after the network.

Computer's Name: hostname

Feeling lost? The command **hostname** will tell you the name of the workstation you are on, and, if available, **host** will give you the network name and number of a computer:

```
$  hostname                              What is name of machine I'm on?
physics                                  The short name.
$  host physics                          What is full name/number of physics?
physics.osrt.edu is 128.193.96.1         The full name.
```

These simple pieces of data are particularly useful in networked computing. You can check if your computer can look up the name of another machine (or of itself), and you can check which machine is feeding a specific window on your screen. The full name obtained from **host** is that which can be recognized from any machine in the world, the short name obtained from **hostname** can only be used locally.

Nameserver Lookup: nslookup

If you want to compute over a network, say to transfer files between machines or to run commands remotely, then your computer must know both the name and numerical address of the machines with which it will network. When everything is working, you need only know the name of the remote machine since then the system translates this name to a numerical address for you. The command **nslookup** is useful for testing the nameserver. Depending upon what is known, it queries the *nameserver* for a computer's name or address. The "nameserver" is a computer somewhere on the network which, when given a name of a host computer such as physics.orst.edu, "serves up" a numerical *IP address* such as 127.31.128.61.

As discussed further in this chapter, the nameserver computer is often quite remote yet is essential for mail systems and networked computing. If your system does not use a nameserver, you must keep a list of machines and their IP addresses in the file /etc/hosts. If you are using a nameserver, the file /etc/resolv.conf will contain the IP address of the local nameserver computer as well as alternative servers (helpful if the regular nameserver goes down or is not reachable). If your machine is the nameserver for the network, your /etc/resolv.conf file may be empty.

It is easy for us to say that the file /etc/hosts should contain the "hostnames" (names and addresses) for all computers you may want to contact now or in the future, yet it is quite a chore to obtain and maintain such a file. The use of a nameserver takes care of this for you. The nameserver is actually a hierarchical system with *domains* or zones of responsibility. Let's say you issue the command:

```
%  telnet physics.orst.edu              Connect me to physics.orst.edu.
```

Your local nameserver may not know about physics.orst.edu, but it does know that if it can't resolve a name (find its address), it should contact one of the national nameservers on the internet. That national nameserver may not know about every specific machine either, but it does know that the nameserver for the *domain* orst.edu is ns1.orst.edu, and it knows the address of that machine. The national nameserver consequently contacts the orst.edu nameserver, gets the information for physics.orst.edu, and then passes it back down the network until your machine get the address. You then can complete your **telnet**.

Here is a sample /etc/resolv.conf file:

domain	orst.edu
nameserver	127.31.128.61
nameserver	127.31.128.245
nameserver	127.31.31.62

This resolv.conf file defines the domain to be orst.edu, the primary nameserver to be ...61, and then two alternative nameservers as well. The system will go through alternative servers in the order given if earlier nameservers fail to perform. If the primary nameserver is not responding, you may notice something like a 1-minute delay while the system makes sure the primary server fails before contacting an alternative.

If the nameserver is not working, remote commands may fail. You will still be able to "**ping**" the remote machine using the IP address rather than the name, but that just proves that you are still connected. To add to your problems, you may also have problems opening new X Window applications and surely will have problems with NFS mounts. If you try to **cd** to an NFS-mounted directory, your shell (command line interpreter) will "hang," that is, not allow any further input. This will also happen to commands like **df** when it tries to show the size of the NFS-mounted file system.

Actually, **nslookup** is a complex command with many options, is not available on all systems, and should be checked via your system's man pages. As an example, we show here some examples of using **nslookup** to test if the nameserver if working, to get an IP address for a hostname, and to get the hostname when we know the IP address:

```
$  nslookup                                          Lookup with no options.
* Can't find server name for address 127.31.128.61:   Timed out
Default Server:  ns2.orst.edu                        Second choice.
Address:  127.31.128.245
>  [ctrl]-d                                          We use [ctrl]-d to exit.
```

Here **nslookup** is unable to contact the primary server and so switches, after a long pause (Timed out), to the first alternative in the /etc/resolv.conf file. If no alternative had been available, **nslookup** would have given a message stating this and then terminated. The prompt > means **nslookup** is in command mode, and we got it out of command mode with [ctrl]-d.

We next ask the nameserver for an IP address of a hostname:

```
$  nslookup                                          Lookup with no options.
Default Server:  ns1.orst.edu                        Primary server is found.
Address:  127.31.128.61
>  physics.orst.edu                                  We ask for a familiar address.
```

```
Server:  ns1.orst.edu                    The name of the server is repeated.
Address:  127.31.128.61
Name:  physics.orst.edu                  The query succeeded.
Address:  127.31.16.10
> nr.tromso.no                           We look up an international address.
Server:  ns1.orst.edu
Address:  127.31.128.61
Name:  nr.tromso.no                      Server returns the address.
Address:  127.231.7.97
Aliases:  ftp.tromso.no
> fake.orst.edu                          We ask for a machine that does not exist.
*** ns1.orst.edu can't find fake:        Server returns an error message:
 Non-existent domain.
> [ctrl]-d                               We use [ctrl]-d to exit.
```

If you do something like this to test your nameserver, you should try several hostnames, including some that you know, as a check. Nameservers can contain lots more information that just IP addresses; for example, they can give routes for delivering mail or give characteristics of the workstation's hardware. In the example below we make a different type of query. We ask for the alphabetic hostname of a computer whose numerical IP address we know, that is, the reverse of what we did above:

```
$ nslookup                               Lookup with no options.
Default Server:  ns1.orst.edu            Primary server found.
Address:  127.31.128.61
> set type=PTR                           We ask for a different type of query.
> 10.16.31.127.in-addr.arpa.             We reverse address and
                                         add the suffix, note ending period.

10.16.31.127.in-addr.arpa.
 Host name = physics.orst.edu
> [ctrl]-d                               We use [ctrl]-d to exit.
```

If your nameserver fails to respond for an extended period, you may want to switch to using the /etc/hosts file. It is a good idea to keep the /etc/hosts file up to date with the remote machines you use the most. Then, after the nameserver fails, move /etc/resolv.conf to /etc/resolv.conf.bak and the system will use the /etc/hosts file instead of the nameserver. Be sure to "move" the /etc/resolv.conf.bak file back to /etc/resolv.conf when the nameserver comes back up.[13] Note that **nslookup** will not work with the /etc/resolv.conf file renamed unless you specify which server to contact using command options. This is how you can check whether the nameserver is working again:

```
$ nslookup - 127.31.128.61               Use the ns1.orst.edu server.
Default Server:  ns1.orst.edu
Address:  127.31.128.61
>
```

---

[13]Move in the Unix or U-Haul sense, remove the original.

Are You There? ping

The command **ping** is an easy and poetic tool for testing network connectivity. It sends regular messages or *packets* to the named remote machine, counts the time till each packet returns home, and takes note if any packets get lost. Generally **ping** continues to send packets until it is stopped by you with a ^c or **delete** command. Under SunOS, ping simply returns a statement that the remote host is *alive* or that there is *no answer.* However, using the -s option on Suns will make its **ping** behave as we demonstrate here:

```
% ping arnor                         Or try /etc/ping, /usr/etc/ping, if ping not in path.
PING arnor.thomas.hal.com:  (127.29.140.13):  56 data bytes
64 bytes from 127.29.140.13:  icmp-seq=0.  time=3.  ms
64 bytes from 127.29.140.13:  icmp-seq=1.  time=2.  ms
64 bytes from 127.29.140.13:  icmp-seq=2.  time=3.  ms
 [ctrl]-c                            User interrupts the program.
--arnor.thomas.hal.com PING Statistics--
3 packets transmitted, 3 packets received, 0% packet loss.
round-trip (ms) min/avg/max = 2/3/3
```

A 1% packet loss is not uncommon or a special matter for concern if the remote machine is not "local." In fact, packet losses greater than 15% are not uncommon on wide area networks, such as those across countries or oceans. On local networks, though, there should be no more than an occasional packet lost. At present, local ethernets attain round trip times which are less than 5 milliseconds, and wide area networks have round trip times as long as hundreds of milliseconds.

Network Interfaces: netstat

The command **netstat -i** shows the network interfaces defined on your machine:

```
$ netstat -in
Name Mtu  Network    Address      Ipkts Ierrs Opkts Oerrs Coll
en0* 2000 127.29.13  127.29.13.9  514       0   534     0    0
lo0  2048 127        127.0.0.1    996       0   996     0    0
```

The first entry is for the computer's own ethernet. The * next to the entry shows that the interface has been *marked down*, that is, shut off. Ethernet interfaces are generally labeled en0, le0, or un0. The entry lo0 is the *loopback.* It is a special software network (no wires) on which the machine talks to itself, as, for example, showing how X Windows communicates with the displays. If the network is marked down, then it may indicate that the system has turned itself off because it found some necessary piece of hardware or software missing. If that is the case, your best approach to solving the problem may be to reboot your workstation. Carefully watch the console for any error messages concerning the network as the machine comes up. (How're your speed reading skills?) Then investigate the indicated problems; it may be as simple as an adapter not responding because of a loose connection that occurred because you moved some wires.

Network Routes: netstat

The **-rn** option on **netstat** shows the default *routes* for your network. Routes are the paths network traffic takes to contact a remote machine. To reach local machines on the same network as your machine, you do not need any extra routes. To reach the rest of the world, you need to define a default route which tells your machine to send all traffic not belonging to your network to this default router. You use **netstat -rn** to be sure you have the default route properly defined, and then **ping** the default router to be sure it is alive:

```
$  netstat -rn                       Show default routes.
Routing tables
Destination     Gateway           Flags  Refs    Use  Interface
127.0.0.1       127.0.0.1         UH       3      0 lo0
default         127.29.13.100     UG       0      0 tok0
127.29.136      127.29.13.99      U        2   1696 tok0
$  ping 127.29.13.100                We ping the default router.
PING thomas.hal.com:  (127.29.13.100):  56 data bytes
64 bytes from 127.29.13.100:  icmp_seq=0.  time=3.  ms
64 bytes from 127.29.13.100:  icmp_seq=1.  time=3.  ms
64 bytes from 127.29.13.100:  icmp_seq=2.  time=4.  ms
 [ctrl]-c                            User interrupts the program.
```

3.9   Reading and Writing Tapes and Floppies

At some point in your affair with computers you will have to transport your files from your friendly home computer to a foreign, possibly weird, one. Since there are a number of electronic networks in place, once you read your files onto any computer either at home or away, you may be able to transfer it to another computer—and possibly the foreign one no less. This is the best way to transfer files, and we talk about it in Chapter 4, *Computer–Computer Interactions*. Transferring your files electronically after you arrive at your foreign host may be possible (and necessary since you're bound to have forgotten something or taken the wrong version). However, this may not be reliable for very large files. If you plan to make electronic transfers after you leave home, you need a system at home with which you can communicate (e.g., with the file transfer protocol **ftp** or **kermit** or via remote login); you will need your files in a form which you can access without your being there, not just stored on backup tapes; and you may need a friend at home who knows your hiding places for backups and will turn your computer on as needed.

If you can't transfer your files electronically, or if you want to be sure, you should transport your files on more than one medium, e.g., on *both* floppy diskettes and cartridge tapes. The tape archive command **tar** (to be discussed soon) produces files on differing media in a format that is easy to understand and (nearly) universal. While we will see it is easy enough to load many files onto a particular type of cartridge tape or a high density floppy, for this to be useful there must be a matching drive at the foreign site able to read them. You will have a better chance for success if you write the tape or floppy from a computer system at home which is the same or similar to the foreign one and if you check before leaving home that the tape or floppy can be read.

To avoid the possible disasters, we suggest the following:

- While you may be lucky and able to run your binary codes on another computer without recompiling, it is most reliable to transfer source codes (even if you are transporting the binary files).

- Rather than have your *archives* spill onto a second medium, store a smaller number of files with each **tar** command, and use several **tar** commands (each diskette or tape is then an independent archive). This is preferred since the continuation which was good at home may not work on a different system.

- Bring along at least one sample input and a listing of the corresponding output to use in testing your programs at the new site. Be confident these runs are "correct" and that they don't require much run time to repeat.

The tar Command

Although there are several commands for archiving files, not all are found on every system (for example **cpio**). Specifically, while many Unix systems have a **backup** command for archiving files, the file structure it produces tends to be more system–dependent than the **tar** format, and so we concentrate on the latter. You should be able to read a **tar** tape, diskette, or electronic file made on another workstation provided you have the necessary drive with which to read it.

Note that the **tar** command is also very useful for producing a single file containing many files, say, of all your projects. This single file is then easily transported or emailed with just one command, and then "untarred" at the other end. This is one way of avoiding the maximum limit for files on a floppy. (As indicated in one of the examples below, one then uses the -f option with a file name rather than a device.)

A command **pax** is available on many machines as a new Posix standard. The **pax** command is more flexible than **tar**, creates archives that can be read by the older **tar** command, and can read **tar** archives as well.

OPTIONS FOR tar

-t	Table of contents of files in archive.
-x	Extract files from tar archive.
-c	Create an archive.
-v	Verbose list of files as read.
-f *name*	Output to file or device *name* for archive.

Creating tar Archives

The **-c** option to the **tar** command creates an archive. In this example we use the option **-f /dev/rmt0** to write the archive to the tape drive. The archive contains all the files and directories below the present working directory (nc in this example):

```
% tar -cvf file.tar *          Create archive of all directories into file file.tar.
% tar -cvf /dev/rmt0 nc        Create archive of nc on device rmt0.
% tar -cv -f /dev/rmt0 nc      Alternative form for above.
```

```
a nc/About, 3320 bytes, 7 tape blocks.   The "a" is for "add."
a nc/doc/mknewsrc.1, 3106 bytes, 7 tape blocks.
a nc/doc/ncc.1, 6503 bytes, 13 tape blocks.
a nc/doc/append.mm, 91031 bytes, 178 tape blocks.
a nc/Makefile, 1464 bytes, 3 tape blocks.
a nc/READ.ME, 2626 bytes, 6 tape blocks.
a nc/License, 4082 bytes, 8 tape blocks.
```

Note that the path names of the files in the archive begin at the directory nc specified on the command line. This means at the time the archive is untarred, the directory nc will be created in the current user's directory and all archived files will be placed in it. In contrast, if we had stated the full path name of the nc directory, the files in the archive would have an absolute path name, for example,

```
% tar -cvf /dev/rmt0 /usr/src/nc        Full path name.
a /usr/src/nc/About, 3320 bytes, 7 tape blocks.
a /usr/src/nc/doc/mknewsrc.1, 3106 bytes, 7 tape blocks.
a /usr/src/nc/doc/ncc.1, 6503 bytes, 13 tape blocks.
a /usr/src/nc/doc/append.mm, 91031 bytes, 178 tape blocks.
a /usr/src/nc/Makefile, 1464 bytes, 3 tape blocks.
a /usr/src/nc/READ.ME, 2626 bytes, 6 tape blocks.
a /usr/src/nc/License, 4082 bytes, 8 tape blocks.
```

Now with the full path name specified, the untarred files will be placed in that directory regardless of the current one.

You may create an archive containing more than one directory by just listing the additional files or directories on the command line as well:

```
% tar -cvf /dev/rmt0 weather asroot     Create archive.
a weather/README 9 blocks.
a weather/how2ftp 5 blocks.
a weather/pricing 7 blocks.
a weather/catds 101 blocks.
a weather/datav.1 15 blocks.
a asroot/str.c 2 blocks.
a asroot/Makefile 1 blocks.
a asroot/asroot.c 8 blocks.
a asroot/asrbsd.c 8 blocks.
a asroot/asr.c 8 blocks.
```

As we have said before, multi-diskette `tars` should be avoided if you wish to read the `tar` on a different system. Some systems allow multi-diskette or multi-volume `tar` archives, but many do not. To prevent your `tar` from spilling over onto a second medium, include a smaller number of files on the `tar` command, and use several `tar`'s.

Listing tar Archives

To list the contents of a `tar` archive (always a good thing to do right after creating one), use the `-t` option in place of `-c`:

```
% tar -tvf nc.tar                              List all files in archive file nc.tar.
-rw-r--r-- 1047 100      3320 Dec 20 00:41:30 nc/About
-rw-r--r-- 1047 100      3106 Oct 27 15:35:22 nc/doc/mknewsrc.1
-rw-r--r-- 1047 100      6503 Apr 28 02:58:16 nc/doc/ncc.1
-rw-r--r-- 1047 100      8698 Apr 28 02:57:49 nc/doc/nclip.1
-rw-r--r-- 1047 100    155636 May 16 22:41:29 nc/doc/man.mm
-rw-r--r-- 1047 100     91031 May 16 22:41:34 nc/doc/append.mm
-rw-r--r-- 1047 100     18501 Jun 02 23:55:48 nc/doc/filter.man
-rw-r--r-- 1047 100      1464 Dec 15 01:45:26 nc/Makefile
-rw-r--r-- 1047 100      2626 Dec 18 19:08:39 nc/READ.ME
-rw-r--r-- 1047 100      4082 Apr 19 16:34:31 nc/License
```

(here the -t option is concatenated with v and f). But be careful. Using the -c option accidently will wipe out your tar.

Reading tar Archives

Once you have files archived onto some medium, it is all too easy to write over them. Better to be safe and spend the money on extra media than to waste hours or days of your time. To read a `tar` archive, first lock your tape or diskette into *read-only*. An error of one letter could erase your data if you don't follow this precaution. On cartridge tapes this means rotating the little cylinder to the closed position; for 8-mm tapes this means sliding the cover in back to close the notch; and on diskettes, this means slipping the tab to open the notch (nice that the procedure is standardized).

To extract all the files in an archive, use the `-x` option instead of the `-t` option:

```
% tar -xvf /dev/fd0                         Extract all files and directories.
x weather/README, 4313 bytes, 9 tape blocks.
x weather/how2ftp, 2185 bytes, 5 tape blocks.
x weather/pricing, 3351 bytes, 7 tape blocks.
x weather/catds, 51239 bytes, 101 tape blocks.
x weather/datav.1, 7647 bytes, 15 tape blocks.
```

To extract all files and subdirectories in one directory:

```
% tar -xvf file.tar newsclip              Extract all files from a tar file's directory.
x newsclip/About, 3320 bytes, 7 tape blocks.
x newsclip/doc/mknewsrc.1, 3106 bytes, 7 tape blocks.
x newsclip/doc/ncc.1, 6503 bytes, 13 tape blocks.
x newsclip/doc/append.mm, 91031 bytes, 178 tape blocks.
x newsclip/Makefile, 1464 bytes, 3 tape blocks.
x newsclip/READ.ME, 2626 bytes, 6 tape blocks.
x newsclip/License, 4082 bytes, 8 tape blocks.
```

In both these cases, the files and directories will be placed in the current working directory of the user since the archives were created without the full path name of the files. If they had been created with the full path names, as in one example above, the files and directories would be copied only in the same location from which they came—regardless of the directory the user is in when the `tar` command is issued.

To extract a specific directory and all subdirectories below it or specific files from an archive, list the full name of the file or directory on the command line:

```
% tar -xvf file.tar newsclip/READ.ME newsclip/License
x newsclip/READ.ME, 2626 bytes, 6 tape blocks.
x newsclip/License, 4082 bytes, 8 tape blocks.
%
```

Note that the name must appear exactly as it does in the archive; if you are not sure of the name, use the `-t` option to get the names first.

Using Tape Drives

While tape drives are the slowest way to store data, they are still and also the most economical for large numbers of data. For this reason we recommend you use tapes to back up your files and your system. Cartridge tapes have made tapes more convenient and less expensive than the old reel systems, yet they are still used in much the same manner. To use your tape drive, you need to know what name your operating system has assigned to it and the system's tape control commands for things like rewind and fast forward.

Two different tape cartridges are widely used on Unix machines today. The 1/4-inch cartridge tape is approximately $6 \times 4 \times \frac{1}{2}$ inches in size. Its two standard formats, QIC-120 and QIC-150, hold up to 120 MB and 150 MB of data, respectively. Most tape drives can read both formats and will automatically switch to the proper one when reading a tape. However, if you are writing a tape to be read on an older drive, you may want to check your manual to see if you can use a special device name to write to the older QIC-120 format.

A newer tape cartridge is the 8-mm tape. This holds 20–40 times more data than a 1/4-inch cartridge and is inexpensive since it is the tape used in home video recorders. It is, however, quite slow. The most common format for 8-mm tapes hold 2.3 GB of data, yet many manufactures are incorporating data compression schemes into their drives to increase the capacity to over 5 GB.

The Unix designation for a tape drive is different on almost every system. Worse yet, different functions on the drives, such as reading at a specific density, are treated as different devices. The default is usually for cartridge tapes to rewind when a `tar` or other operation has completed. If you want to write several archives to a tape, you will want to override this behavior—else successive archives will be written on top of each other and only the last one will remain. To avoid overwriting, override the default by specifying the tape drive as one which does not rewind after it writes (even though it is physically the same drive as the default). Names of tape devices on a few common systems are:

UNIX TAPE DEVICES

Sun OS

/dev/rst0	Tape drive 0.
/dev/nrst0	Tape drive 0 without auto rewind.

SCO

/dev/rct0	Tape drive 0.
/dev/nrct0	Tape drive 0 without auto rewind.

SysV

/dev/rct/0	Tape drive 0.
/dev/rct/0n	Tape drive 0 without auto rewind.

AIX

/dev/rmt0	Tape drive 0.
/dev/rmt0.1	Tape drive 0 without auto rewind.

BSD

/dev/rst0	Tape drive 0.
/dev/nrst0	Tape drive 0 without auto rewind.

The command for controlling the tape drive is often `mt` but may also be `cmt`, `tctl`, or just `tape`:

```
%   mt -f /dev/rst0 erase          Erase the tape in tape drive 0.
```

OPTIONS FOR mt

-f *tapedrive*	Name of the drive.
fsf *n*	Skip past *n* archives.
bsf *n*	Skip back *n* archives.
eof	Place an end of file EOF mark on tape.
rewind	Rewind the tape.
retension	Exercise the tape.
erase	Erase the entire tape.

Retensioning a tape prevents damage by stretching new tapes and by exercising old ones. It is particularly useful with 1/4-inch tape cartridges and is done automatically on some systems. (If your tape drive is taking a long time to initialize itself, this is probably what it's doing.)

The simplest way to use a tape is to place a single archive on each tape. This is common, but if you need to archive large amounts of data from separate file systems, you may want to write more than one archive to the same tape. This is done by using the name of the tape drive which refers to the "no rewind" device so that archives are written one after another and not one on top of another. Each `tar` command will then write a separate successive archive to the tape. To read the archives back, use the "no rewind" device name again and the `mt` command to skip past archives you don't want to read.

PC Floppy Diskettes

Floppy diskettes are more convenient, affordable, and popular than cartridge tapes but not as universal. If you have a PC running a *terminal emulator* program such as *Kermit, Versaterm-Pro, or Telnet*, you can use that PC to make or read copies of your files on floppy diskettes. Programs designed for a PC will *not* generally run under the operating systems present on workstations (or other PCs). The safest approach is to make sure the PC saves the file in *ASCII*, *text*, or *source* form, and transfer these. We discuss this further in Chapter 4, *Computer–Computer Interactions*.

COMPUTER-COMPUTER INTERACTIONS

No man is an island, entire of itself;
every man is a piece of the continent,
a part of the main. ...

—John Donne, *Meditation XVII*

4.1   Introduction

Why Use Different Machines?

Revolutions in computing are becoming regular enough to be the status quo.[1]   In the mid-1970s, DEC Vax made a great contribution to science and engineering by providing distributed computing resources at the laboratory and department level which previously were available only at the institutional or company level.   By the mid-1980s, scientific workstations running Unix provided a comparable level of computing power to small groups and individuals, with national computer networks providing a broadened access to supercomputer centers.   In the early 1990s the workstations were providing computer power comparable to that of the supercomputers of the 1980s—for about the same or less money than the workstations of the 1980s.

Just what is being done with all this increase in computational power?   Much of it is going towards work on problems which could not even be attempted before, such as lattice gauge calculations and hydrodynamic flow around complicated objects; much of it is going towards *visualizations*, that is, producing two and three dimensional pictures or graphs of the numerical results of computations; and much is going towards the analysis and visualization of experimental data of various forms.

In our view computers are complicated objects much like automobiles; there is no one machine which is best for everything and so the more resources a scientist or engineer has available, the better off he or she will be—especially if he or she uses them wisely.   In a

---

[1]As discussed in our chapters on supercomputing, there has been approximately a ten-fold increase in power every 10 years since 1950.

typical scenario, programs may be developed, debugged, and tested on the smaller, slower, and friendlier machines, and then *ported over* to the larger ones for production runs, higher precision, or to speed up the process. While it is often hard to beat the response time and convenience of your own machine, this will not help your productivity much (and that of other users on your system) if your programs take hours to run or if you do not have the tools needed to produce or visualize your results. A rough rule of thumb says if you need to wait much of the day for your results, your progress is suffering too much and you are ready for a more powerful machine. But if you are still correcting your poor computer diction, running test cases, looking at results, and then modifying the code and rerunning, you are probably better off on a local machine.

Open Systems

The term *open systems* has become a popular description of the idea that computers should be able to interact and share resources. The idea is made workable by a number of formal and informal standards to assure that anything, be it printer, disk drive, X terminal, or even workstation from one manufacturer, works with everything else from other manufactures. That being the case, once machines can communicate and share data, a higher level of interconnection becomes possible in which you move your computing among different systems, using each for what it does best. Further, when you sit down at a terminal connected to any open systems machine, the interface you see should look much the same. Ideally the human–machine–machine interface should be seamless; all of your files should be available on all machines without the need to move them, and all of the commands with which you are familiar should be available on all the machines.

An actual example of this *seamless computing* is the following. A user, anita, develops a simulation program on her desktop workstation. Once the program is running, anita wants more computing power. So from the workstation she submits a large batch job to a central, *batch queue manager*. The queue manager reads the request, which includes the types of machines and memory requirements for the job, and finds an appropriate machine on which to run the job. A key point here is that the queue manager finds the machine for anita and watches after her job and its output without anita having to know or care where the job is actually running. In the meantime, anita can view the progress of her job from the local workstation since the remote machine is reading and writing to the same files that the job would if it were running locally.

Once the job is completed, or perhaps even while it is still executing, anita may want to view and print the output in graphical form. Since fast graphics and color printing require expensive hardware, she goes to a visualization laboratory to see the data in graphical form. Once there, she logs onto a graphics workstation and again finds the same files since the queueing manager is reading and writing just as it did on her desktop workstation.

In this example, the user and the user's program were able to move from machine to machine and find the same files and environment. This is because all of the machines used the same physical hard disks to store the user's files. When possible, given differences in workstations, the machines also have the same commands and user programs installed. Since each machine then presents the same *image* to the user, we say this is a *single system image* for the site. Most of this magic is made possible by using remote file systems like *NFS* or *AFS* that are discussed below.

Local Area Networks

A network of some sort is required in order for computers to communicate. As already discussed from a hardware point of view in Chapter 3, *Workstation Setup and Use*, local area networks (LANs) connect machines in a department or building. Most often the LAN is an ethernet. Networks can connect more than Unix workstations and often do connect everything from PCs to supercomputers, yet in order to attain the single-image level of transparency described above with present technology, all of the machines must run some variant of Unix.

One of the nicer things about local networks is that they are not isolated, being interconnected to yet other networks by special-purpose computers called *routers* and *bridges*. The purpose of a router is to keep local traffic confined to the local network and to provide a controlled route for traffic between the local network and other networks and their machines. Routers often connect departmental networks to a sitewide or campuswide *backbone*. A backbone is a special purpose LAN which connects routers rather than computers and thus indirectly interconnects the networks. Backbones are not confined to campus systems. They may be regional or even international.

The internet

The *internet* is the multitude of regional, national, international, and intercontinental networks now used by a large fraction of the industrialized world to exchange computer information. In the United States, most of the computer traffic is carried via regional networks to the national backbone maintained by the U.S. National Science Foundation. This makes the communication free of charge for researchers and educators. In contrast, Europe has many regional networks, and they often are maintained with a more direct expense to the users.

Despite the somewhat fragmented and at times congested nature of the internet, it is still a vast resource of information and communication. The internet is completely democratic, which means that bad information is presented equally with good information. Assuming that you become skilled at using the internet, it can become a tremendous resource. For example, suppose you need a Fortran routine for factoring a sparse matrix. You could post a note to the numerical methods news group `sci.math.num-analysis` asking what other researchers use. A researcher from the University of Melbourne may reply, telling you about the routines available there. If your mate is feeling nice, that researcher may even tell you how to get the routines via electronic mail.

Or perhaps you are having problem with a compiler under AIX (IBM's Unix). So you post a note to the AIX news group. The chances are about equally good for you to get answers from an undergraduate at some university in Europe as they are from one of the compiler designers at IBM. Which answer is more useful is for you to decide.

4.2 Mail Systems

An elementary form of computer–computer communication, which may well account for the majority of network use, is electronic mail. This is the exchange of "messages" or "letters" or "email," with transmission over the communication network watched over by some Unix mail facility. In other words, the user puts a letter in the mail and the system delivers it in due course. This is less direct than the real-time communication provided by the Unix commands `write` and `talk` but is more universal and less of an intrusion into someone else's workspace.

Mail, combined with news groups and bulletin boards, has produced a new type of international communication and (pardon the expression) international networking which has redefined who we may think of as our fellow workers and colleagues. It has also changed long distance collaborations from being painful to being efficient and fun. So much fun, apparently, that studies have found people in a work setting sometimes going through a thousand pieces of mail a day and have found managers restricting other people's mail access in order to increase the progress on managed projects.[2]

On most Unix systems you should be able to get into the most elementary mail system with the command `mail`, `Mail`, or `mailx`. Under *The X Windows System* you can use the X Mail Handler *xmh* which has a nice array of colors and buttons to help you keep your mail organized (you must still write that letter to your folks though). If you regularly use *Emacs* for editing, you may use it also for your mail handling; while not as colorful as *xmh*, it has a nice presentation, lets you do your mail work within your familiar editing environment, and permits an intermix of your mail and Unix files whether you want to or not[3]

Remember, there are two purposes to these mail systems. First, they have editors which permit you to compose letters and then *send* them. Second, they have the ability to let you *read your mail* and save it in an orderly way. While it is easiest at first to keep these two functions separated in your mind, in practice they do get mixed (you can instantaneously reply to a letter as you are reading it or read some old mail while you are in the process of sending out new letters).

Remember, too, to be patient; handling mail from differing computer systems all over the world is one of the most complicated and error-prone activities for a computer to attempt. It requires many links along the way to work perfectly and all systems to agree on ever-changing protocols and naming conventions. Accordingly, problems are inevitable. When you face mail failures, do not just blame the lousy system. Record or print out the details given to you by the system and report all that information to your system administrator.

Also, it is often impossible, or nearly so, for mortals to figure out someone's mail address from the information given in the headers.[4] Thus, it is a good habit to explicitly state your return address in your letters and to get your friends' full addresses before writing to them.

The Unix `mail` command allows you to read incoming mail, send outgoing mail, and customize the way the mail system operates for you. Find details in the `man` pages with:

```
% man mail
```

Once in the mail system, you issue subcommands to personalize the system. Alternatively, you can set the options and aliases in the `.mailrc` file in your home directory (we give a sample on the floppy). Other mailers, such as *emacs*, also use this file.

The Unix mail command operates on two types of mailboxes, your system mailbox, for example, `/usr/spool/mail/rubin`, and your personal mailbox, `/u/rubin/mbox`. The

---

[2]Sproul & Kresler (1991).

[3]In case you care, one author uses emacs and the other mailx.

[4]The header may tell you what your mailer thinks is the path used by the letter to get to you, but you may not be able to return it that way.

system mailbox contains mail which the system has received but about which you have yet to do something. When you invoke a mail program, it automatically saves in your personal mailbox all messages you have read—unless you tell it otherwise. The messages remain (and the file space they occupy gets larger and larger and larger) in your personal mailbox until you file them elsewhere, or better yet, delete them. You put them in order by storing them in "folders" provided by the mail system or in your own (no doubt highly organized) file system. An example of this is,

%	`mail loren`	Start letter to loren on your system.
%	`mail tim pfink hank`	Start letter to 3 users.
%	`mail ghe < junk.file`	Send file to ghe.
%	`mail stetz@comphy`	Start letter to stetz on remote `comphy`.
%	`mail jan@phys.oruni.edu`	Start letter to internet addressee jan.
%	`mail`	List all incoming messages.

Note that you can use simple user names like `loren` or `pfink` only for local users (those with names in the `/etc/passwd` file) and for those distant users whose aliases have been stored in the `.mailrc` file; for example, `ghe` really is `ghe@theo.fisik.orst.edu`.

To process your incoming mail, enter `mail` at the system prompt. For each piece of mail in your system mailbox, the mail program displays a one-line entry similar to the following:

`% mail`	Enter mail system.
`Mail [5.2 UCB] Type ? for help.`	Hello.
`"/usr/mail/lance": 2 messages 2 new`	
`R 1 ken Thu Sep 17 14:36 "Meeting"`	Letter 1, R: read previously.
`M 2 ken Thu Sep 17 14:36 "Cancel Meeting" M`	M: stored in mailbox.
`U 3 pfink Thu Sep 23 4:36 "Book Done" U`	U: unread previously.
`>N 4 alw@bblu Thu Sep 17 5:06 "Delay" > N`	Current: >, new: N.
`&`	Prompt, give subcommand.
`& 1`	Go to letter 1.
`& [rtn] [Ctrl-D]`	Exit, send message.

MAIL SUBCOMMANDS

?	List all subcommands.
headers (h)	List headers of letters.
top *1-3*	Display top few lines of letters *1–3*.
+	Move down to next letter.
-	Move up to previous letter.
=	Give number of present letter.
chdir (cd) *dirname*	Change working directory.
save (s) *1-3 +fname*	Save letters *1–3* into file *fname,* + for appending.
write (w) *1-3 fname*	Save letters *1–3* with no headers into file *fname.*
copy *1-3 fname*	Save letters *1–3* in file *fname,* no delete.
file (folder) *Name*	Store current mbox, switch to mail file *Name.*
reply (respond) (r)	Reply to this letter.
Reply (Respond) (R)	Reply to only sender of this letter.

delete (d) *1-3*	Delete letters *1–3*.
undelete (u) *1-3*	Undelete letters *1–3*.
d *3-7*	Delete letters *3–7*.
dt (dp)	Delete this letter, proceed to next.
!*command*	Execute shell command *command*.
alias (a)	List all aliases' real addresses.
alias (a) *paul*	List *paul*'s real address.
quit (q)	Quit mailer, remove old mail from mail spool.
exit (x) (ex) (xit)	Exit mailer, leave old mail in mail spool.
[rtn] [Ctrl-D]	Exit and send message.

The mh and xmh Mail Handlers

The mail handler *mh* is a flexible system developed by the Rand Corporation. It differs from the other mail programs we discuss in that it is *not* a single command which opens a subsystem but rather a collection of commands. There is, however, **xmh**, an X Windows interface to *mh* which is invoked with the single command **xmh**. The **xmh** command places the entire package of *mh* commands in a friendly environment with buttons and menus. The **xmh** application is compatible with the **mh** commands, so you may choose to use either the same folders or use *mh* if you're reading your mail on a terminal not running X. The setup files .mh_profile and .mh_aliases in your home directory configure **xmh**'s behavior and store personal mail aliases.

All versions of the *mh* system store mail messages in directories which it calls *folders*. The folders are placed in the subdirectory Mail within your home directory, and then within this subdirectory each new mail message is placed in a separate file with a different number as its name. For example, here we look into one of these Mail directories:

`% ls Mail`	List Mail directory.
`drafts/   inbox/   pfink/   rubin/`	Four mh folders.
`% ls Mail/inbox`	List inbox, folder for incoming mail.
`,5  1  2  3  4  6`	Five letters.

The `drafts` folder is used to hold messages temporarily while you are composing a new one or replying to an old one. The `inbox` folder is where *mh* places new mail messages. Notice that message 5 has the , prefix. This indicates a message which has been "deleted" by an *mh* or **xmh** command but which really has only been renamed with a , prefix.

mh COMMANDS

inc	Incorporate new mail into inbox.
scan +*folder*	Scan mail in *folder*, default *inbox*.
show *n*	Show mail message *n*.
comp	Compose a new mail message.
forw +*folder n*	Forward a message to other users.
repl +*folder n*	Reply to the sender of a message.
pick	Pick out messages via content or sender.

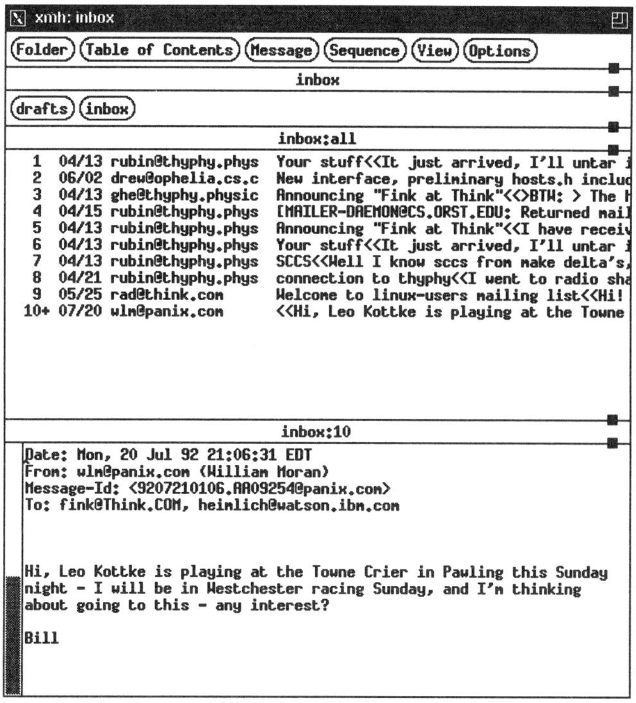

Figure 4.1: The **xmh** mail program.

The **xmh** interface is invoked all by itself or with options:

$	**xmh**	Call xmh and then push buttons.
$	**xmh** *[-path mailpath] [-initial foldername]*	Call xmh with options

As shown in Figure 4.1, the X Windows interface **xmh** gives you several buttons and menus that you may use to receive and sort incoming mail as well as to compose replies or new messages.

The elm and pine Mail Handlers

The mail handlers *elm* and *pine* are menu-driven with on-screen directions and buttons to click. While they are not as powerful or integrated as the Emacs mail facility, they are friendlier and easier for a beginning. For example, you can go through your mailbox (or other folder), by just saying **elm** and following directions:

% **elm**	Just say elm.
Mailbox is '/usr/mail/rubin', 2 messages	Elm tells you all this.
1 Feb 28 Rubin Landau subject	Letter 1.

```
2 Feb 28 Mail Delivery Subs Returned mail      Letter 2.
You can use any of the following commands:    Elm's directions.
d)elete or u)ndelete mail, m)ail a message,
r)eply or f)orward mail, q)uit, To read message, press <return>
j = move down, k = move up, ?= help
```

You now use the arrow or move keys to highlight the letter of interest. Then you give a subcommand to read, reply, save, or delete the letter. In a more advanced mode you give options directly on the command line. For example, to send mail to jan:

```
%   elm -s "subject" jan@thomas.hal.com       Send letter to jan on subject.
```

Elm then puts you in an editor while you compose your letter and prompts you for needed flags. As with the **mail** command, you can also redirect a file as standard input

```
%   elm -s "subject" anita < junk.file        Send junk to anita.
```

elm OPTIONS

-c	Check alias and return.
-f	Read specified folder, not mailbox.
-h (?)	Help - give list of options.
-m	Menu off; more room to see letter.
-s	Subject for letter.
-z	Zero - don't enter Elm if mailbox is empty.

The Emacs Mail Facility

When using Emacs to handle your mail, your letters get copied from the Unix mail spool to an RMAIL file. While you can edit RMAIL like any other file, it is written in a special format designed for using Emacs in the mail mode. Letters are easier to read and write than with the ordinary **mail** command, and if you usually use Emacs for your editing, you should find the Emacs mail system a natural. To use Emacs for your mail you must first invoke Emacs (or have it already running for regular editing purposes). You then switch Emacs to a "read mail" or "send mail" mode and buffer and use the regular Emacs commands with the supplements:

Sending Mail, Emacs

SEND MAIL SUBCOMMANDS

^x m	Enter send mail mode (from within Emacs).
^x 4 m	Enter send mail mode in separate window.
^c ^c	Send correspondence and culminate mailer.
^c ^s	Send correspondence and stay in mailer.
^c ^w	Insert signature stored in $HOME/.signature.

$HOME/.mailrc	File with definitions for aliases.
CC:	In header field for carbon copy.
Bcc:	At bottom for carbon copy.
Fcc:	In header field to copy your out mail.
From	File with your address etc.
^c ^y	Yank selected letter from RMAIL.
^c ^q	Fill paragraphs of yanked mail (makes it pretty).

Reading Mail, Emacs

READ MAIL SUBCOMMANDS

~x rmail	Enter read mail mode (from within Emacs).
h	List headers (summary).
~^h	List headers (summary).
j	Jump to first letter.
>	Jump to last letter.
*n***j**	Jump to letter *n*.
[space]	Scroll down through this letter.
[del]	Scroll up through this letter.
.	Move to top of this letter.
n	Next letter.
~m	Next letter even if "deleted."
p	Previous letter.
~p	Previous letter even if "deleted."
d	Delete letter and move down to next letter.
^d	Delete letter and move up to next letter.
u	Undelete deleted letter.
x	Expunge (really remove) deleted letters.
i *file* **[ret]**	Insert *file* into buffer.
g	Merge new mail.
^u g	Merge other file.
~s *expression*	Search for *expression*.
-~s *expression*	Search backwards for *expression*.
e (x)	Expunge deleted mail from buffer.
o	Output message into RMAIL file.
^o	Output message into Unix file.
s	Save all mail except deletes into file RMAIL.
r	Reply to this letter.
f	Forward this letter.
a	Assign label to this letter for reference.
k	Kill label on this letter.
w	Edit current letter, ^c ^c return to mailer.
^x ^s	Save all mail including deletes into file RMAIL.
q	Quit mailer.

4.3   Electronic File Transfer

Like people, computers communicate in different ways. The simplest, sending notes or mail among users, is done with commands like **mail**. Mail is often restricted to small text files which means books and binary files should not be sent through the mail. There are Unix utilities such as **encode**, which converts binary files into encoded text files so they may be mailed—at least if they are not too big. If they are too big you must split the encoded file into several smaller files which can then be mailed.

How to best transfer files depends, naturally, on how the machines are connected. If both machines are connected to a local network or to internet, the best choice may be **ftp**. The **ftp** program is widely available, powerful, and satisfying to use. It is useful for transferring files between machines with different operating systems such as between a Unix workstation and a VMS or MVS machine.

If the machines are at the same site and their system administrators cooperate, then more transparent communications such as NFS or **rcp** are available. In the other extreme are machines that are connected via modems and telephone lines or by serial, *RS-232* lines. This is common for personal computers which use a modem to talk to a remote Unix workstation or mainframe. For these cases the choices for file transfer are limited to programs such as **kermit** and **uucp**. The **kermit** utility is available on many of the terminal emulator programs on PCs.[5] The **uucp** utility is available on Unix systems and allows for the automatic transfer of files, including mail, between Unix machines via modems. This is one of the oldest methods of networking Unix computers and is still used in some locations.

Another choice for communications over telephone lines is available if both machines are using fast modems, 9600 baud or greater. This is the **SLIP** or **PPP** connection which can be configured to allow users to use the same networking commands on phone lines as they do on the ethernet.

An elementary and obvious fact to remember when establishing communications among any two computers is that they both must speak the same language, that is, the local and host computer must have the same transfer protocol. This transfer protocol permits automatic error checking and retransmission to correct detected errors as well as replacing the **return** and **new line** characters on one system by the appropriate characters on the other (too often an annoying problem). While you may be able to use commands like **save stream** on your emulator program to transfer files, this does not have error checking and, accordingly, should be considered unreliable for all but simple text. Further, if the two computers handle data at differing rates, you must use the slower rate on both machines for communication to occur. And finally, unless the two computers are running the same operating systems with compatible architectures, the files you transfer should probably be *text* or ASCII.

Transferring with ftp

The **ftp** command is a widely available file transfer protocol which works well and quickly on TCP/IP networks (you'll never want to hear the word **kermit** again after using **ftp**).

To use ftp:

---

[5]There may be some understandable confusion here. There is a transfer protocol **kermit** available on most workstations and PCs as well as an emulator program **kermit** which runs on DOS PCs.

- On *local*, issue the **ftp** command with the name of *foreign*

```
%   ftp foreign                          Connect to "foreign."
%   ftp 128.193.96.10                    Connect using IP number.
```

- The file **$HOME/.netrc** describes accounts on remote machines.

- When the connection is established, *foreign* comes back to ask for your user ID on *foreign*. Give your user ID for the foreign machine or just try [Enter] if you have the same user ID on both machines. If that is okay, you will be asked for your password on *foreign*.

- Your life is simpler if you have the same user ID and password on all machines.

- If you must sign on to the other machine (if it complains to you that you are not logged in, for example), issue the **user** command. An example is:

```
ftp>   user rubin                        Tell foreign your user ID.
```

- After telling you that you are logged onto *foreign*, you'll see an *ftp* prompt, ftp>, and you are ready to begin.

- If you want to see your options, just ask with:

```
ftp>   "?"                               List ftp subcommands.
```

Some useful subcommands within **ftp**:

ftp SUBCOMMANDS

ls	List files in foreign's working directory.
pwd	Print name of foreign's working directory.
cd *dirname*	Change directory in foreign.
! *command*	Execute *command* on local.
bye (quit)	End ftp session.
get *file*	Copy *file* from foreign to local.
get *file* -	Get *file* from foreign and send it to the screen.
get *file* |more	Get *file* from foreign and view it using more.
mget *file1 file2 ...*	Multiple get, i.e., copy several files.
mget *	Multiple get all files.
put *file*	Copy *file* from local to foreign.
mput *file1 file2 ...*	Copy multiple files from local to foreign.

Note that while you cannot make all the file manipulations on *foreign* that you can when remotely logged in, you can make enough to do some real damage (the purpose of **ftp** is file transfer, not damage).

- It is safer to begin by orienting yourself with the "list" or "print working directory" command.

- To send a file *from local* to *foreign*, use the **send** or **put** command:

```
ftp>   send file.local file.foreign
ftp>   put file.local file.foreign
```

(On some systems the *file.foreign* designator can be left out, in which case the file named *file.local* will appear automatically on the *foreign* machine.)

- Be patient while files are being transferred; when the transfer is complete, you will be told that it was successful and also the transfer rate achieved. If either machine or network has a heavy load, this may take some seconds.

- Note that if you are **ftp**ing to a CMS machine, you must specify the file name and file type. However, since the **ftp** separator for file name and file type is a period ".", it can look very much like Unix file designators, for example,

```
ftp>   send Unix file cmsname.cmstype
```

- If your Unix file is *unix.file* and you do not give any CMS file name

```
ftp>   send unix.file
```

your CMS file will appear as *Unix file a*.

- To get a file from *foreign* and place it on *local*, you **get** it

```
ftp>   get file.foreign file.local
```

- When you are done transferring files, you **quit ftp** with

```
ftp>   quit                            End ftp session.
```

- As noted before, if you want to transfer many files, it is probably easier to concatenate them into one large file, transfer that large file, and then split it up into subroutine files with **fsplit** or **csplit**. Likewise, you can use the **tar** command to create a file with as many directories and subdirectories in it as you like, transfer this one tar file, and then extract all the directories and subdirectories from the tar file. This assumes you have write privilege on the foreign machine.

- A number of files can be sent or "gotten" with the multiple versions of these commands. For example:

```
ftp>   mget file1 file2 file3          Get these three files.
ftp>   mput file1 file2 file3          Send these three files.
```

Don't take a walk after giving these multiple commands. You will be queried before each transfer as to whether you really want to go ahead with it, unless you use the **prompt** command for no interactive prompting:

```
ftp>   prompt                          Toggle prompt on or off.
Interactive mode off.                  No interactive prompting.
ftp>   mget *.f                        Get all files ending in .f.
```

ftp over internet

Each computer on the internet has a unique name and number, with the name being the familiar one used for much of *mail*. If you know that name or number, you may well be able to transfer files to or from — or even *login* to—that computer in a far away place. In fact, many Unix systems have a *user account* known as *guest* or *anonymous* which, while having limited file access, also has no *password*. If that far-away computer has programs or data which it is willing to share with others, then others can *anonymously ftp* in and copy them. In § 4.4 we give some transcripts of **ftp** sessions which extract files from supercomputer center libraries. Here's a typical session for a Unix user:

```
%   ftp physics.orst.edu              File transfer to computer on internet.
welcome to ...                         Foreign computer responds.


%   ftp 128.193.96.10                 Using machine's IP address.
welcome to ...                         Foreign computer responds.
```

Transferring with kermit

If the file transfer is to or from a personal computer via a modem, you may have to use **kermit**. While the use of **kermit** on the *PC* side may depend on the specific *PC*, it is rather standard on the Unix side.[6] For example, let's start by assuming you are running a *terminal emulator* program on your *PC* which makes it look like a standard computer terminal to the computer on the other end. These emulator programs might be something like *Versaterm-Pro, Red Ryder*, or even just *kermit*. Note, if you are running a windowing environment on your PC, the PC commands may be available on a pull-down menu, so look for them.

```
C:>  kermit                           Run kermit from DOS.
IBM-PC kermit-MS V2.29b 19 Feb 87     DOS's response.
type ?  for help                      More from DOS.
 connect                              Connect me to the host.
```

---

[6]Generally kermit is not supplied by Unix vendors but is available on many sites. Of course you may need kermit to download it to your machine.

```
login                                    Unix's response after it connects.
%  ls                                    Unix, tell me files in this directory.
 file1 file2 file3                       Unix lists three files.
%    kermit -s file1                     Send from Unix to DOS!
Escape back to your local system
 and give a RECEIVE command...
  ^v C                                   To get back to kermit on DOS.
  receive                                Telling DOS's kermit to receive file.
                                         PC now shows it's receiving file.
%                                        Done, back to Unix.
%    kermit -r                           Receive file on Unix from PC.
Escape back to your local system
 and give a RECEIVE command...
  ^v C                                   To get back to kermit on DOS.
 send C:filenew                          DOS, send this file to Unix.
                                         PC now shows it's sending file.
%                                        Done, back to Unix.
%  ls                                    Unix, tell me what I have.
file1 file2 file3 filenew                Filenew has been received.
```

Note that in order for kermit to work on some Unix systems, you must make the transferred file have the Unix mode read/write   -r/w-r/w. You do this with **chmod 777**.

4.4   Getting Programs off the Network

The command **rlogin archie.ans.net -l archie** enters you into a system which searches through lists of available programs and their locations.

Anonymous ftp to NCSA

Here is a transcript of a session which the remote user *rubin* had with NCSA, the National Center for Supercomputing Applications. This is a good example because NCSA permits anyone to sign onto their computers as the user *anonymous*, then enter anything as a password (they prefer your internet address for identification), then browse through their files for software and documentation of interest, and then copy the software and documentation to your home computer. This is also a good idea because the programs are state of the art, supported, and free.

```
%  ftp ftp.ncsa.uiuc.edu             You issue the ftp command.
Connected to zaphod.ncsa.uiuc.edu.    Now wait.
220 zaphod FTP server ready.
Name: anonymous                       Rubin enters anonymous.
331 Send email alias as pw
Password: rubin@phys.oreu.edu
230 Guest login ok, access
restrictions apply.                   Barely in.
ftp>  ls                              Rubin asks to see what's there.
```

```
HDF INDEX Mac PC Unix
README.FIRST Samples                      Etc.
226 Transfer complete.
ftp>  get README.FIRST               Always read this first.
200 PORT command successful.
150 Opening ASCII mode data
connection for README.FIRST (15465 bytes).
226 Transfer complete.
15868 bytes received in 4.599
seconds (3.369 Kbytes/s)
ftp>  ls -l                          Rubin asks for long list.
200 PORT command successful.
150 Opening ASCII mode data
connection for /bin/ls (0 bytes).
total 106
-rw-rw-r-- 1 ftp 53230 Aug 5
 14:39 INDEX
drwxrwxr-x 16 102 512 Aug 30
 16:14 Samples
-rw-rw-r-- 1 ftp 15465 Aug 8
 13:41 README
226 Transfer complete.
ftp>   mget INDEX README             Get me two files.
200 PORT command successful.
150 Opening ASCII mode data
 connection for INDEX (53230 bytes).
226 Transfer complete.                That's one.
150 Opening ASCII mode data
 connection for README (23968 bytes).
226 Transfer complete                 That's two.
24377 bytes received in 5.516
 seconds (4.316 Kbytes/s)
type binary                           To transfer non text files.
ftp>  cd Samples
250 CWD command successful.
ftp>  type binary                     Set to transfer binary file.
200 Type set to I.                    ftp's reassurance.
ftp>  get jet2.hdf
200 PORT command successful.
150 Opening BINARY mode data
 connection for jet2.hdf (121010
bytes).
226 Transfer complete.
121010 bytes received in 109.4
 seconds (1.08 Kbytes/s)
ftp>  type ASCII                      Set back to ASCII.
200 Type set to A.                    ftp's reassurance.
ftp>  quit                            Goodbye.
```

Anonymous ftp to Cornell

Here is a transcript of a session which the remote user *boru* had with Cornell Center for Theory and Simulation in Science and Engineering. Again, you can sign onto their computers as the user *anonymous*, enter your internet address for identification, browse through their files for software and documentation of interest, and then copy the software and documentation to your home computer. It's legal and the software is good. The listing of the file COPYRIGHTS gives more information.

```
$  ftp 128.84.241.33
Connected to 128.84.241.33.
220 ept FTP server (Version 4.1 Fri Aug 28 GDT 1987) ready.
Name: anonymous
331 Guest login ok, send address as password.
Password: boru@phys.oreu.edu
230 Guest login ok, access restrictions apply.
ftp> ls
150 Opening ASCII connection for /bin/ls.
bin dist  etc  incoming  lib  pub  usr
226 Transfer complete.
ftp> cd pub
250 CWD command successful.
ftp> ls
150 Opening ASCII connection for /bin/ls.
COPYRIGHT LASSPTools LASSPTools.demos.tar.Z
LASSPTools.rs6000.tar.Z LASSPTools.sparc.tar.Z
226 Transfer complete.
ftp> get COPYRIGHT                    Display remote file.
ftp> quit
```

The Cornell Theory Center has also made available the *Scientist's Workbench*. This is a software package which brings together and organizes tools and software used for scientific research in a distributed computing environment. To obtain the Scientist's Workbench, **ftp** to info.tc.cornell.edu or 128.84.201.1, and retrieve the file pub/swb/README.TOP.

netlib

In keeping with the our philosophy of sharing and making use of whatever tools are available, we give here some information about getting files off the electronic network. In the previous two examples we have seen how to make an anonymous **ftp** into two supercomputer centers to acquire some of their software and documentation. In this section we show how you can get information about *netlib*, a collection of library packages available for free over the electronic networks. In a following section we discuss *xnetlib*, a new and friendly interface to *netlib*. An excellent guide to the mysteries of networks and address syntax is Frey and Adams (1989). Background about *netlib* is in Dongarra and Grosse (1987) and in a quarterly column published in the SIAM News and SIGNUM Newsletter. To find out more about *netlib* right from your terminal, email in a request:

```
$ mail netlib@ornl.gov          Send mail.
  send index                    The message you send.
```

The response you get tells you how to ask for more and what's available. The information in this section is taken directly from the response, and we acknowledge the documentation and the software. The routines may be state-of-the-art, yet were designed for use by professional numerical analysts who are capable of checking for themselves whether an algorithm is suitable for their needs. One routine can be superb and the next awful. So be careful!

In the preceding request, the internet address `netlib@ornl.gov` refers to a gateway machine at Oak Ridge National Laboratory in Oak Ridge, Tennessee. This address should be understood on all the major networks. Otherwise (and for other libraries):

LIBRARY ADDRESSES

Netlib from Europe	`netlib@nac.no`
"	`netlib%nac.no@norunix.bitnet` (Earn/Bitnet)
"	`s=netlib; o=nac; c=no;` (X.400)
"	`nac!netlib` (EUNET/uucp)
"	`netlib@draci.cs.uow.edu.au`
Statistical Software	`statlib@temper.stat.cmu.edu`
TEXSoftware	`tuglib@science.utah.edu`
Reduce Software	`reduce-netlib@rand.org`

Here are some typical requests you can make of *netlib* via email:

netlib REQUESTS

send *index* **from** *eispack*	Get the full index for library.
send *dgeco* **from** *linpack*	Get routine and all it depends on.
who is *gene golub*	Search in the SIAM membership list.
find *cubic spline*	Keyword search for netlib software.
find *aasen* **from** *linalg*	Bibliographic search.
mailsize *100k*	Set the chunk size used for reply .
quit	End of request (optional).

A list of available packages is given below and in the indices for the individual libraries you would obtain in the full reply. You will also find more information about the packages as well as the names of the authors—who deserve credit when you use their routines.

INVENTORY LIST

a	Approximation algorithms.
alliant	Set of Alliant programs.
amos	Special functions by D. Amos.
apollo	Set of Apollo programs.
benchmark	Benchmark programs and timings.
bib	Bibliographies.
bihar	Bjorstad's biharmonic solver.
bmp	Brent's multiple precision package.
c	"Misc" library for C language.
cheney-kincaid	Programs from 1985 text.
conformal	Conformal mapping.
contin	Continuation, limit points.
core	Machine constants, vector, and matrix.
c++	C++ codes.
dierckx	Spline fitting, various geometries.
domino	Multitask communication, scheduling.
eispack	Matrix eigenvalues and vectors.
elefunt	Elementary function tests.
errata	Corrections to numerical books.
f2c	Fortran to C converter.
fishpack	Separable elliptic PDEs.
fitpack	Cline's splines under tension.
fftpack	Swarztrauber's Fourier transforms.
fmm	Software from Forsythe, Malcolm, and Moler.
fn	Fullerton's special functions.
fortran	Single-double precision converter, debugger.
fp	Floating point arithmetic.
gcv	Generalized cross validation.
gmat	Multiprocessing Time Line and State Graph tools.
go	"Golden oldies" gaussq, zeroin, etc.
graphics	Auto color, ray-tracing benchmark.
harwell	MA28 sparse linear system.
hence	Heterogeneous network computing environment.
hompack	Nonlinear equations, homotopy method.
ieeecss	IEEE/Control Systems Society.
itpack	Iterative linear system solution.
jakef	Automatic differentiation of Fortran routines.
kincaid-cheney	Programs from the 1990 text.
lapack	Numerical linear algebra routines.
lanczos	Cullum and Willoughby's Lanczos programs.
lanz	Large sparse symmetric generalized eigenproblem.
laso	Eigenvalues of sparse matrices.
linpack	Gaussian elimination, QR, SVD.
lp	Linear programming.
machines	Short descriptions of various computers.
matlab	Software from MATLAB user's group.

microscope	Discontinuity checking.
minpack	Nonlinear equations and least squares.
misc	Everything else.
ml	Standard ML of New Jersey.
na-digest	Archive of NA mailing list.
napack	Numerical algebra programs.
news	Grosse's Netlib News column.
numeralgo	Algorithms from "Numerical Algorithms."
ode	Ordinary differential equations.
odepack	Ordinary differential equations.
odrpack	Orthogonal distance regression.
opt	Optimization.
paranoia	Kahan's floating point test.
parmacs	Parallel programming macros.
pascal	Pascal "misc" library.
pchip	Hermite cubics.
pdes/madpack	A multigrid package.
picl	Multiprocessor instrumented communication lib.
pltmg	Bank's multigrid code.
polyhedra	Hume's database of geometric solids.
popi	Digital darkroom image manipulation software.
port	The public subset of PORT library.
pppack	Subroutines from de Boor.
pvm	Parallel virtual machine.
quadpack	Univariate quadrature.
research	Miscellanea from AT&T Bell Labs.
sched	Environment for portable parallel algorithms.
sciport	Portable version of Cray SCILIB.
sequent	Sequent software.
slap	Iterative methods.
slatec	Error handling from the Slatec.
sparse	C sparse linear algebra.
sparse-blas	BLAS by indirection.
sparspak	Sparse linear algebra core.
specfun	Transportable special functions.
spin	Simulation of communication protocols.
stringsearch	String matching.
toeplitz	Linear systems in Toeplitz or circulant form.
toms	Collected algorithms of the ACM.
typesetting	Typesetting macros and preprocessors.
uncon/data	Optimization test problems.
vanhuffel	Total least squares, partial SVD.
vfftpk	Vectorized FFT; variant of fftpack.
voronoi	Voronoi diagrams and Delaunay triangulations.
y12m	Sparse linear system.

xnetlib

Recently developed at the University of Tennessee and Oak Ridge National Laboratory, *xnetlib* is an X-version of *netlib*. We here give some quotes from their documents which you may find useful. Unlike *netlib*, which uses electronic mail to process requests for software and other text, *xnetlib* uses an X Window graphical interface and a socket-based connection between the user's machine and the *xnetlib* server machine to process software requests. Each time *xnetlib* starts up, it contacts the netlib server at Oak Ridge National Laboratory (`surfer.epm.ornl.gov`) to get the latest list of index files. Any new or updated index files may then be downloaded as you wish. At this time there are about 200 of these files, each about a page or two in size. To get files from *xnetlib*, click on *library* (for example) and then select from the list of libraries. Click on the files you want and then click *download*. The index files are stored locally. These are the same files you get by sending for the index by email from netlib.

To receive a copy of *xnetlib* send the message:

```
$  mail netlib@ornl.gov              Unix Mail command.
   send xnetlib.shar from xnetlib    Tell them this.
```

When you receive the `shar` file, remove the mail header, save it to *filename*, type **sh** **filename**, and follow the instructions in the README file.

4.5   Running on a Different Computer

Remote Login: telnet

In a similar manner to `ftp` allowing a user to transfer files across the internet, `telnet` allows users to log onto and work on remote machines as if they were sitting at one of its terminals. How usable this remote login is depends on how well the machines are connected and how well your terminal is recognized by the foreign machine. As the distance between machines increases, and the number of networks that must be interconnected (the number of *hops*), the response time between a user entering a character and the remote machine responding to it increases. You can measure this round trip time with the **ping** command as discussed in Chapter 3. If the ping times are greater than 500 milliseconds, the remote machine will seem unresponsive and you will find it hard to be productive. Slow connections are common when using machines at far-removed different sites. If you are of the patient type, your telnet session will be usable but editing may be difficult.

Telnet has very few options and is simple to use. Like `ftp` you just give the name of the machine you want to connect to as an option:

```
%  telnet itasca.thomas.hal.com       Login to the machine itasca.
Connected to itasca.thomas.hal.com.
Escape character is 'Ĵ'.              The escape character may be Ĵ or î.
SunOS UNIX (itasca)
login:                                Now we can login.
```

Once we get the `login:` prompt, the login is the same as from any other terminal. Telnet will automatically try to set your **TERM** variable for you so the foreign machine knows your terminal type, but nevertheless, you may have to correct it if the remote machine does not know about the name it was sent as your terminal type.

To end the telnet session, log off the remote machine. If the connection is *hung*, that is, you have stopped getting a response, you will not be able to log off and so you should use the telnet escape character to get a telnet prompt and then quit the telnet session. The telnet escape character may be either ^] or ^t. You will also get the telnet prompt if telnet does not recognize the remote hostname you use. In this case you are not connected to the foreign machine but are just running telnet. You can **quit** telnet or tell telnet to **open** some other machine.

```
%  telnet itsca.thomas.hal.com          Itasca is misspelled.
itsca:  unknown host                    No host by this name.
telnet>  open itasca.thomas.hal.com     Use the open command.
Trying...                               It takes a while.
Connected to itasca.thomas.hal.com.
Escape character is '^]'.
SunOS UNIX (itasca)
login:      ^]                          Use the escape character to get
                                        to the telnet prompt.

telnet>  quit                           Use quit to end the session.
Connection closed.
%                                       Telnet session ended.
```

Logging On to a Non-Unix System

Telnet is useful for connecting to Unix machines and often works for non-Unix systems such as VAX. If you want to connect to a non-Unix machine, you may have to use a different program.

VM and MVS Using tn3270

The standard Unix program **tn3270** emulates an IBM 3270 terminal and can be used to log onto VM and MVS systems that are running TCP/IP. Since the two systems have such different assumptions about terminal protocols, the emulation is not perfect and it may not be adequate for heavy use. A *map* file is used to map the keyboard you are using to the 3270 function keys. The default mapping is for the pf keys to be mapped to the sequence **escape** numerical key. Here is a list of the standard default keys. If you use **tn3270**, you will want to set up your own map file so that special function keys on your keyboard work with the 3270 emulation.

telnet for VMS

An easy way to connect to a DEC VMS machine is to open an **xterm** window using the **-v** option, see Chapter 5, *Looking through X Windows*. This creates a **vt100** emulation which, while generic for Unix, is in fact a DEC terminal. Use this window to telnet to the VMS machine.

<u>tn3270 MAPPING</u>

pf1	[esc]1	wordnext	[esc]f
pf2	[esc]2	wordprev	[esc]b
pf3	[esc]3	down	^n
pf4	[esc]4	left	^b
pf5	[esc]5	right	^f
pf6	[esc]6	up	^p
pf7	[esc]7	clear	[esc]
pf8	[esc]8	delete	^d
pf9	[esc]9	clear	^l
pf10	[esc]0	eraseeof	^k
pf11	[esc]-	backtab	^a
pf12	[esc]=	enter	^j
backtab	[esc][tab]		

4.6   Unix to Unix

Considering that they are getting different systems to talk to each other, telnet and ftp work amazingly well. Yet there are smoother interfaces available for Unix workstations, and if you interconnect them on a regular basis, these are recommended. The Unix remote commands **rlogin**, **rsh**, and **rcp** provide this more transparent interface by letting you treat the remote computer effectively as another file or directory on your own machine. You can then login, run commands, and copy files on the remote machine with the same ease as you do locally (which we hope is easy).

The magic that allows remote access is a file called .rhosts in the user's home directory on the remote machine. This file lists the names of accessible computers and the users who may access them. To use a remote machine, your machine and login name must be listed in the remote machine's .rhosts file. For example, now the user bohr wants to log into the machine *phyl* from the machine *theo*. In bohr's home directory on the machine *theo* he creates the file .rhosts that looks like this:

theo bohr	bohr will be logging in from theo.
theo.copenhagen.ne bohr	Same entry with full hostname.

To avoid confusion over the full hostname, theo.copenhagen.ne in this case, and the short name, theo, we include an entry for each; multiple entries cause no problems. With the .rhosts file so prepared, we can use the remote commands. If your login name is the same on both the local and remote machine, you do not need to include your login name in the .rhosts file.

Remote Login: rlogin

The command **rlogin** logs you into a remote machine in a manner similar to **telnet**. If your user ID is the same on each machine, you only need to declare the machine on which you want to log in:

```
%   rlogin phy1                    bohr logs in remotely to phy1.
                                    The login takes a few seconds.
%   hostname                       To check if we're there, we ask.
phy1                               phy1 introduces itself.
%                                  Prompt is a shell on remote machine.
```

Since one % looks like another %, when dealing with remote machines, it is useful to have the hostname of the machine in your prompt (see dotfiles in Appendix A).

If you are prompted for your password instead of receiving a new prompt, it indicates that your .rhosts file is not being properly handled. You can, of course, trust the computer with your password, but that is somewhat of a nuisance. If your login name is different on the remote machine, then give the -1 option to the rlogin command which will then accept your login name on the remote machine and pass it along:

```
theo%   rlogin phy2 -1 niels       bohr's name is niels on phy2.
phy2%   hostname                    Note prompt with hostname.
```

To terminate your remote login session, issue the **exit** or **logout** command on the remote machine. If this does not work, then use the escape sequence ˜. to make **rlogin** break the connection.

Commands from Remote Shell: rsh

The remote shell command **rsh** allows you to execute a command on a remote machine without actually logging onto that machine. Beware that on some Unix System V machines, **rsh** is the name for the *restricted shell*, in which case you get a remote shell by issuing the **rshell** or **rcmd** commands. The command **rsh** uses the same .rhosts file as does **rlogin**, yet while **rlogin** will prompt you for a password if it has trouble with the .rhost file, both **rsh** and **rcp** require a properly functioning .rhosts file. If the .rhosts files is not properly configured, these commands will issue an error message and quit.

In the example below, big brother bohr wants to find out if his students are working on phy1 (as they were told to), and so he runs the command **who** remotely on the machine phy1:

```
%   rsh phy1 who                   Remote shell, computer name, command.
pfink     console Mar 16 17:58
ghe       ttyp0   Mar 16 17:58  (slip-serv)
```

The remote shell runs in your home directory on the remote machine — just the same as when you log in at home. To execute a command that is not in your home directory, you must either give the path name relative to your home directory or issue the **cd** command to change the directory to it.

```
%   rsh phy1 pwd                   Run pwd on phy1.
/u/bohr                            In bohr's home directory with rsh.
```

Now bohr uses **rsh** to explore his home directory on phy1:

```
%  rsh phy1 ls -CF                    List in columns for remote phy1.
Mail/    bin/
News/    proj/
%  rsh phy1 ls -CF proj               Look at the directory proj.
bin/     src/
runs/
                                      Note path is relative to home directory.
%  rsh phy1 ls -CF proj/bin           Now look at remote subdirectory.
calcL*        bigjob*
%  rsh phy1 ls -CF /u/bohr/proj/bin   Use full path name
                                      to get to the same directory.

calcL*        bigjob*
```

Now bohr wants to run one of his programs on phy1. To do this, he has to change directory and then run his **runs** command. While the change directory command **cd** and bohr's program **runs** are separate commands, they must be concatenated as a single command for **rsh** to execute. To do this, separate the commands with a semicolon (the standard Unix procedure to run two commands sequentially) and surround all of the commands with quotes:

```
%  rsh phy1 "cd proj/runs; /u/bohr/proj/bin/calcL"
```

Or, you can "escape" the semicolon by placing a \ directly before it:

```
%  rsh phy1 cd proj/runs \; /u/bohr/proj/bin/calcL
```

The \ tells the shell not to place any special meaning on the next character and instead to just pass it along. In either case the remote shell gets the semicolon and interprets it as a command separator.

To really make use of someone else's resources, we may also need to include I/O redirection in our remote commands. In this example bohr runs a remote command with standard input from the file data.in, a file also located in the runs directory on the remote machine. Since we again need to concatenate several commands, the whole mess is enclosed in quotes:

```
%  rsh phy1 "cd proj/runs; /u/bohr/proj/bin/job < data.in"
```

For another level of complication we can take the input file from our local machine while running the command remotely:

```
%  ls                                 Local list.
ch4.tex    ch4.div    ch4.ps          What's on theo.
%  rsh phy1 lp -dps < ch4.ps          Use local ch4.ps as
                                      input for the remote command.
```

Here we have printed a local file on a remote machine by running the `lp -dps` command on the remote machine with a redirected input from the local file `ch4.ps`.[7]

The same methods work for output as well as input. Here bohr runs the program remotely and directs the output to a local file:

```
%  rsh phy1 /u/bohr/proj/bin/calcL > run1.out
```

In case you have different names on different machines, the `rsh` command accepts the same `-l` options as does `rlogin`. So when bohr wants to run commands on phy2, he gives the `-l` option to tell phy2 his login name is niels, not bohr:

```
%  rsh phy2 -l niels who              Remote command with different user id.
```

Remote Copy: rcp

In the preceding examples it would have been more convenient to already have the files on the remote machine and then copy them back to our local machine when done working. In this way we avoid both worrying about a number of things at once and issuing a long and error-prone command. This is possible by using the remote copy command `rcp`. In general, the `rcp` command works like the standard copy command `cp`, but with the additional features of being able to specify a remote machine as well as your user ID on the remote machine. Like the `rsh` command, `rcp` goes to your home directory on the remote machine. To copy a file to or from another directory, you must specify the path name for the file relative to your home directory. For example, to copy your `.cshrc` file from machine to machine:

```
%  rcp local.file remhost:rfile      Copy local file to remote one.
%  rcp .cshrc remhost:               Copy local .cshrc file to machine remhost.
%  rcp remhost:.cshrc .              Copy remote .chsrc file to local machine.
```

When no file name is specified for the second machine, the file will have the same name as it had on the first machine.

In our next example, bohr copies some input files on the local machine to the remote machine phy1 and then runs his program on the remote machine. When the program is completed, he copies the output files back to his local machine:

```
%  ls
setup.data     inputs                User bohr has two input files.
%  rcp setup.data inputs \
   phy1:proj/runs                     He copies both
                                       to remote machine's directory runs.

%  rsh phy1 "cd proj/runs; \         Run remote job with
   /u/bohr/proj/bin/calcL"            input files.
                                      After the job has completed,
%  rsh phy1 ls -l proj/runs          check for the output files.
```

---

[7]There are more elegant ways to do this using Unix remote printing facilities.

```
-rwxr----- 1 bohr     10908 Mar 10
 09:53 setup.data
-rwxr----- 1 bohr     40696 Mar 10
 09:53 inputs
-rwxr----- 1 bohr   2158225 Mar 10
 22:34 data.output
%  rcp phy1:proj/runs/data.output .    Copy output file to local machine.
```

As with the other remote commands, you can also specify your user ID on the remote machine if it is different from your user ID on the local machine. This is done by using the same notation as for the **mail** or **finger** commands. Here bohr copies a file to **phy2** where his user ID is niels:

```
%  rcp calcL.c niels@phy2:myprog        Remote copy with 2 names.
```

There are two options that make **rcp** very handy, namely, **-r** to indicate recursive copy, and **-p** to preserve modification dates and file permissions. The **rcp -r** command copies a directory and all of the files and subdirectories below it. The **rcp -p** command preserves modification dates and file permissions; this helps make the remote files look just like they do at home as well as being useful for utilities such as **make**. For example:

```
%  rcp -rp src remhost:newproject      Recursive, permissive copy of src.
```

copies the complete directory src to the machine remhost. In the process, it creates a new directory src under the directory newproject on the remote machine. The **-p** part of the option preserves the modification times of all of the files.

4.7 Network File System (NFS)

So far we have shown you how to copy files between machines, log onto remote machines, and run commands on remote machines. While these Unix remote commands make computing on more than one machine easy, it is still far from the envisioned "transparent computing environment" mentioned earlier. The problem is that each machine has its own file storage, and therefore, if you log onto a different machine, you will get a different home directory and different files. You can, of course, try to maintain multiple sets of files and programs using **rcp**, but this is an ever increasing pain and waste of resources, especially as the scope of your problem and the number of machines you use grow.

The solution is to have only a single home directory on a single machine holding the hard disk containing your files. The other machines then *mount* these disks using a remote file system like NFS or AFS. To the user each machine appears to have the same hard disk. In practice, an NFS-mounted hard disk has the same look and feel as a local disk except it is slower, especially for writing files, and naturally its access is susceptible to network disturbances. The machine that actually contains the hard disk which other machines use is called a *fileserver*. It may be a general purpose workstation or a special purpose machine. In fact, with NFS any machine can be both server and importer of files.

Owing to the finite nature of transmission times, NFS is only useful when the sharing is at the same site, preferably on the same network. It also requires that the system administrators for each machine cooperate in configuring and sharing file systems. Configuring NFS mounts is not that complicated but it is beyond the scope of this book. One requirement worth mentioning is that each user hoping to share his or her files must have the same user ID and group id on all machines. If you have a different user ID on the remote machine, the files will look like they belong to different user and NFS will not let you edit or create files.

It is possible, and at times even desirable, to mount directories to machines of different computer architectures.[8] This does create problems, however. First, programs compiled under one architecture will not run on a machine with a different architecture. Second, the user's setup files, such as .profile, may contain options or set paths that work on one machine but not on others.

4.8   DOS, Macintosh to Unix Transfers

For a number of reasons you may want to transfer files between Unix and your PC. For instance, you may want to work on files with your laptop computer while traveling or with your PC at home and then use the PC files on your workstation. To be safe you should transfer only ASCII or binary files (text or numbers but no control characters). Thus you should not transfer executable files or internal files from applications such as word processors. On your personal computer you may need to tell your word processor or application program to *save file as, text* or ASCII or to read the file in as text or ASCII. If it is source code that you transfer between systems, you will need recompile it; if it is text for a word processor, you will need to reformat it; if it is source code for a *text processing program* such as *Nroff* or LATEX, the formatting is always done locally anyway.

A difficulty which may arise in transferring files between workstations and PCs is that there are several conventions used for ending a line and starting a new one. In the DOS transfer commands below you may notice our use of options to replace the sequence CR-LF (carriage return–line feed) with NL (new-line character) and to interpret a [ctrl-z] (ASCII SUB) as the end-of-line character. Additionally you need be careful with the \ (BACKSLASH) character since it has special meaning to Unix. Furthermore, while Unix is case sensitive with its file names, DOS is not; DOS assumes all names are uppercase. For more information, use the **man** command on your local system.

After you have the text file in the proper form to transfer, there are two basic approaches you can follow. The first is possible if your personal computer and workstation can be connected together, say, by cable or modem. You can then use a terminal emulator program (such as **NCSA telnet, kermit,** or **Versaterm**) on your PC and transfer the file with one of the transfer protocols (such as **kermit** or **ftp**) contained in the emulator program. The second approach is to use floppy disks (diskettes) to transfer files.

When using floppies for transfer, it is best if your PC runs Unix and you write your disks in **tar** format.[9] If your PC is a DOS or Mac machine, your Unix workstation must have the appropriate software to read or write floppy formatted for your type of PC. On the IBM workstations the commands **dosread** and **doswrite** reads and writes DOS files from floppies. For other workstations there is the *Mtools* collection of DOS commands. If your Unix cannot emulate DOS read and write commands, you then must read the DOS

---

[8]Architecture refers to the arrangement of memory and the organization of the CPU. We discuss architecture in Chapters 12 and 13.

[9]Techniques with **tar** have been discussed already in Chapter 3, *Workstation Setup and Use*.

files from the floppy onto a DOS machine and use a terminal emulator program on the DOS machine with its macros to transfer the files to the workstation.

DOS Transfers under AIX

Three commands are needed to use a DOS floppy disk under AIX. The **dosdir** command is the equivalent of the **dir** command in MS-DOS and shows the contents of the floppy disk. The commands **dosread** and **doswrite** transfer programs from and to the floppy.

Read 1 File from DOS Diskette to Unix

	Insert DOS diskette into the floppy drive.
`$   cd dirname`	Get into desired Unix directory.
`$   dosread -a fname`	Read from DOS floppy to Unix.

The **-a** option must be used for all text files since it corrects for line feed, carriage return differences between Unix and MS-DOS format files.

Write and Check 1 File to DOS Diskette from Unix

	Insert DOS floppy.
`$   cd dirname`	Change to desired Unix directory.
`$   doswrite -a unixfile dosfile.tex`	Write to DOS floppy.
`There are 977920 bytes of free space.`	The voice of DOS.

Note that the DOS floppy needs be formatted before writing to it. This can be done on your PC or with the AIX command **dosformat**. For more information on this and other DOS commands, check the manual with **man dosread**. As a further example, now we examine and read the Fortran program ZROOTS.FOR from a floppy:

`$ dosdir`	List files on floppy.
`VANDER.FOR   ZROOTS.FOR`	The files.
`There are 976896 bytes of free space.`	The voice of DOS.
`$ dosdir -l`	Long list of DOS directory.
`VANDER.FOR 769 Mar 26 1992 17:45:25`	One line of many.
`There are 976896 bytes of free space.`	The voice of DOS.
`$ dosread   -a   ZROOTS.FOR`	Read ZROOTS.FOR from floppy.
`$ ls`	List files in current directory.
`ZROOTS.FOR`	Yes, it's there now.
`$ mv ZROOTS.FOR   zroots.f`	Rename for Unix.

Write Entire Directory to DOS Diskette

To copy an entire directory from Unix to DOS, place the following few lines in a file (we call ours dos.dir). This file is a shell script that takes the output file names from the list command **ls** and uses them as file names for the **doswrite** command:

`dosfiles='ls'`	List files, set to variable `dosfiles`.
`for i in $dosfiles`	Go through list of names.
`  do`	Repeat loop.
`  doswrite -a $i $i`	Write 1 file onto floppy.
`  done`	

To run this script, make the file executable (x) with the command **chmod x dos.dir**, and then issue the **dos.dir** command. If you want the file to go into an already existing DOS directory named `pcfiles`, change the **doswrite** line above to:

% doswrite -a $i /pcfiles/$i   Write to DOS directory.

Transfer Entire Directory, DOS to Unix

Let's say we have a DOS directory `notes`, all of whose files we want to read into Unix. The steps are similar to the above. First insert the floppy. Next, get into the Unix directory where you want the DOS files copied. Then create the Unix file (we call it `dosread.dir`):

`#!/bin/ksh`	Use ksh (see Chapter 10).
`dosfiles='dosdir notes'`	List DOS files in directory notes.
`for i in $dosfiles`	Repeat for each file name.
`  do`	
`  dosread -a notes/$i $i`	Read from floppy directory notes.
`  done`	

To write all files in the current Unix directory to the DOS directory `notes`, you need replace the **dosread** line above with the **doswrite** line:

% doswrite -a $i /notes/$i   Read into DOS directory notes.

DOS Transfers Using Mtools

There is a public domain collection of tools known as *Mtools* used for manipulating DOS floppies and their files from within Unix systems. If you are on an IBM machine you may as well use the native **dosread, doswrite,** and **dosdir** command package. If not, then your local Unix may have *mtools* (try **man mtools**) or you may be able to get it free off the network.

On the next page we give *mtools'* collection of commands, each of which emulates the DOS command without the *m* in front.

Mac Diskette to Unix

The technique here is less direct than using DOS floppies since there are no native MAC commands on workstations (other than on a MacII running AUX, which are rare). In this case you need either a serial (cable or modem or Appletalk) or TCP/IP (ethernet) connection between your Mac and the workstation or mainframe. Then you transfer the files with either **ftp** or **kermit**.

MTOOLS COMMANDS

mattrib	Change DOS file attribute flags.
mcd	Change DOS directory.
mcopy	Copy DOS files to/from Unix.
mdel	Delete DOS file.
mdir	Print working DOS directory.
mlabel	Label a DOS volume.
mmd	Make DOS subdirectory.
mrd	Remove DOS subdirectory.
mread	Read (low level) DOS file to Unix.
mren	Rename existing DOS file.
mtype	Print contents of DOS file.
mwrite	Write (low level) Unix file to DOS.

CHAPTER 5

LOOKING THROUGH X WINDOWS

Turn your face away
from the garish light of day, ...

—Charles Hart, *The Phantom of the Opera*

The good news is that there is graphical user interface (GUI=gooey) for Unix workstations, which runs on machines from all manufactures, and has many of the nice mouse and graphical features found on the window environments of PCs. This standard system is called *The X Window System*, or "X" for short. It was developed at MIT and is supported by a consortium of industry leaders, including DEC, Hewlett-Packard, Sun, IBM, and AT&T. The bad news is that the documentation for X does not lend itself to a casual perusal while searching for a piece of needed information. To be fair to the casual peruser, even the serious user may get confused after facing the extent of the documentation with its continual revisions and the complication of the local blending of hardware and software. Nevertheless, the X Window System works very well, is pleasant, improves your working efficiency, and by becoming the standard user interface for all workstations, is very much helping make "transparent computing environment" a reality.

From an administrative point of view, the X of the X Window System might stand for eXtra large and eXtra heavy. The X program itself requires at least 25 MB of memory to get stored on your hard disk and at least 16 MB of random access memory to be run by your computer. And if that is not enough, X also puts significant demands on your workstation's processing power. As expected, meeting all these hardware requirements places eXtra demands on your pocket book.

There are several versions of X in existence to add to the challenge of X programming, and you should not be too surprised to find pieces of each running on any one machine. While it's commendable that the X consortium keeps turning out new versions every couple of years, it's overwhelming for the vendors to keep integrating the new releases into their products. The versions and releases of X currently in use are *X11 R3*, *X11 R4*, and *X11 R5*. These versions are not completely compatible, and so as you migrate from one to the next, you might be required to change your setup files and options.

The X Window System uses a *client–server* model for displaying graphics. Your display is considered the *server* when X is running on your display. The programs which place graphical objects on the display are *clients* of this server. As a consequence of the standardization of X, any machine on the network can open a window on your server and run a client—unless you are wise and knowledgeable enough to forbid it.

In this chapter we try to help the beginner get started with X and learn to take advantage of some of its many features. Along the way we present discussions and examples which should help the more experienced user personalize their X environment for that custom look. In concluding, we'll prove again one major advantage of a standard interface is that many programs and applications become available for it. A few of these applications are commercial packages, such as the symbolic manipulation programs, while most are freeware available over the network. Some of the free X applications have already been discussed in Chapter 4, *Mail Systems*.

5.1   Starting Up X

Many vendors and local support groups have provided their own methods for users to start up the X Window System. As you might expect after our introductory grumbling, even on one machine the method may differ if you are at the console or at an X terminal.[1] Frequently Unix itself starts up X without any user encouragement. In that case, Unix both initiates X and opens a special window on the display asking you to log in. Once you have logged in, the login window may drop out of view and your customized *environment* may be created on the screen (or the default if you have been lazy).

Another common method for starting X is to log in in your normal way, and then issue the command **xinit** or **xtstart**. The programs run by these commands, as well other X programs, are usually kept in the directory /usr/bin/X11. You should add this directory to PATH in your .profile, as described in Chapter 3, *Workstation Setup and Use*, and in Appendix A. If you are so inclined, you may browse through this directory to see some of the X commands available to you.

Once you have started X, you probably will see the screen turn gray, see one or more windows appear, as in Figure 5.1, and see the mouse pointer become activated (it's usually a small arrow). If you have trouble locating the mouse pointer on the screen, just roll the mouse around on its pad to get the pointer jumping around. While discussing mice, please note that from now on we will be lazy and suggest you move your "mouse" into some object on the screen when we really mean move your mouse's pointer. Keep your mouse on its pad; in fact, we recommend that you always keep your mouse on a clean mouse pad for precision of motion and protection of mouse.

As far as X is concerned, all mice have three buttons. While some mice may actually not have three buttons, operationally X assumes they do. For mice with only two buttons, depressing both simultaneously is equivalent to depressing the middle button:

X MOUSE BUTTONS

left	Number 1.
right	Number 2.
middle (or 1 + 2)	Number 3.

If you can get your hands on your computer now, try moving the mouse around on

---

[1] In § 5.8 we discuss the class of devices known as "X terminals" or "X stations."

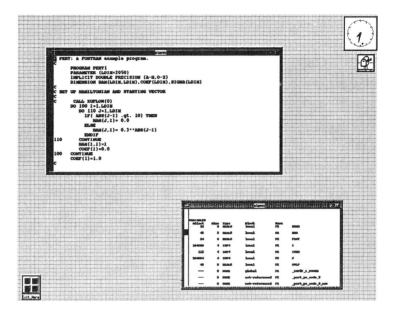

Figure 5.1: X11 and Motif window environment.

the screen. Notice what happens when the mouse is pointed at various objects (parts of the screen) and different buttons are clicked or held down. Don't worry too much about "breaking" or confusing the system with your clicking; just try to get a feel for how the components making up X work. When you confuse or damage X beyond repair, just kill X and start again using the procedures described below.

Stopping X

If you have followed our suggestion to go pointing and clicking, you may well have a confused X and so need to terminate X. As with most things in X, a universal and simple method does not exist, so you need experiment:

- Close all edit sessions and quit programs before stopping X. Use the Unix commands **ps -ef** or **ps aux** to see if your processes are still running, and if so, **kill** them.

- Look for a *window* labeled something like Exit Here or login. Move the mouse into this window, enter the Unix command **exit** or **logout**; this may shut down X.

- You may have a pull-down menu item for Shut Down, Quit, Reboot, or Restart. Click on the gray background to pop up the menu; these may terminate your X session, possibly after asking you for a confirmation of your desires.

- An effective, if somewhat inelegant, method for stopping X on some systems is to simultaneously depress the **Ctrl**, **Alt**, and **Backspace** keys. You then will be told that the X server has crashed—as if this is the beginning rather than the end of your problem; don't worry, this is your intention.

The difficulty in terminating the X Windows System is that in addition to the window manager and X itself, virtually every item you see on a screen, such as Figure 5.1, is a separate, active program. To shut down X properly, you must kill all of these programs and terminate them in the proper order. If you do not, you run the risk of Unix becoming very stern with you and not letting you log off until you do something about your *stopped jobs*.

5.2　Managing Windows

As we discuss in detail later, the X *window manager* is a program which runs under X and controls the format, features, organization, placement, and response of X's windows. While you can run X without a manager, it is much more convenient and faster to have it managed. There are a number of free window managers available over the network. They are free and each produces a characteristic feel and look. It is these window managers which tailor X and give it the capability of making your workstation appear like a PC. In addition to the window manager, there are desktop programs such as *xdt* which convert your screen into a symbolic desktop with icons representing various files and functions, similar to what you find on the Macs. These desktop interfaces are excellent guides for providing beginners a tour, but tend to get in the way for power users.

Motif Window Manager: mwm

The Motif Window Manager, mwm, is very popular and almost standard for many applications and manufactures. It has a pleasant 3-D look, is easy on the eyes, is relatively simple to use, and works rather similarly to MS *Windows* by Microsoft. The twm window manager is our alternative choice. It is not as pretty as *Motif*, yet is faster and better met our needs for closure; the speed is important if you are a power user with many open windows.

The Motif Window Manager is part of the Motif Graphic User Interface (GUI). Motif itself is a *tool kit* which follows the standard style for X applications adopted by the Open Software Foundation (OSF). This standardization is helpful to you since the menus, scroll bars, buttons, and extras will be much the same for different applications, so you don't have to learn new ones all the time. As more applications get written using the Motif GUI, the entire X Windows System should become more uniform and easier to use. At present we find an uneven adherence to the standards in applications, yet with enough similarity to still be effective.

Window Manager Setup: .mwmrc

The Motif Window Manager uses a .mwmrc file to configure such things as button functions and menu items. If you do not have this file in your home directory, find the system default file system.mwmrc in the directory /usr/lib/X11/system.mwmrc, copy it to .mwmrc in your home directory, and then customize this one for your own needs and desires. We will give examples to help you configure mwm and its startup file .mwmrc, and we give a sample .mwmrc in Appendix A and on the floppy. If you are using a window manager other than Motif, such as *Open Look* or *twm*, the configuration procedures are similar, but you will need a somewhat different startup file.

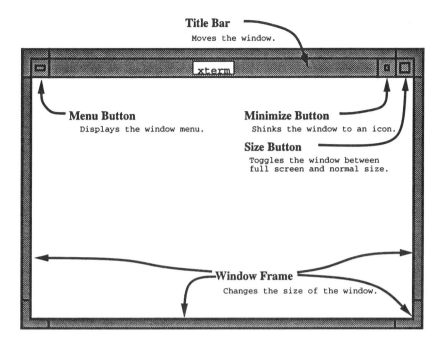

Figure 5.2: Parts of a Motif window.

Manipulating Windows with Motif

The window which X displays for you is officially an "*X client*" served by the X Window System. As you study Figure 5.2 note that the Motif Window Manager puts a frame around all X clients for good looks as well as for ease in moving, resizing, iconifying, and closing them. To see what we mean, grab your mouse and:

- Open a new window, possibly by clicking on the *terminal, high function terminal (hft)*, or the *shell* button on the menu.

- Notice that as you move the mouse from the screen background into an X Window, the pointer changes and the window outline brightens. This is more than cute since the changes denote different functions that have become possible; for example, you can output into any window but input only into the bright window.

- When the mouse is placed "on" the window frame but not yet "in" the window, the mouse pointer becomes a small arrow up against a stop, → |. The direction of the arrow and the form of the stop varies for different parts of the frame (flat stop at sides, right angle stop in the corners).

- Move the mouse onto a window frame until the new arrow and its stop appears. Hold down the leftmost mouse button now and move the mouse. The window changes dimensions. This is known as *dragging* out the corner or side. You can stretch each side or corner in the direction the arrow is pointing.

- Move the mouse to the wide horizontal bar on the top of the window, but not quite into the narrow frame above it. This is called the *title bar.* The pointer now changes to a heavier arrow without any arrow stop. Notice that the title bar has four parts, or buttons. Dragging the long central part where the window's title is written moves the window.

- Move the mouse onto the title bar, hold down the left mouse button, and then drag the mouse until the window slides into to a good viewing position for you.

- On the right-hand side of the window's top (see Figure 5.2) are two buttons (we'll discuss the single, right-side button soon). The left-most of the two right buttons has a big square on it; the one to the right of it has a small square. Click the left button with the left mouse button and notice that this causes the window to completely fill the screen.

- Click the left mouse button again while the mouse is on the left-most of the two right buttons on the top, and notice that the window now shrinks back down.

- The button on the top right of the window with the small square is both cute and useful. Again using the left button of your mouse, push the top left button of the window and notice that the window shrinks into an *icon* (small symbol) which positions itself in some out of the way place, possibly even hidden under an existing window which you'll have to move to uncover the icon.

- When you locate that icon, hold the mouse over the icon and quickly click the left button twice. If you get this right, the icon will be converted back into a working window.

- Now move the mouse pointer to the left of the title bar and hold the left mouse button down. Notice that a menu of window operations similar to that in Figure 5.3 pops up. To get rid of the menu, move your mouse (with the left button still depressed) into some other region of the window or background and *then* release the button. (Or you may release the mouse button and the menu will remain until you click your left mouse button on the background.) Clicking the mouse on a menu item is your way of ordering the item.

- Some of the functions you can see on the menu, such as *Move, Size, Maximize,* and *Minimize,* are the same ones you can accomplish with mouse strokes. Others, such as *Lower* and *Close* are new. *Lowering* a window causes other open windows to appear on top of the current window. *Raising* a window causes that window to appear on top of other open windows. In contrast, *closing* a window is *not* cosmetic; it removes the window from the screen and kills any programs running in the window. You can raise a lowered window from the background, but not a closed one from the dead.

- Select a menu function such as *Lower* by holding down the left mouse button and moving the mouse over to this item. Release the button to select the item currently under the mouse. To actually activate the command, you may also have to also click in the window you want to lower.

- Now raise the window you have just lowered by choosing *Raise* from the menu. You may also have to click in the window you want to raise (or lower some on top). In

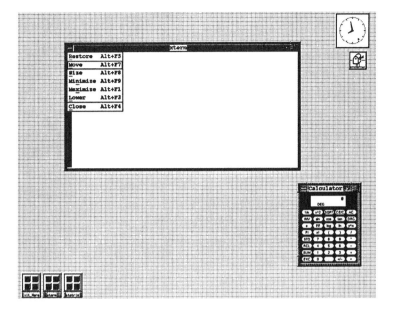

Figure 5.3: A Motif window menu.

twm there is a list of open windows kept in the corner of your screen and you can activate them from there.

- Next bring the menu up and then make it disappear without selecting any menu item. Just move the mouse off the menu and release the left button. If the menu still remains on the screen, click the mouse button again in any window and the menu will disappear (see § 5.2, *Menus*, for more details).

Notice that there are keys (often function keys) listed to the right of each menu item in Figure 5.3. Typing a key is equivalent to selecting the menu item. This may be faster than using the mouse once your hands are on the keyboard.

Active Window

Remember, *only one window at a time can receive input from the keyboard*. This window is *in focus* or *active*. All other windows can display output simultaneously (in the time-sharing, or round-robin, sense) with each other as well as with the window in focus. However, only the in-focus window can receive input.

By clicking on windows, notice that the Motif Window Manager highlights the border of the in-focus window. The in-focus window is not necessarily the window on top. There are two ways to determine which window gets the focus. In one, the keyboard focus automatically follows the pointer and the window in which the mouse resides receives the focus. In the other method, you must click your mouse in the window you want in focus.

The process of placing a window in focus or activating it can be combined with that of raising a window on top of all others. In *auto raise* the window automatically is raised

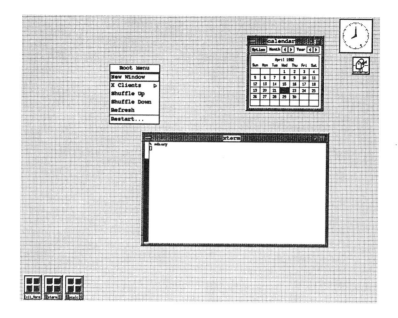

Figure 5.4: The window manager's root menu.

when it receives the focus (we prefer this option). Without auto raise, you must click on
the window frame with the left mouse button to raise the window—even if it is active. Use
the .Xdefaults file to tell X what your choice is, as follows:

! Focus policy		This is comment line.
Mwm*keyboardFocusPolicy:	explicit	Add ! to deactivate.
! Or		
!Mwm*keyboardFocusPolicy:	pointer	Remove ! to activate.
! And select auto raise	True or False	
Mwm*focusAutoRaise:	True	Add ! to deactivate.
!Mwm*focusAutoRaise:	False	Remove ! to activate.
!		

Menus

Clicking your mouse on the screen's background, that is outside of any window, will cause
the menu of applications and window operations shown in Figure 5.4 to pop up. Usually
each of the mouse buttons (and sometimes some combination of them) bring up different
menus. Of course, the default on your particular system depends on your vendor and your
diligent local support group. Move your mouse off the menu before releasing the button.

Now depress a mouse button (try the left one first) while the mouse pointer is on the
screen background—again not while in an actual window. *While holding down the mouse*

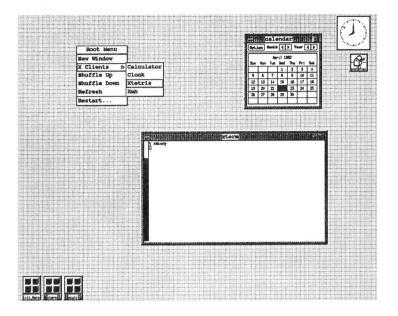

Figure 5.5: Cascading menus.

button, select a menu item by moving the mouse to the menu line you want and *then* releasing the mouse button once the item is highlighted. To avoid errors, relax, hold your hand steady, and release the button gently.

If you decide while in a menu that you don't really want to make *any* selection, keep the mouse button depressed and move the mouse off the menu to the screen background (or some open window). Once in safe territory, relax and then release the button. The menu should then disappear. If the menu remains, then you must explicitly click the mouse somewhere else on the screen to get rid of the menu.

Some menu items have submenus or cascading menus as options, such as the boxes seen to the right of the menu items in Figure 5.5. Until you have developed some mouse dexterity, such as with classes at your local video game arcade, you may find invoking these submenus a small challenge. Examine the cascade menu items available to you by pulling down a menu item, sliding sideways over to the cascade box, and pulling down one of them (always keeping your left mouse button depressed). Remove the cascade menu by keeping your mouse button depressed, sliding your mouse to the background, and then releasing your mouse button. Select a cascade menu item by releasing your mouse button when the mouse is sitting on your desired menu item.

5.3 Standard X11 Options

Most X applications use the same command line options. Here are some useful ones:

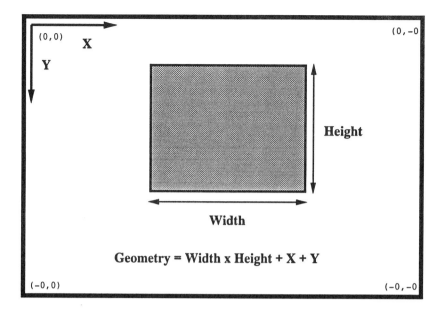

Figure 5.6: X11 screen coordinates.

X OPTIONS

-display *host:n*	Location of the X server.
-geometry $w \times h + x + y$	Window size and location.
-bg *color*	Window background color.
-fg *color*	Text and graphics color.
-fn *font*	Text font.
-iconic	Initial window to be icon.
-title *strings*	Window header title.

5.4   The Geometry of X11

Before we begin personalizing X, let's orient ourselves to the geometry of the X display. Consider Figure 5.6. The upper left corner of the screen is the origin $(x, y) = (0, 0)$. The x coordinate increases from left to right while the y coordinate increases from top to bottom. To place a window in a particular location, we give the window size and coordinates as width×height±x±y. A negative coordinate means the coordinate is referenced from the corner opposite the origin. So +0+0 is the upper left corner and -0-0 is the lower right corner. To place an 80 column by 40 row **xterm** window at the top of the screen and 100 pixels from the *left*, you issue the Unix command:

```
%   xterm -geometry 80x40+100+0          Top left (slightly right).
```

To place a 100×100 size **xclock** at the top of the screen and over 200 pixels from the *right* of the screen, you issue the Unix command:

```
%  xclock -geometry 100x100-200+0
```
Top right (slightly left).

5.5 Personalizing X Windows

Your X system uses a few dotfiles in your home directory to configure just about everything; they determine which X utilities and programs to run at startup, which window management system to use, and which fonts and colors you will see. Dealing with these files can be a little overwhelming if all you want to do is change the size of your font from young-programmer's size to middle-aged professor's size. We present *Sample Dot Files* in Appendix A and on the floppy and encourage you to modify our dotfiles to your preferences and system (but do keep backups). If you want to customize your display with something really personal, feel free to skim through the 600 page X User's Guide.

To see these and other normally invisible dot files, issue the **ls -a** Unix command:

```
$ ls -a                                List all files including dot ones.
./          .cshrc      .mwmrc      .xinitrc   bin/
../         .kshrc      .profile    Mail/      proj/
.Xdefaults  .login      .sh_history News/      src/
```


X Configuration: .Xdefaults

The behaviors, fonts, and colors for X Windows System applications are set by configuration lines in the .Xdefaults file in your home directory. Many applications also follow the defaults which are set in the directory /usr/lib/X11/app-defaults. But the .Xdefaults file will override them. Each line in the .Xdefaults files configures an attribute of an X program. For example,

`program*attribute:  setting`	Generic line in .Xdefaults.
`xterm*background:  LightSkyBlue3`	Set background color for xterm.

Notice that when you make a change in your .Xdefaults file, you may not see the change immediately because the .Xdefaults file is usually read only when the X server starts up (particularly in the latest releases of X). To have your changes take effect immediately without your having to kill and restart X, you must tell X to reread your configuration file. You do that by going to your home directory and issuing the Unix command:

```
%  xrdb -load .Xdefaults
```
Reload configuration (dot) file.

X Startup: .xinitrc and .xsession

On systems which give you a special login window or dialog box, the file `.xsession` in your home directory determines the startup applications. On systems where you personally start X by entering a command such as **xinit** or **xstartup**, the `.xinitrc` file in your home directory is used (as shown by that last **ls -a** command). In either case the startup files are just *scripts*, that is, small programs run by the default shell (usually `sh`). For example, a line in `.xinitrc` makes the choice between the prettier *Motif Window Manager* **mwm** and the simpler but faster **twm**.

You should check if you already have some of these dot files in your home directory. If you do not, X will use the defaults supplied with your system. For a startup file appropriate to your system, check with your local system administrator or in the system documentation provided by your vendor. You can try the samples given in Appendix A, although your locally supplied setup file should require fewer modifications in order to work just right.

Customizing Motif

In § 5.6, *Your Workspace: xterm*, we will provide examples of using menu items. Before we do that we suggest you make your X life more pleasant by becoming more familiar with how the Motif Window Manager **mwm** works. Specifically, by modifying the `.mwmrc` file in your home directory, you customize menu items and mouse buttons to include routine tasks.

When your login account was first created and Unix initialized you, it probably gave you a general purpose `.mwmrc` file. If you do not now have such a file in your home directory, look for the standard `.mwmrc` file contained in `/usr/lib/X11/system.mwmrc` and copy it into your home directory. (We have provided a sample `.mwmrc` in Appendix A and on the floppy.) Look at this `.mwmrc` file with your favorite editor—but first make a copy, say to `.mwmrc.bk`, just in case your customizations leave the system in shreds. The file may look rather confusing at first (and at last), but follow a basic rule of Unix survival is to ignore most of the file and worry only about the parts that interest you and which you can understand.

In `.mwmrc` there should be a section that looks something like this:

```
# Root Menu Description
Menu RootMenu
{
"Root Menu"          f.title
no-label             f.separator
"New Window"         f.exec "xterm &"
"Shuffle Up"         f.circle_up
"Shuffle Down"       f.circle_down
"Refresh"            f.refresh
no-label             f.separator
"Restart..."         f.restart
"Quit"               f.quit_mwm
}
```
.mwmrc file.

The left column is the menu which appears when you click on the background with **mwm**. You may also note some other menus, like *Default Window Menu Mwm Window Menu*. These additional menus appear when you click on an individual window's menu button (the one to the left of the window), in contrast to the menus which appear when you click on the background. Looking at this *Root Menu* you see how several functions are accomplished in **mwm**. The menu has a name, in this case *Root Menu*, and each line in the menu has two fields. The first field is a string or label which appears in the menu, and the second is a command to be executed when the user selects that menu line.

The first two lines in this `.mwmrc` file really don't do much. The `f.title` just gives the title for the menu, while the `f.separator` draws a line in the menu to separate the title from the menu items. Notice that `f.separator` is also used to separate the `Restart` and `Quit` operations. The third item, `"New Window" f.exec "xterm &,"` is of more interest. Selecting it executes the program **xterm**, which in turn opens a new window on your screen. What's interesting is the technique. You can insert lines in your `.mwmrc` file to create menu lines to run *any* command, even a shell script.[2] To run your own command, add a line to the menu with a label, then the **mwm** command `f.exec`, and then the command you want to run. Here is an example of a menu item to bring up a calculator:

"Calculator" f.exec "/usr/bin/X11/xcalc >/dev/null 2>/dev/null &"	Calculator window.

Notice first that the menu item label "Calculator" is surrounded by quotes. Next notice that the **mwm** command `f.exec` executes the following Unix command in the Borne shell. The command string which actually runs the calculator program is also surrounded by quotes and appears exactly as it would if you were typing a command line in the Born shell (or its cousin, the Korn shell). It is important to also observe that the command string ends with an ampersand `&` so it will be executed in the *background*; otherwise, the window manager would be stalled waiting for the menu command to complete.

The redirector `>` in our Unix command string redirects the standard output and its standard error to `/dev/null`. The device `/dev/null` is a black hole where you send data you never care to see again. It is generally a good practice to redirect output from menu commands to this black hole because there is no hope of seeing this output anyway and this will keep the window manager from being disturbed by your blunders.

Finally, notice that in the code line we're examining we used the full path name for the calculator program. This may not be necessary since the window manager uses the same path as the login shell, but it does not hurt to be sure. Using full path names also makes the command more robust since systems and procedures change, and it eliminates any ambiguity you or others may have as to what program is executed. For example, on our current system there are two different **xterm** programs, `/usr/bin/X11/xterm`, which came with the system, and `/usr/local/bin/X11/xterm`, which is a newer version we got from a friend. By using the full path name, we ensure which one will run.

Let us now return to modifying the `.mwmrc` file. After you add the new menu line, the window manager must reread the file before the changes are affected. The easiest way to do this is to use the menu item marked *Restart* which makes **mwm** run `f.restart`, which in turn makes the window manager reread the setup files and start over. There is the danger

---

[2]In § 5.6 we show how to use **xterm** to run commands inside their own window.

that an error in the new `.mwmrc file` (like unmatched quotes) will cause **mwm** to die or work improperly. If you are lucky enough in this case to still have an X window available, you can work within that window to fix the mistake, kill **mwm**, and then restart by issuing the command (from the command line):

```
$  mwm &                                Restart mwm.
```

If the window manager is really confused, you should kill the X Windows System, use your terminal in its text mode to fix the file, and then restart X.

Now, if you are really going to be playing around with your X environment a lot, a safer way to personalize it is to use a shell command for the window manager which switches back and forth between the default and your personal `.mwmrc`:

```
$  alt ctrl shift !                     Toggle between .mwmrc files.
```

Yes, this really does mean striking the `alt`, `ctrl`, `shift`, and `!` keys all at the same time (easy for you concert pianists out there). A dialog box should appear asking if you want *Toggle Behavior.* If you click on *Yes,* **mwm** restarts using the system defaults. Toggling again makes **mwm** restart using your `.mwmrc` file.

The remaining menu lines in the preceding example are built-in window manager commands. To avoid interruption of your personal games you may want to move these to a separate, cascade menu controlled by a different mouse button. These cascade menus are convenient for grouping similar commands. To make one, first create a new menu and then add a menu line to the root menu. Here is an example in which we add a `Tools` line to the `RootMenu`:

```
# Root Menu Description    Menu RootMenu {
"Root Menu"          f.title
no-label             f.separator
"New Window"         f.exec "xterm &"
"Tools"              f.menu Tools
"Shuffle Up"         f.circle_up
"Shuffle Down"       f.circle_down
"Refresh"            f.refresh
no-label             f.separator
"Restart..."         f.restart
"Quit"               f.quit_mwm
}
```

Now we add a new `Tools Menu` to our `.mwmrc` file:

```
Menu Tools                          Create cascade menu.
{
"Tools"   f.title
"Xrn"     !"(xrn)&"
"xcalc"   !"(xcalc)&"
"xlock"   !"(xlock)&"
}
```

Button Bindings

The .mwmrc file can also be used to define which buttons do what in various places. This is useful because you can create separate menus for each mouse button and you can also use it to change the behavior of mouse clicks on windows and icons. For example, let's say you always use the left mouse button to do things such as drag windows. To change this to the right mouse button, go to your .mwmrc file in your home directory and locate Button Bindings which look something like these:

```
Buttons DefaultButtonBindings
{
<Btn1Down>       frame|icon  f.raise
<Btn3Down>       frame|icon  f.post_wmenu
<Btn1Down>       root         f.menu RootMenu
<Btn3Down>       root         f.menu RootMenu
Meta<Btn1Down>   icon|window  f.lower
Meta<Btn2Down>   window|icon  f.resize
Meta<Btn3Down>   window       f.move
}
```

There may also be other button listings in the .mwmrc file with labels such as Explicit Button Bindings or Pointer Button Bindings. The specific set of bindings mwm uses is controlled by the line in .Xdefaults:

```
Mwm*buttonBindings:   DefaultButtonBindings | Choose button binds.
```

Changing the label from Default Button Bindings to one of the other bindings or perhaps to the name for your own set of bindings forces mwm to use the new button bindings. Once again, the change will not take place until after you restart mwm.

It is rare in our experience for a user to change the way the basic button bindings work in mwm. The sample .mwmrc file shows some examples of additional key button bindings you may find useful. In the example below, we add the Tools menu created previously to the right mouse button, button number 2, by adding the following line to the DefaultButtonBindings:

```
<Btn2Down>     root    f.menu  Tools
```

The <Btn2Down> part of this line says that when the middle button is clicked on the screen background or on root, the function f.menu is executed to bring up the Tools menu. (The f.menu Tools command is the same one used in the Tools Menu to bring up the menu.)

Deciphering the other lines in the button bindings is pretty straightforward. For example, the sixth line, `Meta<Btn1Down>` `icon|window` `f.lower`, says that if button 1 is pressed down with the meta key (usually labeled [ALT]) while the mouse pointer is on an icon or in a window, then the function `f.lower` is executed. This in turn sends the icon or window behind other objects on the screen.

5.6   Your Workspace: xterm

The **xterm** window is where you do most of your work in X. Think of it as a terminal custom built to your specifications. Since each such terminal is created with the **xterm** command, they can uniquely yours and as many in number as want. This is both fun and useful because it takes only one command or click to create a new window and make your very expensive workstation look just like a personal computer.

Choosing Screen Fonts and Colors

The first step in customizing your **xterm** is to select font sizes for text, and colors for the foreground and background, which will help you view the windows comfortably. (We suspect the default fonts and colors were selected by some plaid-panted programmer after spending all night writing code and drinking Coke.) Fortunately the setup is easy. You first examine the available choices; then you decide which names you prefer placing in the `.Xdefaults` file in your home directory so they become the defaults. A standard set of options for **xterm** is:

```
%  xterm -display host:n -geom wxh+x+y \
     -fn font -bg color -fg color -e command
```

Now let's make these more suitable for you. If you do not have a color screen, go ahead and ignore the color option. (We actually find black and white displays easier to read.)

Figure 5.7 shows some standard X11 monospaced fonts and their aliases. Changing fonts in your **xterm** window is not as simple as in Macintosh applications where you just choose a font from a menu. (The *X11 R4* and *R5* **xterms** do have font menus, but you need to set up the menu before using it.) The present standard, *X11 R3*, has a total of 157 different fonts to experiment with (counting all of the different type faces and sizes) and the new *X11 R4* has more than 400. While not all vendors supply every font, some provide additional fonts for a more distinctive look. The large number of fonts means that a naming convention was needed which completely specifies the characteristics of every font. The new *X11 R3* naming convention is consistent with the X documentation's fondness for succinctness:

```
adobe-courier-bold-r-normal--18-180-75-75-m-110-iso8859-1
```

The **xterm** command to get an 18-point courier font is:

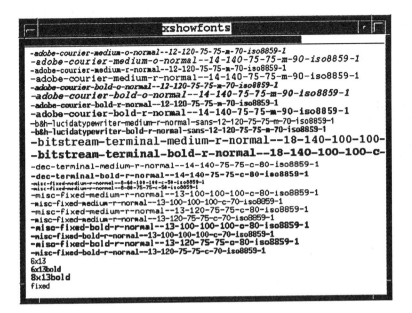

Figure 5.7: A sample of X11 monospaced fonts.

```
$  xterm -fn \
    adobe-courier-bold-r-normal--18-180-75-75-m-110-iso8859-1
```

Is this a bit much? Fortunately, wild cards can be used to shorten the name and still unambiguously specify the font:

```
$  xterm -fn '*-courier-bold-r-*-18-*'     Short version.
```

Notice the quotes ' ' are used so the shell does not try to fill in the *'s. You also can use `-courier-bold-r--18-` to prevent substitution for the *'s if the quotes become too difficult, as they may when you try putting commands into a `mwm` menu.

Font names become even more confusing when you encounter the local aliases by which any given font may be known. For example, the font above may also be called *cour.b.18* and *courb18*. You clearly need some help before making your choice and, fortunately, the system comes through for you. The command `xlsfonts` lists all of the fonts available on your system in both the *X11 R3* naming convention and any aliases. The list may be long, so you may want to pipe it to `more` or direct the output to a file:

```
$  xlsfonts | more        Examine fonts through more.
$  xlsfonts > fontfile     Store fonts in file.
```

As usual, the list tells you the names of the fonts but not what the fonts look like. To preview the fonts, you may use the `xfontsel` command, if it is available.

It is generally best to use `xterm` fonts in which each character is of the same width (like on a typewriter) because *monospaced* fonts preserve the alignment and spacing of the output from the system. Choose fonts that look good to you, and then test them with the command:

```
$   xterm -fn font_name                    Examine fonts.
```

The X Window System also gives you the option of selecting colors for the background, foreground, windows, and fonts. Colors are a little simpler than fonts. Many color terminals have 256 colors available, but the limited memory on less expensive satellite terminals, such as X terminals, limits the options to 16. There may be programs available on your system to preview the colors:

```
$   xcolors                                Show available colors.
$   xterm -fn font_name -bg color -fg color
```

Setting Defaults in .Xdefaults

Once you have found fonts and colors you like, you will want to use them in **xterm** as the default choice. You do this by adding your choices to the .Xdefaults file. Here are some lines to configure an **xterm** the way we like it:

```
xterm*Font:     *-courier-bold-r-*-18-*        In .Xdefaults file.
xterm*background:    LightSteelBlue
xterm*foreground:    Black
```

Notice that we did not use any escape characters or quotes for the font name. Since the .Xdefaults file is not read by the shell, the *'s will not be expanded. We can also set other characteristics of **xterm** in the .Xdefaults file. Ones we have found pleasant are:

```
xterm*cursorColor:     Red
xterm*fullCursor:      true
xterm*scrollBar:       true
xterm*saveLines:       1000
xterm*VT100.geometry:          80x25+0+0
xterm*loginShell:      true
```

The cursorColor line sets the color of the **xterm** cursor; we use Red since it stands out well. The fullCursor true line causes a block cursor to be used; we find that full cursor stands out better. The scrollBar and saveLines lines set the maximum number of lines back to which you can scroll.

Copy and Paste

Copying and *pasting* with **xterm** is easy and similar to the operations with PC windows. You can even cut and paste from one window to another, which also means from one application to another. This is particularly useful in editing files and in composing and modifying Unix commands, since you can copy job numbers or terrible file names.

Copy Depress the *left* mouse button. As you drag it over the text you want selected, the text is highlighted. Releasing the mouse button copies the selected text to the X clipboard (which you cannot view). To select a word, click twice on it; to select a line, click three times on it.

Paste Move the cursor to the position where you want the text to be placed and then depress the *middle* button (or both buttons on two-mouse systems). In order for an editor to accept your paste, the editor must be in the insert or input mode. Emacs will use your copy once it's on the clipboard—but with Emacs' own conventions.

As an example, let's say you are mailing a note to anita and want to include a listing of the files in which she will find your program. You just pull down a menu to open another window, give the ls kabs/src command to get the listing, select for copying the file names by dragging with the *left* button depressed, and paste that list into your letter (which is in a different window) by depressing the *middle* mouse button. Before pasting, you must be sure your editor or mail program is in the input mode. Then you have to click your mouse to place the cursor where you want to paste the text. Your selected list remains on the X clipboard until another item is cut.

You can also use the X mouse for copying text from one file into another or even from one machine to another. Just open a window, log into the remote machine, and when you have placed the information you need on the remote window, select it in the same way. To place the information on the screen, you can display the file using more, your editor, cat, or whatever works for you.

Experienced users know that there's a long standing bug in xterm which causes it to hang, or stop, if you paste too large an amount of text. How large? Sorry, we can't tell you in advance. That will depend upon your system.

Unix Commands and Remote Login

Being able to run multiple windows becomes very useful when you use options to run specific commands with your xterm windows. For example, using xterm -e runs a program inside an xterm window, so that when the program terminates, the window closes. Your Unix command is the argument following the -e option. Here's some examples:

```
%   xterm -e vi .Xdefaults        Edit .Xdefaults file in new window.
%   xterm -e rlogin theo          Remote login with new window.
```

The first line starts up a window running vi .Xdefaults. After you have completed your editing and you terminate vi, the window will close. The second line opens a window which automatically logs you onto the theoretical physics machine theo (as discussed in Chapter 4, *Computer–Computer Communications*). You can even avoid the hassle of entering your password and user ID when the window opens, if you have the same user ID on both machines and a .rhosts file in your home directory on the remote machine with the name of your local machine in it.

As also discussed in Chapter 4, you can use the commands telnet or tn3270 in a window to log onto machines that do not have rlogin available. For example, to connect to an IBM mainframe running the VMS operating system and do it using a separate window:

```
%   xterm -e tn3270 osuvm                    Emulate 3270 terminal for VMS.
```

It is somewhat of a fine point, but one which can be frustrating for those who care, that when you give commands with **xterm**, they run directly without opening a shell (starting an independent command line interpreter). If you want to run a command inside a shell, you must explicitly open the shell and *then* run the command:

```
%   xterm -e /bin/sh -c "ls /usr/*"     Open a shell, execute command.
```

This opens the Borne shell, lists all usr files in a window (the wild card * is evaluated by the shell), and then runs **mail** for the user. The quotes are optional here but are good practice for those times when several commands are placed on the line as a group.

Adding xterm Windows to mwm Menus

Now that you understand how to use **xterm** windows, you can include them into the **mwm** menus to obtain a very convenient system. We define a new window menu:

```
# Window Menu
Menu Window
{
"Windows Menu" f.title
no-label        f.separator
"New Window"   f.exec "xterm -fn *-courier-bold-r-*-18-* &"
"Big Window"   f.exec "xterm -fn *-courier-bold-r-*-18-* \
        -geom 80x45+100+20&"
"Fridge Window" f.exec "xterm -fn *-courier-bold-r-*-18-*\
        -geom 80x25+200+20-r rlogin &"
"Telnet to OSU" f.exec "xterm -fn *-courier-bold-r-*-18-*\
        -geom 80x25+200+20-r telnet orst.edu &"
}
"Who"          f.exec xterm -fn fixed -bg black -fg yellow \
        -geom 80x25-0-0 -r /bin/sh -c who ; read ans &"
```

The New Window line just opens a simple window. Since no geometry is given, the default size, placement, and colors will be used. The Big Window line opens a large window. With the Fridge Window line, we create a window for automatic login to a remote machine, and with the line Telnet to OSU, we create a window for telneting to a computer on the northwest frontier.

The Who menu item is a cute, but not too useful, example of running an arbitrary command. It opens a small window in the upper left-hand corner of the screen listing your fellow users currently on the computer (even computer types like company). Typing a [Return] in the window closes it.

xterm and Your Unix Shell

It is tiresome to hear endlessly about communications problems. You always wish those with them would be quiet. Communication problems will haunt the Unix shell unless it

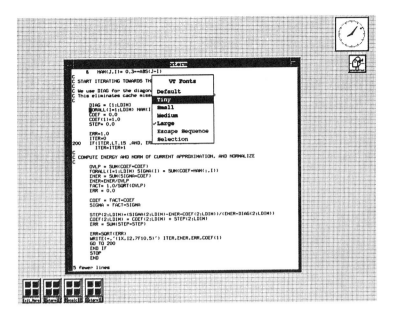

Figure 5.8: The `xterm` menu.

knows what type of terminal you are using. This important datum is contained in the TERM variable. Normally `xterm` sets its own TERM variable, or `termcap`, to **xterm**. However, if you log onto another machine, it may not recognize the `xterm termcap` and instead assume you are one of the standard choices: `vt102`, `vt100`, and `ansi`. All of these `termcaps` have a common root and may provide all the information needed to communicate.

When the size of your **xterm** window is changed, your friendly Unix system must be made aware of the change in order for scrolling and editing to work properly. This is handled automatically in most cases, and the old standby program **resize** may not be needed. Be aware that if you log onto a remote machine, particularly a non-Unix machine, it may not be able to handle changing window sizes or even a window size which is not the standard 25 × 80. In this case the remote machine may use the the top 25 lines of the display and ignore the rest.

xterm Menus

The **xterm** window has three different popup windows, and in this section we'll show how to get to them and what they do. Specifically, we describe the use of the *X11 R4* menus; the *X11 R5* are very similar. To pop up the **xterm** menu:

- Place the mouse in a **xterm** window.

- Hold down [Ctrl] key and depress the left button for the `Main Options` menu.

- Hold down [Ctrl] key and depress the middle button for the `VT Options` menu.

- Hold down [Ctrl] key and depress the right button for the Fonts menu (Figure 5.8).

This will not work if you are in a special window, such as the one created by Emacs. The *Main Options* menu comes up with the option *Log To File* which we find quite useful. The first time you select it, a file *xtermLog* is created in your home directory and whatever appears in the xterm window gets written into this log file. Selecting *Log To File* again stops the logging. Although we have not had much use for the other options, you might.

Depressing the [Ctrl] + middle button on the menu brings up the *VT Options* or *Modes* menu. Here you can toggle on and off various options which customize your xterm to make it the type of terminal you would build for yourself. These same options can be set on the command line or in .Xdefaults. The *soft reset* and *full reset* options are used to resuscitate a display that has advanced to a strange state. They are both safe to use, but since *full reset* clears the screen, it should NOT be used when you are using an editor.

The third menu is extremely useful. It is a font menu. If your system has been properly installed, the font menu will change the font used in the xterm window. If you are not satisfied with the fonts available, you can set them to your favorite ones by adding to your .Xdefaults file lines such as these:

xterm*fontMenu*font1*Label:	Unreadable	Label for menu item.
xterm*VT100*font1:	nil2	Very small font.
xterm*fontMenu*font2*Label:	Tiny	
xterm*VT100*font2:	5x7	
xterm*fontMenu*font3*Label:	Small	
xterm*VT100*font3:	6x10	
xterm*fontMenu*font4*Label:	Medium	
xterm*VT100*font4:	7x13	
xterm*fontMenu*font5*Label:	Large	Menu item five for R5 only.
xterm*VT100*font5:	9x15	
xterm*fontMenu*font6*Label:	Huge	Menu item six for R5 only.
xterm*VT100*font6:	10x20	

A cute use to make of the font menu is to have one of the fonts be the tiniest font available. You then start a program in a window, and after you are sure it is running well, select this tiny font (the window size will automatically shrink too). Then you move the window to either side of the screen and continue to work in other windows as you keep an eye on the running program and its output in its tiny window.

xterm: Tektronix 4014 Emulator

The xterm window provides a Tektronix 4014 emulator which is needed for some graphics programs. The emulator works on many systems but it only provides monochrome line drawings and rather crude letters and symbols. We cover the uses of the emulator in Chapter 6, *Graphics and Visualization*. You open a 4014 window (Figure 5.9) either from the VT Options menu or more likely from the command line with a -t option to the xterm command:

```
%  xterm -t                          Open Tek 4014 window.
```

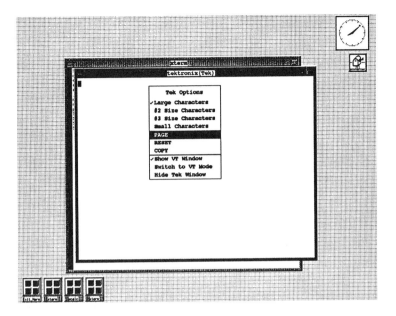

Figure 5.9: The Tek Options menu in **xterm**.

The VT Options menu allows you to switch between a Tektronix and VT102 window. You can switch between a Tektronix window for graphics and a VT102 window for text (there is no provision for automatic switching). When using the Tektronix window, be sure your Unix TERM variable is set to *tek 4014* or perhaps just *4014*:

```
%  export TERM=tek            Set TERM for tek emulation.
%  export TERM=4014           Set TERM for tek emulation.
```

The option *tek* usually refers to a Tektronix 4012 emulation, but the differences between 4012 and 4014 are not great.

In case you have yet to share the experience, the Tektronix window behaves differently enough from a normal window for the uninitiated to believe something must be wrong. First, the fonts are often unreadable. Second, the screen does not scroll normally; when the cursor reaches the end of the screen, it moves to the top right half of the screen and begins again there. After finishing with that section, it moves to the top left and just writes on top of whatever is there (an old trick used by professors to get students to erase boards). To keep the new lines from overwriting the old ones, you must clear the screen. This is accomplished with either the **clear** command or by finding the appropriate option in the menu. There are different menus which come down when you press [Ctrl] plus mouse buttons in a Tektronix window, Figure 5.9. You can change fonts by using the *Tek Options* menu = [Ctrl] + middle button. The menu all has the items: *tekpage, tekreset,* and *tekcopy.* The buttons *tekpage* and *tekreset* clear the screen and reposition the cursor respectively.

The X Windows System's Tektronix emulator has the ability to interface with programs

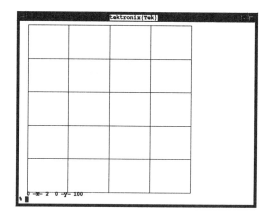

Figure 5.10: A simple plot using the Tektronix emulation in **xterm**.

which present their output on a *Tektronix terminal*. This type of terminal uses the cursor's position, GIN mode, and graphics input mode to make line drawings or position text. Extra care is needed since the original Tektronix 4014 never had a mouse, and how your application interfaces with the emulator will depend upon the application. For example, moving the mouse button while in the GIN mode moves the cursor, and pressing a mouse button transmits the cursor coordinates to the application. Yet this also sends an "l," "m," or "r," depending on the mouse button pressed.

We give more details of how to use the Tektronix emulator in Chapter 6, but if you are too excited to wait, try opening a Tektronix window now and moving into it to get the plot in Figure 5.10:

```
% xterm -t                              Open Tek 4014 window.
% echo "1 50" |graph| tplot -Ttek       Plot for system V.
% echo "1 50" |graph| plot  -Ttek       Plot for BSD.
```

5.7 Local Server and Remote Client

Here is a sample session in which we run the X client program *idraw* on a remote machine with the IP number 128.193.96.41. We then view the ouput of *idraw* through an X window on the local machine with IP number 128.95.7.2. You must know the IP numbers or properly–registered hostnames ahead of time, or get them with the commands: **echo $DISPLAY**, **hostname**, **host**. Be aware that each X terminal has its own IP number, and that it is different from that of the main computer.

```
local$  xhost +128.193.96.41          Tell local who will be host.
128.193.96.41 being added to access control list
local$  telnet 128.193.96.41          Connect to remote in same window.
   ...                                Login to remote machine.
```

remote$ **csh**	Run c shell.
remote$ **setenv** DISPLAY 128.95.7.2:0	Tell remote where to display.
remote$ **idraw**	Run *idraw* on remote, window on local.

5.8 X Terminals

Although running a windowing environment is a drain on the computing power of a workstation, modern workstations (and even PCs) have become powerful enough to service a large number of windows simultaneously. Taking this one logical step further, it is even possible to have one workstation service a number of X Windows on different terminals or workstations simultaneously.

A terminal engineered to run the X Window System remotely from the Unix workstation is called an *X terminal* or *X station*. X terminals have become very popular as a way to provide the benefits of a graphics and windowed display to multiple users without incurring the expense and management of multiple, full-powered workstations. While these terminals contain rather substantial computing power themselves, they are still terminals in that they cannot function without the central workstation providing the terminal with operating system, programs, memory, and CPU cycles. The CPU within the X terminal is used only to draw the screen, but because drawing a high resolution color screen is a computationally intensive chore, this lightens considerably the load on the central computer.

The X terminal runs an X server, which in turn receives the drawing commands and transmits the user's key and mouse commands back to the applications. The X terminal is connected to the central computer via a *TCP/IP* network, usually *ethernet*. This means each X station has an independent *hostname* and *IP address* and will place some amount of increased traffic on the communications network. On a more technical level, an X terminal has a fast graphics processor and enough memory (typically several Megabytes) to support all of a single user's windows. To save memory and expense, X stations may have fewer colors than the console, usually 16 rather than 256. X terminals can even be a DOS computer, some of which run a very nice X Windows System. In those cases, the computer can have its own DOS existence (if you call that living).

5.9 X Clients

An *X client* is a program designed to run within the X Window System and be served by X (thus "client"). There are many clients available (though probably not all on your system), and most are in the public domain. If your system does not have a particular X client you need, you can probably get it from a friend. Here are some of the ones available, with an asterisk indicating our recommendations.

X CLIENTS	
aquarium	Watch the fish.
bitmap	Bitmap editor.
dclock	Digital clock.
heXcalc	Programmer's calculator.

X CLIENTS

ico	Animate icosahedron or other polyhedron.
idraw*	Drawing editor (like MacDraw).
maze	Automated maze program.
muncher	Draw interesting patterns.
oclock	Display time of day.
olwm	OPEN LOOK window manager.
pbmlife	Portable bitmap rules of Life.
plaid	Plaid-like patterns.
psycho	Animate an icosahedron.
puzzle	15-puzzle game.
resize	Set TERMCAP and terminal settings to current window size.
roids	Dodge and shoot flying rocks.
scale	Resize bitmap image.
smoothim	Smooth and reduce noise in image.
spaceout	Animated space display.
startx	Robust X Window start.
tvtwm*	Tom's Virtual Tab Window Manager.
twm*	Tab Window Manager (useful on a slow X terminal).
vpuzzle	Shuffle your display like an old puzzle.
worm	Draw wiggly worms.
worms	Animate worms.
xauth	X authority file utility.
xbiff*	Mailbox flag.
xcalc*	Scientific calculator.
xcalendar*	Calendar.
xclipboard*	Clipboard.
xclock*	Analog / digital clock.
xcolors	Display all color names and colors.
xconq	Strategy game.
xconsole	Display console messages.
xcpustate	Display system usage.
xcutsel	Interchange cut and selection.
xdb*	Display bitmap in a window.
xdbx*	Interface to dbx debugger.
xdecide	Decision Making Tool.
xdm	Display Manager.
xdpr	Dump X Window to printer.
xdpyinfo	Display information.
xdvi*	Display dvi file.
xedit	Simple text editor.
xev	Print contents of X events.
xeyes	Watch over your shoulder.
xface	Display face savers.
xfade	Fade between strings.
xfig	Interactive generation of figures.

xfish	Workstation-to-aquarium conversion.
xfontsel	Point-and-click font selection.
xgc	X graphics demos.
xgif*	Display GIF (*) pictures.
xgraph*	Plot graph from data.
xhost*	Server access control.
xim	File format for digital images.
xinit*	X initializer.
xkill	Kill X client.
xless	File browsing program.
xload	Load average display.
xview	View images.
xlock*	Lock X display until password entered.
xlogo	X Window System logo.
xlogout	Simple logout button.
xlsatoms	List interned atoms defined on server.
xlsclients	List running client applications.
xlsfonts*	List fonts.
xlswins	Display server window list.
xmag	Magnify part of screen.
xman*	Manual page display program.
xmandel	Mandelbrot and Julia sets.
xmap	Display world map.
xmessage	Display message.
xmh*	MH message handling system.
xmodmap, xprkbd	Modify keyboard.
xmoire	Display changeable vector pattern.
xmoon	Current moon phase.
xperfmon	Monitor performance.
xphoon	Display phase of the moon
xplaces	Snapshot and print of windows.
xpostit	Post-it^{RG} notes.
xpr*	Print window dump.
xprop	Display property.
xpseudoroot	Create pseudo root window.
xpuzzle	Another V11 puzzle game.
xrainbow	Life's beautiful.
xrdb	Resource database utility.
xrefresh	Refresh an X screen.
xrn*	Interface to usenet news system.
xrotmap*	Rotate HSB colormap on your friend's display.
xrsh*	Start remote X shells (clients).
xscope	Protocol viewer.
xset*	Set user preferences.
xsetroot*	Set root window parameters.
xshow	Show bitmap files.
xshowcmap	Show colormap.

X CLIENTS

xsol	Play solitaire.
xtartan	Draw tartans as window backgrounds.
xterm*	Terminal emulator.
xtetris	Game.
xtoxim	Convert X Window dump to `xim` file.
xtrek	Space shoot 'em up game.
xtroff	Troff previewer.
xv*	Manipulate images.
xwatchwin	Watch window on other X server.
xwd*	Dump window's image.
xwps	Convert window to Postscript.

PART II

TOOLS

## CHAPTER 6

INTRODUCTION TO GRAPHICS AND VISUALIZATION

Enough of Science and of Art;
Close up those barren leaves;
Come forth, and bring with you a heart
That watches and receives.

—William Wordsworth, *The Tables Turned*

In line with the "survival guide" nature of this book, here and in the next chapter we assist you in understanding and experiencing scientific graphics and visualizations. Since visualization changes on a nearly daily basis and is the subject of research conferences, we will not attempt the condensation of several book-worths of material into these two chapters. Instead, in this chapter we introduce and discuss the hardware and software. In the next chapter we give specifics on how to use several systems which should meet your elementary needs.

6.1 Graphic Devices

Graphic devices have changed rapidly with the changes in computers over the last decade or so. A few years ago the primary graphic devices were Tektronix storage scopes, model 401x displays, and pen plotters. Color graphics were generally only available at central, shared facilities, and 3D graphics were still done with the help of large mainframes. Today, color displays dominate the workstation world, with high resolution, color displays being expensive but common. The general availability of graphics displays has made windowing environments the normal user interface for all computers, from PCs to supercomputers. And, more recently, specialized *adapters* (circuit boards which go inside your computer) to support fast 3D image rendering, visualizations, and animation have become available even for personal computers.

Printers have pretty much kept up with the graphics displays. Dot matrix and ink jet printers can be excellent, if slow, for text, and at least useful for graphical output. We recommend the higher resolution and faster laser printers for scientific work with graphical programs. In particular, those incorporating a microprocessor designed for the *PostScript* page formatting language are now readily available and work very well with graphics and scientific text processing such as LaTeX and TeX. And as if to eradicate the sighs from those of us who swooned over the transient beauty of our high resolution color terminals, color laser printers are finally becoming less expensive and more available.

The pioneering Tektronix displays and Hewlett Packard pen plotters were analog devices. The electron beam and pen moved from data point to data point drawing a line as they moved. In contrast, today's devices are all *bit mapped*. A scanning beam turns individual picture elements on and off. Colors are obtained via this beam containing three components, each of which controls different color picture elements. The display screen itself is physically composed of an array of these picture elements, or *pixels*, each of which lights up with some color or brightness. For high resolution screens these may be 1280 pixels × 1024 pixels × 256 colors.

If each pixel were just turned on or off by the electron beam, then that information could be stored in a single bit and there would be a simple 1:1 mapping of each bit to each pixel. Yet more information than 1 bit is needed for color (or even gray scale) displays, and so graphic displays typically employ a *2-, 4-*, or *8-bit format* to describe the color of each pixel. The latter format is common in the more powerful systems discussed here. In the 8-bit format, the bits represent numbers in the range $0 \rightarrow 2^8 = 256$, with each number in turn representing a color. The actual *bit map* is contained in an area of RAM known as the *screen buffer*, with each consecutive group of 8 bits describing a single pixel. In common jargon, one skips a step and speaks of looking at the bit map on the screen.

Many typical displays employ the *RGB* color model for colors. In this model, all colors are represented as particular blends of the three primary colors red, green, and blue, with differing intensities possible for each primary color. There are an extensive number of colors possible with this system, as well as confusion over how colors are produced. The confusion arises from there also being 8 bytes used to determine the intensity of *each* of the primary colors. There are 256 reds × 256 greens × 256 blues for a total of $2^{24} = 16,777,216$ possible colors (if you count different intensities as different colors). Yet we just said that even the more powerful systems use just 8 bytes/pixel. The trick is that when you use a color graphics display, you first choose a *palette* of 256 colors (which includes the intensity levels) out of the over 16 million possibilities, and from then on you just choose from the same 256.

The image you actually see on the screen is being created by an electron beam (or beams for color) moving across the screen. The beam starts in the *top left* corner, scans from left to right at about 35,000 KHz, and jumps down one pixel each time it reaches the right edge of the picture, as indicated in Figure 6.1. After reaching the bottom of the picture, it jumps or flicks back to the top left and repeats the process. Since the process is typically repeated with a frequency greater than 60 Hz, people normally do not notice the screen flickering (your eye's flicker fusion rate is about 50 Hz). The process whereby this electron beam scans across the screen and appropriately excites each individual pixel is called *rastering*, and the file with the *bit map* of the screen is also called a *raw raster file*.

Computer Displays

Screen specifications are given both in pixel width times height and diagonal screen size. Buying a larger display for your computer but keeping the same graphical adapter gives you a larger image. Because the bit maps stay the same, the "dots" just get bigger, and

data begin

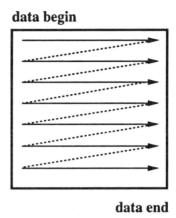

data end

Figure 6.1: Row-major order used in scanning video screens and for input data.

this means the resolution or clarity of the image decreases. It is the same as with a large TV screen. A smaller, 19-inch screen is quite suitable for a single user at a close distance, while a large, 34-inch display works well for demonstrations or classroom use where the viewers are far away (and therefore need a large image but cannot resolve the larger dots).

Some common display types, resolutions, and sizes are[1]:

DISPLAY CHARACTERISTICS

Macintosh SE	512 × 342, monochrome, 9" diagonal
Macintosh II	640 × 480, 256 colors, 13" diagonal
IBM PC, VGA	640 × 480, 16 colors, 12" diagonal
IBM PC, SVGA	1024 × 768, 256 colors, 14" diagonal
Sun SPARCstation	1150 × 900, monochrome, 19" diagonal
IBM RS 6000	1280 × 1024, 256 colors, 19" diagonal
HP Model 900	1280 × 1024, 256 colors, 16", 19" diagonal

A number of other factors also influence how readable the screen is. These include the *refresh rate* and the presence of *interlacing*. Typically computer displays are refreshed, or redrawn, at 60 to 70 Hz. A higher refresh rate means a smoother display for fast graphics. A common problem occurs when the room lighting and computer screen each flicker (strobe) near the same frequency, in which case the screen's flicker becomes noticeable. This is a common problem in the United States where there is 60 Hz fluorescent lighting in most offices.

Interlacing is when the screen is drawn twice, the electron beam of the second drawing scanning between the lines of the first drawing. This is used to give television pictures and cheap computer displays increased resolution.

---

[1]Most manufactures offer several displays. This list is only a sampling.

The X Window System

Having a high resolution display is not enough. You still need a program in order to use the display. That program frequently is provided by the *X Window System*, X for short. The system provides support for input devices like keyboards and mice, as well as protocols to let users manipulate windows with graphics in them. As discussed in Chapter 5, *Looking through X Windows*, the working environment is pleasant, friendly, and becoming universal; yet it is challenging to modify and taxing on your system resources.

6.2 Laser Printers

Laser printers have become the standard for both text listings and graphics. The advantages are numerous. They produce clear text, are quiet, and are faster than the mechanical printers they have replaced.[2]

There are disadvantages to laser printers, however. To start with, they cost more than mechanical printers. Furthermore, laser printers use similar printing engines to those used in copiers, and just as copiers require frequent and sometimes costly maintenance, so do laser printers. Finally, since laser printers produce quick copies of book-like quality, they are open to misuse when treated as copiers or libraries.

PostScript

The language *PostScript* or *ps* has become a standard for sending text and graphics to printers. PostScript is a page-description language developed and licensed by Adobe Systems. It was specifically designed to communicate the description of a printable page to a raster-output device, such as a laser printer, and is responsible in part for the desktop publishing revolution.

PostScript laser printers contain a fairly powerful computer which compiles the ps files sent to it and then generates the raster or dot-matrix files sent to the laser printing engine. The powerful microprocessor, a high memory requirement, and the licensing fee for the PostScript language are all reasons for the added expense of a PostScript printer. For example, a typical low-end PostScript printer may have a Motorola 68000 processor and 2 MB of memory, which is equivalent to an Apple Macintosh computer.

The PostScript files produced by graphics programs, or *text filters*, are readable text files—at least in the sense that C or Fortran programs are readable. Although you may find them complicated and confusing, we encourage you to look at some to get an idea of the information they tell the printer. Most users create and print PostScript files without ever looking at the files themselves or knowing anything about the PostScript language. PostScript is meant to describe a page to a printer and does not have to be understood or even viewed by humans. PostScript files are recognized as such by the first line of text in the file containing the two characters %! and by the .ps suffix to the file name. All PostScript files begin with lines like these:

---

[2]Just as the speed of mechanical printers vary, so do the speeds of laser printers. The fastest printers, the ones that send us monthly statements, are still mechanical.

```
%!PS-Adobe-2.0
%%Creator:  dvips Copyright 1986-91 Radical Eye Software
%%Title: tch.dvi
%%Pages:  6 1
%%BoundingBox:  0 0 612 792
```

PostScript Fonts

As with other computer fonts, PostScript fonts are numerous and take up too much space. There are several basic and familiar fonts and hundreds more that many feel they must have. Unless you really have a specific need or exotic tastes, the basic fonts will probably be adequate. Printers generally come with a basic dozen or so fonts, with the actual number depending a lot on how you count. There are hundreds of additional fonts for those who feel they must have more to be complete.

Some common PostScript fonts are:

AvantGarde-Book	**Bookman-Demi**
Bookman-Light	**Courier-Bold**
Courier-Oblique	Courier
Helvetica-Bold	Helvetica-Narrow
Helvetica-Oblique	Helvetica
NewCenturySchoolbook-Bold	*NewCenturySchoolbook-Italic*
NewCenturySchoolbook-Roman	**Palatino-Bold**
Palatino-Italic	Palatino-Roman
Συμβολ (Symbol font)	**Times-Bold**
Times-BoldItalic	*Times-Italic*
Times-Roman	✳❂☐❖✦✺■✳❂❖▼▲ (Zapf Dingbats)

A fundamental difference between PostScript fonts and others, such as X or Macintosh fonts, is that PostScript fonts are defined by their outline. What is stored is not a map of the bits making up the actual characters, but rather a description of how to draw them, or more precisely, their outlines. The advantage of *outline fonts* is that they can be precisely scaled to an infinite number of sizes, even factional sizes, and still look good. Fixed size bit map fonts, in contrast, are harder to scale and often contain rough corners. Outline fonts are drawn with the full resolution of the printer instead of the fixed resolution in which the bit map was created. This book was set using PostScript Times and Helvetica fonts rather than the LaTeX Computer Modern Fonts. Therefore when we printed the final draft on a 1200 dots-per-inch PostScript printer, everything looked the same, only smoother, than our normal 300-dots-per-inch low resolution printer.

Encapsulated PostScript

A special format of PostScript files is *encapsulated PostScript* or *eps*. Encapsulated PostScript was designed to allow graphic material from one program to be transferred and used in a document produced by another program. This goes beyond the usual role of PostScript files as an intermediary between programs and printers. A number of word processors and graphics programs such as *Frame Maker*, *Corel Draw*, and LaTeX are able to *import* encapsulated PostScript drawing from such programs as *Gnuplot* (whose use we recommend and describe in Chapter 7, *Scientific Graphical Tools.*)

If your application says it imports encapsulated PostScript, it actually does require encapsulated PostScript; straight PostScript will not work. You can identify encapsulated PostScript by the first lines of the document. They should look something like this:

```
%!PS-Adobe-2.0 EPSF-1.2
%%DocumentFonts:   Times-Bold
%%Pages:  1
%%BoundingBox:   65 493 550 786
%%EndComments
```

The key is the EPSF label in the first line. The rest of the file varies depending on the application that wrote it.

PCs as Graphics Terminal Emulators

We have found personal computers, even of modest power, to be a useful and economical extension of the computing power of workstations and supercomputers. In part, the editors, word processors, drawing programs, and user interfaces on the PCs are often more advanced than those on scientific machines. Further, it is also possible to use an inexpensive PC as a graphics terminal to a larger computer—often at a much lower cost than a dedicated terminal—and then combine the better features of both systems. For example, as discussed in Chapter 3, *Workstation Setup and Use*, and Chapter 4, *Computer–Computer Interactions*, you can make diskettes on the PCs containing ASCII copies of your workstation files and then transport them to another location, mail them around the world, use a local PC to work on them, or transfer them to another machine.

To use a personal computer as a terminal to another computer requires two basic things: a connection to the other computer and a program which permits your PC to *emulate* the behavioral characteristics of one of the standard terminals. The connection can be one of several possibilities, with the type of connection influencing the type of emulation. One type of connection is through the modem port or serial port on the PC; if connected to an actual modem, it permits you to use the phone lines to communicate with other computers. If the computer you want to communicate with is nearby, you can run a serial (RS232) cable from the serial port on your PC to a serial port on the big computer. Another type of connection is through an *ethernet* port to a TCP/IP network. This requires you to have an ethernet card in your computer to send and receive data with the correct protocol. Finally, we mention that there are systems that connect PCs together (such as *Apple Talk, Tops, PhoneNet, LocalTalk*) which are useful in their own right, but also may contain a *gateway box* or connection to TCP/IP networks. These often open up a wider world to many PC users.

The software or terminal emulation program you need depends on what type of connection you have. For a PC running DOS with a simple serial connection, the common–domain emulator program *kermit* (which also contains the kermit file transfer protocol) will probably be adequate as a text terminal. However, it may not be adequate as a graphics terminal emulator for your application.

For a Macintosh on a serial connection, we recommend the commercial product *Versa Term Pro* by Synergy. It is also excellent for a TCP/IP connection, although in the latter case you can use the free *NCSA telnet.* You can use *Versa Term Pro* for text and color graphics by emulating DEC and Tektronix terminals, with automatic switching between them. In fact, we find that a good combination to use is Versaterm Pro on your Mac and Gnuplot on your workstation; since Versaterm automatically emulates a Tektronix display, you can do your plotting over the network without the need to run X Windows on your PC.

If your PC has a connection to the TCP/IP networks, either directly or through a gateway, then we recommend the two programs *NCSA telnet for the IBM PC*, and *NCSA telnet* for the Macintosh. These programs can be obtained free over the network from the National Center for Supercomputing Applications or for a nominal charge through the mails (see § 6.4). The *telnet* from NCSA lets you have simultaneous connections (multiple windows) to any number of computers on the network, and to transfer files rapidly with `ftp`. Further, you can emulate color graphics terminals and switch to text terminals including DEC VT 102 and Tektronix 4014.

We have found the use of PCs as adjoints to workstations invaluable in our work. By using a PC as a terminal to the workstation, we can look at some graphics output in a Tektronix window on the PC. We then can import that image into the PC and use the drawing program on the PC to polish up the graph for publication.

6.3 Basic Scientific Graphics

You are getting comfortable with your new workstation. You have learned to use the X Windows System and you have even gotten some of your programs to run. Now you want to make a simple $x - y$ plot of your results, the bread and butter of science. You page through your graphical workstation's systems manuals but find nothing about plotting data. Something must be wrong. You have spent many tens of thousands of dollars on your new system, in part for its color graphics.

Despite everything you may have heard about Unix being good for scientific computing, it has always been weak in basic scientific graphics. In the next chapter we discuss how to do scientific graphics on your workstation without spending thousands more. We will examine several systems which produce scientific graphics ($x - y$ plots) and some 3D plotting. These are bread-and-butter, public domain systems for scientists and engineers, but they may be all you need for now. And they certainly are a good place to start before buying more specialized systems.

Symbolic Mathematics and Spreadsheets

A theme we hope is coming through in this book is:

> *Don't be a computational bigot. Make use of whatever tools you have available to help you get your job done, even if it means more than one type of computer or operating system.*

The same is true for graphics and visualization. There are excellent packages available on PCs, many of which fit in well with desktop publishing and PostScript printers. Furthermore, some spreadsheet programs which are also available for workstations have competent 2D and 3D graphics, which are particularly convenient if you are using a *spreadsheet* for data processing.

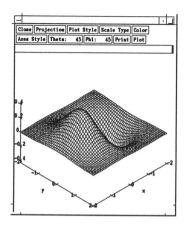

Figure 6.2: A visualization produced by Maple V.

Finally, we should mention that symbolic manipulation programs, such as *Maple, Mathematica,* and *SMP*, are recommended for what they do. While such programs are assuming a greater and greater role in large-scale computing, for the present their emphasis is more on symbolic manipulation than numerical solutions and simulations. Yet they can be used to generate code to be compiled and can solve problems which previously were only approached numerically. More to the present point, these packages tend to have 2D and 3D plotting routines which are breathtakingly beautiful and straightforward to call. They clearly are the approach of choice if the function you need visualize can be written analytically. For example, to make a color version of Figure 6.2, issue the *Maple V* command:

```
>  plot3d(x*exp(-x2-y2),x=-2..2,y=-2..2,grid=[49,49]);
```

6.4 Visualization

You may find yourself at times having experimental or computational data you need to understand, yet which is not understood well as a plot of x versus y, or even as a *surface* $z(x, y)$. Examples of this might be the velocity of a fluid as it flows around some surface, or the value of the electric potential near a complicated 3D conductor. Often in these cases the interesting science (or program bugs) manifest themselves as a deviation from what is otherwise regular behavior. It is just that which we would like to extract from pages and pages of data. This is what computer *visualization* is all about. For example, to use color to represent the velocity (or z) as it varies in the x and y directions, you need a tool to produce 2D color images from data, such as in the visualization in Figure 6.3. (Yes, even though $z(x, y)$ is in some sense three dimensional since there are three variables, in the world of visualization this is called 2D data because there are two independent variables.) You may even want *animation*, that is, to look at a number of similar images as a function of time.

The real world, of course, contains functions of more than just two variables, yet our brains and terminals seem to conspire to limit our perceptions to views of only 2D surfaces

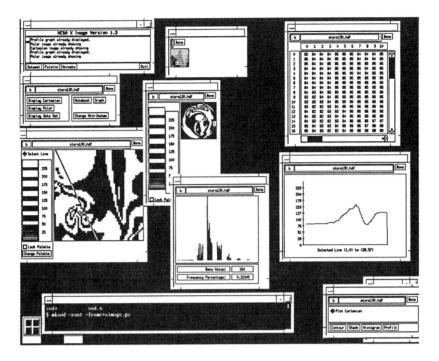

Figure 6.3: A visualization produced by NCSA X Image.

(3D if extended to *virtual reality*). There are visualization tools which *slice* or *dice* data sets into smaller sections to be viewed on our terminal screens and retinas. Some of these tools are available from national supercomputer centers or laboratories (in the United States we have obtained visualization programs from Cornell, Livermore, and NCSA).

The world of visualization may seem confusing until the meanings of some words are clearer. As discussed in the introduction to this chapter, your display screen is composed of an array of *pixels*, each of which lights up with some color or brightness. For high resolution screens there may well be 1280 x 1024 pixels x 256 colors or more. For the *X Image* system, an *8-bit format* describes the color of each pixel. This translates into $2^8 = 256$ colors (yet you can choose your 256 color–*palette* from over 16 million possibilities). The visualization program's input data element $z(x, y)$ must, accordingly, be scaled to an integer value in the range $0 \rightarrow 255$ to represent a color.

A *raw raster file* contains the 8-bit data for row–major–order rastering, with each line following an earlier one, as in Figure 6.1. This linear array of just the z values (colors) for the pixels, rather than the set (x, y, z), is the input to visualization tools such as *X Image* (the x and y values are implied by the row and column numbers). Note that your standard Fortran program also stores matrices in linear form, but they are in column-major order, and consequently must be transposed before being visualized (C language matrices are stored in row-major order). This is one of the tasks accomplished by data formatters such as NCSA's *HDF*.

NCSA X Image

The Software Tools Group at the University of Illinois' National Center for Supercomputing Applications, NCSA, develops and supports a free set of software tools for the analysis and visualization of data. The tools are available through anonymous ftp or through regular mail facilities (we give a sample ftp session with NCSA in Chapter 4, *Computer–Computer Interactions*).

The NCSA packages are designed for scientists and engineers to use on their own workstations or PCs, and share an aim similar to this book, namely, of giving people the "opportunity to concentrate on their science and enlarge their potential for discovery."[3] While some of the programs in the *NCSA Scientific Visualization Software Suite* are meant for the Macintosh II (not Plus or SE), a good number also exist for Unix machines with X Windows. These are powerful packages designed for serious scientific work and require you to read the documentation, which for each package is roughly the size of this chapter. Here we discuss briefly just *X Image*.

The *X Image* program produces several varieties of color images of a function z of two variable (x and y), as well as contour plots (constant z surfaces), shaded plots (gray scale appropriate to a laser printer), profiles of slices through the data ($z(x, y)$ versus x), and histograms (frequency of z versus x). Some of its options include: display of input data in spreadsheet form (but not in ASCII format); color visualization of 2D data (raster displays) in Cartesian ($z(x, y)$) and polar formats; plotting of data as color contours and in gray scale; creation and manipulation of palettes (mapping of color to z values); color histograms (frequency of z versus z); animation of multiple visualizations; correlated selection between image and data windows.

Using this package means reading in your data with one datum for each pixel of the image, and then using the push buttons in various windows to visualize your data from differing perspectives. It is tremendous fun, is friendly to use, and can give you insight into your work not previously possible. For example, refer to Figure 6.3. If your eyes are good, you may be able to notice:

- The upper right-hand corner is a display of the data set used as input in which you use the window's scroll bars for moving through the data. The window is obtained by pressing the button *Display Data Set* in the control window (the second window down on the left).

- The large window in the middle left is a Cartesian visualization of the data. It is a plot of color (scaled z value) versus x and y (the colors are lovely if you could only see them). The steps give the key to conversion of input data (z's) to color. This Cartesian display is obtained by pressing the button *Display Cartesian* in the control window.

- The large window in the center is a polar visualization of the data. It is a plot of color (scaled z value) versus r and θ (rows = r, columns = θ). This polar display is obtained by pressing the button *Display Polar* in the control window.

- In the lower right-hand corner of Figure 6.3 we see the graph window which is opened by pressing the *Graph* button in the control window.

---

[3]NCSA on-line documentation.

- In the middle right of the screen there is a profile of the data set, that is, a plot of z as it varies along the slanted line drawn through the Cartesian display of the data. To get this type of plot we first need to toggle the switch in the upper left corner of the Cartesian plot until it gets to *Select Line*, then use our mouse to draw a line through the Cartesian plot of the data, and then press the *Profile* button in the graph window. You obviously can use this to produce $z - x$ or $z - y$ plots as well.

- In the lower middle of the screen is a histogram of the data, that is, a plot of the frequency of some z value versus z. It is obtained by pressing the *Histogram* button in the *graph* window.

- In the top middle is the shaded plot of the data set (no color) obtained by pressing the *Shade* button in the graph window.

- Notice the log book in the upper left-hand corner of the screen. It tells you what the system is doing, if your command is accepted, and if not, then why not. Keep your eye on the log as you play.

- Finally, if you press the *Contour* button in the graph window, you obtain a color contour of your data set (not shown here). This is an outline of the constant z values in the Cartesian display of your data.

Data Input, HDF Files

If perchance you (or your ever-helpful system manager) are grabbing X Image over the network, we recommend you also grab the *HDF* package. Hierarchal **Data Format** is a general purpose file format which can be used for the storage and transfer of *both* 32 bit floating point data as well as raster images. The software runs on supercomputers, workstations, DOS PCs and Macintoshes and has the added advantage of making the transfer of graphical data among machines convenient. Once you get the HDF library (it is called `[libdir]/libdf.a` or `-ldf`), you need to include the library when compiling the program making HDF calls:

```
$ f77 prog.f -o prog [libdir]/libdf.a    Fortran, f77=compiler's call.
$ cc prog.c -o prog [libdir]/libdf.a     C language call.
```

Here, too, you should read all the README files NCSA keeps on line and study the needed documentation. But if you can get away with it, reading only the *Calling Interfaces* document might be adequate. Our program to convert ASCII files to HDF is[4]:

```
      PROGRAM HDFORM
c     Read In Ascii Data, Order on x, y
c     Convert To HDF
c     x = data(1,j,k), y = data(2,j,k) V(x,y) = data(3,j,k)
c     data.hdf = output, mat = input
      IMPLICIT REAL*8 (a-z)
      REAL*4 mat
      DIMENSION data(3, 33, 33), mat(33,33)
      INTEGER shape(2),ret, DFSDsetdims, DFSDputdata,i,j,k
```

---

[4]Courtesy of T. Mefford.

```
c    input 7
     Open(7, file='tape7', status='unknown')
     Do 90 j = 1, 33
       Do 80 k = 1, j
c  read in x,y V(x,y)
       read(7,99) data(1,j,k), data(2,j,k), data(3,j,k)
 80 continue
 90 continue
 99 format(3e16.8)
c************* 2 variable sort to order data
     Do 15 i = 1, 1089
       Do 17 j = 1, 33
         Do 12 k = 1, 33
         If (j.eq.1) go to 10
         If (data(1,j,k).gt.data(1,j-1,k)) go to 10
         temp1 = data(1,j,k)
         temp2 = data(2,j,k)
         temp3 = data(3,j,k)
         data(1,j,k) = data(1,j-1,k)
         data(2,j,k) = data(2,j-1,k)
         data(3,j,k) = data(3,j-1,k)
         data(3,j-1,k) = temp3
         data(2,j-1,k) = temp2
         data(1,j-1,k) = temp1
 10    Continue
         If (k.eq.1) go to 12
         If (data(2,j,k).gt.data(2,j,k-1)) go to 12
         temp1 = data(1,j,k)
         temp2 = data(2,j,k)
         temp3 = data(3,j,k)
         data(1,j,k) = data(1,j,k-1)
         data(2,j,k) = data(2,j,k-1)
         data(3,j,k) = data(3,j,k-1)
         data(3,j,k-1) = temp3
         data(2,j,k-1) = temp2
         data(1,j,k-1) = temp1
 12    Continue
 17 Continue
c******* set mat to log(data(3) value)
     Do 30 k = 1, 33
       Do 20 j = 1, 33
         data(3,j,k) = Dlog10(Dabs(data(3,j,k)+1.d-12))
         mat(j,k) = Sngl(data(3,j,k))
 20    Continue
 30 Continue
c    hdf output
c    shape = size of each dim, ret = return to hdf sub,
c    2=ndim, mat=input matrix of data for hdf
c    2 hdf subs to ''set dimensions'' & ''put data in data.hdf''
     shape(2) = 33
     shape(1) = 33
     ret = DFSDsetdims(2,shape)
     ret = DFSDputdata(' data.hdf',2,shape,mat)
     END
```

A related program available from NCSA is *NCSA Reformat/XReformat* for Unix based systems. This converts a variety of non-HDF files, such as FITS, TIFF, GIF, Sun, raw raster files, and X Window dumps, to HDF.

6.5   High-Performance Graphics

The simple *line graphics* produced by plotting programs are not sufficient for complex, interactive visualizations. High performance graphics require 3D primitives and the ability to modify parts of the figure without having to constantly redraw the whole thing. Animation is also important for interactive graphics, that is, the ability to produce and observe a sequence of similar images. It, too, is best done with specialized software and hardware. As becomes clear by considering just the magnitude of the numbers involved, when the material we want to view gets really complex, like with a million graphic elements per second, special hardware support is mandatory.

In the past, such high-performance graphics were the domain of supercomputers with specialized graphics devices (like MVS with IBM 5081 graphics displays). Now the porting of mainframe graphics standards to workstations and the availability of graphics adapter boards for workstations are making high performance graphics more affordable. And (as if this were all planned) the high performance RISC workstations are providing the needed processing power.

There is, unfortunately, a problem using high performance graphics hardware with the X Window System. Since the X protocol is designed to hide the hardware from the application, it tends to conflict at times with graphics hardware containing support for interactive drawing, shading, and transforming 3D images. An additional problem arises from high-performance graphics systems, such as PHIGS, which explicitly obtain and process graphics input simultaneously with X's event-driven input. Conflicts may well arise when these two views are forced to coexist, such as drawing animated figures inside a Motif window. Consequently, it is typical to find slower, high-performance graphics on an X Window display than on a simpler (and less expensive) specialized system. It makes sense, then, to match your software and hardware needs to each other.

GKS, PHIGS, and PEX

The Programmers Hierarchical Interactive Graphics System *PHIGS* is an extensive set of standards to create the interface between an underlying graphics system and an application demanding high-performance, interactive graphics. An example of such an application is the computer assisted design of engineering structures, or the rendering of molecular images in computational chemistry. PHIGS itself is a superset of the older graphics kernel system *GKS* and its 3D extensions. PHIGS and GKS share fundamental primitive attributes, graphics input, error processing, and control. In fact, many PHIGS implementations include a GKS compatibility option.

As the name states, PHIGS is a hierarchical graphics system. This means it has graphics structures which themselves contain other graphics structures—somewhat like a robot arm in which the whole arm or each structure within the arm can be manipulated. PHIGS structures get bound to output primitives only when a structure is displayed. This means that structures are created and manipulated in a generic modeling space and then transformed for display from a particular viewpoint.

A recent extension to PHIGS known as *PHIGS+* adds lighting, shading, color, depth cuing, and advanced primitives to the PHIGS geometric primitives and gives the system the tools needed to meet future needs. Another recent extension or union is *PEX*. There is a standard for combining PHIGS, PHIGS+, and the X Window System server, and it's part of the *X11 R5* release. Whether it is included on your particular system depends on your vendor.

Using graPHIGS

The IBM implementation of PHIGS is called *graPHIGS*. It was initially developed and released for graphic system 3250's and 5080's attached to IBM mainframes. Version 2.1 of graPHIGS provides support for workstation use with X under *AIX* Unix. Here is a simple PHIGS program adopted from an IBM graPHIGS demonstration. It draws a basic structure—a red square with a white border—and applies a transformation to the structure based on user input:

```
#include <afmnc.h>
main() {
 int wsid = 1, viewid = 0, strid = 1;
 int n4[1] = {4};
 int lcview,major,class,minor;
 float matrix[9],lcpos[3];
 static float oldpos[2] = {1.0,1.0};
 static float pts[8]={1.0,1.0,1.0,-1.0,-1.0,-1.0,-1.0,1.0};
```

The graPHIGS API is initialized with the following two lines:

`GPOPPH (" ",0);`	Open graPHIGS.
`GPOPWS (wsid,"*","X ");`	Open a workstation.

The open graPHIGS call `GPOPPH` puts the graPHIGS API into the open state, and the open workstation call `GPOPWS` opens one graphics workstation with the specified identifier *wsid*.

The next section of code creates a geometric structure with the specified identifier, *strid*. The actual geometry and attributes are placed inside this structure:

`GPOPST(strid);`	Open structure.
`GPINLB(1);`	Insert label 1.
`GPINLB(2);`	Insert label 2.
`GPEF  (2);`	Set edge.
`GPIS  (2);`	Set interior style solid.
`GPICI  (2);`	Set interior color RED.
`GPECI  (1);`	Set edge color WHITE.
`GPPG2 (1,n4,2,pts);`	Add 2D polygon.
`GPCLST();`	Close structure.

In this example, polygon edge attributes and polygon interior attributes are inserted into the structure, followed by a 2D polygon. Two label elements are added with the insert label call `GPINLB`. These labels allow us to insert and delete elements between the two labels at a later time. The next lines of code display the geometry on the screen:

`GPARV (wsid,viewid,strid,1.0);`	Link root to view.
`GPUPWS(wsid,2);`	Update workstation.
`GPCHMO(wsid,2,3,2);`	Choice: event mode.
`GPLCMO(wsid,1,2,2);`	Locator: sample mode.

The geometry structure must be associated with a workstation view before it can be displayed. We associate the *root structure* with the default graPHIGS API view 0, specified by the identifier *viewid*. Next, we use the update workstation call GPUPWS:

`do {`	Until mouse hit.
`GPSMLC(wsid,1,&lcview,lcpos);`	Get mouse position.
`if (lcpos[0] != oldpos[0]`	
`c || lcpos[1] != oldpos[1])`	
`{`	
`  oldpos[0] = lcpos[0];`	
`  oldpos[1] = lcpos[1];`	
`  GPSC2 (lcpos,matrix);`	Calculate scale matrix.
`  GPOPST(strid);`	Open edit structure.
`  GPDELB(1,2);`	Delete between labels.
`  GPMLX2 (matrix,3);`	Insert new matrix.
`  GPCLST();`	Close structure.
`  GPUPWS(wsid,2);`	Update workstation.
`{`	
`  GPAWEV(0.0,&major,&class,&minor);`	Check for events
	while (class != 4).
` GPCLPH();`	Close graPHIGS.
`}`	

Inside the loop, GPSMLC samples the position of the locator device (mouse pointer). The locator position is returned as (x, y, z) coordinates in the variable `lcpos`. If the new and old locator positions are different, the shape of the square is modified by editing the structure containing the square. The GPSC2 call creates a new 2D scale matrix which is then inserted into the structure using the set modeling transformation 2D call GPMLX2. Also inside the input loop, the graPHIGS API event queue is checked with the await event call GPAWEV. The loop terminates if the returned class equals 4 (mouse button pressed). This program can be compiled on a IBM RS6000 with graPHIGS installed using the following command (the **-lgP** option links the graPHIGS library):

% cc -o square square.c -lgP   Compile & link graPHIGS.

CHAPTER 7

SCIENTIFIC GRAPHICAL TOOLS

7.1 Introduction

If I can't picture it, I can't understand it.

—Albert Einstein

In Chapter 5 you learned how to use the X Window System, the graphical interface which has been adopted as a standard for many workstations. We hope you read that chapter and are comfortable working with X. In the preceding chapter we presented an introduction to graphics and visualization, the devices, the techniques, and the availability. We also acquainted you with the fact of life that despite all the publicity about scientific workstations, basic scientific graphics has always been a weak point with Unix systems.

In this chapter we discuss in more detail how to use several scientific graphical tools (applications) with X Windows. The tools we discuss all work under X. All are available free over the network (if your system does not already have them). And all produce output for PostScript devices, thereby permitting laser printing and inclusion in documents. We hope their inclusion is a step towards making Unix a better system for you as a scientist or engineer.

7.2 Unix Plot Utilities

Most Unix implementations do contain a basic, perhaps primitive, graphics system. The basic calls consist of drawing a point, a line, a circle, or an arc. These are usually called `plot(3)` utilities since the documentation for them was originally in § 3 of the Unix manual. There is also a collection of numerical and graphical commands available as part of Unix System V. This collection is called the *Unix System Graphics*, or *AT&T Graphics* for short, and contains commands similar to these we will discuss. Since the AT&T graphics system is not supported or fully implemented on many systems, and because many of its output devices are by now obsolete, we do *not* discuss or recommend it. However, it can lead to confusion if you find a file with AT&T graphics commands (they, too, have a `plot` command).

The command `plot` on BSD Unix, or `tplot` on System V Unix, translates the `plot(3)` calls so that they may be displayed on one of several different output devices.[1] Which devices are supported depends on your system. Generally the output devices permitted by the software include Tektronix 4014 terminals, HP plotters, HP graphics terminals, and some older types of dot-matrix printers (a basic law of computing states that *whatever the type of printer supported, it is not the type you have*). Also available on your system, or at least on the network, are *filters* to produce the PostScript form of output from either Unix `plot(3)` routines or from Tektronix 4014 graphics codes.

You may use these plotting calls within your own program or interactively with a simple $x - y$ plotting program called `graph`. To start with, it is probably better to work interactively while you learn how to make the calls, experiment on how to fit the graph on the paper, and check that there really are data in your files. We use the `graph` command to demonstrate how to use the `plot` package, and then we show a simple program which includes calls to the C graphics routines.

Locating Unix Plotting Functions

First you need to determine what, if any, parts of the `plot` graphics package your system contains. Start by checking with `man` to find the `plot/tplot` and `graph` commands, and then check if the system has the basic `plot` library:

```
%   man tplot                          Print man pages on tplot.
tplotCommand
Purpose
   Produces plotting instructions for a particular workstation.
Syntax
   tplot [ -TWorkstation ] [ File ]
Description
   The tplot command reads plotting instructions from standard
   input or a specific file and writes instructions for the
   specified workstation to standard output.   ...
```

While the manual entry tells us what types of output devices are supported, the manual pages are often outdated or simply incorrect. You may be forced to experiment. Nevertheless, the **-k** options on `man` is useful when hunting for topics, and while it is mainly BSD systems which have the **-k** option, if your system has it, you should see something like this:

```
%   man -k plot                          Print plot's man pages.
pac (8) - printer accounting info        Not anything we want.
plot (1G) - graphics filters             Plot filter.
plot (5) - graphics interface            BSD's §5 = file format.
plot:  openpl et al.   (3F)
     - f77 library interface
plot:  openpl, et al.   (3X)
     - C graphics interface
```

---

[1] We refer to `tplot` in this chapter to avoid confusion. If your system has `plot`, the same examples and options work, only the name is different.

If you become confused by the command **plot** and the plotting routines, you can ask the **man** command for the specific **plot(3)** system calls (the 3 in **man** command):

```
%  man 3 plot
PLOT(3X) UNIX Programmer's Manual PLOT(3X)
NAME
   plot:  openpl, erase, label, line, circle, arc, move, cont,
   point, linemod, space, closepl - graphics interface
SYNOPSIS
   openpl(), erase, label(s),char s[]; line(x1,y1,x2,y2)
   circle(x,y,r), arc(x,y,x0,y0,x1,y1), move(x,y), cont(x,y)
   point(x,y), linemod(s), space(x0,y0,x1,y1), closepl()
DESCRIPTION
   These subroutines generate graphic output in a
   relatively device-independent manner.
```

Finding **graph** is easier:

```
%  man graph
graph Command
PURPOSE
   Draws a graph.
SYNTAX
   graph [ -gGrid ] [ -hSpace ] [ -l"Label" ] [ -mStyle ] ]
   -rSpace ] [ -s ] [ -t ] [ -uSpace ] [ -wSpace ]
   -a [Number [LowerLimit]] ] [ -cCharacter [ -b] ] [ -x [ -l]]
   LowerLimit [UpperLimit [Space]] ] ] [ -y [ -l ]
   [ LowerLimit [UpperLimit [Space]] ] ]
DESCRIPTION
   The graph command reads pairs of numbers from standard input.
   Each pair is the x and y coordinates of a point on a graph.
   The command writes the graph to standard output.
NOTE: The tplot command processes the output of the graph
   command for printing.
```

Using tplot and graph

The command **graph** may meet your needs if you want a quick plot. To use **graph**, you first create a file data (any name is acceptable) of $x - y$ coordinates separated by spaces which **graph** reads to produce a graph in **plot(3)** output (see unreadable listing in Figure 7.1). Since **graph** produces Tektronix output, you next open an X Window which emulates a Tektronix 4014 terminal:

```
%  xterm -t
```
Start Tektronix emulation.

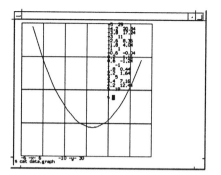

Figure 7.1: A screen dump of the graph produced from **graph** with data in file data (shown in an **xterm** window).

(Alternatively, you could use a PC and a terminal emulation program such as *MS-Kermit* to view the Tektronix output.)

We now move into this Tektronix window, check with the usual Unix commands that we are really in the directory with the data file, and then issue the **graph** command:

```
%   graph < data | tplot -Ttek                Plot from Tektronix window.
```

You pipe the output of **graph** through **tplot** to produce a graph you can see on the Tektronix emulation. The results are shown in Figure 7.1. Both **graph** and **tplot** read their inputs from stdin and send their outputs to stdout. Accordingly, your only option **-Ttek** is a type of output device. There are options for **graph** to make log plots, to set minimum and maximum values for the axis, and more:

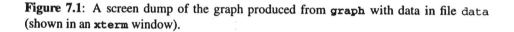

GRAPH OPTIONS

-a *n L*	Automatic abscissas, spacing *n* starting at *L*.
-b	Break line after label (string in quotes).
-c *c*	Character *c* used to mark data points.
-g *n*	Grid, n= 0, none; 1, ticked; 2, full (default).
-l *label*	Label or title for graph.
-m *n*	Mode for drawing lines.
-x l *xl xy g*	l (el) indicates logarithmic axis. First numerical
-y l *yl yh g*	argument is lower limit for that axis; next two,
	upper limit and grid spacing, are optional.

Using plot(3) inside Programs

The **plot(3)** commands are listed below. All the arguments except *s* are integers; *s* is a string pointer:

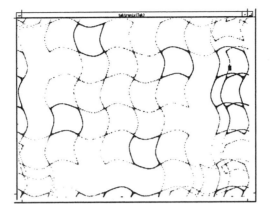

Figure 7.2: Figure produced by program `pictures` and `tplot` command.

PLOT SUBCOMMANDS

openpl()	Initialize display, actually a no operation.
erase()	Clear screen.
label(*s*)	Place label *s* at current location.
line(*x1, y1, x2, y2*)	Draw line from *(x1,y1)* to *(x2,y2)*.
circle(*x, y, r*)	Draw circle, center *(x,y)*, radius *r*.
arc(*x, y, x0, y0, x1, y1*)	Draw arc, center *(x,y)*, from 0 → 1.
move(*x, y*)	Move to *(x,y)* without drawing line.
cont(*x, y*)	Draw line from the current point to *(x,y)*.
point(*x, y*)	Draw point at *(x,y)*.
linemod(*s*)	Set type of line drawn, styles: *dotted,* *solid, longdashed, shortdashed, dotdashed.*
space(*x0, y0, x1, y1*)	Set coordinates of the drawing space, *(0,1)* = (lower left, upper right) corners.
closepl()	Close `plot` and flush all output.

To compile the program, you first must link the appropriate `plot` library (`-lplot`) as well as the math library (`-lm`). To link directly with the Tektronix library, substitute `-14014` for `-lplot`. If you want to pipe your output through `tplot` to view it on a Tektronix emulator, try either `/usr/lib/libplot.a` or `/usr/lib/lib4014.a`. In the first instance, we compile `pictures` and produce Figure 7.2 with:

```
%   cc -o pictures pictures.c -lplot -lm      Compile picture.
%   pictures | tplot -Ttek                    View pictures.
```

You can also write programs which use the `plot(3)` subroutines to make plots directly. This is an easy and simple way to make basic black and white graphs each time you run your program, a helpful feature in debugging.[2]

BSD systems come with a set of Fortran-accessible subroutines, which unfortunately

---

[2]The GNU Graphics package provides color extension to the `plot(3)` functions.

are not usually present with the Unix systems now for sale. If you have these C subroutines, it is straightforward to call them from Fortran. Below is a C version of a simple plotting routine to draw the "Wallpaper for the Mind."[3]

| ```c
/* Draws WALL PAPER for the MIND
/* Using basic Unix plotting functions
/* Scientific American, September 1986 */
#include <math.h>
 main()
{
    double x, y,a, xold;
    double pi = 3.1415926535897931160E0;
    int ix,iy;
    double randMax= 2147483647;
    int i;
    int seed;
    int N=30000;
    srandom(getpid());
    a = random();
    x = (a/randMax) * pi;
    a = random();
    y = (a/randMax) * pi;
    a = random();
    a = pi - (a/randMax)*0.07;

    openpl();
    space(-400,-400,400,400);


    for(i=0;i<N;++i){
        xold =x;
        x = y -sin(x);
        y = a - xold;
        ix = (x+0.005)*100.0;
        iy = (y+0.005)*100.0;
        point(ix,iy);
    }
    closepl();
}
``` | Defines math functions.<br><br><br><br><br>Max value from random.<br><br><br><br>Assign random value to 3.<br>Parameters defining graph.<br><br><br><br><br>Open a plot.<br>Defines plot space:<br>$(x,y)$ values of ll and ur<br>for corners of drawing.<br>Draw 30,000 points.<br><br><br><br><br>Draw point at $(ix, iy)$.<br><br>Close plot, flush all output. |

Filters for Printing Plots

Figure 7.1 shows an output from **graph**. It is a screen dump of our X terminal obtained by using the commands **xwd** and **xpr**. There are better ways to get hard copies of your output. On some systems, for example, **tplot** supports printers or plotters directly—but do not get too excited. These are older printers and you may not have your specific printer

---

[3] Dewdney (1986).
```

supported. A more general approach to obtaining hard copy is to convert your output to the PostScript format with *PostScript converter* or *filter* and then print it out with a laser printer or save it to a file with a .ps suffix. Most of the figures you see in this book were produced this way.

Adobe Systems, the developers of PostScript, licenses a package of PostScript filters that many vendors include with their systems. These include the commands **psplot** and **ps4014** as well as **enscript** for printing text on PostScript printers. The **psplot** command is a simple filter used much like **tplot**:

```
%   pictures | psplot > pict1.ps          Save PostScript output.
%   pictures | psplot | lp                PS output sent directly to printer.
```

The **ps4014** command is used in a similar manner but with the Tektronix output from some other program, or from a plotting program that has been linked with the **lib4014.a** library, or from the output of **tplot**. There are a number of options for **ps4014** which allow for shifting the image, scaling it, or rotating it. For example:

```
%   graph < data | tplot -Ttek | ps4014 -R -S4 | lp
```

This example rotates the previous graph example, scales it so the width is 4 inches, and then sends it directly to the printer.

7.3   Xgraph-Easy Graphs with X11

The *Xgraph* program written by D. Harrison of the University of California is an excellent tool for everyday scientific plotting. It is simple to use, very fast, colorful, widely available (free over the network), versatile, and interfaces well with X Windows. It also has a broad range of output formats: PostScript printers, HPGL files, and *Idraw* files.[4] While Xgraph has enough options to handle rather technical material, it can also be run by a novice on the simplest of data files. By default, Xgraph will label the axes, produce appropriate tick marks, generate a legend, and use different colors or styles for multiple data sets. Furthermore, the commands may be given from a Unix command line or placed directly in the data file. The graphs are plotted in separate windows, and there can be quite a few open at once. This is easy for the novice. It is also easy to get the output from the plot window by choosing menu items with mouse buttons.

---

xgraph *options =WxH+x+y -display host:display.screen file...*

Input

The format for Xgraph's input data file is similar to **graph**. The data consists of a number of *data sets,* each set separated by a blank line.[5] In the simplest case this is identical to the data file used before, namely, just lines of $(x\ y)$ values with no commas. Usually, however, it is better to include some labels. Here is an example of an edited version of the

---

[4]Output to Idraw is quite valuable because you can fix up a graph for publication (which doesn't necessarily mean making your theory agree with the data).

[5]Alternatively, you can give Xgraph data from the standard input.

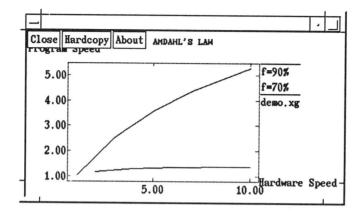

Figure 7.3: Output from the command `xgraph demo.xg`.

file `demo.xg` we will use in Chapter 12 to show Amdahl's law:

```
TitleText:   PROGRAM SPEEDUP VERSUS FRACTION VECTORIZED
Ticks:   true
BoundBox:   on
YUnitText:   Speedup
XUnitText:   % Hardware Speedup s
"f=90%"
1 1.00
3 2.5

"f=70%"
1 1.00
10 2.7027

2 1.1765
10 1.3699
```

The Xgraph plot window created from this file is shown in Figure 7.3. The first five lines are *options*. They title the plot, draw axes with tick marks, and place text along the *y* and *x* axes (we list more options below). They really are options and so can be left out, although if included, they need to be separated by spaces. After the options are three *data sets*. The first two are shown with the name of each data set enclosed in double quotes (the trailing double quote is optional). The last data set uses a blank line to separate it from the preceding one. When plotted, the data are labeled with the data set name, or with the file name (in this case `demo.xg`) if no other name is given.

Up to 64 independent data sets can be displayed with Xgraph, and it automatically uses different colors and/or line styles for each set. (If you look closely at Figure 7.3, you will notice that the curve for $f = 70\%$ is missing; that's because it was yellow and this is a black and white screen dump of a color display and not a true hardcopy in which the colors are replaced by line types.)

There is a flexibility in specifying the data file of which you may want to take advantage. Let's say you have discontinuous data points which you do not want connected with lines (or you want to draw a picture with hidden lines). You do this by including an optional *directive* on the line with your data:

`1.9 4.7`	Data with no directive.
`draw 1.9 4.7`	Data with "draw" directive, same as above.
`move 4.7 1.9`	Data with "move" directive.

If the directive is *draw* (the default), a line will be drawn between the previous point and the current point. If the directive is *move*, no line will be drawn. The directive *move* is always assumed for the first data point in a set.

Xgraph Window

Give the Unix command:

`$ Xgraph demo.xg`   Plot my graph.

The Xgraph program will read the data and information in demo.xg (a copy of which is on the floppy) and create a new window like that in Figure 7.3. This displays your graph with all the data sets and with a legend in the upper right corner. You can *zoom in* on a portion of the graph by depressing a mouse button in the area of interest and sweeping out a box with your mouse. Xgraph then opens a new window containing just that portion of the graph. You can create a whole bunch of Xgraph windows like this until you get just the one(s) you like. Or, you can plot other data sets and have those Xgraph windows on the screen, too. (It is a good idea to close unneeded windows—especially on an X terminal—since they use up lots of memory.)

Xgraph Options

Xgraph is further controlled by a large number of options. You can learn about them with the **man Xgraph** command. Most of these options can be specified in several ways. One way is on the command line in a cryptic form:

% xgraph -option *option data* **data.xg**   Command line options.

The options may also be placed in your .Xdefaults file (see examples in Appendix A) or in a more verbose form within the data file itself. Option specifications in the data file are similar to the .Xdefaults file specification except the xgraph name is omitted. Some of the more useful options which you should try out are given in the Table below. Note that the verbose form is for use within the data files and it also uses the *option data*.

IN-LINE OPTION	IN-FILE OPTION	DESCRIPTION
-9 *mydata*	*mydata*	*mydata* labels 9th data set.
-bar	BarGraph	Bar graph, xsee too -brb, -nl.
-bb	BoundBox	Boxed graph, no grid (see too -tk).
-brb *base*	BarBase	Bar graph's base value; default 0.
-brw *width*	BarWidth	Bar graph's bar width; default 1 pixel.
-lnx	Logx	Logarithmic x axis; grid = power of ten.
-lny	Logy	Logarithmic y axis; grid = power of ten.
-lw *width*	LineWidth	In pixels for data, lines; default 0 (thin).
-lx *xl,xh*	xLowLimit,xHighLimit	Low and high x limits; for manual zoom.
-ly *yl,yh*	yLowLimit,yHighLimit	Low and high y limits; for manual zoom.
-m	Markers	Mark data points distinctively.
-M	StyleMarkers	Mark data points distinctively for color.
-nl	NoLines	Do not connect data; for points need -m.
-p	PixelMarker	For data points; with -nl for scatter plots.
-P	LargePixel	For data points; with -nl for scatter plots.
-rv	Reverse Video	For black and white displays.
-t	TitleText	Use *Text* as plot's title.
-tf *fontname*	TitleFont	9x15, helvetica-18 (default), ...
-tk	Ticks	Ticks not grid lines; see, too, -bb.
-x *unitname*	xUnitText	Ordinate name; default x.
-y *unitname*	yUnitText	Abscissa name; default y.

Xgraph Hardcopy

Notice in Figure 7.3 that the *xgraph* window contains three buttons: *Close, Hardcopy,* and *About.* The *Hardcopy* button is interesting. Depressing it produces a menu:

HARDCOPY OPTIONS

Output device	HPGL, PostScript, Idraw.
Disposition	Send output "to device" or "to file."
File or device name	Device (as in `lpr -P`, or file.
Maximum dimension	Maximum size of plot in centimeters.
Include in document	Produce output for inclusion in other documents, e.g., PostScript with bounding box for `psfig`.
Title font family	Name of font for title.
Title font size	Size of title fonts in points.
Axis font family, size	Fonts for axis and key.
Ok, cancel	Proceed or cancel hardcopy.

Xdefaults for Xgraph

The colors, screen fonts, and geometry of the Xgraph window are set using typical X declarations. The geometry is set in the `.Xdefaults` file as discussed in Chapter 5, *Looking through X Windows,* or from the command line as:

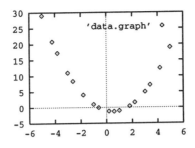

Figure 7.4: Gnuplot's plot of data points.

```
%  xgraph [ other options] =WxH+x+y    Set geometry.
```

This specifies the initial width × height and the (x, y) location of the Xgraph window. Other options can be set in your .Xdefaults file, Here are some typical ones:

```
xgraph.TitleFont:    Rom10
xgraph.LabelFont:    Rom14
xgraph.Device:       PostScript
xgraph.ZeroColor:    Red
```

7.4 Gnuplot

Gnuplot is a versatile, 2D and 3D graphing package which makes Cartesian, polar, surface, and contour plots. It is available through *archie* (see §4.4) or via anonymous ftp from a number of sites (we used ftp.gnu.ai.mit.edu = 18.71.0.38). While Gnuplot is versatile and fast, it is not as friendly as the menu-driven programs found on PCs. Yet Gnuplot runs on a number of systems including Unix, VMS, and DOS, and produces output formatted for a large variety of devices including dot-matrix printers, HP pen plotters, HP Laserjet printers, Tektronix terminals, X terminals, and PostScript. So even though we present our examples using Gnuplot on an X Window System, you should be able to use the same procedures to produce the same plots on a PC or any system emulating a Tektronix terminal. Gnuplot has been our personal choice for 2D and 3D graphics with Unix, although *ACE/gr* has just replaced it in our hearts for 2D work.

You begin with a file of $(x\ y)$ data points, say, data.[6] When you issue the **gnuplot** command, you get a new window with the Gnuplot prompt gnuplot>. Gnuplot has many commands to plot data, and we use just a few here. You should read the **man** pages and experiment. The plot in Figure 7.4 is obtained from the following session:

---

[6] A sample data file is on the floppy as data.graph.

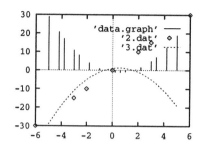

Figure 7.5: Output from the Gnuplot for three data sets with impulses and with lines.

`% Gnuplot`	Start Gnuplot program.
`G N U P L O T`	
`Copyright (C) 1986, 1987, 1990`	
`Colin Kelley, Thomas Williams`	
`Send bugs and comments to`	
`pixar!bug-gnuplot@sun.com`	
`Terminal type set to 'x11'`	Type of output we want.
`gnuplot>`	The Gnuplot prompt.
`gnuplot>` **`plot "data"`**	Plot data file data.

The general form of the 2D plotting command within Gnuplot is:

> **`plot`** {**ranges**} *function* {**`title`**} {**`style`**} {**`,`** *function* ...}

GNUPLOT OPTIONS

with points	Default. Plot symbol at each point.
with lines	Plot lines connecting the points.
with linespoint	Plot lines and symbols.
with impulses	Plot vertical lines from x axis to points.
with dots	Plot small dot at each point (scatter plots).

It is important to notice that all file names or directories are in quotes (single or double); in fact, any name referring to a Unix object which is not a Gnuplot keyword must be in quotes. If you forget the quotes, Gnuplot responds with so informative an error message as to make you nostalgic for Unix:

`gnuplot>` **`plot data`**	FAILS! We forgot ' '.
`  undefined variable:   data`	Not a clear error message.
`gnuplot>` **`plot 'data'`**	THIS WORKS.

Let's now add two more data files so that we have:

data		2.dat		3.dat	
-5	29	-6	-30	-5	-29
-4.2	20.84	-3	-15	-4.2	-20.84
-3.8	17.24	-2	-10	-3.8	-17.24
-3	11	0	0	-3	-11
-2.6	8.36	2	10	-2.6	-8.36
-1.8	4.04	3	15	-1.8	-4.04
-1	1	6	30	-1	-1
-0.6	-0.04			-0.6	0.04
0.2	1.16			0.2	-1.16
0.6	-1.24			0.6	1.24
1	-1			1	1
1.8	0.44			1.8	-0.44
2.2	1.64			2.2	-1.64
3	5			3	-5
3.4	7.16			3.4	-7.16
4.2	12.44			4.2	-12.44
5	19			5	-19

In Figure 7.5 we plot a number of graphs on the same plot using these several data files and the command:

```
plot 'data' with impulses, '2.dat', '3.dat' with lines
```

You will note that the input files are separated by commas and that a single quote is used around the file names here (double quotes also work). Note, too, that we have started to get fancy by using a **with** command to set the plot style. Explicit values for the x and y ranges are set with the plot options:

```
gnuplot>    plot [xmin:xmax] [ymin:ymax]  "file"   Generic.
gnuplot>    plot [-10:10] [-5:30]  "data"          Explicit.
```

Input Data Format

The format of the data file read into Gnuplot is not confined to x-value y-value. You can read in a data file in the C *scanf* format string xy using the **using** option in the plot command[7]:

```
plot 'datafile { using { xy | yx | y } {"scanf string"}
```

This format explicitly reads selected rows into x or y values while skipping past text or unwanted numbers:

```
gnuplot>    plot "data" using "%f%f"          Default, 1st x, 2nd y.
gnuplot>    plot "data" using yx "%f %f"       Reverse, 1st y, 2nd x.
```

---

[7]Since it is common for Unix programs to use the C scanf format for reading in files, it is a good idea to have a C book handy even if you avoid programming in C.

```
gnuplot>  plot "data" xy using \                    Use row 2,4 for x, y.
   "%*f %f %*f %f"
gnuplot>  plot "data" using xy "%*6c %f%*7c%f"
```

This last command skips past the first six characters, reads one x, skips the next seven characters, and then reads one y. It works for reading in x and y from files such as:

```
theta:   -20.000000 Energy:   -3.041676
theta:   -19.000000 Energy:   -3.036427
theta:   -18.000000 Energy:   -3.030596
theta:   -17.000000 Energy:   -3.024081
theta:   -16.000000 Energy:   -3.016755
```

Note that since the data read by Gnuplot are converted to floating point numbers, you should use %f to read in the values you want.

Besides reading data from files, Gnuplot can also generate data from user-defined and library functions. In these cases the default independent variable is x for 2D plots and (x, y) for 3D. Here we plot the acceleration of an harmonic oscillator:

```
gnuplot>  k = 10                      Set value for k.
gnuplot>  a(x) = .5*k*x**2            Analytic expression.
gnuplot>  plot [-10:10] a(x)          Plot analytic function.
```

A useful feature of Gnuplot is the ability to plot the combination of analytic function plus numerical data. In this example and in Figure 7.6 we compare the theoretical prediction for the period of a simple pendulum to the experimental data, as might be done in an introductory physics laboratory. Here and on the floppy is the exp.data data file:

# length(cm)	period (sec)
10	0.8
20	0.9
30	1.2
40	1.3
50	1.5
60	1.6
70	1.7
80	1.8
90	1.9
100	2.0

(Note that the first line of text is ignored since it begins with a # .) We plot this with:

```
%  gnuplot                                Start Gnuplot program.
. . . . . . . .                           Long-winded introduction.
gnuplot>  g = 980                         Set value for g.
gnuplot>  y(x) = 2*3.1416*sqrt(x/g)       Period T = y, length L = x.
gnuplot>  plot "exp.data", y(x)           Plot both data and function.
```

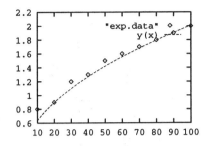

Figure 7.6: Output from Gnuplot when plotting the combination of data from a file and an analytic function.

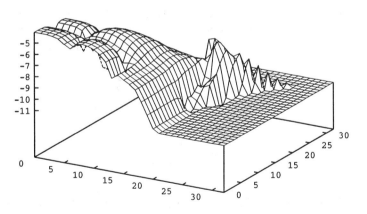

Figure 7.7: Surface plot of the optical potential for the proton interaction with ^3He as a function of momenta k and k' produced by Gnuplot (courtesy of T. Mefford).

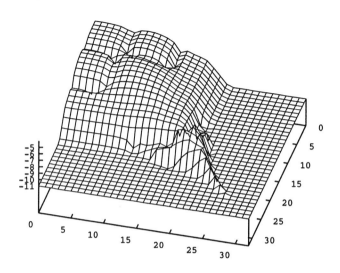

Figure 7.8: Rotated surface plot.

Gnuplot Surface (3D) Plots

Most of our discussion of 2D plots can be extended to 3D or surface plots. The surface plot command is **splot**, and it is used in the same manner as **plot**—with the obvious extension from (x, y) to (x, y, z). As discussed with *X Image*, a surface is often specified just by giving its z values for successive rows, for example:

-4.043764	Data for 3D plot.
-4.047083	
$\vdots$	
-11.000000	
-11.000000	

This is part of the file gnu3d.data on the floppy with *strips* of z values separated by spaces. Since there are no explicit x and y values given, Gnuplot labels the x and y axes with the row and column number. Axis labels and titles can be specified explicitly. These data produce the *hidden line* surface in Figure 7.7 with the following commands:

```
gnuplot>  set hidden3d              Hidden line plot.
gnuplot>  set nokey                 No label.
gnuplot>  splot 'gnu3d.data' w l    Surface plot with lines.
```

Im T(E)

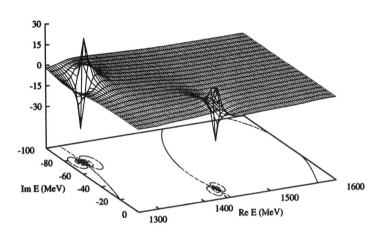

Figure 7.9: Surface plot of antikaon–nucleon T matrix as a function of complex energy produced by Gnuplot (courtesy of G. He).

While viewing the plot in one of the X Windows, you modify its viewing angle, labels, or scale by entering text in the command window. The command to do this is:

```
gnuplot>  set view rotx, rotz, scale, scalez
```

GNUPLOT VIEWS

rotx	Rotate about x axis 0 to 180° (default 60).
rotz	Rotate about z axis 0 to 360° (default 30).
scale	Scale entire plot (default 1.0).
scalez	Scale z axis (default 1.0).

The changes occur when you redraw the plot using the **replot** command. For example, Figure 7.8 is obtained after producing Figure 7.7 by issuing the commands:

```
gnuplot>  set view 30, 105        Move over and up.
gnuplot>  replot                  Redraw with the changes.
```

As another example for specifying data, we start with a data file containing the z values for an even 36×16 grid in x and y values. To create our plot we then set the sampling rates. We take **samples** as the number of points on the x axis, and **isosamples** as the corresponding y sampling rate:

```
gnuplot>    set samples 36              Number along x axis.
gnuplot>    set isosample 16            Number along y axis.
gnuplot>    splot 'ip' with lines using z '%f'
```

To now get more realistic, below is a sample session in which (x, y, z) data are read in from the file ImT.dat. A 3D surface is then plotted, but without hidden lines removed, along with a contour plot projected onto xy plane. The plot is in Figure 7.9.

```
gnuplot>    set nokey
gnuplot>    set view 120, 25
gnuplot>    set xrange [1300:1600]
gnuplot>    set yrange [-100:0]
gnuplot>    set zrange [-30:30]
gnuplot>    set xtics ("1300" 1300, "" 1331.15297, \
      "1400" 1400, "" 1434.57747, "1500" 1500, "1600" 1600)
gnuplot>    set ytics -100, 20, 0
gnuplot>    set ztics -30, 15, 30
gnuplot>    set xlabel "Re E (MeV)"
gnuplot>    set ylabel "Im E (MeV)"
gnuplot>    set param
gnuplot>    set contour
gnuplot>    set cntrparam levels 10
gnuplot>    set terminal postscript eps "Times-Roman" 14
gnuplot>    set label "Im T(E)" at 1450, -100, 60
gnuplot>    set output "ImT.ps"
gnuplot>    splot 'ImT.dat' w l
```

The form of the data is:

```
1300.00000 -0.00100 -0.00001
1303.00000 -0.00100 -0.00000
1306.00000 -0.00100 +0.00000
```

Labeling the Graph

Gnuplot has limited flexibility in labeling its plots. Only a single font is used and the size and type of font is determined by the output device or terminal selected. A plot, such as Figure 7.10, is titled with the **title** option to the **plot** command:

```
gnuplot>    plot "data" title "Name"          "Ex..." = title.
```

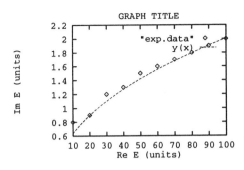

Figure 7.10: Output from Gnuplot with Title and axis labels.

A key explaining the meaning of the data points is placed in the upper left-hand corner of the plot by default. It is removed with the `set nokey` command:

```
gnuplot>    set nokey                    Remove explanatory key.
```

Or if you'd rather, the key can just be moved by supplying `set key` with (x, y) coordinates:

```
gnuplot>    set key -2,25; replot        Move key, redraw plot.
```

The title of the data points used in the key can be set using the `title` option to the `plot` command. The default is to use the name of the data file or function being plotted:

```
gnuplot>    plot "data" title "Name"     Title for key.
```

The figure itself can be titled and the axis labeled with another `set` command:

```
gnuplot>    set title "GRAPH TITLE"      Title the figure.
gnuplot>    set xlabel "Re E (units)"    Set x axis label.
gnuplot>    set ylabel "Im E (units)"    Set y axis label.
gnuplot>    replot                       Plot with additions.
gnuplot>    set zlabel "z (units)"       Set z axis label.
```

The title *GRAPH TITLE* is placed in the top center of the figure. The position of the label depends on the output device—which means your plot can look different on the printer than it does on the screen. You can adjust the position of the axis labels from their default by supplying positive or negative offsets from the default values (yes offsets, not absolute positions):

```
gnuplot>    set xlabel "x (units)"; replot   Set label, redraw plot.
gnuplot>    set xlabel "x (units)" -10,10     Move label up 10, left 10.
gnuplot>    set xlabel                        Clear label.
gnuplot>    set xlabel "x (units)" 0,0        Use default position.
```

Alternatively, an arbitrary label may be placed anywhere on the graph with the **set label** command:

```
gnuplot>  set label tag "label text" at x,y,z right|left|center
```

Here **tag** is an optional number to reference the label. The last option is the justification relative to the specified (x, y) point. By default, the text is placed flush left against the (x, y) point. Actually, the label text and the (x, y) or (x, y, z) points are optional as well; however, the label defaults to " " and the location defaults to $(0, 0)$, neither of which we find too useful. The label can be hidden (for example, to produce a clean–looking graph) using the **set nolabel tag-number** command:

gnuplot>	**set label 1 "T" at 2,3 center**	Create title.
gnuplot>	**set nolabel 1**	Hide the label.
gnuplot>	**show label**	Shows all defined labels.

Xdefaults for Gnuplot

The colors, screen fonts, and geometry of the Gnuplot X Window are set using typical X declarations. The geometry is set from the command line:

```
%  gnuplot -geom 200x200+10+100                    Set geometry.
```

Other options can be set in your .Xdefaults files; here are some typical ones:

```
gnuplot*background:     white
gnuplot*geometry:       640x450+0+0
gnuplot*font:           fixed
gnuplot*textColor:      black
gnuplot*borderColor:    black
gnuplot*axisColor:      black
gnuplot*line1Color:     red
gnuplot*line2Color:     green
```

Saving and Loading Gnuplot Commands

So far you have been in an interactive mode when entering Gnuplot commands. Since we hardly ever get anything right the first time, we prefer redrawing the plot until we get it right and then saving the final commands which worked for us. You can place your commands in a file ahead of time, but you may find it's better to let Gnuplot save them for you and then edit the saved file afterwards. The **save** command places the text of all commands used to define the plot in a file. With the **functions** option, it saves just the user-defined functions; with the **variables** option, just the variables; and with the **set** option, just the set values:

gnuplot> **save "demo.plt"**   Save plot commands in file.

The saved command file is an ordinary text file containing the Gnuplot commands as shown in the following example (we have edited out the list of default values):

```
set terminal x11
set nogrid
set key
set nolabel
set label 1 "(Weekend)" at 5,25,0 center
set title "From Gnuplot Demos"
set trange [-5 :   5]
set xlabel "" 0,0
set xrange [1 :   7.96]
set ylabel "" 0,0
set yrange [0.5 :   99.9]
set zlabel "" 0,0
set zrange [-10 :   10]
set autoscale t
set autoscale xy
set autoscale z
set zero 1e-08
plot 'data.dat' using "%*s %f" \
 title "data" with impulse
```

You can edit this file or create one from scratch. Any line that starts with a # is a comment and is not read by Gnuplot. You load this plot file either by naming it on the command line or by using the **load** command from within the Gnuplot window:

gnuplot> **load "demo.plt"**   Load command file.

If a file is named on the command line, Gnuplot reads the file, executes each command as if it had been typed in interactively, and then exits.

The **pause** command is useful in creating interactive Gnuplot scripts or in letting the viewer watch as a plot is composed. The form is:

gnuplot> **pause n "Prompt"**

This commands prints out the *Prompt* string and then waits n seconds. If $n = -1$, **pause** waits for the user to hit [Ret]. If $n = -0$, it does not pause at all:

gnuplot> **pause -1 "Hit return"**   Waiting for your return.
gnuplot> **pause 3**   Wait 3 seconds.

If you want some commands, such as setting the terminal type, to run every time you start up Gnuplot, you put them in your home directory in the (invisible) file .gnuplot. This file is read each time Gnuplot is started.

Printing Plots

Gnuplot supports a number of printers including PostScript ones. The basic method of printing plots is:

1. Set "terminal type" for your printer.

2. Send the plot output to a file.

3. Replot figure for new output device.

4. Quit Gnuplot (or get out of Gnuplot window).

5. Print file from Unix.

   You could also import the file into a word processor to have it appear in a document or into a drawing program to fix it up just right.[8] To see what type of printers and other output devices are supported by Gnuplot, enter the **set terminal** command without any options into a gnu window:

gnuplot> **set terminal**

```
eepic EEPIC -- extended LaTeX picture environment
emtex LATEX picture environment with emTeX specials
epson_60dpi Epson-style 60-dot per inch printers
hpljii_300ppi HP Laserjet series II with 300 pixels/in
kc_tek40xx Kermit-MS tek40xx terminal emulator - color
km_tek40xx Kermit-MS tek40xx terminal emulator - monochrome
latex LaTeX picture environment
nec_cp6c NEC printer CP6 Color
postscript PostScript graphics language, small characters
psbig PostScript graphics language, big characters
epsf1 Encapsulated PostScript graphics, small characters
epsf2 Encapsulated PostScript graphics, big characters
qms QMS/QUIC Laser printer (also Talaris 1200 and others)
tek40xx Tektronix 4010 and others; most TEK emulators
unixplot Unix plotting standard (see plot(1))
x11 X11 Window System
```

Here's an example of creating a PostScript figure and printing it:

```
gnuplot>  set terminal postscript        Choose local printer type.
Terminal type set to 'postscript'        Gnuplot response.
gnuplot>  set term postscript eps         Another option.
gnuplot>  set output "plt.ps"             Send figure to file.
gnuplot>  replot                          Plot again so file is sent.
gnuplot>  quit                            Or get out of gnu window.
```

---

[8]To edit the output of *Gnuplot* with *Idraw*, you select *unixplot* as the terminal type for the output file, pass the output through *plot2ps*, and then open the *Gnuplot* file with *Idraw*.

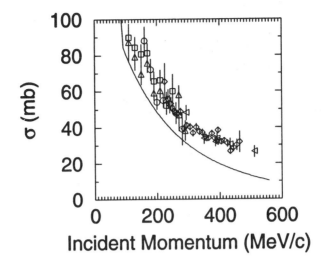

Figure 7.11: Output from ACE/gr with data points and curve (courtesy of G. He).

```
gnuplot>  lp plt.ps
```
Print file.

A more direct way to print Gnuplot figures is using the **lasergnu** command from Unix:

```
%  lasergnu -Pps -p 'plot "data"'
```
Print plot.

The **-P** option is followed by the name of the printer, **ps** in this case, and the **-p** option sets PostScript output. The **plot** command is surrounded by single quotes so that it forms one argument. Another form for the **lasergnu** command prints a figure from a Gnuplot file such as those created with the **save** command:

```
%  lasergnu -Pps -p -f myplot.plt
```
Print myplot.plt

The two forms can be combined. The plot file is read first, and then the **plot** command is executed:

```
%  lasergnu -Pps -p -f setplot.plt 'plot "data"'
```

7.5 ACE/gr: Exploratory Graphical Analysis

ACE/gr is a brand-new plotting package written by Paul J. Turner of the Oregon Institute of Science and Technology (anonymous ftp from amb4.ese.ogi.edu [129.95.20.76] in pub/acegr). It runs under the X Window System, contains data analysis tools such as curve fitting and Fourier transformations, and produces publication–quality results (something the other packages do not uniformly do). Furthermore, it meets our criteria of being widely applicable (it runs under X Windows), being free, and supporting a number of drivers for PostScript, HPGL, and FrameMaker. The plot given in Figure 7.11 was produced with the command:

```
$  xmgr -p kp.param -xydy kp.points -xy kp.data
```

The file `kp.param` contains ACE/gr's description of the plot produced by an interactive session with ACE/gr. The input data files are of the form:

kp.data file	kp.points file
@legend string 5 "tc0.triumf"	
.37086E+01 .24101E+03	180 72 6
.74172E+01 .23291E+03	200 54 4
⋮	⋮

7.6   Pdraw, 3D Plotting for X and PostScript

Pdraw was written by K. H. Toh of the University of California. It takes a file of $z(x, y)$ values and renders them into 3D curves in a box which can be rotated, projected onto a plane, and drawn in various ways. With enough curves or contour graphs as input, or by judicious choice of options, you can construct a surface. Pdraw runs with X10 and X11 Windows and produces PostScript output for printing or inclusion in documents. While we provide some information here, you can obtain more with the **man pdraw** command.

Pdraw Input File

The input data file (plot file) consists of alternating (x, y, z) values in the form:

xmin xmax ymin ymax zmin zmax	Lower and upper bounds for plot.
ncurves	Number of curves to plot.
npts1	Number of points for each plot.
z1	
z2 ...	
npts2	Begin second set of points to plot.
z1	
z2 ...	

Pdraw Options

Plotting options are specified either on the command line:

```
% pdraw [-options] plotfile1 plotfile2 ...
```

or in an `options-file`. Other than the usual X Window System options, the most useful options are:

PDRAW OPTIONS

-v *vx vy vz*	View along axis from $(0, 0, 0)$ to (vx, vy, vz).
-o *options-file*	Options in options-file (shown later).
-P*printer*	Specify printer for ps plot, default $PRINTER.
-s *scale*	Scale for ps plot, default 1.0.
-e	Unequal x, y, and z scales, make cube-like.
-h	Draws polygons with hidden lines.
-nosort	No sorting for hidden-line option.
-print	Automatically prints plots.
-ps	Turns off PostScript plotting.
host:display	Open window on host and display.

PDRAW IN–FILE OPTIONS

xlabel *LABEL*	Label for x axis, default "X-Axis."
ylabel *LABEL*	Label for y axis, default "Y-Axis."
zlabel *LABEL*	Label for z axis, default "Z-Axis."
toplabel *LABEL*	Label on top, default "3DLinePlot."
equalscale *on(off)*	$x - y$ scaling, default off.
postscript *on(off)*	For PostScript plot, default off.
printplot *on(off)*	Send PS file to printer, default off.
printer *PRINTER*	Define printer, default $PRINTER.
line *on(off)*	Draw line, default off.
linechange *on(off)*	Change line types, default off.
marker *on(off)*	Draw marker, default off.
markerchange *on(off)*	Change marker types, default off.
hiddenline *on(off)*	For hidden-line drawings, default off.
nosort *on(off)*	For hidden-line drawings, default off.
scale *{0.1 - 1.0}*	Scale for PS plot, default 1.0.
xticks *{1 - 20}*	Number of x-divisions, default 2.
yticks *{1 - 20}*	Number of y-divisions, default 2.
zticks *{1 - 20}*	Number of z-divisions, default 2.

Viewing and Hardcopy

Once the Pdraw window is open, the view can be altered with the mouse buttons and from the keyboard:

PDRAW MENU BUTTONS

h(l)	Rotate sideways.
j(k)	Rotate up or down.
o	Orginal view.
a, s, d, f	$90°$ rotations.
x	Project onto yz plane (constant x).
y	Project onto zx plane (constant y).
z	Project onto xy plane (constant z).

This view will remain for printing. When you push the button in the Pdraw window to
Quit, you will be asked in the command window if you want to print the file:

```
Type return (or n/q) to send the plot to the -Pps printer:
```

If your print command aborts or you kill it with [cntrl]-c, you may also be left with the
intermediate PostScript file `dataplot.ps`.

CHAPTER 8

USING FORTRAN AND C WITH UNIX

When I read some of the rules for speaking and writing
the English language correctly ... I think
Any fool can make a rule
And every fool will mind it.

—Henry David Thoreau

8.1 Compilers

The Fortran language you find on your workstation will probably be some variation of *FORTRAN 77*, a nickname for *American National Standards Institute (ANSI) FORTRAN standard ANSI X3.9 - 1978.* It is most likely an optimizing compiler and probably a quite good one if your system has RISC architecture.[1] The Fortran 77 compiler is usually invoked by the **f77** command.[2] Regardless of your computer system, your Fortran will probably be a superset of Fortran 77, that is, it will do everything ANSI Fortran should do and more. Likewise, the C compiler probably meet the ANSI definitions and more too. The C language compiler is usually invoked by the **cc** command—although different systems may have additional names for compilers meeting additional standards.

While these workstation compilers have not in the past had all the bells and whistles of those on the larger mainframe computers, they are now improved and actually offer some advantages. First of all, they are so much alike that it is possible to write a Fortran or C Language source program on one workstation and have it compile and execute—without alteration—on another workstation. Second, because the standards also refer to the numerical precision of various operations, when you get your Fortran or C program running on another workstation, it will produce the same numerical answers to the level of precision specified. And, finally, the Unix file system's structure is nicer than those on many mainframes.

---

[1]Chapter 12 describes *RISC and Supercomputer Architectures* and Chapter 13 describes *Programming RISC and Vector Machines.*

[2]Under AIX, the Fortran compiler may be called **xlf** or **f77**.

A challenge to scientists and engineers trying to create, modify, and run numerically intensive programs on workstations is to do it without all the tools and consultants available on and around mainframe computers. While Unix does have an excellent set of tools for program development, in our view they appear geared more towards the computer scientist who may write sophisticated programs but with less numerical orientation than the computational scientist. The debugging and organizational challenges can be great for the large, sometimes hand-me-down, programs run by scientists and engineers, and this is one of the main motivations for writing this book.

In this chapter we provide examples of running various compilers and some general hints. In Chapter 9 we give a more technical description of *Different Compilers and Their Options*. In Chapter 10 we discuss some *Unix Tools* which we believe are especially valuable to Fortran and C users, and in Chapter 11 we give some general *Scientific Programming Hints*. In Chapter 13 we'll have information for those interested in *Programming RISC and Vector Machines*. But first, some words to the wise.

Warnings

To avoid outdated bugs, be sure to obtain and run the latest version of the compiler on your workstation. To avoid mismatch bugs, be sure the versions of the compiler and of Unix you are using are compatible. This can be checked by contacting a systems manager or manufacturing representative. Be careful about running a system with several compilers installed, for example, different versions of the same compiler or perhaps different flavors of C or Fortran. You may not be able to mix object files, and one compiler may *break* the links of a previous one (they may share the same library names but have different contents).

Naming Conventions and Stages

As nice as it might be for the neophyte, you cannot just tell the computer the name of your file containing Fortran, C, or Pascal source code and have the answers from the program returned to you. As indicated in schematically frightening detail in Figure 8.1, there are a number of stages the computer (and to a lesser extent you) must go through to convert those lines of source code to an executable program. Once you have that executable program, you can just tell the computer the program's name and it will run. In rare cases, it might even produce the answers you have been waiting for so patiently.

What is usually just called *compiling* actually involves a number of stages. We indicate in Figure 8.1 the compiling, linking, running, and debugging stages, as well as typical suffixes of associated files. Depending on how hard you work, the stages may include:

COMPILING STAGE & ASSOCIATED PROGRAM

preprocessing	cpp, ratfor
compiling	f77, cc
assembling	as
linking	ld
running	a.out
debugging	dbx, xdb, sdb
profiling	gprof, prof

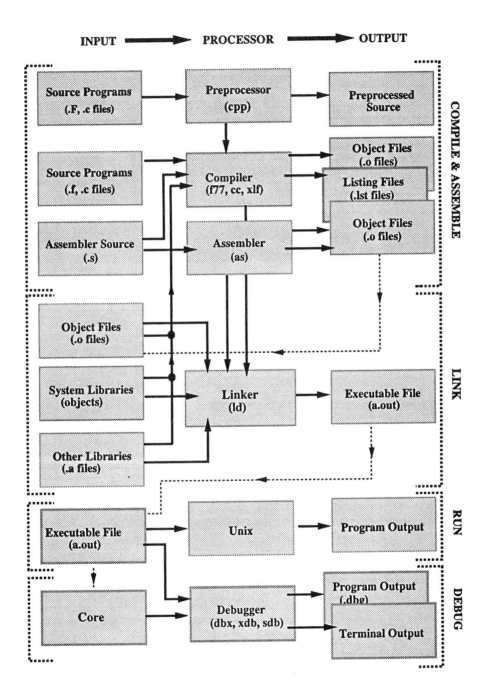

Figure 8.1: The stages in compiling and debugging along with the associated files.

The conventional Unix names for the files used during these various stages are:

COMPILING FILES

sub.f	Fortran source programs.
sub.c	C language source (unrelated to C shell).
sub.p	Pascal source programs.
sub.o	Object programs when -o not used.
a.out	Default name for executable code.
sub.obj	Intermediate object code (discard).
sub.dbg	Used by debuggers sdb, dbx, xde, and xdb.
sub.i	Intermediate debris from compilation errors or C code preprocessed by cpp needing compiling.
sub.il	Inline expansion code templates.
sub.lst	Source listing with map and error messages.
sub.List	Source listing with map and error messages.
sub.s	Code to be assembled.
sub.tcov	Output from tcov (Sun).
sub.d	Run statistic for profile with tcov (Sun).
sub.r	Code to be preprocessed by Ratfor.
sub.e	Code to be preprocessed by EFC.
sub.F	Code to be preprocessed by cpp.
mon.out	File produced for analysis by prof (ULTRIX).
/lib/libc.a	C library.
/lib/libm.a	Math library.
/usr/lib/libcl.a	Math and I/O libraries.
/usr/include/f77	Directory searched by INCLUDE statement.
/usr/lib/libF77.a	General Fortran library.
/usr/lib/libI77.a	Fortran I/O routine library.
core	Listing of entire memory, remove it.

It is important to understand the existence of these various files for at least two reasons. First of all, you may find files in various directories which you'll need to identify as either debris left over from intermediate compiling stages or valuable resources. Second, as indicated in Figure 8.1, compiling does not have to be a one-shot-and-its-all-over affair which converts source to executable code. For example, the source prog.f, after being run through the preprocessor and compiler, produces the object file prog.o. (And prog.f could have been produced from sub.F by the preprocessor.)

The *object file* prog.o is a compiled or *binary* code which tells the computer in *machine language* just what you want it to do. Yet object files are not complete programs because they need to be combined or *linked* together with other subroutines by the linkage editor (either explicitly by calling it up or implicitly, when a compiler is called) to make an *executable* file. Executable files can be loaded into the computer's memory (just by telling Unix their name) and run. This is the reason they are also called *load modules*. The other subroutines needed to produce a complete program are either provided by you or some *library*. The final executable program may have the same name as the source code file, such as prog, but without the .f or any other extension. If you are not choosy, the executable will turn out to be a.out. And finally, if you have given the proper options and after successful compilation, the debugger can treat your executable as input and assist you to interactively debug your program.

Since object and executable files are written in a *binary* code, they cannot be viewed with the usual text editors or Unix commands like more and cat.[3] You can, however, use them again and again even in a variety of programs. In fact, even your executables can be saved and run many times; there is no reason to relink all the objects before a run unless you have changed one or some of the objects.

8.2 Sample Program and Tutorial

You may recall from Chapter 2, *Getting Friendly with Unix*, our Fortran program area.f which calculates the area of a circle. In case you don't, here it is again for you to run as a sample Fortran program (you will also find it on the floppy):

`PROGRAM area`	This is main program.
`c`	Space helps readability.
`c area of circle, r input from terminal`	Say what's happening.
`c`	
`DOUBLE PRECISION pi, r, A`	Uppercase for clarity.
`c Best value of pi for IEEE floating point`	Comment.
`pi = 3.14159265358979323846`	Set value of π.
`c read r from standard input (terminal)`	
`Write(*, *) 'specify radius'`	Appears on terminal.
`Read (*, *) r`	Input from terminal.
`c calculate area`	
`A = pi * r**2`	
`c write area onto terminal screen`	
`Write(*,10)'radius r =',r,' A =',A`	* for terminal.
`10 Format(a20, f10.5, a15, f12.7)`	
`STOP 'area'`	Stop, write name.
`END`	

1. To gain some experience with your computer system, try entering the preceding program into a file or copy it from the floppy. Then use the procedures being covered in this chapter to do the following:

   (a) Compile and execute area.

   (b) Check that the results are correct; good input datum for testing is $r = 1.0$, since then $A = \pi$. (Check if $r = 1$ works (without the decimal point).)

   (c) Try your program with $r = 2.$ and see if the area increases by a factor of 4; then experiment.

---

[3]In spite of our innately rebellious nature, we cannot even tell you it will do no harm trying to view binary code on your terminal since viewing a binary file may well confuse or lock up your terminal and make your program buggy. If you can't resist, go ahead and try it. It's not our file or system.

2. This Fortran program takes the input *from* and places the output *to* the *terminal screen*. Revise this program so that the input comes from and the output is placed into separate *files*.

3. Revise this program so that it uses a main program to do the input and output, and a subroutine to do the calculation. Check that it still runs properly.

4. Now go back and try the exercises at the end of Chapter 1 which explore your system's numerical limits.

8.3   Compiling Source Code

After you have entered and checked your source code with an editor, you *compile* it. Although we may emphasize Fortran, the Pascal and C compilers work similarly, and on most Unix systems you can even mix together the object or .o files produced by the Fortran and C compilers. However, this can be a little tricky. We consequently save a more detailed explanation for you *power users* until Chapter 10, *Unix Tools*.

Compiling with No Options

When a Fortran source code in prog.f is compiled, and no -o option is specified, the executable program is placed in the file a.out, like this:

```
%  ls                              List files.
prog.f                             Just a Fortran source code.
%  f77 prog.f                      Compile code in prog.f.
Compiling FORTRAN Program:         f77 tells you.
prog.f:                            Unix says working on this.
MAIN limits:                       Limits is the MAIN program.
%  ls                              You ask what's here now.
a.out prog.f                       Compiled, linked program in a.out.
%  a.out                           You run by entering name.
1 9.500000000  6.082209587         The output now follows.
```

As you can see, the Fortran, Fortran I/O, and math libraries are automatically linked. Linking other libraries requires the -1 option.

Essentially the identical procedure is used with the C compiler. You use **cc** in place of **f77** and prog.c in place of **prog.f**:

```
%  cc prog.c                       Compile C code in prog.c.
%                                  Nothing, if no errors.
%  ls                              You ask what's here.
a.out prog.c                       Compiled, linked program in a.out.
%  a.out                           Run executable by entering its name.
1 9.500000000  6.082209587         Output now follows.
```

In circumstances when your C compiler does not automatically include the math library, you instruct `cc` to include it with the `-lm` option:

```
%  cc -lm prog.c
```
Compile C code including math library.

Source (Program) Listing

It is always important to have a recent listing of your source codes produced by the compiler. The listing shows you what the computer thinks you have entered (and thus shows you spacing and spelling errors), gives the statement numbers to which error statements refer, and shows the compilation errors at the points where they occur. Additionally, if you give the compiler the appropriate options to produce variable attributes and program reference maps, they,too, too will be placed in the listing (we find them invaluable in debugging, and highly recommend you use them). The compiler usually places the source listing in a file with the suffix `.list`, `.l`, or `.lst`. You can then either print or (preferably) examine the listing with an editor. For example:

```
%  xlf -qsource prog.f
```
AIX compile with simple source listing.

⋮

⋮
Compiler information given.

```
%  xlf -qsource -qattr -qxref prog.f
```
AIX compile + list, attributes, x ref map.

```
%  f77 -v -V prog.f
```
ULTRIX or UX verbose compile.

```
%  f77 -V +R prog.f
```
UX verbose compile + references.

```
%  vi prog.l
```
Examine source listing.

Compiling with -o Option

If we include the `-o` option in the compile command, we do not get stuck with the nondescript `a.out` as the program name but instead get to choose a name with some meaning. Here's an example:

```
%  f77 myprog.f -o exname
```
Place executable in `exname`.
```
Compiling FORTRAN Program:
```
`f77` tells you what it's doing.
```
myprog.f:
```
Compiling this.
```
MAIN limits:
```
```
%  ls
```
List files.
```
exname myprog.f myprog.o
```
Executable, source, object.
```
%  exname
```
Execute program in `exname`.
```
1 9.500000000 6.082209587
```
The output now follows.

You can see from this example that the source code (`.f`, `.c`) must be in the current directory, and the `.o` files are left in the current directory (unless you instruct otherwise with options).

8.4   Dealing with Object Files

Source programs need not be contained in one file only. In fact, for big programs it is
best to divide the code among a number of smaller files, perhaps by using the commands
fsplit or **csplit** to place each subroutine in its own file. This often makes debugging
simpler and faster, and also facilitates your ability to keep the object files and use them
again and again in different programs.

In the next example, the program poly uses the function subname stored in the file
sub.f. To compile, we simply include the names of both files and again use the -o option
to tell the compiler what to name the compiled program:

```
%  ls                              Check what files exist.
bigprog.f                          A big Fortran code.
%  fsplit bigprog.f                Split up bigprog.f into subs.
poly.f sub.f                       The individual subs are listed.
%  f77 poly.f sub.f -o poly.       Compile .f's, object in poly.o.
Compiling FORTRAN Program:         f77 tells you what it's doing.
poly.f:                            Compiler's output.
MAIN:                              Main program in poly.f.
sub.f:
subname:                           Subprogram subname in sub.f.
%  ls                              List contents of working directory.
poly poly.o sub.o                  Executable and two object files.
poly.f sub.f                       Main's source, subprogram's source.
```

Since object codes and executables are composed of low–level commands specific to
your particular machine, *object codes and linked modules (executables) may not run on
different machines (even if they are running Unix); you can't take them with you.* You
may, however, find some solace in appreciating that since object files are machine language
codes, you can link together object files produced by the Fortran and C compilers—if they
both follow the same naming and data transfer conventions.

Compiling a Subroutine

```
%  ls                              List files.
sub.c                              One C language source.
%  cc -c sub.c                     sub.c = source, -c = option.
%  ls                              List files.
sub.c sub.o                        One C language source, one object code.
```

Here the -c option instructs the compiler to just compile the source code *without* automatically calling the linkage editor (**ld**) to produce an executable file. The object code of
sub.c is automatically placed in sub.o.

Unresolved and Undefined References

Sometimes the compiler gives you an error message with words of the sort "unresolved or undefined references or symbols." This does not refer to the opinions of your former employers or the analysis of your dreams but rather indicates that you have told the compiler to produce an executable file but have not given the compiler all the subprograms needed. The compiler has searched its internal libraries without success and is asking you to supply these subprograms or tell the compiler where to find them. We now will suggest some ways to do that.

Compile and Link

To *link in* some existing object files with the program you are compiling, tell the compiler to include the already compiled .o files (the compiler automatically calls the linkage editor). For example:

```
%   f77 poly.f sub.o -o prog          Compile poly, link sub, executable = prog.
%   prog                              Execute prog.
P0 = 1.,  P1 = -1.  P2 = 1.  P3 = -1. Output from prog.
```

In this example, poly.f got compiled, sub.o was linked in, and the executable was placed in prog.

Linking Object Files into Executables

Let's say you have a number of object files that you have compiled yourself or extracted from a library. You want to combine them all into an executable file or *load module* which can be placed in the computer's memory and be executed. As indicated in Figure 8.1, you can invoke the *linker* for this purpose, but you usually do it indirectly by calling the compiler (your old friend now) with the -o option for objects:

```
%   f77 (or cc) -o prog sub1.o sub2.o   Link two .o's into executable = prog.
%   f77 (or cc) -o prog *.o             Alternative to link all .o's.
```

The executable program is placed in the file prog since that is the name specified after the -o option.

Link Objects and Libraries

The **man** pages for **f77** or **cc** usually indicate the *libraries* needed by the compiler and they will be automatically included when you compile. If the object files you want are located in another library, you need not extract them from the library yourself (and thus make extra copies in your directory) but instead can have the compiler (linker) do the extraction for you by again using the -o option for objects:

```
%   f77 -o prog sub.o libe1.a libe2.a   Link .o and libes into executable prog.
```

Here the libraries (.a suffixes) are linked in the order specified and the executable is placed in the file prog since that is the name specified after the -o option. An alternate approach (or possibly substitute—depending on your system), is to have the compiler search through the system libraries by giving it the *-1library* option flag like this:

```
%   f77 -l libe1 -o prog          Search libe1.a for subroutines.
%   cc -lm -o prog                Include math library.
%   cc -o prog sub1.o sub2.o /usr/lib/libfor.a /usr/lib/libsys.a
```

Because the compiler is only calling on the linker to link in the libraries (as in Figure 8.1), the C compiler can be used as well to link in Fortran libraries.

In the C language you also have the option of using the statements:

```
#include <file-name>              Include file-name.
#include "file-name"              Include file-name.
```

These commands cause source statements in the named files to be embedded with the rest of the source code. The first form is usually for the system libraries and the second for personal ones. To get the system I/O routines (like printf) and the math functions (like sin), you do something like this:

```
/* Sample C Program with includes */
# include <stdlib.h>              Search /usr/include.
# include <stio.h>                 ''
# include <math.h>                 ''
# include <time.h>                 ''
# include "mylibe.h"              Search source file's directory.
```

If you also want to link in **blockdata** declarations (if they are not being picked up automatically) as well as your own **library** mylibe.a, you include them on your **f77** or **cc** command:

```
%   cc -o prog blkdata.o lib1.a \
        /usr/lib/libfor.a /usr/lib/libsys.a
```

Be careful to preserve the above order (or go ahead and try a different one and see if prog will run).

8.5   General Compiler Options

As we have seen above, the Fortran and C compilers produce object code from source code and link together object codes and even libraries into executable *programs*. Let wonders never cease, they do even more if you ask them to with *options* in the **f77** or **cc** command:

```
%   f77 -options prog.f
```

Here *options* can be rather extensive; in this chapter we give some basic ones, and in the next chapter we'll give some more specialized ones. The *options* available for your particular machine's compilers are described in your local reference manual or in the manual pages accessible via the `man f77`, `man cc`, etc., commands. Note that while single-letter options are case sensitive, they can be concatenated to other option letters (and in the order of your choice!) to make up new words which *Scrabble* would never allow.

COMPILER OPTIONS

-c	Compile `.f` or `.c` to object `.o`; no link.
-l	Include nonstandard library of subroutines.
-lm	Include C math library.
-D	Treat d (debug) statements as source.
-o *prog*	Name executable *prog* not `a.out`.
-O	Optimization (has levels).
-w	Suppress warning messages.
-g	Generate *global* symbol table for debugger; (debug after program is running).

Optimization Option

Work gets done more quickly if programs run more quickly. While it may not be a wise investment of your time to spend days to obtain a few seconds speedup in a rarely used program, a 30% or more improvement on a real time-hog may well conserve valuable computer resources and friends. This is the subject of many hot coffee-break discussions. In fact, in Chapter 11, *Scientific Programming Hints*, and in Chapter 13, *Programming RISC and Vector Machines*, we discuss some methods for optimizing your program to match a particular computer's hardware or to better adhere to the method behind the madness of some particular compiler.

Here we indicate that many (and particularly RISC) compilers contain optimizers which produce faster running code than can the typical user's manual optimization. For example, the compiler may check if a variable defined within a *do* loop ever changes and, if not, remove its definition to outside the loop. Since the variable will not be continually redefined, this will speed up the program.

Modern compilers are getting better and hardly ever make a mistake at optimizing. Yet in the real world of computational science with large, complicated, and convoluted programs which may not have been written with the best programming techniques, a conservative view is probably prudent. For instance, if there was a reason for you to place the definition of a variable within the *do* loop and the compiler was not clever enough to realize it, the compiler–optimized program may run faster but give incorrect answers.

As a general rule, optimization increases compilation time, uses more memory during compilation, sometimes finds errors which previously caused no problems, and by taking a more global view of your program, tends to lose the connection between source– and object–code lines. We therefore suggest that when you debug your programs, or get them running on a new machine, you first compile and run them with no optimization. When the results look right (agree with a known analytic result or with the output from a run somewhere else), try a gradual increase in the level of optimization, checking at each step that the results are still correct. While we appreciate that this conservative approach is a waste of time for a perfect compiler, it seems to us a small investment considering the time spent on developing the code and the importance of its results.

A very good approach to optimizing is for you to inspect the changes made by the compiler before they are put into effect. Some RISC compilers, for example, have pre-processors which convert your source code to *optimized* code which you can examine or modify. This gives you the possibility to see what the compiler is doing, correct it if it is wrong, and, if you like it, call the new source your own.

Not All Compilers Are Equal

Although all Fortran 77 and ANSI C language compilers can be made to follow the same respective sets of general rules, the compilers on most workstations are actually supersets of the standards — meaning they can do more than the minimum. To see just what your compiler is capable of and how to make it perform, use the **man** command with the name of the compiler. Here's an example:

```
%   man f77 (or xlf or cc)            Read man pages.
%   man ar cc dbx dbxtool f77cvt
%   man fpr fsplit gprof ld make
%   man prof as asa strip lintfor
%   man ratfor matherr prof
%   f77 -help                        Ask f77 for help with options.
%   f77                              Without options, also for help.
```

In this chapter we have used basic compiler options which should be the same on all compilers. The more specific optimization options tend to be compiler dependent and we will review some in the next chapter.

8.6   Executing Programs

To execute a program, you just enter the name of the file containing it:

```
%   prog                             Just give file name to execute.
```

If the prog file is not executable, it can be made so (at least in the grammatical sense) with one of these commands:

```
%   chmod +x prog                    Make prog executable.
%   chmod 766 prog                   Set mode and make executable.
```

In the next section we'll show you some details about your choices for input and output under Fortran and Unix. If you do not want to use the standard input and output, you can specify I/O with the Unix redirectors > and <:

```
%   prog < infile  > outfile         Run prog, input infile, output outfile.
```

8.7　Redirecting I/O and Piping

As you may recall from Chapter 2, *Getting Friendly with Unix*, each Unix command has a *standard input* and *standard output* associated with it. These are the assumed defaults when you compile and run. Actually the system is quite flexible and you can (or can at least try to) make any file or device serve as input or output. This frees you from having to type in the input for your program from your terminal and having to read its output on a screen. This permits some serious computing using numerous input and output files and a rapid filling of all the space on the disk. You can, additionally, get really organized and arrange your programs so that different kinds of input data are read from differing *devices* (*aka units* or *tapes*) and then store those files in appropriate places. You may find that as your programs get more powerful, you will need more and more complicated input just to control what they do. You may however, also find that it is nearly impossible to type in a complicated sequence of control characters without errors (and consequent disasters). For this reason, working from a master input file and making only small changes in it is a great time-saver and disaster-avoider.

Unix's flexible input and output includes *redirection* and *piping* (which you are familiar with from our discussions in Chapter 2). These systems save you time and file space and can speed up the computation by permitting the computer to look ahead and plan for the work it must do. Redirection and piping allow you to tell a command to read its input from some file and write its output to some other file. Piping allows you to tell a command to read its input from another command's output or even to read its input from the output of a string of several commands without explicitly writing intermediate files. Unfortunately, not every command gets its input from standard input or sends its output to standard output, in which case Unix cannot redirect or pipe using these commands.

8.8　Fortran I/O

The **man** pages for each Fortran compiler give specifics for input and output. You probably should read them since I/O is the area where your program must interface with your computer hardware, and this often causes trouble.

Fortran Preconnected I/O Units

As we have said before, the Unix operating system has a flexible file structure which treats files, devices, and commands in much the same way. Specifically, since each command has a standard input, output, and error, and since piping between commands is possible, you can use Unix to run your executable files and to keep track of your input and output (I/O).

The point for you to keep in mind with Fortran I/O is that you must tell it how to connect up with the Unix file system. Specifically, Fortran does not even deal with *files* but rather with *logical units*, or just *units*, or historically *tapes*, and you must tell Fortran which Unix file or device to associate with its input and output units. Since the convention in Fortran is to have unit 5 as input and unit 6 as output, Unix takes this one step further and automatically *preconnects* the following devices and units:

FORTRAN PRECONNECTED UNITS ⇔ UNIX DEVICE

5	Standard INPUT (stdin).
6	Standard OUTPUT (stdout).
0, 7, 2 (*one only*)	Standard ERROR (stderr).

Using other units in your Fortran code requires you to first connect them with the **open** statement. We discuss that below. If units 5 and 6 are not preconnected for your system, then you will have to **open** them, too.

List-Directed, Formatted I/O

The simplest method for Fortran input and output is called *list directed, formatless,* or *free format*. In this case you place an asterisk * in place of an explicit line number for the format statement. Of course you no longer can personally control the form of the output or be assured that it will remain constant as your output numbers change; yet list-directed output saves a lot of time in getting started and is often all you need. Likewise, unless your input files are sequential and have appropriate separators between the data, the input directed by the list will not be clear. Here are some sample I/O's using the preconnected (default) units:

`Write (6, *) E, m`	List directed (*) write to unit 6 (default).
`Read (5, *) E, m`	List directed (*) read to unit 5 (default).
`Write (6, *) 'input energy, mass'`	input... appears on stdout (terminal).

You probably noticed that using the asterisk * *also* as a Fortran unit number automatically gave you the preconnected (default) units. As a consequence, if you are running from your terminal without redirection and want screen output, you can be lazy:

`Write (*, 999) E, m`	Formatted write to standard out (terminal screen).
`999 Format(2 f10.3)`	An explicit format statement.
`Read (*, 999) E, m`	Formatted read from standard in (terminal keyboard).

And you can really be lazy if you use list-directed I/O to and from your terminal:

`Write (*, *) 'key in energy, mass'`	key... appears on stdout (terminal).
`Read (*, *) E, m`	Input from terminal.
`Write (6, *) 'E, m =', E, m`	6 is stdout, list directed.
`Print *, 'E, m =', E, m`	Print always goes to standard out.
`Read *, E, m`	List directed, standard in.
`Read E, m`	List directed, standard din.
`Read 999, E, m`	Formatted, standard in.
`Write (6, '(2f10.3)') E, m`	6 is standard out, internal format.

Finally, the standard input and output can also be redirected to ordinary Unix files, here called `infile` and `outfile`:

`%  prog > outfile`	Redirect output to `outfile`.
`%  prog < infile`	Redirect input to `infile`.

Here *prog* contains Fortran statements of the form:

`Read  (5, *)  mass`	Fortran read from 5 (standard in).
`Write (6, *)  mass`	Fortran read from 6 (standard out).

Unformatted I/O

It is important to realize that your Fortran I/O statement usually does two things. First it does the obvious: move external data into central memory or central memory data to an external device. Second, as a necessity for the moving, it often must format or convert the data to or from its internal or binary representation to that (usually ASCII) used on the external device. There are three advantages to avoiding this conversion: 1) unformatted data occupy less room in memory, 2) the conversion and often subsequent reconversion is a slow process which may use a large fraction of the run time of your program, and 3) conversion between binary and decimal representations is not exact, that is, precision is lost. If your program, for instance, uses a large number of the same input data or uses large scratch files during your calculation, this would be a good place to use unformatted I/O. Formatless read/write statements look just like the usual ones except there is no format statement number and no * indicating list direction:

`Read (5) E, m`	Formatless read from unit 5, no conversion.
`Open (7, file = 'mine',`	
`1 form = 'unformatted')`	**Open** statement.
`  Read (7) e, m`	Formatless, no conversion.
`  Close (7)`	Optional.

However, as indicated in the next section, you may have to **open** the logical units if they are not preconnected or if you want to use a file.

Connecting Your Own I/O Units

As indicated in the preceding section, part of the power of Unix is the uniform way it treats devices, files, and commands. You can take advantage of this by having the different logical units 1–99 of your Fortran programs correspond to different storage devices, terminals, line printers, or even parts of memory. The connection between logical units and Unix files is done with the **open** statement and its options—an example of which we have just seen. Here are some more:

To write to the standard output (your screen, unless you redirect the output) use the following Fortran statements:

`Open   (6, status ='unknown')`
`Write (6, 900) mass`
`900 Format(f7.2)`
	Open 6, create if doesn't exists.
	Write to unit 6.

Open and Write to a Sequential File Named `tape7`:

`Open (7, file = 'tape7',`
`1 status = 'unknown')`
`Write (7, 900) mass`
`900 Format(f7.2)`
`Write (7, '(f7.2)') mass`
`Write (7, *) mass`
`Close (7, status = 'delete')`
`Close (7, status = 'keep')`
	
	Internal format.
	List-directed format.
	Disconnect, delete file.
	Disconnect, save file.

To read the existing, sequential file `tape8` from `unit 8`, we must **open 8** and (for insurance) **rewind 8** before reading from it:

`Open(8, file = 'tape8', status = 'old')`
`Rewind 8`
`Read (8, 900) mass1`
`900 Format(....)`
`Read (8, *) mass2`
`Close (8)`
	Old since exists.
	Make sure at top.
	
	Disconnect now.

You saw that when we opened the sequential file, the pointer pointed to the first record and each read or write caused it to move ahead one record.

To create and open a new, sequential file **nu** as well as a temporary, or scratch, sequential (and formatted) file:

`Open (8, file = 'nu', status = 'new')`
`Open (7, file = 'temp',`
`1 status = 'scratch')`
`Read (8,900) mass1`
`900 Format(....)`
`Write (7,900) mass1`
`Open (unit#, file='fname', status='unknown`
`1 (new,old,scratch)', access='sequential(direct)',`
`2 form='formatted(unformatted)', err=888,`
`3 iostat=ios)`
	Create new file.
	Open scratch file
	
	Generic Form.

We see in the generic form (which has nondefault options in parentheses) that `fname` is the Unix file to be opened, `status` gives the present status of `fname`, `access` indicates whether this is a sequential or direct access file, form tells whether you will be making formatted or unformatted reads and writes to this file, the number given for err is the statement number where the program should go if an error such as end of file occurs, and ios is a variable which is given the value 0 if no error occurs and a value > 1 if an error occurs.

It is important to remember to use form = 'formatted' for formatted, list directed, or ascii I/O, that is, a conversion between ascii and internal representation of data. Accordingly, here's an efficient and accurate formatless I/O for storing intermediate results:

```Open (8, file = 'temp', form = 'unformatted')```
```Write (8) mass1```
```...```
```Rewind 8```
```Read (8) mass1```
	Formatless write.

At this point you may be confused by the need for the status option and the location of the pointer as you open a file. As shown in the table below, the answer depends upon whether the file already exists or not and upon whether an implicit or explicit open statement was made.

	Implicit Open	**Explicit Open**		
status	...	'new'	'old'	'unknown'
exists	beginning	error	end	beginning
no exists	beginning	beginning	error	begin

Now we give a code fragment which shows how to *write to an existing file*, that is, how to get to the end of the file and to write over the end-of-file record (this really is just Fortran, not Unix):

```   Parameter (true = .true.)```
```   Open (16, file = 'extant', status = old)```
```c   position to end of file```
```   Do While (true)```
```   Read(16, *, end = 888)```
```   End Do```
```c   backspace & write over end of file record```
```999 Backspace 16```
```   Write (16, *) Mass```
	Define logical.

Printing Fortran Output

Within the Fortran language there are a number of options permitting you to control the form of your printed output. These often appear as *carriage control* characters placed in the first column of printed output. If you send your Fortran output file to a printer with the **cat, lp,** or **print** commands, you may well find the characters 1, 0, +, - appearing in the first column of your output—as well as ugly output. To obtain the proper output, you must pass your output file through a filter, such as **asa** or **fpr**, to convert these characters into signals for the printer or screen. For example:

`%  prog > fort.out`	`prog` generates output file.
`% asa fort.out	lp`	Convert output, pipe to printer.
	Or if that doesn't work...
`% fpr fort.out	lp`	Convert output, pipe to printer.
`request id is ti-8 (1 file)`	In printer queue.
`% prog	asa	lp`	Run, convert, print.
`% prog	asa	more`	Run, convert, view on screen.

Conversely, if your print file does *not* have carriage control characters in its first column—but is used with a print command which assumes it does—you may lose whatever character was in this first place as well as obtaining ugly output. An editor can help.

8.9   C Language I/O

As was true with Fortran I/O, you must tell the C language how to connect up with the Unix file system if you want to input or output information to or from your C program. In contrast to the complexity of Fortran's dealing with logical units which you had to associate with Unix files, C deals directly with Unix files. Specifically, the standard input, output, and error streams of C are the standard input, output, and error devices of Unix:

C File Pointer	Unix Device	Unix Default
`stdin`	standard input	keyboard
`stdout`	standard output	screen
`stderr`	standard error	screen

These units are preconnected and are accessed with the `printf()` and `scanf()` functions. The functions `fprintf()` and `fscanf()` are the file versions of `printf()` and `scanf()`, and they are used to read and write arbitrary or standard files.

To actually read from or write to one of the nonstandard files, it must be open and Unix must know our intention. And to be safe and neat good little chaps, we close the file when we are done. This is accomplished with the `fopen()` and `fclose()` functions for Unix files or with the `tmpfile()` function for temporary (scratch) files. In this example, we open the file `myin` for reading and the file `myout` for writing:

```#include <stdio.h>```	Contains file definitions.
```main()```	
```{```	
``` int n;```	
``` double e, m;```	
``` FILE *ifp, *ofp;```	
```printf("Hello Everybody \n");```	Print to stdout.
```fprintf(stderr,"Opening file myin.\n");```	Print to stderr.
```ifp = fopen("myin","r");```	Open myin for reading.
```ofp = fopen("myout","w");```	Open myout for writing.
```fscanf(ifp,"%d %f",&n, &e```	Read an integer & float.
```fprintf(ofp,"N= %d charge= %f\n",n, e);```	Output.
```fclose(ifp);```	Close input file.
```fclose(ofp);```	
```}```	

This code fragment uses the conventional identifiers ifp and ofp for *input file pointer* and *output file pointer*. This example indicates just two modes for opening files. Other modes are:

C OPEN FILE MODE

r	Read text.
r+	Read or write text.
w	Write text.
w+	Write or read text.
a	Append text.
rb	Read binary (same as text for Unix).
wb	Write binary (same as text for Unix).
ab	Append binary (same as text for Unix).

Care is needed here since writing to an existing file will overwrite it and because function calls are needed between the reads and writes to the same file. A perusal of the reference manual is appropriate.

8.10 Libraries

A *library* is a collection of subprograms from which a program you write can borrow needed subroutines. The library entries are usually object codes in such a form that the linker box in the center of Figure 8.1 can extract from the library those subroutines your program calls but has yet to find (or, in plain English, unresolved external references). The uncalled subroutines in the library are not included in your executable.

You are free to write and collect your own library or to use the system libraries supplied with your system as well as third-party packages such as IMSL, NAG, SLATEC, ESSL, and SAS. These latter packages are comprehensive and powerful, and we strongly recommend their use. Libraries are generally good to have around since they save you from having to program your own subroutines as well as providing you with efficient, modern algorithms—possibly even optimized for your particular hardware and software. In fact, because different versions of the same libraries are often available on both workstations and supercomputers, lending from the local version of your library is often a quick and painless way to at least partially optimize your program to the local system.

Creating, Updating, and Including

You create your own library or *achieve* several compiled subroutines into a library libename.a with the archive command:

```
%  ar -cvr libename.a sub1.o sub2.o    Create libename.
```

Here *.o can also be used to replace the actual names of the object files. To *update* or *replace* an already existing library with the subroutine newsub:

```
%  ar -rv libename.a newsub.o          Replace newsub.
```

Once you have created your libraries, you must include it into your executable (load module). This is done most directly by using the -1 compiler option. For example, to include libe1.a:

```
%  f77 -l libe1 -o prog               Search libe1.a for subs.
```

The -1*libname* option causes the linker to search the library lib*libname*.a in order to eliminate unresolved external references. Because a library is searched when its name is encountered, if a file contains an unresolved external reference, the library containing the definition should be placed after the file on the command line. Details are found with the man pages for ld. On some systems libe1.a may have to be in directory /lib. or /usr/lib—unless you specify other search paths with additional options. But beware that including libraries is order–sensitive.

Libraries can also be included with the C language compiler. For example:

```
%  cc -o prog sub.o /usr/lib/libfor.a /usr/lib/libsys.a \
     /lib/lib.a /usr/lib/lib.a
```

8.11   Minimizing Response Time

Unix provides a multi-user, multi-tasking environment. This means you share computer resources with other users and with other tasks the computer does on its own, like mail handling and printing. It is an experimental fact that everyone's productivity decreases significantly with even a small increase in response time.[4] For this reason it is to everyone's benefit to use the system's resources wisely; the response time will not be annoyingly long and the number crunching jobs will still have a chance to get a good mouthful.

---

[4]Doherty and Pope (1986).

Running jobs at low priority is a good way to keep computing-bound jobs (those which run the central processing unit for long periods of time) from slowing down interactive use of the computer. The Unix command `nice` lets you run your background jobs at low priority. The `nice` command accepts priority numbers from 1 to 20, where higher numbers mean more niceness to others, that is, lower priority. For example, to execute the program `number.cruncher` at low priority in the background, you enter:

```
%   nice -20 number.cruncher &        Low priority run, Bourne shell.
%   nice +20 number.cruncher &        Low priority run, C shell.
```

Another strategy for using processor resources wisely is spreading the load, that is, performing work outside of periods of peak usage. In fact, Unix has the command **batch**, which permits you to enter a job into a *batch* queue, as well as a command **at**, which permits you to schedule the time when you want your job to run. The advantages of *batch* over, say, just a *background* job is, first, that batch jobs are automatically at a low priority and, second, that the batch queue can be set so that only a small number of batch jobs (possibly 1) are running at a time. In this way the batch jobs progressively terminate without competing with other batch jobs. (Having a large number of jobs running simultaneously wastes memory and system time.)

Being nice to the system does not ensure that the system will be nice to you, namely, not kill your job if you log out of the system to get some lunch. Fasting is one solution. We prefer the `nohup` command which tells Unix not to hang up on you.[5] For example:

```
$ksh   nohup prog < infile  > outfile       Execute prog, no hangup.
$ksh   nice -5 nohup prog < infile > outfile  Execute, no hangup.
```

The regular Unix commands just follow the `nohup` and `nice` commands.

And, finally, if you are concerned with minimizing response time, we remind you that the computer's memory is also finite. As we discuss in more detail in Part III's examination of virtual memory, there may be a number of jobs trying to share *central memory* at one time In the extreme case the total memory needed may be larger than fits into central memory forcing the system to use *virtual memory* and greatly increasing the time for all of the jobs to complete.

8.12 Mixing Fortran and C

An amazing aspect of Unix is that programs written in Fortran, C, or Pascal can call subprograms compiled in the other languages. For this to work properly, however, respect must be paid to the differences in data types and argument–passing conventions in the different languages. We outline two possibilities here, calling a Fortran subprogram from a C program and calling a C procedure from a Fortran program. (We do not discuss Pascal explicitly, but do give some of the comparisons in the tables.) If the data structures with which the programs deal are complicated, you will probably need a good knowledge of each language. We recommend Loukides (1990), and your manufacturer's documents.

---

[5]You may want to refer to our discussion in Chapter 3, *Workstation Setup and Use*, where we indicated how the C shell `nohup` could be set in the `.cshrc` file.

Corresponding Data Types

If your C program uses a data type not available in Fortran (or vice versa) it is difficult to program up an interlanguage call. The corresponding data types are shown in the table below.

C	Fortran	Pascal
char	CHARACTER	CHAR
signed char	INTEGER*1	PACKED -128..127
unsigned char	LOGICAL*1	PACKED 0..255
short signed int	INTEGER*2	PACKED -32768..32767
short unsigned int	LOGICAL*2	PACKED 0..65535
signed int (long int)	INTEGER*4	INTEGER
unsigned int	LOGICAL*4	
float	REAL (REAL*4)	SHORTREAL
structure of 2 floats	COMPLEX	
double	REAL*8	REAL
structure of 2 doubles	COMPLEX*16	
char[n]	CHARACTER*n	PACKED ARRAY[1..n]

If the data are stored in arrays, not only must you ensure that the data types are matched, but you must also convert between the different subscripting schemes used in the two languages. Specifically, Fortran stores arrays in column–major order while C and Pascal store them in row–major order (yet with different origins for the subscripts). Accordingly, the same location can have data with different meanings in different languages:

Location	C Element	Fortran Element	Pascal Element
lowest	a(0,0)	a(1,1)	a(1,1)
	a(0,1)	a(2,1)	a(1,2)
	a(1,0)	a(3,1)	a(2,1)
	a(1,1)	a(1,2)	a(2,2)
	a(2,0)	a(2,2)	a(3,1)
highest	a(2,1)	a(3,2)	a(3,2)

Argument Passing

When a function is called in the C language the actual value of the argument passed to the function. In contrast, Fortran always passes the address in memory (a *reference pass*) where the value of the argument is to be found. To keep your function from processing the numerical value of an address when it thinks it is dealing with the actual value of a variable, follow these two rules.

- When calling a Fortran function from C, make all arguments in your C program pointers. Generally this is done with the address operator, &.

- When you want your C function to be called from Fortran, declare the arguments as pointers in C.

Calling Fortran from C

In order for your C program to be able to call functions in Fortran, you may need to modify your C code somewhat. Here are some hints:

- Pass all arguments to the Fortran subprograms as pointers.

- Append an underscore _ to the called Fortran subprogram names since Fortran does that to its subprogram names. (There may be some colors of Unix for which no underscore should be added.)

- Use lowercase letters for the names of external functions, unless the Fortran subprogram being called was compiled with a -u option (or the equivalent as discussed in Chapter 9). This option retains the uppercase letters. (On some systems the C compiler automatically converts the subroutine's name to lowercase unless you instruct it otherwise.)

Sample Fortran from C

The C program in `c_fort.c` on the floppy calls the Fortran subroutine in `area_f.f`.

C main: `c_fort.c`

```/* PROGRAM c_fort */```
```main()```
```{```
```/* area of circle, r input from terminal */```
```extern double area_f_();```
```double r, A;```
```printf("specify radius ");```
```scanf("%lf",&r);```
```A = area_f_(&r);```
```printf("radius r=%10.5f A=%12.7f\n",r,A);```
```}```
	A C main with Fortran function.
	
	Fortran function, _ appended.
	
	Read r from terminal.
	Argument r passed as a pointer.
	Write to screen.

Fortran subroutine: `area_f.f`

```   double precision function area_f(r)```
```c area of circle, r input from terminal```
```c```
```   DOUBLE PRECISION pi, r```
```   pi = 3.14159265358979323846```
```   area_f = pi * r**2```
```   return```
```   END```
	
	Best pi for IEEE floating point.

Here's a more complicated example in which the Fortran subroutine gauss, containing array and integer arguments, is called from a C program:

C main:

```#include <stdio.h>```	
```#include <math.h>```	
```#define MAXN 100000```	Allows N up to 100000.
```extern void gauss_(int *,int *,double *,\```	This is ANSI C style.
``` double *, double[],```	
```double[]);```	
```float a,b;```	Input: a,b are float.
```int N;```	Input: N is integer.
```{ double x[MAXN],w[MAXN],adoub,bdoub,ans=0;```	
```int index,job;```	
```job = 0;```	Uniform scaling a-b.
```adoub = (double) a;```	Convert floats to doubles.
```bdoub = (double) b;```	
```gauss_(&N,&job,&adoub,&bdoub,x,w);```	Call to Fortran with pointers.
```for (index=0;index<N;index++)```	Summation of terms.
```ans += exp(x[index])*w[index];```	
```return(ans);```	Return answer to caller.
```}```	

Fortran subroutine: ```gauss.f```

``` subroutine gauss(npts,job,a,b,x,w)```	
```c rescale gauss-legendre grid points and weights```	
```c npts = # points, x, w = points and weights.```	
```c```	
``` integer*4 npts,job,m,i,j```	
``` real*8 x(npts),w(npts),a,b,xi```	
``` .....```	Assign x and w.
``` end```	

Compiling, C Calling Fortran

The multilanguage programs actually get mixed when you tell the compiler which object files to link together. There is a sample ```Makefile``` on the floppy which does this. The tricky part is that to call Fortran from C, you must explicitly include the Fortran library (automatic in Fortran but not in C). If your main (top level) program is in C, use **cc** for the linking:

```% cc -c c_fort.c```	Compile C main program.
```% f77 -O -c area_f.f```	Compile Fortran function.
```Compilation successful for file area_f.f.```	Fortran's reply.
```% cc -o c_fort c_fort.o area_f.o -L/usr/lang/SC0.0 -lF77```	
	Link with **cc** under SunOS 4.x
```% cc -o c_fort c_fort.o area_f.o -lxlf```	Link with **cc** under AIX.
```% c_fort```	Now run program.
```specify radius 1.```	You're asked and you reply.
```radius r= 1.00000 A= 3.1415927```	The computer's reply.

Calling C from Fortran

To call C procedures from your Fortran program, you may need to make some modifications in your Fortran code. Here are some points to keep in mind:

- While both the underscore _ and the dollar sign $ are legitimate characters in C names, do not use them as first characters. Names beginning with _ are reserved names in C and in some Fortran libraries, and $ is used by Unix for shell variables.

- Let's say you have called a C procedure as a Fortran subprogram, call Csub. Because Fortran normally converts subprogram names to lowercase and appends an underscore _ to them, you may have to explicitly make the name of the C-called function end with an underscore, Csub_.

- The returned value from a C procedure is ignored if it is "called" by Fortran, call Csub, but not in a Fortran function call, ECOM = E(p). In the former case you may as well give the C procedure a void type, whereas in the latter it cannot be void.

- To avoid having Fortran convert names to lowercase, use the -U option (or the equivalent as discussed in Chapter 9).

- Avoid the name main unless it's for a Fortran program or a C top-level main function.

- Avoid the use of C library names and reserve words.

- With some Fortrans, arguments can be passed by methods different from the default in Fortran by using the %VAL and %REF keywords in the argument list of a subprogram. %VAL causes the actual argument to be passed, while %REF causes the argument to be passed by reference to its memory location.

Sample C from Fortran

The Fortran program in fort_c.f on the floppy calls the C subroutine in area_c.c.

Fortran main: fort_c.f

```
      PROGRAM fort_c                            Fortran main with C subroutine.
c area of circle, r input from terminal
      DOUBLE PRECISION r, A, area
      Write(*, *) 'specify radius, e.g.  1.0'
      Read (*, *) r                             Read r from terminal.
c calculate area via call to C procedure.
      A = area_c(r)                             C procedure.
c write area onto terminal screen
      Write(*, 10) 'radius r =', r, 'A =', A    Write to terminal.
 10 Format(a20, f10.5, a15, f12.7)
      STOP 'fort_c'
      END
```

C subroutine: `area_c.c`

```double area_c_(p)```	Procedure area called from Fortran.
```/* Note _ */```	Append an underscore to the name.
```/* double area_c(p) */```	Alternative to above for some systems.
```double *p;```	Fortran passes a pointer.
```{```	
``` double pi, r, a;```	
```pi = 3.14159265358979323846;```	Best pi for IEEE floating point.
```r = *p;```	For clarity, assigned to a local variable.
```a = pi * r*r;```	Calculate area.
```return(a);```	
```}```	

Compiling, Fortran Calling C

The multilanguage programs actually get mixed when you tell the compiler which object files to link together. There is a sample `Makefile` on the floppy which does this. Since your main program is in Fortran, you need use **f77** to link the `.o` (object) files. You, of course, need **f77** to compile your Fortran source and **cc** to compile your C source:

`%   f77 -O -c fort_c.f`	Compile Fortran main.
`Compilation successful for file fort_c.f.`	Fortran's reply.
`%   cc -O -c area_c.c`	Compile C procedure.
`%   f77 -o fort_c fort_c.o area_c.o`	Link, executeable in fort_c.
`%   fort_c`	Give program name to execute.
`specify radius, e.g.  1.0 `**`1.0`**	You respond to program.
`radius r = 1.0 A = 3.14`	Computer's reply.
`STOP circle`	Computer's reply.

8.13   Porting Code to Unix

In general it is straightforward to port standard Fortran to Unix since Fortran does not deal much with the organization of memory. Because this is where the problems occur, porting C code may be more difficult. The main problems may be with static variables, EQUIVALENCE, and COMMON blocks. In particular, RISC machines usually have an architecture designed to work with 32-bit words whereas other systems may not. So if your code depends on word length, you must be careful and possibly use some of the compiler options to force your previous word length. The code you get may be slower than optimal, but at least you will have something working while you rewrite your programs.

Fortran Static Variables

Fortran programmers often assume that future calls to a subroutine will find the values for variables in that subroutine that were left there on a previous call. This is usually *not* the default under Unix but can be imposed by specifying a *static* implementation of variables.

This can be done on some compilers (see Chapter 9) with options when compiling the subroutines:

```
%   f77 -K sub.f                    Static for HP-UX f77.
```

Static variables can also be obtained by using the SAVE statement in your subprograms; as for example:

| Implicit SAVE | Make all variables static. |
| SAVE x1, x2 | Make just these two variables static. |

In some compilers, such as XL Fortran, local variables are static by default. With these compilers there is still the option to declare variables as STATIC or AUTOMATIC (new value on each call) in the Fortran declaration statement:

COMPLEX Za, Zb /(4.2, 9.6)/, Ze	Three complex numbers.
STATIC x/1.0/	Static variables can be initialized (default).
Automatic y	Automatic variables cannot be initialized.

Common Blocks and Equivalences

You may recall that when we declare variables to single or double precision (REAL or REAL*8) we are telling the compiler to store them respectively in words 4 and 8 bytes (B) long. Placing single-precision arrays or variables before double-precision arrays in COMMON blocks can cause alignment problems even though this is acceptable Fortran. For example, consider the Fortran code

REAL a(3)	Single precision.
REAL*8 b(2)	Double precision.
COMMON a, b	This determines alignments.

This leads to variables in memory of the form

8B		8B		8B		
a(1)	a(2)	a(3)				
			b(1)		b(2)	

The problem is that the COMMON statement forces the 8B word b(1) to begin on a 4B boundary rather than on an 8B one. Some compilers refuse to accept this, while others might accept it but produce a slow code. The solution is to place larger variables, such as double-precision ones, before smaller' variables, such as single-precision ones, in the COMMON block.

Likewise, the equivalencing of variables without regard to their data alignment may cause problems (TYPE CONFLICTS) or slower–running code. For example, the legitimate Fortran code

REAL a(2)	Single precision.
REAL*8 b(2)	Double precision.
EQUIVALENCE a(2), b	This fixes alignments.

leads to variables in memory of the form:

8B		8B		8B	
a(1)	a(2)				
	b(1)		b(2)		

The problem again is that the EQUIVALENCE statement forces the 8B word b(1) to begin on a 4B boundary rather than on an 8B one. You must remove such equivalencing.

Different Results from Different Machines

An annoying and sometimes disturbing side effect of running your programs on a different machine is that you may get different results. This is often the case when you are moving your programs from an older architecture to a workstation. The reason is that in the past, computers used proprietary floating point representations and binary arithmetic. Virtually all modern computers now use the IEEE standard. Except for minor differences, this means that with modern machines you should get the same results from your program regardless of which vendor's hardware you use.

Moving Unformatted Fortran Files

If the computers you are porting your program to and from have different floating point format, moving unformatted data between machines will certainly fail. The simplest and safest method to move unformatted Fortran between machines of different architectures is to write a short Fortran program which reads the data files and then writes them into a text file. You first do this on the machine you are moving from, and then reverse the operation on the new machine. If you have a large number of data to move, this method may be undesirable. In that case check with the hardware vendor for utilities to ease the process. In particular, the **assign** command under UNICOS can be used to force Fortran files into the IEEE standard format.

Unix File I/O

Porting programs from a non–Unix operating system to Unix invariably involves rewriting the Fortran statements controlling input and output. Unix has a very simple model for file I/O. The options used for optimizing I/O on other systems, such as asynchronous reading and writing under MVS, are meaningless under Unix. File names and unit numbers will also need changing to conform to Unix's naming scheme.

You want to be aware also that although Unix workstations can often match the computational speed of older mainframes, they still lack the speed of their bigger cousins in reading and writing files to hard disk. For this reason you may wish to retune your programs for the slower Unix disk. For example, if your program contains *check points* which periodically write out the values of all of its data into a file, you may want to decrease their frequency to decrease the time spent writing files.

Miscellaneous Fortran Porting Points

- Most compilers have options to accept a form of Fortran more standard to another machine (described in next chapter). This can save you lots of work at first.

- If you want to convert your source code to all capital letters, use the Unix utility `tr`:

```
%  tr '[a-z]' '[A-Z]' oldsub NEWSUB        Transpose lower to uppercase.
```

- If you want to check the size of the COMMON blocks used in each subprogram or the size of the individual subroutine objects, you may have to compile each subprogram separately.

DIFFERENT COMPILERS AND THEIR OPTIONS

9.1 Why This Chapter?

In the last chapter we saw how to perform operations with the Fortran and C compilers using basic options. That is all that is needed for starters and may well be all that you ever will need if your programs are standard f77 or ANSI C with no special features. However, these compilers have many other options which you may find useful. For example, if you need to debug your program, get a fully referenced listing of it, or optimize it, then you will want to use the options. In particular, we find the full listing and cross-reference maps invaluable for debugging (and for that reason we have <u>underlined</u> the appropriate options in the tables). As before, the options are set off from file names with a minus sign:

```
%   f77 -options prog.f
```

In the sections which follow we give some of the options available for IBM, HP, DEC, and Sun compilers. While the basic options discussed in the previous chapter should still apply for whatever computer you use, the more specific ones given in this chapter are machine dependent. Even though all the compilers conform to ANSI standards, the compilers are supersets with additional, nonstandard features. In using our tables, be aware that they are not complete. They are intended to be reminders or indicators of what to look for on your system. And the options may change with time. You should read your local reference manual or scroll through the manual pages with the man f77 (cc) command. Remember, also, that single-letter options are case sensitive and can be concatenated with other option letters.

9.2 Sun Fortran f77

The Sun Fortran compiler is called **f77** and is a superset of Fortran 77. It contains many extensions and many options and even provides compatibility with VMS Fortran if the Fortran converter **f77cvt** is used. The naming convention for files is the same as given in Chapter 8 (see Figure 8.1), yet with some local extensions:

FILE NAMES

sub.d	Input file for **tcov** test coverage.
sub.F	Fortran source code, prepossessed by **cpp**.
sub.for	VMS source code, **f77cvt** converts it to **f77**.
sub.vf	VMS source code, **f77cvt** converts it to **f77**.
sub.il	Inline expansion files (with -O).
sub.S	Assembler source code for **cpp**.
sub.tcov	Output from **tcov**.
mon.out	File for analysis by **prof**.
gmon.out	File for analysis by **gprof**.

Sun Options

OPTIONS

-a	Generate .d files for **tcov** profiling.
-align *block.name*	Align Common *block.name* on page boundaries.
-ansi	Identify non-ANSI extensions.
-c	Compile only, do not link, make .o file.
-C	Check that array bounds are not exceeded.
-dalign	Use double load/store instructions for speed.
-e	Extended source lines ($\leq$ 132 characters).
-f	Align data & Commons on 8-byte boundaries.
-f*processor*	Invoke floating point accelerator.
-F	Preprocess .F files to .f files.
-g	Create global symbol table for debugger.
-help	Display list of options.
-i2	2 byte integer & logicals.
-i4	4 byte integer & logicals (default).
-I*path*	Also search *path* for include files.
-l*lib*	Link with object library *lib*.
-L*dir*	Also search *dir* for library routines.
-N*suboptions*	Fix for **f77** table overflows.
-o *prog*	Name output file *prog*.
-onetrip	Perform Do loops at least once if reached.
-O*(1,2,3)*	Optimize; 1: peephole, 2: partial, 3: global.
-p	Setup for profiling with **prof**.
-pg	Setup for profiling with **gprof**.

-pic	Produce position independent code.
-pipe	Use pipes & CPU, not files, during compilation.
-S	Create only . s (assembly language) file.
-time	Report execution times during compilation.
-u	Make default variables type UNDEFINED.
-U	Do not convert uppercase letters to lower case.
-v	Verbose listing of compiler's progress.
-w[66]	Suppress warning messages; -w66 for f66.

Sun Q Options

Q OPTIONS

-Qoption *prog opt*	Pass *opt* to program *prog* = **as, cc, cg, cpp, f77pass1, iropt, inline, ld, optim.**
-Qpath *pathname*	Search directory *pathname* for alternate program versions.
-Qproduce *sourcetype*	Produce *sourcetype* = .o, .s code.

9.3   DEC Fortran Compiler

The command **f77** invokes the DEC Fortran 77 compiler which produces object code in the *RISC ULTRIX* extended *coff* format. In addition to the Unix standard . f file, the input source files may have . for or . FOR suffixes. Object files are produced with the standard . o suffix but are deleted if an executable is formed. Those source codes containing suffixes . F, . r, or . e are preprocessed respectively by **cpp, ratfor,** or **efl.** Intermediate . i files are compiled with no further preprocessing. For example:

```
%   f77 -o obj a.f b.f        Compile a.f, b.f, executable in obj.
%   f77 -c -O1 a.f b.f        Compile a.f, b.f, create .o files.
%   f77 -c -o obj -O3 a.f b.f Compile subs, object in obj.
```

If the environment variable DECFORT is set, its value is used as the name of the compiler to invoke. If the environment variable TMPDIR is set, its value is used as the directory for temporary files.

Loading DEC Libraries

The standard library /usr/lib/libc.a is loaded with the *-lc* loader option and not a full path name. The wrong library can be loaded if there are files with the name libc.a in the directories specified with the *-L* loader option or in the default directories searched by the loader.

DEC Fortran Options

f77 OPTIONS

-1	Perform DO loops at least once if reached.
-66	Allow FORTRAN-66 extensions (same as **-nof77**).
-automatic	Local variables on run-time stack, default: **-static**.
-bestGnum	Provide data needed for **-Gnum** option.
-C	Run-time check of array and string bounds.
-c	Compile only, do not link, make .o files.
-check_bounds	Same as **-C**.
-col72	Treat source lines as ending in column 72.
-cord	Run **cord** after linking, reduces cache conflicts.
-cpp	Run **cpp** before compiling.
-d_lines	Compile lines with D in column 1, else comments.
-extend_source	Treat source lines as ending in column 132.
-F	Preprocess with **efl** or **ratfor**, result in .f files.
-fpe0, -fpe	Terminates if floating point overflow, invalid data.
-fpe1	Continue execution if floating point overflow.
-fpe2	Continue and warn if floating-point overflow.
-fpe3	Continue and warn (if check underflow) if overflow.
-fpe4	Continue, warn, and count floating point overflows.
-G *num*	Max *num* bytes of Common accessed.
-g0	No global debugging information in the object file.
-g1	Global debugging information, default.
-g2, -g	Global debugging information, set **-O0**.
-g3	Global debugging information for optimized code.
-I	No **cpp** search for #include files in /usr/include.
-I*dir*	Directs **cpp** to search for #include files in directories.
-i2	2B default integer and logical variables.
-i4	4B default integer and logical variables (default).
-K	Leave intermediate files.
-L	No search standard directories for libraries.
-L*dir*	Search *dir* for libraries before standard directories.
-l*string*	Search *string* libraries for **ld**.
-nocpp	Do not run **cpp** before compiling.
-noextend_source	Treat source lines as ending in column 72 (default).
-nof77	Allow Fortran 66 extensions.
-noi4	2 byte integer & logicals (same as **-i2**).
-O0	Disable optimization, no unassigned variable check.
-O*(1,2,3)*	Optimize; *1*: local, *2*: global, *3*: additional global.
-O4, -O	Inline expansion of small procedures (default).
-o *prog*	Name output file **prog**, a.out unaffected.
-onetrip, -1	Perform Do loop at least once if reached.
-P	Setup for **-cpp** option.
-p0	Disable profiling (default).
-p1, -p	Setup for profiling with **prof**.
-pg	Setup for profiling with **gprof**.

-R	Use for `ratfor` options.
-r8	8B floating point constants.
-static	Statically allocate local variables (default).
-std	Warnings for nonstandard language.
-U	Do not convert uppercase letters to lowercase.
-U*name*	Removes initial definition of *name*.
-u	Make default variable type UNDEFINED.
-V	Verbose listing of compiler's progress.
-v	List compiler passes.
-vms	Make system behave like VAX Fortran.
-w	Suppress warning messages.
-w1	Suppress warnings about unused variables.

DEC Keyword Options

The keyword options are specified as **-name keyword** where keyword may be abbreviated.

f77 KEYWORD OPTIONS

-align commons	Align commons on 2- and 4-byte boundaries.
-align norecords	Align records on the next available byte.
-assume noaccuracy-sensitive	Reorder for improved performance.
-assume backslash	Treat backslash literally in character.
-assume dummy-aliases	Assume dummy arguments share locations.
-assume recursive	Permit recursive Functions & Subroutines.
-check bounds	Run time check of subscript and substring bounds.
-check overflow	Trap on integer overflow as well as floating point.
-check underflow	Warning for floating-point underflows.
-show code	Machine language listing if -v also invoked.
-show include	Show text from INCLUDE in listing if -v also invoked.
-show xref	Show cross-reference map if -v also invoked.
-stand semantics	Warnings of non-ANSI usage.
-stand source_form	Warnings of tab formatting, lowercase characters.
-stand syntax	Warnings of non-ANSI syntax extensions.
-warn noalignments	Warnings for non-naturally aligned data.
-warn declarations	Warnings for undeclared symbols (same as -u).
-warn nogeneral	Suppress warning level messages (same as -w).
-warn nounused	Suppress unused variable warnings (same as -w1).

9.4   IBM XL Fortran Compiler, xlf

The IBM *XL Fortran* and *XL C language* compilers run under AIX and are optimized for the IBM RS 6000 (XL stands for Exceptional Family—which tells you something about previous compilers). These compilers produce highly optimized code and descriptive diagnostics, accept the XL precompilers, and interface well with the powerful **dbx** debugger. If you write standard Unix **f77**, you should have little trouble with **xlf**—although handling its default, extended precision may give slightly more precise results than expected. If you are using *makefile* (see Chapter 10, *Unix Tools*) with the **f77** command, you need only add a line, F77 = xlf, near the top of the makefile and replace all occurrences of **f77** with **${F77}**. The rest of the makefile should then keep on working.

The command **xlf** or **f77** is used to compile Fortran source code (.f files), process assembler source code (.s files), and link object files (.o files) (see Figure 8.1). As before, this Fortran command automatically calls the linkage editor to produce an executable object file, unless the -c option is invoked. Some standard calls are:

%	xlf	Call for help, try it.
%	xlf -qsource -qattr=full \	
%	-qxref=full sub.f	Full listing.
%	xlf -O -c -v sub.f	Optimize & compile sub.f verbose.
%	xlf -Ocv sub.f	Same as above.
%	xlf -O -o prog main.o sub.o	Assemble executable prog.
%	xlf -O -o prog prog.f	Produce executable prog from entire program prog.f.

You will notice here that the -o option always takes an argument and that the commands— but not the options—are case insensitive (*unless* you give the -k option).

xlf Options

There are two classes of options available with **xlf** (three if you include placing them in the source code file with directives). The first is the usual *flag* options specified as —*option(s)*. The second is the *q options* which override the initial compiler settings.

xlf FLAG OPTIONS

-#	Give compiler progress data, invoke nothing.
-1	Execute DO loops at least once (if reached).
-B*pre*	Make *pre* prefix to program names.
-c	Compile only; do not call the linkage editor **ld**.
-C	Run-time check of array and string bounds.
-D	Compile lines with D in column 1, else comments.
-g	Generate global symbol table for debugging.
-I*dir*	Search directory *dir* for INCLUDE.
-k	Accept free-form Fortran code (mixed case).
-l*key*	Search library file *libkey.a* for subprograms.

-L*dir*	Search in directory *dir* for *-lkey* files.
-N	Give help for -N*x num* option.
-N*x num*	Specify internal table size *num*, x = B, C, D, N, P, A, Q, T, or S.
-o *prog*	Name executable *prog* (not a.out).
-O	Optimize code (takes levels).
-p	Generate simple profiling support code.
-pg	Generate extensive profiling support code.
-Q	Include ("inline") appropriate subprograms.
-Q*x*	Include specified subprograms, +*sub* include, -*sub* exclude, ! none.
-t*x*	Apply -B option prefix to the *x*, x= c: compiler, a: assembler, l: linker.
-u	Use undefined IMPLICIT data typing.
-U	Case-sensitive Fortran code.
-v	Verbose information on the compiler's progress.
-w	Suppress low level warning messages.

xlf q Options

xlf q OPTIONS	
attr	Produce attribute listing of referenced names.
dbcs	*DBCS* characters permitted.
dpc	Promote constants to double precision.
extchk	Check interface and mismatched Commons.
extname	Underscore suffix to external names.
fips	Full ANSI Fortran 77 flagging.
list	Listing of object file.
listopt	List options.
noi4	Give `integer`, `logical`'s 2B length.
nofold	No compile-time evaluation of constant and floating point expressions.
nomaf	No multiply-add instructions.
noprint	No listing.
noobj	No object file.
phsinfo	Phase information on screen.
recur	Allow recursive subprograms.
rndsngl	IEEE single-precision standards.
rrm	Run-time rounding mode.
saa	SAA Fortran flagging.
source	Source listing.
stat	Timing and size statistics in listing.
xref	Cross-reference listing (for debugging).

The **xlf** q options are specified as *-qoption* where *option* is an on/off switch such that, if **x** is the option, **-qx** turns the option on and **-qnox** turns the option off. For example:

```
%   xlf -qsource -qcharlen=1000 sub.f    2 q options & compile sub.f.
%   xlf sub.f -qnosource -qstat          2 other q options & compile sub.f.
```

Here **-qsource** tells the compiler to produce a source listing, and **-qnosource** tells the compiler not to produce a source listing.

The preceding q options override the initial compiler settings.

xlf -q Options' Suboptions

The q option can also have a suboption value, or in fact several suboptions of the form:

-qoption=suboption1:suboption2: ... :suboptionN

The suboptions include:

xlf SUBOPTIONS

attr = full	List all attributes, referenced or not.
charlen = *num*	Maximum length for character data.
ci = *num1*	ID numbers of conditional includes.
flag = *sev1:sev2*	Severity level of diagnostics reported, *sev1* in listing, *sev2* at terminal.
halt = *sev*	Stop if error $\geq$ severity *sev* .
xref = full	Full cross-reference listing (helps debugging).

9.5   HP Fortran 77, f77, fc, and fort77

The Fortran compiler on the HP-UX Unix system is called **f77** or **fc**. (Since **fc** conflicts with the K shell's **fc** command, **f77** is preferred.) The other compiler under HP-UX, **fort77**, is a POSIX-compliant interface to the **f77** compiler.

The options below are passed to the compiler on the command line or through the FCOPTS environment variable.

HP f77 OPTIONS

-A*exceptions* **(-a)**	Errors for non-ANSI feature.
-a	Warnings for non-ANSI features.
+A	Align data on 2B, not 4B, boundaries.
+apollo	Apollo domain compatible defaults.
-c	Compile only (no link), produce .o file.

-C	Check for range.
-D	Lines with D in col.1 are source, else comments.
+DA*architecture*	Generate code for specified architecture.
+DS*architecture*	Schedule for specified architecture.
+e	Enable non-HP code compatibility.
+E*secondary*	Enable specific non-HP compatibility.
-g	Global symbol table for debugging.
-G	Set up for profiling with **gprof**.
-I2	2B integers and logicals.
-I4	4B integers and logicals (default).
-I*dir*	Search *dir* too for $INCLUDE files.
-K	Retain subprogram's variables (static memory).
-l*name*	Search /lib/*lname*.a & /lib/*lname*.sl, then /usr/lib/*lname*.a & /usr/lib/*lname*.sl.
-L	Program listing to the standard output.
-L*dir*	Search *dir* first for libraries.
+N*tableN*	Set compiler's table sizes.
-o *obj*	Name object file *obj*, not a.out.
-onetrip	Execute DO loops at least once.
+O*optlevel*	Optimize at *optlevel* = 1, 2, 3.
-p	Set up object files for profiling with **prof**.
+Q*dfile*	Read *dfile* for compiler directives.
-R4	4B floating point constants (default).
-R8	8B Floating point constants.
+R	Cross-reference map and symbol table.
+T	Trace back for run-time errors.
-u	Undeclared implicits ($\equiv$ IMPLICIT NONE).
-U	Uppercase for external names (default, lower).
-v	Verbose compilation report.
-V	List source in .l file.
-w	Suppress warning messages.
-Y	8- & 16-bit native language support strings.
+U	Case sensitive, except for keywords.
+z	Short displacement, position independent code.
+Z	Long displacement, position independent code.

The HP f77 compiler also has W (or +Q) options:

f77 W OPTIONS

-W*c,arg1–argN*	Pass *arg1–argN* to subprocess c, c = r: ratfor, a: assembler, l: linker.
-W d, -Q, *dfile,* **-s**	Send options -Q *dfile* & -s through compiler.
+Q *dfile* **+s**	Send options -Q *dfile* & -s through compiler.

9.6   C Language

Essentially all of what we have said about using the Fortran compiler with Unix also applies to the C compiler (you do have to use `cc` in place of `f77` and `sub.c` in place of `sub.f`, but that is just logical). For example, the command:

```
%   cc prog.c sub.o -o prog
```

compiles the file `prog.c` containing C source code, creates a file `prog.o` containing an object code, and then automatically invokes the linkage editor `ld` to link `prog.o` and `sub.o` with all the C startup and library routines. The resulting executable program is placed in the file `prog`.

Further options can be given with a "-," or concatenated with earlier **-options**. Options can also be included in the source code—in which case they apply to individual subprograms or even just sections of individual subprograms:

```
/* code fragment of option in source */
#pragma options langlvl=saa halt=s source
```

The `cc` command also accepts further files as arguments, such as object programs produced by earlier `cc` or `f77` runs or entire libraries. The object files, together with the results of compilations, are linked (in the order given) to produce an executable program. By default the executable is `a.out`, although as indicated above, this can be altered with the -o option:

`%   cc  -O -c -v sub.c`	Optimize, compile `sub.c` verbosely.
`%   cc   -Ocv sub.c`	Same as above.
`%   cc   -O -o prog main.o sub.o`	Assemble executable `prog`.
`%   cc   -O -o prog prog.c`	Produce executable `prog` from complete C program `prog.c`.

Since the default returned value from a C program is random, if you want to return a specific value, you must either `call exit` (or `call atexit`) to terminate the process or leave the `function main()` with a `return expression;` construct.

Including libraries with `cc` is order sensitive. It is usually done with the `-lname` option which causes the linker to search the library `lib.names1` or `libname.a`. Since a library is searched when its name is encountered, if a file contains an unresolved external reference, the library containing the definition must be placed after the file on the command line. Details are found with the **man** pages for `ld`. To get more information on line, try:

`%   cc`	Without options for help.
`%   cc -help`	Ask Sun C for help with options.

Below we give a description of the `cc` options available with Sun, HP, DEC, and IBM C compilers. Although this seems repetitious since major options like -o and -c are the same for both `f77` and `cc` and for all manufacturers, there are differences in the other options (the same letter sometimes has different meanings to different compilers).

9.7 Sun C Compiler cc

The Sun's C language compiler is invoked with the `cc` command. When debugging or profiling, object programs are compiled using the `-g` or `-pg` option respectively, and the same options should be used when these objects are linked with the `ld` command.

SUN cc OPTIONS

-a	Produce `.d` files for profiling with `tcov`.
-align _block	Page-align global uninitialized data.
-Bbinding	Static/dynamic (nonshared/shared) lib binding.
-c	Compile only, do not link, makes `sub.o`.
-C	Tell C preprocessor `cpp` to retain comments.
-Dname	Define symbol *name* to `cpp` ($\equiv$ `#define` directive).
-E	Run source through C preprocessor `cpp`.
-fprocessor	Use specific floating point accelerator.
-g	Global symbol table for debugging.
-go	Additional symbol table information for `adb`.
-help	Display list of options.
-Ipath	Also search *path* for include files.
-llib	Link with object library *lib*.
-Ldir	Also search *dir* for library routines.
-M	Macro preprocess for `makefile` dependencies.
-o out	Name output file `out`.
-O1,2,3,4	Optimize; *1* peephole, *2* partial, *3* global.
-p	Setup for profiling with `prof`.
-P	Preprocess with `cpp` only.
-pg	Set up for profiling with `gprof`.
-pic	Produce position independent code.
-pipe	Use pipes & CPU, not files, during compilation.
-R	Merge data & text segments for `as`.
-S	Create only `.s` (assembly language) file.
target_arch	Compile for processor architecture.
-temp=dir	Use *dir* as temporary file directory.
-time	Report compilation times.
-Uname	Remove *name*'s definition in `cpp`.
-w	Suppress warning messages.

Sun cc Q OPTIONS

-Qoption *prog opt*	Pass *opt* to program *prog* = `as`, `cc`, `cg`, `cpp`, `f77pass1`, `iropt`, `inline`, `ld`, `optim`.
-Qpath *path*	Search directory *path* for alternate program versions.
-Qproduce *type*	Produce *type* = `.o`, `.s` code.

9.8   HP C Compiler cc, c89

The C language compiler on the HP-UX Unix system is called **cc** or **c89**, the latter being the POSIX-compliant version. The options are passed to the compiler on the command line or through the CCOPTS environment variable. (Being a commercial product, the options **-A, -G, -g, -O, -p, -v, -y, +z, +Z** are sold as optional equipment.)

HP cc OPTIONS

-A_mode_	Compilation standard to be used;
	c- Kernighan,Ritchie, a- ANSI X3.159-1989.
-c	Compile only (no link), produce .o file.
-C	Inform **cpp** to leave C-style comments.
-D_name_	Define _name_ to **cpp**, as if by #define.
-E	Run only preprocessor **cpp**.
-g	Global symbol table for debugging.
-G	Setup for profiling with **gprof**.
-I_dir_	Search _dir_ also for $INCLUDE files.
-l_name_	Search /lib/_name_.a, /lib/_name_.sl,
	/usr/lib/_name_.a, /usr/lib/_name_.sl.
-L_dir_	Search _dir_ first for libraries.
-n	Mark output file from linker "shareable."
-N	Mark output file from linker "unshareable."
-o _obj_	Name object file _obj_, not a.out.
-O	Optimize at level 2 (≡ +O2).
-p	Setup object files for profiling with **prof**.
-P	Run **cpp**, output in sub.i.
-q	Mark output from linker "demand loadable."
-Q	Mark output from linker "not demand loadable."
-s	Strip symbol table information from linker output.
-S	Compile sub.c, leave assembly sub.s.
-t_x,name_	Substitute subprocess _x_ with _name_.
-U_name_	Remove initial _name_ definition in **cpp**.
-v	Verbose compilation report.
-w	Suppress warning messages.
-W_c, arg1–argN_	Pass _arg1-argN_ to subprocess c.
-y	Setup for static analysis.
-Y	8 & 16b native language support strings.
-z	No address 0 binding, null pointer detection.
-Z	Allow referencing of null pointers.
+z	Short displacement, position independent code.
+Z	Long displacement, position independent code.

HP cc Ambiguities

HP-UX makes specific choices on handling some of the intentional ambiguities in Kernighan and Ritchie's (1978) _The C Programming Language_. The ambiguities include:

cc AMBIGUITIES

char	`Char` type treated as signed by default.
pointers	Accessing NULL pointer object (-z option).
identifiers	≤ 255 significant identifier characters.
types	int $\geq$ short, long $\geq$ int, int/ long can hold pointer.

These choices can be modified with the compatibility mode (**-Ac**) options.

9.9 DEC C Compiler

The **cc** command invokes ULTRIX's RISC C compiler including the C preprocessor. It produces object code in RISC extended coff format (the default), binary or symbolic ucode, or binary or symbolic assembly language. You can get more information with the **man** command for **cc, dbx, ld, pixie, prof, what,** and **monitor.** The production of object files and executables follows the standard forms, except for some of the optimization. For example:

`%  cc -c sub.c`	Compile C source to object `sub.o`.
`%  cc prog.c`	Compile C source to executable `a.out`.
`%  cc -c sub.s`	Compile assembly source to object `sub.o`.
`%  cc -c sub.i`	Compile preprocessed C subroutine.
`%  cc -c -O3 sub.c`	Compile C source to ucode `sub.u`.
`%  cc -c -j sub.c`	Compile C source to ucode `sub.u`.

A nice feature of DEC's compiler is its production of default symbols which are useful when porting code to other systems. These symbols include:

cc DEFAULT SYMBOLS

unix	Any UNIX system.
bsd4_2	Berkeley 4.2 Unix.
ultrix	ULTRIX only.
mips	Any RISC architecture.
MIPSEL	Little endian variant of MIPS architecture.
host_mips	Native compilation environment.

As also occurred with the Fortran compiler, the standard library /usr/lib/libc.a is loaded by using the **-lc** loader option and not a full path name. Accordingly, the wrong library may be loaded if there are files with the name libc.astring in the directories specified with the **-L** loader option or in the default directories searched by the loader.

DEC C Libraries

If the environment variable COMP_HOST_ROOT is set, its value, rather than the default slash (/), is used as the root directory for all pass names. If the environment variable COMP_TARGET_ROOT is set, its value, rather than the default slash /, is used as the root directory for all include and library names. This affects the standard directory for #include files, /usr/include, and the standard library, /usr/lib/libc.a.

DEC cc OPTIONS

-c	Compile only, do not link, make .o files.
-cord	Run cord to reduce cache conflicts.
-cpp	Run cpp before compiling, default.
-nocpp	Do not run cpp before compiling.
-E	Run only C macro preprocessor, set -cpp.
-f	No promote expressions of type float to type double.
-feedback file	Used with -cord for prof file.
-g0	No global debugging information in object file.
-g1	Global debugging, limited if optimized, default.
-g2, -g	Global debugging information, set -oo.
-G *num*	Max *num* bytes accessed from global pointer.
-g3	Global debugging information for optimized code.
-I*dir*	cpp searches for #include files in *directory*.
-I	No cpp search for #include files in /usr/include.
-j	Compile and leave ucode object in .u file.
-ko *prog*	Name ucode loader's output *prog*.
-k	Pass options starting with -k to ucode loader.
-L*dir*	Search only *dir* for libx.a and libx.b.
-o *prog*	Name output file prog, a.out unaffected.
-O0	Disable optimization.
-O1, 2, 3	Optimize; *1* local, *2* global, *3* additional.
-O*limit num*	Max opt routine size, default 1500 blocks.
-P	Setup for -cpp option.
-p0	Disable profiling (default).
-p1, -p	Setup for profiling with prof.
-pg	Setup for profiling with gprof.
-signed	All char declarations = signed char, default.
-unsigned	All char declarations = unsigned char.
-std	Warn of nonstandard language.
-S	Symbolic assembly language in .s file.
-U*name*	Remove initial definition of name.
-v	List compiler passes.
-volatile	All variables treated as volatile.
-varargs	Warnings for varargs.h macros.
-w	Suppress warning messages.
-V	List version of driver, passes.
-Y*environment*	Compile C programs for *environment*.

9.10   IBM C Compiler cc, xlc

The *XL C* and *XL Fortran* Unix compilers are optimized for the IBM RS 6000. These compilers produce highly optimized code and descriptive diagnostics, accept the XL precompilers, and interface with the powerful **dbx** debugger. They are, accordingly, an improvement over the past. The **xlc, cc, c89** commands are used to compile XL C source code (.c files), process assembler source code (.s files) and object files (.o files). The different commands are the same except for the default language level (the langlv option). With **cc** this is extended, while with **xlc,c89** it is ANSI. The ANSI is most portable. As before, **cc, xlc,** and **c89** automatically call the linkage editor to produce a single executable object file unless the −*c* option is invoked. Some typical commands are:

% **xlc**	Call for help, try it.
% **xlc -O -c -v sub.c**	Optimize, compile sub.c verbose.
% **xlc -lm prog.c**	Compile prog, link math libe math.h.
% **cc -Ocv sub.c**	Same as above.
% **c89 -Ocv sub.c**	Same as above.

IBM C Options

There are two types of options available when invoking the XL C language (three if you include placing them in the source code file with directives). The first is the usual flag options specified as −*option(s)*. The second is q options which are used to override the initial compiler settings.

xlc FLAG OPTIONS

-#	Display data on compiler's progress.
-B*prefix*	Make *prefix* prefix to program names.
-c	Compile only; do not call the linkage editor **ld**.
-C	Write comments in **cpp**'s output.
-D*name*	Define *name* (≡ #define), default 1.
-E	Preprocess but do not compile.
-F*x*[:*stanza*]	Alternate configuration file *x, stanza*.
-g	Produce debugging information.
-I*dir*	Search directory *dir* for INCLUDE.
-l*key*	Search library lib*key*.a for subprograms.
-L*dir*	Search directory *dir* for -l*key*.
-o *prog*	Name executable *prog* (not a.out).
-O	Optimize code.
-p	Generate simple profiling support code.
-pg	Generate extensive profiling support code.
-P	Preprocess, no compile, output to .i file.
-Q	Include (inline) appropriate subprograms.
-t*x*	Apply -B option prefix to the *x*,
	x= **c** compiler, **a** assembler, **l** linker.
-U*name*	Undefined *name* (≡ #undef directive).
-v	Verbose compiler progress information.
-w	Suppress low-level warning messages.
-y*x*	Compile-time rounding of constants.

xlc q Options

Other options are specified as -q*option* where *option* is an on/off switch such that if x is the option, -q*x* turns the option on and -q*nox* turns the option off. For example:

```
%  xlc -qsource -qcharlen=1000 sub.c    Two q options + compile.
%  xlc sub.c -qnosource -qstat          1 on + 1 off q option + compile.
```

Here -qsource produces a source listing while -qnosource produces none. These q options override initial compiler settings:

xlc q OPTIONS

attr	Attribute listing of referenced names.
dbcs	*DBCS* characters permitted.
extchk	Check external name types and function calls.
list	Listing of object file.
listopt	List options.
nofold	No compile-time evaluation of constant, floating point expressions.
nomaf	No multiply-add instructions.
noprint	No listing.
noro	No read-only string literals.
phsinfo	Phase information on screen.
rndsngl	IEEE single-precision standards.
rrm	Run-time rounding mode.
source	Source listing.
stat	Timing and size statistics in listing.
xref	Cross-reference list (for debugging).

The q option can also have a suboption value, or in fact several suboptions, of the form:

-q*option=suboption1:suboption2: ... : suboptionN*

xlc q SUBOPTIONS

attr = full	List all attributes, referenced or not.
chars = signed	Sign `char` data.
flag = *sev1:sev2*	Severity level of diagnostics reported, *sev1* in listing, *sev2* at terminal.
halt = *sev*	Stop if error $\geq$ severity *sev*.
langlvl = *langlvl*	Compilation language level *langlvl*= `ansi`, `saa2`, `saa`, or `extended`.
pgmsize = *p*	Large (l) or small (s) table size for compiler.
spill = *size*	Size of register allocation spill area.
xref = full	Full cross-reference list (helps debugging).

UNIX TOOLS AND TIPS

In Chapter 2, *Getting Friendly with Unix*, we provided our eclectic minimanual of essential Unix tools. Those are the basic survival skills needed to navigate through file systems and manipulate files. We assume you have mastered those skills and are ready now for some more powerful ones. While you may not have found Unix friendly in your Chapter 2 encounters, we believe after experiencing some of the powerful and useful features of Unix in this chapter, you really will begin to like Unix. Again, we will not try to be exhaustive but instead to concentrate on those features we have found valuable in our scientific work. To learn about further features or about more options than those we illustrate, we recommend the **man** pages. More complex commands like **awk** may require you to read a detailed description in one of the Unix books listed in the *References*.

10.1 Unix Toolkit

The Unix operating system introduced the idea of a *toolkit*. That is, rather than having a few generalized and complex utilities programs, the system contains a toolkit of small and simple programs which the user combines to perform sophisticated tasks and to create custom programs. For example, suppose we want to count how many users with group id 20 are listed in the /etc/passwd file. The fourth field in the /etc/passwd file is the group id:

```
larke:WsvQ64KOjG94w:350:20:Ed Larke:/u/larke:/bin/ksh
```

To count the number of lines which have 20 in the fourth column, we use **cut** to grab the fourth column, **egrep** to extract those lines with 20, and then **wc** to count the number of words. While we will explain some of these basic Unix utilities later, the point here is that a single command line is all we need to complete the task:

```
%  cut -f4 -d':'  /etc/passwd |egrep 20 |wc -1
   54                              Output from command.
%                                  Prompt, i.e. done.
```

Because Unix treats files, commands, and devices all pretty much as files, and since most of these tools will take their input either from files or from other commands (or standard input if no file name is given), this juxtaposition of tools is general and powerful.

Translate Characters: tr

The **tr** command translates one group of characters into another set. This is often used to change uppercase to lowercase or vice versa. The command does not accept a file name so its input must be through the standard input. For example, to convert the capital characters 'A' through 'Z' in file upper.f into 'a' through 'z' in file lower.f:

```
%   tr '[A-Z]' '[a-z]' < upper.f > lower.f
%   tr -s " " " " < paper.tex          Remove multiple blank spaces.
```

In the second command we used the **-s** option to squeeze multiple occurrences of a character (in this case blanks) into a single occurrence of that character.

Smart File Splitters: split, csplit, fsplit

When transferring, moving, or searching through a large number of Fortran or C subroutines, it is often easier to copy all the subroutines into one file and then work with just the one large file rather than many small ones. For example, to copy all files with .f or .c suffixes into the one file all, first create all (perhaps with **cat**) and then concatenate all subroutines into all:

```
%   cat *.f >> all               Add all .f files to end of all.
%                                Unix returns prompt when done.
```

If you want to compile all, which for Fortran requires a file ending with .f and for the C language requires a file ending with .c, you now move all to all.f or all.c:

```
%   mv  all  all.f               Renames all to all.f for compiler.
%   mv  all  all.c               Renames all to all.c for compiler.
```

Note, if you had first created all.f and then tried

```
%   cat  *.f  >>  all.f          Copy all .f files to end of all.f,
```

Unix would say you were naughty by trying to copy a file onto itself.

When you are done working with all.f or all.c, it is **split** back into individual subprograms with the **split** commands:

```
%   fsplit  all.f                Break all.f into individual subs.
%   csplit  all.c                Break all.c into individual subs.
```

After splitting (but before *you* and the computer split) it's a good idea to remove the big file:

```
%  rm all.f (all.c)                        Conserve disk space.
```

By having some @PROCESS or similar compiler directive statements preceding your sub-routine declarations may keep **fsplit** or **csplit** from knowing where that subroutine begins. The **spilt** command is a general utility that will break up any text file into small parts. It is useful for splitting files into small pieces for mailing.

Sort

sort will order a file or standard input. You can choose which field to sort and can **sort** either alphabetically or numerically.

SORT OPTIONS

+*i*	Skip *i* fields, sort on the *i+1* field.
-*i*	Stop sorting after the *i* field.
-t'*c***'**	Use *c* as the character which separates fields.
-b	Ignore blanks.
-n	Sort by numerical value.
-r	Reverse the order of the sort.
-u	Remove any duplicate lines.
-f	Merge upper and lowercase.
-d	Dictionary order.

You can sort by number or name. To find the largest files, sort the output of **ls -s**:

```
%  sort +3 -t':'  -n /etc/passwd        Numerical sort on 4th field.
%  sort /etc/passwd                     Alphabetical sort.
%  ls -s | sort -n                      Numerical sort for large files.
```

Word Count: wc

The **wc** command counts the number of lines, words, characters, or bytes. With no options, it prints out all three counts and the file name:

wc OPTIONS

-l	Count lines.
-w	Count words.
-c	Count bytes or characters.

For example, we can obtain statistics on several Fortran files:

```
%  wc cswap.f dogleg.f enorm.f fdjac1.f
    78   329   2285   cswap.f            Lines, words, characters, file name.
   195   866   5667   dogleg.f
   127   493   3542   enorm.f
   168   795   5320   fdjac1.f
```

Pattern Search: grep, fgrep, egrep

The **grep** command is so widely used it has become a verb. To **grep** a file is to find lines in it which match a specified pattern. This simple function quickly becomes indispensable once you learn how to use it. Yet in its attempting to be overly friendly (some may say to confuse the casual user), Unix systems provide three different versions of **grep**: the original **grep**, fast grep **fgrep**, and extended grep **egrep**. Other than nostalgia, there seems little reason to use the original **grep**. Since **egrep** is generally as fast as **fgrep**, we simplify things by just using **egrep**. The entire **grep** family accepts either file names or standard input. For example, to search all Fortran files in the current directory for the word gauz:

```
% egrep gauz *.f                        Search all Fortran files for gauz.
bij.f:          common /gauz/ npts(3), kode(3)
readin.f:       common /gauz/ npts(3), kode(3)
udz1v.f:        common /gauz/ npts(3), kode(3)
vkabs.f:        common /gauz/ npts(3), kode(3)
```

Because **egrep** is case sensitive, "gauz" will not match "GAUZ." To make **egrep** ignore case, use the **-i** option (or **-y** on some systems):

```
% egrep -i bigmat *.f                   Search for bigmat, ignore case.
readin.f:       float BIGMAT[1000][1000])
readin.f:       ferd[i] = ferd[i] * BigMat[i][j]
```

It is also possible to use **egrep** to match one of several patterns and to use *wild cards* in the patterns:

```
% egrep "parallel|distributed" Mail/*   Search Mail for either
                                        parallel or distributed.
oldmail:  parallel processors.          A match for parallel.
oldmail:  distributed computing.        A match for distributed.
```

Next we use *regular expressions* and wild cards to search for patterns. First we search for all lines that start with "alpha":

```
% egrep '^alpha' data                   Search through file data.
alpha = 0.76353 sigma = 6.8336
alpha = 0.78453 sigma = 7.0835
alpha = 0.80463 sigma = 7.5638
```

Since only a single file is searched in this example, **egrep** does not bother printing the file name.

There is also a veto option **-v** to **egrep** which *excludes* lines containing the objectionable regular expression:

```
% egrep -v '^C' prog.f                  Print lines not starting with "C."
% egrep -v '^$' prog.f                  Print all except the blank lines.
```

Manipulate Columns: Cut, Paste

Cutting and *pasting* columns of text or numbers is very useful to the computational scientist, for example, in preparing data for input to a graphics program or in preparing a manuscript for publication.[1] The cut command extracts one or more columns using either a fixed charter count or a field in a file. We start in this example with the file data:

3.9737	8.93737	10.8833	9.6363	File data.
4.0567	9.26556	11.3576	9.7935	
4.6345	9.73457	10.8833	9.8963	

Let's say you want to extract the first and third columns for plotting. Since the lines all have the same number of characters for each column, we could tell cut to "grep" the first through the sixth characters in order to capture the first column, and then to grab the sixteenth through the twentieth characters to capture the second column. We grab the seventh character as well in order to get the blank which separates the columns:

```
$  cut -c1-7,16-22 data        Cut 2 columns from data.
3.9737 10.8833                  The output.
4.0567 11.3576
4.6345 10.8833
```

Note that the -c option specifies which characters to cut. We could also use the fact that a blank separates the columns to tell cut that it should grab the first and third columns. The -d option tells cut what character separates the fields and the -f option tells cut which fields to grab. The -f and -c options cannot be mixed:

```
$  cut -d' ' -f1,3 data         Cut first and third fields.
3.9737 10.8833                  Same results as above.
4.0567 11.3576
4.6345 10.8833
```

This example would also work if the columns were separated by tabs. The only change would be to give the option -t'[tab]'.

Problems may arise with the -d or -f options if the file is not uniformly formatted, for example, if the number of spaces between fields or the number of digits in each number varies. To remove multiple spaces, use the tr command, as shown above, and connect to the cut command via a pipe:

```
$  tr -s " " < data |cut -d" " -f1,3    Squeeze out blanks, then cut.
3.9737 10.8833
4.0567 11.3576
4.6345 10.8833
```

---

[1]These commands are from System V and may not be available on BSD-based systems. In that case use the Emacs editor.

The **paste** command combines columns from separate files into a single file. We can start with two data files and combine them so the columns are side by side:

data1 file	data2 file
7.81737	10.93737
8.24556	11.73567
9.17457	12.52343

```
$   paste data1 data2 > data3          Combine files into data3.
$   cat data3                          List data3.
8.93737 10.93737
8.24556 11.73567
9.17457 12.52343
```

Compare Files: diff, cmp

Often we need to know the differences between files. For text files we get the differences with **diff** and for binary files we use **cmp**. If no output is given, then the files are the same:

```
%   diff prog.f prog2.f              Compare two Fortran programs.
%                                    No output, identical files.
%   diff pert2.f pert3.f             Another example.
4c4                                  Line 4 in pert2.f, line 4 in pert3.f.
<   PROGRAM PERT2 ...                Lines in file 1.
>   PROGRAM PERT3 ...                Lines in file 2
```

If you are tired of no one giving you a yes–no answer anymore, then the **cmp** command is for you (particularly since you do *not* want to read or print binary files). As an example, we ask the shell if the program pert in rubin's directory is the same as the one in the present directory:

```
%   cmp /u/rubin/pert pert            Compare binary, executable, files.
/u/rubin/pert pert differ:   char 25 line1
```

Unix's File Editor: sed

The editors *Emacs* and *vi* are used to make changes in files interactively. Yet sometimes you want to make particular changes in many files or repeat the same editing again in the future, or to do editing from the command line of Unix and pipe the results to yet other commands. For these purposes, which are not as esoteric as they may appear at first, **sed** is indispensable. For example, suppose your files contain data of the form 1.12D+33, but your graphics program doesn't like the D for an exponent. Or suppose you want to convert your paper from *nroff* to LaTeX. Or perhaps you want to delete all lines containing the string copyright (c) by IBM from a group of files.[2] These operations of substitution and deletion make **sed** a must to learn (you'll have time in your jail cell).

The **sed** command, like **awk**, which we describe next, are used as a programming language to create **sed** scripts. These scripts are useful for complicated or repetitive debugging chores. Quite often, **sed** is used on the command line with simple options. These options are of some historical interest since they are based on **ed**, the old Unix line editor now mercifully extinct and forgotten. When used from the command line, only a subset of the full **sed** options is needed.

sed OPTIONS

-e s/*pat1***/***pat2***/**	Substitute *pat2* for one *pat1* per line.
-e s/*pat1***/***pat2***/g**	Substitute *pat2* for every *pat1* per line.
-e /*pat1***/d**	Delete lines with *pat1*.
-e y/*str1***/***str2***/**	Substitute characters in *str2* for those in *str1*.

In our first example we start with the data file graph.dat containing $x - y$ pairs:

4.05D-09 11.35D+03	File graph.dat
9.73D-09 9.89D+03	
10.8D-09 9.63D+03	

We must change the D to an e for our graphics program. Rather than do this by hand with an editor, we use **sed**, which is quicker and gives us a tool to edit future files:

```
%   sed -e "s/D/e/g" graph.dat  |  xplot   Edit and pass directly to xplot.
```

Notice that, if we had not added the **g** option for global changes, only the first D per line would have been changed:

```
%   sed -e "s/D/e/" graph.dat                  Leave off the g and use standard output.
4.05e-09 11.35D+03
9.73e-09  9.89D+03
10.8e-09  9.63D+03
```

In the next example we first delete all comments from a Fortran file, that is, all lines starting with a c or C, and then use the **y** option to translate all uppercase letters into lowercase (the same function as **tr** provides):

```
%   sed -e "/^[c,C]/d" prog.f >prog2.f   Strip comments and put into prog2.f.
%   sed -e \
    "y/abcdefghijklmnopqrstuvwxyz/ABCDEFGHIJKLMNOPQRSTUVWXYZ/" \
    prog.f > prog2.f
```

---

[2]This is a joke. We don't really advocate deleting copyright notices.

General Text Selection: awk

The **awk** command is another text selection and manipulation tool. Some call it the most popular Unix tool of its type, while others call it incomprehensible and **awk**ward. We have heard rumors that there are users who write 500-line **awk** scripts and still function in polite society, but we doubt it. Personally we use **awk** only in situations where we can't get other Unix tools like **sed** and **grep** to work. In its simplest form, **awk** selects a line from a file according to some pattern, like **grep**, but is much more general. We present here a few examples of **awk** but refer interested readers to the *References* for more information.

The form of an **awk** command is:

```
%   awd pattern {action}                        Generic awk.
```

One of the more useful tricks of **awk** is to be able to select all text between two patterns. For example, select all lines in an output file between the words Gaussian points and Gaussian weights, you use a command like this:

```
%   awk "/Gaussian points/,/Gaussian weights/" output.dat
```

To see more of the power of **awk**, here we print out each line in a file for which the previous line starts with zk(1):

```
%   awk ' prev =="zk(1),"{print} {prev=$1}' output.dat
```

In this last example, you will notice that every time a line is read, the first pattern on the line $1 is assigned to the variable prev. Then when the next line is read, the pattern prev =="zk(1)," is tested. If the pattern is true, then the action {print} is taken and the line is printed. You will also notice that the next action {prev=$1} does not have a pattern before it and therefore is always taken. The two **awk** pattern-action pairs are surrounded with single quotes to group them as a single option to **awk**.

10.2   Shell Programs (Scripts)

There used to be a time when being a system programmer bought some respect, even if the system programmer was kept in a glass room. Well, Unix has changed all that. Anyone can system program. In fact, shell programs (or *scripts, exec's, command files, run files*) are powerful and simple techniques which saves much time and aggravation.

A shell program or *shell script* is an ordinary text file containing commands which will eventually be read by the shell. The script is written for any of the Unix shells you have available, with most users using **sh** or **ksh** since these shells provide a simple and easy-to-use programming language. The Korn shell is a superset of the older Borne shell, so you may start by writing your scripts for the simpler Borne shell and incorporate Korn shell features as you need them. The C shell provides a very flexible programming syntax, but it is also rather cumbersome. We present the basics of programming in the Borne shell with some Korn shell enhancements.

Script Execution and Arguments

For our first try we created a shell script in the file try:

```#!/bin/sh` `echo "The number of arguments is $#"` `echo "They are $*"` `echo "The first is $1"` `echo "The number of arguments is $#"` `exit```	**sh** shell's file try.

You will want to try this and the following scripts out on your system. Because scripts are ordinary text files, you may use your favorite editor to create them or read them from the floppy. To start, notice that the first line is #!/bin/sh. This tells Unix to use the Borne or sh shell. This is interesting since any line beginning with a # is usually a comment, but the combination #! is special. It says that this file should be interpreted using the program that follows. In this case it is /bin/sh, although /bin/ksh is also possible. This must be the first line of the file, and in fact, #! must be the first two characters. Traditionally, shell scripts that don't start with #! are assumed to be Borne shell scripts, but since this convention is broken by some newer systems, it is always a good idea to declare what shell you want.

Some lines in the script have the form echo "$1". This command echoes, that is, prints on your screen, the first argument given to the script when it is executed. Similarly, $2 is the second argument, $3 the third, and so on. Two special variables are also useful. The variable $* stands for all the arguments, and the variable $# for the number of arguments.

After the file try has been created using the editor, we make it executable:

```
%   chmod +x try                        Make file try executable.
%   ls -l try                           Check for x rating.
-rwxr-xr-x   1 pfink  \
 usr      96 Nov 25 22:04 try
%   try red blue green                  Run the script in try.
The number of arguments is 3
They are red blue green
The first is red
```

Loop through Arguments: for

Sometimes we may want to loop through a list of files executing some commands on each file. The for loop is used for this purpose:

```for *variable* in *list*` `do` ` statement` `done```	Execute statement on each loop. Close the do with done.

If the *list* option is not given, the `for` condition loops over the arguments to the shell script. Now we run `bigmat` with file names as arguments to the shell command:

```#!/bin/sh```
```if [$# -ne 1]```
```then```
``` echo "This script needs at \```
``` least one argument."```
``` exit -1```
```fi```
```for file```
	Loop over the arguments.

```do```
``` echo "Running program \```
``` bigmat with input $file."```
``` bigmat < $file```
	Variable file contains the next argument.

```done``` ```exit```	

If-Then-Else

Shell scripts may contain simple `if-then-else` structures like Fortran or C:

```if [test]```
```then```
``` command```
```else```
	`Else` is optional.

``` command``` ```fi```	`if` always finishes with `fi`.

The *test* may deal with file characteristics or numerical/string comparisons. Although the left bracket here appears to be part of the structure, it is actually another name for the Unix **test** command (located in `/bin/[`). Since `[` is the name of a file, there must be spaces before and after it as well as before the closing bracket. To use the Korn shell's built-in **test** command, replace the single pair of square brackets with `[[ ]]` a pair of double brackets.

TEST OPTIONS, FILE TESTS

-s *file*	Test if *file* exists and is not empty.
-f *file*	Test if *file* is an ordinary file, not a directory.
-d *file*	Test if *file* is a directory.
-w *file*	Test if *file* has write permission.
-r *file*	Test if *file* has read permission.
-x *file*	Test if *file* is executable.
!	**Not** operation for **test**.

TEST OPTIONS, NUMERICAL COMPARISONS

$X -eq $ Y	Test if $X is equal to $Y.
$X -ne $ Y	Test if $X is not equal to $Y.
$X -gt $ Y	Test if $X is greater than $Y.
$X -lt $ Y	Test if $X is less than $Y.
$X -ge $ Y	Test if $X is greater than or equal to $Y.
$X -le $ Y	Test if $X is less than or equal to $Y.

TEST OPTIONS, STRING COMPARISONS

"$A" = "$B"	Test if string $A is equal to string $B.

TEST OPTIONS, NOT (!)

"$A" != "$B"	Test if string $A is not equal to string $B.
$X ! -gt $Y	Test if $X is not greater than $Y.

The next example is a script that takes one argument, a file name. If the file exists, it is used as the input for the user's program. If the number of arguments is incorrect or if the input file does not exist, the script prints out a message and exits:

```
#!/bin/sh
if [ $# -ne 1 ]
then
     echo "This script needs one argument."
     exit -1
fi
input="$1"
if [ !  -f "$input" ]
then
     echo "Input file does not exist."
     exit -1
else
     echo "Running program bigmat with input $input."
     bigmat < $input
fi
exit
```

Case

While we may use a series of *if–then–else* constructs to test a variable against several forms, it is much easier to use the case statement. This is done in the first script below. In the second script we use wild-card matches with the case statement. This takes one argument and matches it against several patterns in the case statement. If the pattern matches the argument, then the script prints out a statement:

`case $key in`	Match the variable `$key`.
`    `*pattern1*`)`	Test match to *pattern1*.
`        statement`	If `$key` matches *pattern1*, then execute `statement`.
`        ;;`	Each pattern ends with `;;`.
`    `*pattern2*`)`	Test match to *pattern2*.
`        statement`	If match, then execute `statement`.
`        ;;`	
`esac`	Close the `case` with `esac`.

`#!/bin/sh`	
`case $1 in`	Match the first argument.
`  in.date)`	
`    echo "Argument is in.date."`	
`    ;;`	
`  *.f)`	Matches anything that ends in `.f`.
`    echo "Argument is a Fortran \`	
`file name."`	
`    ;;`	
`  *.c)`	Matches anything that ends in `.c`.
`    echo "Argument is C file."`	
`    ;;`	
`  in|out)`	Use `|` for 'or'
`    echo "Argument is either the \`	
`word in or the word out."`	
`    ;;`	
`  *)`	This will match anything.
`    echo "Argument does not match \`	
`any the patterns."`	
`    ;;`	
`esac`	

Unix Commands inside Shell Scripts

Any Unix command or program may be executed from within a shell script by just issuing the command as you would on the command line. To "capture" or record the output of a command and assign it to a variable, the command is surrounded by forward quotes ` `` `. You have already encountered an example of this capture in the sample script for reading DOS floppies given in Chapter 4, *Computer–Computer Interactions*:

`#!/bin/sh`	Use Borne shell.
`dosfiles=`dosdir notes``	List DOS files on the floppy.
`for f in $dosfiles`	Repeat for each file name.
`do`	
`  dosread -a notes/$f $f`	Read from floppy's directory notes.
`done`	

Although this script will do the job, there are two problems with it. The first is that while the **dosdir** command does list all DOS file names, it also produces a line stating how much free space is available:

```
%  dosdir                          The AIX command.
CONFIG.SYS
CALL.EXE
There are 216064 bytes of free space.
```

Consequently, the script thinks this last line is part of the list of file names, but because the shell will be unable to locate any files with these names, it will complain to you. Accordingly, we filter out the last line by piping **dosdir**'s output through **egrep**. The second problem is that the DOS file names are all in uppercase letters, and we prefer lowercase name for Unix files. To solve that problem, we use the **tr** tool described in § 10.1, *Unix's Toolkit*, to convert the file names to lowercase.

The improved script looks like this:

`#!/bin/sh` `dosfiles=`dosdir notes| egrep -v \` ` "bytes of free space"`` `for f in $dosfiles` `do` `   lf=`echo $f|tr '[A-Z]' '[a-z]'`` `   dosread -a notes/$f $lf` `done`	Script to strip off comments. Repeat for each file name. Set lf to lowercase name. Read from floppy-directory notes.

Arithmetic in Shell Scripts

The Borne shell does not have any built-in ability to evaluate simple arithmetic statements. This is all right because the Unix command **expr** performs simple mathematics as well as numerical comparisons from the command line:

```
%  expr 3 + 2                      Add 3 and 2.
5                                  The shell's answer.
```

These numerical comparisons are only for integers, with mandatory spaces separating the integers and operators. Operators that are special shell characters, like * or |, must be preceded with an backslash \ or surrounded by quotes. The permitted operations are:

expr OPERATIONS

$x + y$	Add two numbers.
$x - y$	Subtraction.
$x * y$	Multiplication.
x / y	Division.
$x \% y$	Remainder.
$x < y$	Returns 1 if true 0, if false.
$x <= y$	Less than or equal to.
$x = y$	Test for equal to.
$x != y$	Test for not equal to.
$x >= y$	Greater than or equal to.
$x > y$	Greater than.
$x \mid y$	x if $x \neq 0$, else y.
$x \& y$	x if both x and $y \neq 0$, else 0.
$x : y$	String compare. See manual.

From within a shell script you use **expr** to increment a variable by assigning the output of **expr** to the variable:

`N='expr $N + 1'`	Increment N by one.

We use this idea in the example below in which we run the user program `bigmat` with input files given on the command line and with the output stored in a different file for each input file name. The output file names are `output.N` where N is used as a counter:

`#!/bin/sh`	
`N="1"`	Be sure to initialize N.
`for file`	Loop over the arguments.
`do`	
`  outfile="output.$N"`	Create output file name.
`  echo "Running bigmat - input:\`	
` $file output:  $outfile."`	
`  bigmat < $file > $outfile`	
`  N='expr $N + 1'`	Increment N.
`done`	
`exit`	

10.3 Interactive Shell Tips

Re-Executing Commands

While none of us gets the respect he or she deserves, Unix at least listens and remembers what we say—as witnessed by the C and K shell's **history** command. This command not only recalls your previous commands but also lets you re-execute and even repair them (better than going around saying, "Gee I wish I had said that."):

```
%  history                              You issue the history (or his) command.
   30 ls                                Here's your list.
   31 cd comphy/book/chapters
   32 ftp bigblue
   33 mail
   34 print malebox
   35 history                           The history command above.
%
```

Notice that the commands are listed in the numerical order in which they have been issued during the present login. As a result, the last one, number 35, is at the bottom of the list. Some uses of this list are:

REPEAT COMMANDS

!!	Repeat last command (csh).
!*n*	Repeat command number *n* (csh).
!*pattern*	Repeat command starting with *pattern* (csh).
^*old***^***new***^**	Change *old* to *new* in last command.
!*n***:s/***old***/***new***/**	Repeat command *n* with substitution (csh).
r	Repeat last command (ksh).
r *n*	Repeat command number *n* (ksh).
r *pattern*	Repeat command starting with *pattern* (ksh).

Here are some examples which show that if you know **history**, you may relive it:

```
%  history                              Tell me my last commands.
   30 ls                                This is the 30th command since login.
   31 cd comphy/book/chapters
   32 ftp bigblue
   33 mail
   34 print malebox
   35 history                           This is the command given last.
%                                       Your turn.
%  !!                                   Repeat last command (or r).
   36 history                           Unix tells you what's going on.
   31 cd comphy/book/chapters             Here's your history again.
   32 ftp bigblue
   33 mail
   34 print malebox
   35 history
   36 history                           2 history's since you repeated it.
%  !31                                  Repeat command #31.
31 cd comphy/book/chapters              Unix tells you what's going on.
```

```
%                               Your turn.
%   !f                          Repeat previous f... command.
32 ftp bigblue                  Command #32 is being repeated.
  ^male^mail^                   Correcting spelling of male.
  print mailbox                 Corrected command.
%   !31/book/BOOK               Rerun # 31, substitute for book.
%   cd comphy/BOOK/chapters     The corrected command.
```

Command Line Editing with ksh

The Korn shell has an additional feature which allows you to edit the current or past commands using *vi*-like or *Emacs*-like commands. You choose the editor by setting the environmental variable VISUAL to the editor you want.[3] In *vi* mode, hit [escape] then use the *vi* movement keys (h, j, k, l) (but not the arrow keys) and *vi* commands to edit the Unix command. Entering [return] submits the edited command to the shell.

In *Emacs* mode, hit [escape], then use the *Emacs* movement keys (^p, ^n) (but not the arrow keys) and *Emacs* commands to edit the Unix command. Entering [return] submits the edited command to the shell.

Stop and Go

You start a job from your terminal, waiting impatiently as it executes. You know you have better ways to spend your time. What's a person to do? Well, Unix's C and K shells provide job control tools to deal with such a dilemma. With *job control* you suspend a program from the *foreground* (that high priority category in which terminal jobs run for quick response) and, if desired, place it in the *background* where it executes detached from your terminal. In both cases this frees your terminal for other work while keeping the program running in the computer's memory. You may return the job to foreground at any time. (While it seems like a foregone conclusion that all users have multi-windowing terminals, someday you may find yourself at poor Cascadia State College with a "dumb" terminal and then you'll have more respect for these commands.) The requisite commands are:

JOB CONTROL

ctrl-z	Suspend running (foreground) job.
bg	Place suspended job in background.
fg	Place bg/stopped job in foreground.
jobs -l	List background jobs.
command **&**	Execute *command* in background.
kill -9 *jobid*	Kill job (get *jobid* from **ps** command).
command1; *command2*	Execute *command1*, then *command2*.

With job control you can execute any number of jobs at once, although only one job may be in the foreground. Yet, in a multi–windowing environment such as *X Windows*

---

[3] See Chapter 3 on *Workstation Setup and Use* for a discussion of setting environmental variables.

or Sun Windows, each window may have an active foreground job as well as background ones. Because background jobs requiring terminal input stop and wait to be placed in the foreground, it makes sense to place compute-bound jobs in the background and switch among several active jobs as they progress from computation to interactive input.[4]

A common use of job control, especially during program development, is switching between editor and compiler. Suspending and continuing an editor is faster than reloading it. This becomes significant as the files get larger, or if you switch a lot, or if your system is being used a lot. Further, this places you back into your file at your previous location.

You may find that you like job control so much that you edit several files at once, using `ctrl-z` to suspend one editing session and `fg` to continue another. To be this controlling you must specify which jobs to continue—else `fg` or `bg` applies to just the last job. To find out what the computer knows about the jobs you have given it, use the `jobs` command. It will give you a number to reference your job, its status, and the command you entered to execute the job. For example:

`% jobs`	Tell me about stopped jobs.
`[1] Stopped vi myprog.c`	A suspended editing.
`[2] Stopped vi myotherprog.c`	
`[3] Stopped cc canonical.c`	
`% bg 3`	Place job #3, compilation, in background.
`% jobs`	Prompt means OK, but I'll check.
`[1] Stopped vi myprog.c`	
`[2] Stopped vi myotherprog.c`	
`[3] Running cc canonical.c`	See #3 run.
`% fg 2`	Resume editing `myotherprog.c`.

In the next example we suspend a job, run it in background, check its status, and then work on something else while waiting for Unix to tell us the background job is finished:

`% ls`	List files in my current directory.
`% myprog.c test-data`	A C source code and some data.
`% cc myprog.c`	A foreground compilation.
`  ctrl-z`	Enter stop-command *before* prompt.
`Stopped`	Unix says foreground job stopped.
`% bg`	Place last job into background.
`[1] cc myprog.c`	Unix talks about your background job.
`% jobs [1]`	You ask for the status of job #1.
`Running cc myprog.c`	Unix tells what's running.
`% lpq`	Tell me about line-printer queue.
`no entries`	At most, Unix says nothing's waiting.
`[1] Done cc myprog.c`	Without prodding, Unix says it's done.
`% ls`	List files in working directory.
`a.out* myprog.c test-data`	`cc` created the `a.out`.

---

[4]Compute-bound or CPU-bound jobs are those which require enough central-processing time before they complete, to make other jobs wait. They are problems for a time-sharing system, like Unix, in which the CPU switches continuously among all the active processes.

Running into the Future

Sometimes you may not want to execute your job right now. It may be so demanding on the system as to ruin the response tim, or you may want to get home to a still-hot dinner and just know you won't if there's hot output. Here's an example of how to run the program **happyBday** at 8 AM on May 24, say,

```
%  at 0800 may24 happyBday              Run happyBday at time.
```

The **batch** command is akin to **at**, yet **batch** has more intelligence. It will automatically queue your jobs and let only one run at a time. By using **batch**, you may submit a batch of jobs at once and not have them load down the system unreasonably or waste time by competing with each other to finish. To use **batch**, enter the **batch** command, then enter your Unix command in the same manner as you would from the command line, and then end your submission with a ^d:

```
%  batch                                Enter the batch command.
happyBday 2>&1 >outfile                 Enter the job.
 ^d                                     End submission with a ^d.
```

When the job has completed, the system will send you mail. The command **atq** will show all **batch**–jobs in the queue or **at**–jobs waiting to be processed. If you want to put a command off for a while (say 200 seconds), try

```
%  (sleep 20; command)&                 Run command after 20 seconds.
```

Here the **&** places the command in the background. Semantically you'll see that there is another command which seems to belong here. The **time** command times how long it takes to execute a command, as for example:

```
%  time happyBday                       Time how long to execute happyBday.
```

We use the **time** command to see how long it takes to run our programs.

10.4   The Make Utility

The **make** command invokes a very powerful utility for making or assembling programs from source codes and libraries. In spite of its power, **make** is quite easy to use since it's smart. It will compare the modification times of the source code files needed to create your program, and if some source has been modified in the time since its object was created, **make** will automatically recompile those source routines which have changed. Though **make** is smart, it can't read your mind. So instead, it reads the file makefile or Makefile in the current directory to find the rules for making a program. A simple makefile looks like this:

`# Makefile for program kabs`
`kabs:  kabs.f`
`  TAB   f77 -O -o kabs kabs.f`
	The program `kabs` depends on `kabs.f`.
	Line is indented with a TAB.

Here the first line is simply a comment. The next states that the *target* program we want to make, `kabs`, depends on the file `kabs.f`. If the file `kabs.f` has been modified since the target `kabs` was created, then `kabs` will be rebuilt by executing the commands on the following lines. It is important to note that *the command lines must be indented with a tab character.* In the next example, the single command line says to recompile the program using f77. To **make** the program, issue the command **make** with a target name:

`%  make kabs`	Make the program `kabs`.
`    f77 -O -o kabs kabs.f`	The system compiles the program.

In the preceding example, the program only depended on one file. **Make** becomes particularly useful when the program is made up of many files; for example:

`# Makefile for program kabs`
`kabs:  kabs.o graf.o`
`      f77 -O -o kabs kabs.o graf.o`
	The program `kabs` depends on two files.

This `makefile` states that the program `kabs` depends on two object files. No rule is stated for compiling the object files, so **make** uses its built-in rules. It will assume there is a C or Fortran source code in the present working directory and use it to make the object files; in this case it will look for `kabs.f` and `graf.f` or `kabs.c` and `graf.c`. Since `kabs` depends on the object files, **make** will check if they are current before making `kabs.f`. The file `kabs.o` implicitly depends on `kabs.f`, and so **make** will check the modification time of `kabs.f`. If it has changed since `kabs.o` was created, **make** will recompile the object file. It will then do the same for `graf.o`. After this, **make** will check the modification times of the object files and compare them to the target `kabs`. If either object file has been modified, **make** will run the command line which recompiles (links) `kabs`. The exact result of executing **make** depends on the state of the source. Here is a sample run:

`%  make kabs`	Issued from working directory.
`    f77 -c kabs.f`	Build `kabs.o` object file.
`    f77 -O -o kabs kabs.o graf.o`	Then build the target.

The built-in rules for making object files look like these:

`.c.o:` `      $(CC) $(CFLAGS) -c $<`	Rule for making object files from C programs.
`.f.o:` `      $(FC) $(FFLAGS) -c $<`	Rule for making object files from Fortran programs.

These are only two of several built-in rules. You may find these rules by issuing the command **make -p** or sometimes by looking in the /etc/make.cfg file. Notice that the rules use variables for the name of the compiler and for the options or flags passed to the compiler. There is also a special flag $< which stands for the name of the file. You may set and use the variables for the compilers and flags as well as creating your own variables.

Anatomy of a Makefile

`# Makefile for kp archive`	Define a lists of object files.

`LIBOBJ = albmom.o energy.o \`
`  prntio.o`
`OBJ = kp.o bimom.o handle.o \`
`  graf.o`	

`FC = f77`	Define the Fortran Compiler.
`FFLAGS = -O $(DEBUG)`	Define flags for Fortran compiler
`all: kplib.a kp kabs`	Define dummy target all.
`kp:   $(OBJ) kplib.a`	kp depends on all
`    $(FC) $(FFLAGS)  -o kp \`	files defined inOBJ
`$(OBJ) kplib.a`	and kp library.
`kplib.a:   $(LIBOBJ)`	To make the kp library,
`    ar r kplib.a $(LIBOBJ)`	use the **ar** command.
`kabs:`	To **make** kabs,
`    cd kabs; make kabs`	change directory & issue **make**.
`clean:`	Dummy target for
`    /bin/rm *.o`	cleaning up the directory.

Notice that **make** with no options uses the first target in the makefile. Traditionally, there is a dummy target called all and we have defined an all above. After that, we change to the directory kabs, which contains a makefile, and issue **make**.

10.5   Source Code Control System (SCCS)

The source code control system SCCS is a set of commands which helps you keep track of the changes made to source code (or any text) files.[5] It's like a friendly librarian and accountant for your files who even helps you restore your files to the condition they were in at some previous time. The SCCS is particularly handy when a group is making changes to the same source code or a single person likes to try out lots of changes but keeps forgetting how to get the code back to where it runs.

Like saving receipts for your income tax, most of us know we should use SCCS but never get around to making the time investment. Accordingly, we show you three simple steps which afford you the benefits of SCCS quickly:

---

[5]SCCS is a System V command. A similar system RCS is available under BSD.

SCCS SUBCOMMANDS

admin -i *file.f s.file.f*	Put subs under SCCS control.
get *s.file.f*	Retrieve, read only.
get -e *s.file.f*	Retrieve, read/write (e = edit).
get -p *s.file.f* | **more**	Retrieve, just peak.
delta *s.file.f*	Store changes.
prs *s.file.f*	List revisions.

Placing Files under SCCS

The SCCS stores your file and the history of changes you have made to it in a file with an s. prefix. So, the first step in using SCCS is to place your files under SCCS administration, that is, to makes the s. files. Yet before we do that, add a comment line near the top of each subprogram that looks something like this:

```
C %W%  latest revision %G% %U%    Comment near top.
```

When you print your program containing this comment, SCCS will fill in the special variables %W% with the date and version number. However, if you don't add such a line, SCCS will complain with a very cryptic message as though you made a real error.

We start by using the **admin** command to place the file under SCCS administration. Notice that there is not a space between the **-i** flag and the name of the file:

```
$  ls                              Look at what we have.
Makefile whet.f                    A makefile and a simple program.
$  admin -iwhet.f s.whet.f         Place the program under SCCS.
$  ls
Makefile s.whet.f whet.f           The s. file and original.
$  rm whet.f                       We remove the original.
```

Getting the Latest Version

The **get** command is able to retrieve the latest, or any past, version of your program:

```
$  ls
Makefile s.whet.f
$  get -e s.whet.f                 Get latest version for editing.
1.1                                Version 1.1.
new delta 1.2                      These changes will become version 1.2.
198 lines                          Book keeping.
$  ls
Makefile p.whet.f s.whet.f whet.f  p.whet.f is a flag for SCCS.
```

To get a past version , use the **prs** command to list past versions and **get** **-r** to retrieve the version you want:

```
$  prs s.whet.f                                        List versions of whet . f.
s.whet.f:                                              prs lists the deltas.
                                                       Most recent is version 1.3.

D 1.3 92/04/06 09:37:44 pfink \
  3 2    000/000/198
MRs:
COMMENTS:                                              Comments the user made about changes.
Optimized for superscalar.

                                                       The next delta, 1.2.
D 1.2 92/04/06 09:31:08 pfink\
  2 1    000/000/198
MRs:
COMMENTS:
Added new timing print out.

                                                       The original version is 1.1
D 1.1 92/04/06 09:13:22 pfink \
1 0    198/000/000
MRs:
COMMENTS:
date and time created 92/04/06 \
09:13:22 by pfink
$  get -r1.1 s.whet.f
1.1
198 lines
$  get -r1.1 s.whet.f                                  Get read-only copy of the original.
1.1
198 lines
$  ls
Makefile s.whet.f whet.f
```

Saving Changes

Incorporating the changes, what SCCS calls *deltas*, into your file produces a new version of your source code. You do this by issuing the **delta** command with the name of the SCCS file. Then SCCS gives you the chance to describe this version of the code:

```
$  ls                                                  We have editable version of whet . f.
Makefile p.whet.f s.whet.f whet.f
$  delta s.whet.f                                      Save the changes.
Type comments, terminated with
End of File character or blank line.
Added new timing print out.                            Our comments.
                                                       Terminate comments with a blank line.
1.2                                                    This is version 1.2.
```

```
2 inserted
0 deleted
193 unchanged
$ ls
Makefile s.whet.f
```

Statistics

No lines deleted

Editable and **p** files have been removed.

10.6   Unix Debugging Tools: D, dbx, xdb, ...

Wi' lightsome heart I pu'd a rose
Frae aff its thorny tree,
And my fause luver staw[6] my rose,
But left the thorn wi' me.

—Robert Burns, *Ye Flowery Banks*

We continue to bemoan the fact that debugging a large scientific program is more of a challenge than it has a right to be. In the next chapter we will discuss things you as a programmer can do to meet this challenge. Here we indicate some Unix tools which will help you debug your C, Fortran, or Pascal programs. One tool lets you keep your own books and just use the D compiler options to print out the information you need for debugging. Other tools call in outside help, namely *debuggers*. The most generally available debugger is **dbx** — or some similar combination of letters. This valuable tool is further improved by using it in an X Windows interface known as **xde**, and we recommend it highly.

D Compile Options

One standard debugging technique is to print out the values of variables and constants from different parts of your program to check that they are being transferred correctly. Another debugging technique is to build a simple test case right into your program and then to check that it continues to give a known answer even after you make those "harmless" modifications. Once these debugging structures are built into your program, you just leave them there permanently—without having to execute them. You do that by commenting them out with a d or D in column 1. For example:

`subroutine sub1`
`...`
`d       write(6,999) 'at 999, x, y =', x, y`
`d 999 format( (a), 2f10.3)`
	d in col. 1.
	d in col. 1.

If this is done with the traditional C in column 1, you must go back and modify the source code to uncomment them. With a d in column 1 you uncomment these statements by invoking the **D** (for debugging) option of the Fortran compiler:

```
%   f77 -D sub1.f
```

Option makes D statements = source.

---

[6]False lover stole.

Or alternatively, you may place debug directives in the source file:

`$debug on`	Treat D statements as source.
`$debug off`	Treat D statements as comments.

Prerequisites for dbx

Another approach to debugging does not require you to modify your original C, Pascal, or Fortran source codes. Instead, you use a *debugger* to provide you with an environment to selectively execute just parts of your program, to print out selected variables when desired, and to trace through variables as they change while your program runs. The **dbx** debugger does this for you. On the one hand, **dbx** is a source level debugger. This means that even though it is running your object code, it is smart enough to direct you to the statement in your source which has caused the problem in your object code. On the other hand, **dbx** is also a symbolic debugger, which means it is smart enough to tell you the name and value of the variable at which your program is having its difficulties and not just the binary value of the location in memory where something is amiss.

As indicated in our discussion of *Different Compilers and Their Options* in Chapter 9, in order to use these types of debuggers you must first compile your entire program with the **-g** option invoked. The compiler then produces the global variable tables needed by the debuggers to convert addresses located in virtual memory to the name of the source subprogram and the line number within that subprogram. While this information is usually provided by default (that is, without explicitly invoking -g option), explicitly invoking the -g permits tracing back to your program's variables, data, and structures. If your executable, or even a subroutine within your executable, is not compiled with the -g option, or if symbol references are removed with the **strip** command, the symbolic capabilities of **dbx** are limited. Furthermore, if you are using C or Fortran preprocessors, such as **cpp, ratfor,** or **elf,** you may want to generate and save the intermediate (`.i, .f`) files since they provide information to help **dbx** find the bugs.

Optimization and debugging have conflicting approaches to processing your program, so *you should run the debugger on nonoptimized code only.*[7] After the bugs are removed, you continue to leave the debugging option on as you increase the level of optimization. Finally, when the program enters the production stage, turn off all storage of global symbol tables. The exception to this rule occurs when the bug occurs only at higher optimization levels, in which case you may as well try the debugger with your optimized but buggy code.

Some of the **subcommands** given from within **dbx** (when you see the **(dbx)** prompt) include:

---

[7]On some systems such as DEC's ULTRIX, the **g** compiler option must be specified as **g0, g1** (default), **g2 = g, g3** depending upon the optimization level of your code. Only **g3** is acceptable with optimized code—although it may result in inaccuracies.

dbx SUBCOMMANDS

help	Tell me what I may command.
run	Execute the program.
print *var*	Display value of *var*.
where	Print currently active procedures.
stop at *line*	Suspend execution at *line*.
stop in *proc*	Suspend execution in subprogram *proc*.
cont	Resume execution.
edit	Invoke **vi** editor.
step	Execute 1 line.
next	Step to next line (skip over calls).
trace *line*	Trace execution of *line*.
trace *proc*	Trace calls to *proc*.
trace *var*	Trace changes to *var*.
trace *exp* **at** *line*	Print *exp* when *line* reached.
status	Print trace/stops in effect.
delete *number*	Remove trace or stop *number*, or all.
screen	Switch **dbx** to another virtual terminal.
ignore	No signal trap when application called.
call *proc*	Call *procedure* in program.
whatis *name*	Print declaration of *name*.
list *linei, linef*	List source *lines*.
registers	Display register set.
quit	Exit **dbx**.

There are more subcommands available for use with **dbx**. If you use the X Windows interface **xde**, many subcommands as well as needed documentation are available via pull-down menus and buttons. We recommend it! As your programs get more complicated or your problems more subtle, you may need to check the **man** pages for details. For example, if your program has a fault which keeps it from executing and causes a core dump to be produced, **dbx** can examine the state of the program when it faulted, something we mere mortals dare not do.

Sample dbx Runs

As an example, let's say our old program area.f from Chapters 2 and 8 has somehow been corrupted and no longer gives correct answers. It compiles fine and runs fine, but we must have inadvertently changed something in viewing the file. (The problem is that we have lost an asterisk in the line which calculates the area, so that it now reads A = pi * r*2 rather than A = pi * r**2; but let's assume only superuser knows this and won't tell us.) We compile area.f in our usual way and store the executable in area. We now use **dbx** to examine the program during execution. (If **xde** is available, you can push buttons rather than give the subcommands.)

%	**f77 -wO area.f -o area**	Compile, optimize, object in area.
%	**dbx area**	Begin debugging the executable area.
%	**(xde area)**	Alternative X Window interface for **dbx**.

```
dbx version 3.1 for AIX.
Type 'help' for help.
reading symbolic info ...warning:
 no source compiled with -g
(dbx)                                    (dbx) = dbx promp.
(dbx) quit                               Get out of dbx, need -g option.
%                                        The shell's prompt returns.
% f77 -g area.f -o area                  Compile, optimize, object in area.
```

When we are told that we forgot to invoke the **-g** option, we quit **dbx** and then compile properly. Now we are really ready to start debugging. We make execution of the program stop at critical points called *breakpoints* with the **dbx** subcommand **stop**, move on from there with the **step** subcommand, and use the **dbx** subcommand **print** to examine a variable's value:

```
% dbx area                               Begin debugging executable area.
dbx version 3.1 for AIX.
Type 'help' for help.
reading symbolic information ...
(dbx) list 1,20                          We tell dbx to list lines 1:20.
1 PROGRAM area
2 c
3 c area of circle, r input from terminal
4 c
5 DOUBLE PRECISION pi, r, A
6 c calculate pi
7 pi = 3.141593
8 c read r from standard input (terminal)
9 Write(*,*) 'specify radius'
10 Read (*, *) r
11 c calculate area
12 A = pi * r*2
13 c write area onto terminal screen
14 Write(*,10) 'radius r =', r, ' A =', A
15 10 Format(a20, f10.2, a15, f12.3)
16 STOP 'area'
17 END
(dbx) stop at 14                         We set breakpoint.
[1] stop at 14                           dbx's confirmation.
(dbx) run                                Run program now.
specify radius                           The program's query.
 2                                       We enter 2
[1] stopped in area at line 14           dbx stops area.
(dbx) print radius                       We ask for value of radius.
"radius" is not defined                  Our mistake, it's called r.
(dbx) print r                            We ask for value of r.
2.0                                      dbx tells us value of r at breakpoint.
[1] stopped in area at line 14           dbx stops area,
14 Write(*,10) 'radius r=',r,'A=',A        and lists line.
```

(dbx) **continue**	We tell **dbx** to continue.
radius r = 2.00 A = 12.566	**area**'s output.
STOP area	**area**'s output.
execution completed	Message from **dbx**.
(dbx) **print pi**	We ask for value of *pi*.
3.1415929794311523	**dbx** gives *pi* at breakpoint.
(dbx) **status**	List active **dbx** command.
[1] stopped in area at line 14	Command # 1 active.
(dbx) **delete 1**	Remove command #1, breakpoint.
(dbx) **list 12**	List line 12.
12 A = pi * r*2	Line from code with error.
(dbx) **edit**	You edit area.f to insert missing *.
(dbx) **quit**	Get out of debugger.
% **f77 -wO area.f -o area**	Recompile area.f.
% **area**	We rerun program.
specify radius	
2.0	
radius r = 2.00 A = 12.566	The right answer.

Again notice that you must recompile the program after editing and then use **dbx** on the new program.

TECHNIQUES FOR POWER USERS

SCIENTIFIC PROGRAMMING HINTS

But, Mousie, thou art no thy lane,[1]
In proving foresight may be vain:
The best-laid schemes o' mice an' men
Gang aft agley.[2]

—Robert Burns, *To a Mouse*

11.1   Aims of Programming

In computational sciences we use the computer's power to solve problems which defy analytic solutions or to understand realistic systems at a depth greater than otherwise possible. To be successful at this we need powerful hardware and powerful software. And sooner or later if you try to do something new or different enough, you will have to write your own programs. As indicated in the introductory chapter, we view programming as an art which blends elements of science, mathematics, and computer science into a set of instructions that tell the computer how to accomplish a scientific goal. In addition, it should contribute to science and engineering by encouraging collaboration. Accordingly your programs should:

- Give correct answers, without which other aims are irrelevant.

- Be simple, easy to read, and have evident logic.

- Document themselves so that the programmer and others understand them.

- Be easy to use.

- Be easy and safe to modify for different computers.

- Be passed on to others to use and develop.

---

[1]Not alone.
[2]Go often askew.

The computer itself will catch most of your errors of diction, yet it will not correct your errors of style, mathematics, or science. What constitutes the best programming style is continually debated within the computer science community. We will add our two bits by giving some hints in this chapter. Our discussion is too brief to be more than reminders and if you need more, you might check the references.

Before discussing any programming techniques, you probably first need to get some experience with the numerical characteristics of your computer. Specifically, if you haven't yet done the exercises at the end of Chapter 1, *Introduction*, we suggest you do them now.

11.2   Top-Down Structured Design

True creative artists follow their own rules. Here are some suggested rules which may help you on the road to becoming a creative programmer.

- Put off as long as possible the actual writing of your program. Concentrate instead on clarifying, understanding, and defining the problem to be solved. You will want your program to solve the correct problem and you will want to know when it has succeeded.

- Invest time choosing the best *algorithm*, that is, the set of rules the computer follows to solve your problem.

- Keep in mind that while some algorithms may appeal to your sense of elegance (or simplicity), they may not work well for your problem. Consequently, plan to use several algorithms in different parameter regimes, and then analyze each for precision, efficiency, and ease of use.

- An algorithm which is best for one type of computer architecture, for example, *scalar*, may not be best for another type, for example, *vector* or *parallel*.

- A program which is clear and simple will usually end up being less buggy. While it may take more computing time, this usually saves you time. Most importantly, it may help your project reach a successful completion rather than being abandoned in frustration.

- The planning of your program should be from *top, down to bottom*. This means you first outline the major tasks of the algorithm, always keeping the big picture visible. Arrange the major tasks in the order in which they need be accomplished. This will be the most basic outline.

- Next, plan the details of each major task, making sure to break these tasks into subtasks (which may turn out to be subprograms or groups of subprograms). In your outline, this will be the next level of complexity.

- You need to continue breaking up your tasks into smaller ones until you feel you are essentially writing a subroutine.

- Strive to keep the flow through the program *linear*, as indicated in Figure 11.1, with a minimal amount of jumping around.[3] Avoid the Ping-pong of computed *go to*.

---

[3]In Chapter 14 on *Parallel Computing*, this principle is modified for a parallel computer where multiple, central processors work simultaneously on one problem.

- Do not become overzealous with modularization. If a subroutine is very small and often called, the overhead time for the calls may be relatively expensive. In this case (especially for vector programs) the compiler will optimize better if you combine often-called and related program units into one.

11.3   Modular and Object-Oriented Programming

We have already introduced the *modular* concept of breaking up the tasks of a program into smaller and smaller ones, and then programming up these smallest tasks as subprograms. In general, your programs will be clearer and simpler if you make them modular.[4] You may end up getting more work done as you finish off small pieces of your task. You may even be able to isolate the hard part and make it someone else's chore.

Object-oriented this and that is an overly used phrase in today's computing world. Often these object-oriented systems have little or nothing to do with *object-oriented programming* (OOP). Object-oriented programming has a precise definition. Although the object often refers to some graphical interface, the concept is actually quite general. The *object* can be a component of a program. Of interest to us is OOP's programming paradigm which aims to simplify writing large programs by providing a framework for reusing components developed and tested in previous problems.

A true object-oriented language has four characteristics[5]:

Encapsulation Encapsulation is associating the data in an object with the code or methods for accessing the data. The data are hidden from direct manipulation and are accessed only via the *methods*.

Inheritance A hierarchy of definitions is established with objects inheriting characteristics, including code, from higher-level objects.

Polymorphism Polymorphism is the concept that different objects or routines may have *methods* with the same name. Although multiple routines with the same name may seem like the road to chaos, this is a powerful idea. For example, two different *objects*, a car and a rocket, may have *methods* with the name mass. A routine then alters the mass of either by using the object mass method without needing to know the type of object on which it acts.

Abstraction Abstraction allows the programmer to concentrate on the problem's solution rather than on details of implementation. How this abstraction is achieved in an object-oriented language is sometimes controversial. Generally, object-oriented languages do not rely upon data types as traditional languages do. This allows more general routines, such as general sort routines, that will work with any type of data.

Some practical hints for incorporating modular programming philosophies into your programs are:

- Write many small subprograms, each of which accomplishes limited tasks.

---

[4]This may not be good for vectorization on a supercomputer, but you can always recombine the subprograms after they are debugged and running.

[5]Smith (1991), Pinson and Wiener, (1991).

Linear Sequence

Figure 11.1: A simple (linear) sequence of actions.

- Give each subunit well-defined input and output which gets passed as arguments (preferably not in COMMON or with an EQUIVALENCE).

- Make each subprogram reasonably independent of the others. You then can test them independently and use them again and again in other programs.

While you can view in a single glance small programs written for some simple project, when you have tens or hundreds of thousands of lines of code, the complexity will boggle the mind unless your program is modular and you have your outlines or flow charts to consult.

11.4 Structured Programming

You should always be striving to build *structures* into your programs which clearly reveal their contents and logic. The physical structuring of your code can be built in by using successive indentations for different sections (ignored by the compiler); by the frequent and judicious use of comment and blank lines[6]; and by using upper- and lowercase letters to improve clarity (the Fortran compiler is case insensitive and the C compiler can be instructed to be also).

On a more conceptual level, modern high-level languages contain several building blocks to provide structure to programs; they are also sufficient for all programming needs. Some common structures are illustrated in Figures 11.1–11.5. These logical building blocks start with the linear sequence, Figure 11.1, and include:

Repeat Loop *N* Times, Figure 11.2: *Do* all instructions up to the end of loop indicator *Endo N* times.

If–Then–Else, Figure 11.3: *If* a certain condition is met, *Then* execute some instructions, or *Else* do something else. When one of these possibilities is finished, this sequence ends.

Repeat Loop Unknown Number Times, Figure 11.4: *While* some condition is met, keep repeating these instructions. If the condition is no longer met, go to statements beyond *Endwhile*.

---

[6]Avoid non-commented blank lines since they will not always be accepted by compilers.

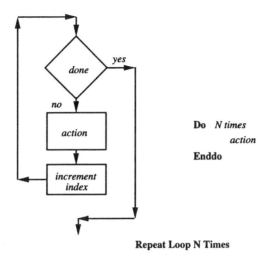

Do   *N times*
     action
Enddo

Repeat Loop N Times

Figure 11.2: The Repeat Loop *N* Times structure and pseudocode.

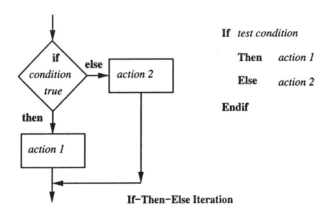

If   *test condition*

     Then   *action 1*

     Else   *action 2*

Endif

If–Then–Else Iteration

Figure 11.3: The *If–Then–Else* structure and pseudocode.

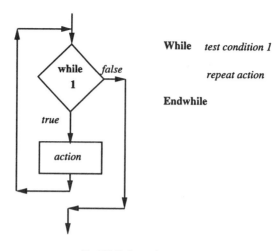

While   *test condition 1*

        repeat action

Endwhile

Do While Iteration

Figure 11.4: The *While* structure and pseudocode.

You will note that these structures have well-defined beginnings, ends, and conditions for their action, all of which help make the program's flow clearer. Of course, actual programs often contain more complicated logic; yet as we see in Figure 11.5, these basic structures may be combined for a richer structure.

For optimal use of the *If* statements, that is, faster running code:

- Use block or logical *If* statements rather than computed *If* statements. When a computed *If* statement is required, you can avoid jumping around too much by making the next statement a target point.

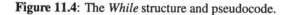

- If the test in your *If* statement involves an *And/Or* operation, use the leftmost positions for the conditions most likely to be satisfied.

11.5   Programming Hints

Some specific programming hints which may help you implement the preceding general rules for writing programs are:

- Use *compiled* languages if you want to use your program on a wide class of computers or want to use common libraries of subroutines. (BASIC is an *interpreted* language.)

- Use the standard version of the language if you want to *port* your code to another computer or have it run immediately on future systems.   (Avoid local language extensions.)

- Add plenty of comments and documentation as you write the code, with at least a short description in each subprogram. This will help keep your mind on track and be useful later (a natural act for those who talk to themselves or keep a diary).

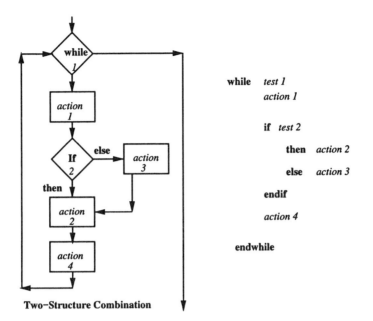

Figure 11.5: A combination of *While* and *If–Then–Else* structures.

- Use descriptive names for variables and subroutines like `mass` and `temp`, keeping them similar to the variables employed in standard texts and papers. Describe your variables in comment statements.

- To be safe, declare all variables (do not use the `IMPLICIT` statement in Fortran unless you make it an `IMPLICIT UNDEFINED`). Combined with cross-referenced maps, this helps you pick up spelling, typographical, and forgetfulness errors.

- Use only standard *structures* and avoid convoluted logic.

- To show the content and structure of your statements, use plenty of spaces and indentations within statements and blank comment lines around them.

- Do not use *Go To*, except in standard *structures*.

- In Fortran, use statement labels only for `Continue` and `Format` statements.[7]

- Avoid `EQUIVALENCE` statements. They make the logic hard to follow.

- To avoid hard-to-diagnose errors and an opaque code, don't manipulate `COMMON` blocks.

- Be cognizant that compilers make errors too. You'll want to be particularly careful if your programming is subtle or clever or highly convoluted. Comparing results

---

[7]Because of limited space, our examples don't always follow this rule.

derived with different levels of *optimization*, different flags, or reorganized program parts may help reveal compiler bugs (the least-optimized answer is usually your best bet).

11.6   Optimization and Efficiency

Your valuable time and patience, and your computer time, will all benefit from optimized code. If your program runs more quickly, you (and all other users) will probably get your debugging done more quickly, your results back more often, and on to something else. Yet common sense tells us that unless the personal time you gain from making the program run faster *exceeds* the personal time you spend speeding the program up, you may as well let the computer do the extra work. If you are going to go to the trouble of optimizing your code, then you will want to work on the *hot spots*, that is, those places in your program where the computer spends much of its time (they are usually a small fraction of the total program). Optimizing a part of your code which costs little CPU time hardly ever pays.

Another factor to consider is that a conflict exists between the rules for clear and portable programming and those for optimized programming. Changes a programmer makes to optimize a code can make the code less transparent and more machine dependent.

When thinking about whether to optimize or not, it may be helpful to recall that the time a computation takes is determined by the efficiency of the numerical algorithm used, as well as the efficiency of your programming. The efficiency of algorithms is studied in numerical analysis. In your haste to solve the real problem, you won't want to ignore it. However, you may not always want the most efficient algorithm. If, for example, your problem has an exceptionally large range of input parameters (or even unknown input parameters), you may prefer a slower, more *robust* algorithm which is less likely to break down under nonoptimal conditions (a Jeep, rather than a Jaguar).

As we discuss various specifics regarding optimized programming in this chapter and in Chapters 12-14 on supercomputers, you may find it useful to remember that modern compilers have been designed to take your code and optimally adapt it to the computer's hardware. This leads to a golden rule:

To assist compilers and other users, make your programs standard and clear.

In fact, if you use one of the preprocessors, it will show you what the optimized source code looks like, so you may take it, or leave it, or adopt it as your own.

Debugging and Optimization

You will want to use the lowest–level optimization during program development and debugging because many compilations will be needed to remove grammatical errors. With low-level optimization, you can take advantage of any interactive debugging tools available such as **dbx**, **sdb**, **xdb**, or **cdbx** or the ones invoked with compile-time options. (We discussed these in Chapter 10, *Unix Tools*, or you can refer to the **man** pages.)

If you are going to use your program repeatedly for *production* runs and if it takes more than a few seconds to run, then you want to have the compiler *optimize* it. Once your program has been debugged and tested, run the same test cases using successively higher levels of optimization during compilation. Beware, higher optimization will demand more compilation time and more storage—especially for complicated programs into which the compiler really sinks its teeth, and so you may run out of time or memory.

If compilation fails or the results are different at higher optimization, you may have to use a less-optimized version. While this will be a rare occurrence with the better compilers available today, it is more likely with some of the very large and complicated codes used by computational scientists. If you experience a failure, check that it is not being caused by uninitialized variables which may have been acceptable at lower optimization levels. (A cross-reference map is handy for checking that variables have been defined before use.) In more sophisticated debugging where core dumps are examined, extra care may also be needed because the optimized program may still have variables in registers which have not yet been placed back in memory when the core is dumped.

Input/Output and Optimization

A compiler's optimization of input/output (I/O) is usually not too effective, and so writing efficient code is very important. Here are some hints:

- Use unformatted I/O whenever possible. This avoids the conversion between data storage schemes and will lessen the processing time. It also uses less storage and retains precision better than formatted I/O.

- For each I/O statement, process as many items as possible. Each call to the system's I/O routines can handle around 20 items, so bundling will minimize the number of calls to these routines.

- Use implied *Do* loops in your I/O statements. This permits the compiler to transfer larger blocks of data. For example:

`write(4)  ((b(i,j),i =1,10),  j=1,20)`	Better performance.
`read(5,10)  (a(i),  i = 1,  10,  n)`	Poorer, n unknown to compiler.

- It is convenient to bunch the I/O statements all together in one subprogram. Then you will know where to make modifications when porting code.

Variables, Expressions, and Optimization

- Use variables of 4 bytes length and avoid using `INTEGER*2` and `LOGICAL*1` variables.

- Because fetching variables from afar in memory takes extra time, use local variables in the numerically most intensive loops in your program. Avoid using passed variables (subroutine arguments) in I/O statements or in calls to other subprograms, `EQUIVALENCE`d variables, variables in `COMMON`, and loop indices. You can accomplish this by assigning a local variable to a frequently referenced argument or `COMMON` variable:

`SUBROUTINE Sub(dummy)`	`dummy` is the dummy argument.
`local = dummy`	Local variable now equals `dummy`.
`local = local**43`	Local variable changed, no effect on `dummy`.
`. . .`	Further work with `local`.

- When setting a local *scalar* variable equal to a frequently referenced COMMON variable, make sure to set the COMMON variable back to the local variable before exiting from that section of code:

`COMMON x`	Variable `x` in unlabeled COMMON.
`temp = x`	`temp` is local variable.
`y = temp**2`	
`temp = temp**99 + 2*temp ...`	
`. . .`	And even more use of `temp`.
`x = temp`	Reset `x` = final `temp` value.

- COMMON blocks each require distinct addressing, so group elements into the same block to minimize the number of blocks:

3 addresses needed (BAD)	1 address needed (GOOD)
`COMMON /com1/ a`	`COMMON /joint/ a, b, c`
`COMMON /com2/ b`	`c = a + b`
`COMMON /com3/ c`	
`c = a + b`	

- When arranging COMMON blocks, place variables occupying smaller amounts of memory before ones occupying larger amounts. This reduces addressing. For example:

`COMMON /big/ x(1000), y`	Poor—small variable later.
`COMMON /small/ y, x(1000)`	Better—scalar variable first.
`COMMON /bigger/ b(5000), c(500), d(50)`	Poor—small array last.
`COMMON /smaller/ d(50), c(500), b(5000)`	Better to ascend.

- To avoid jumping around in memory, to make better use of registers, and to give the compiler a better chance to optimize, accumulate partial sums in local scalar variables rather than in arrays:

BAD code	GOOD code

`    sum(i) = 0`
`    Do 10 j = 1, 99`
`10 sum(i)=sum(i) + a(i,j)**4`
	`    temp = 0`
	`    Do 10 j = 1, 99`
	`10 temp=temp + a(i,j)**4`
	`    sum(i) = temp`

- Pass subroutine arguments in a COMMON block rather than as actual arguments (parameters) in order to avoid the overhead associated with passing arguments to subprograms. Beware that the use of ENTRY statements with arguments may not reset all arguments in the subprogram to their current value. Also be aware that even though this may lead to a faster program, it is *not* good object-oriented programming and makes the program's logic more difficult to follow.

- If your program contains a short *Do* loop which gets referenced frequently, you increase the program's speed by expanding or *unrolling* the loop into *in-line code*; for example, by including the subprogram's statements in the main program. The price for this decrease in overhead is a decrease in modularity and clarity.

- If you wish to make subscripting and indexing more efficient, expand or combine smaller arrays until they are of the same size as the larger ones with which they are processed.

- Because Fortran stores arrays in *column-major order* (and C in row-major order), have the left-most index of an array vary most rapidly (right-most for C). If a variable is used as an index, make the rightmost index the variable:

SLOWER	FASTER

`   SUBROUTINE Sub(x,n)`
`   REAL*8 x(n,8)`
`   Do 10 i =1, 8`
`10 x(7,i) = c`
	`   SUBROUTINE Sub(x,n)`
	`   REAL*8 x(8,n)`
	`   Do 10 i = 1, 8`
	`10 x(i,7) = c`

- The compiler will try to be smart enough to look inside your *Do* loops, pick out expressions which are constant or duplicated as the loop index varies, and then store them while the loop executes. This is known as *Invariant Code Reduction*. As a good programmer you help the compiler pick out these constant expressions by placing them in parentheses (operations within parentheses are performed before those without) or by placing them at the *left ends* of expressions. For example:

Not recognized (BAD).	Duplicate/constant recognized (GOOD).

`Do 10 i = 1, 99`
`   a = b*x*y*z`
`   c = d*y*z*x`
`   e = x*y + f`
`   g = h*y*x + z`
`10 continue`
	`Do 10 i = 1, 99`
	`   a = b * (x*y*z)`
	`   c = d * (x*y*z)`
	`   e = (x*y) + z + f`
	`   g = h*((x*y) + z) + h`
	`10 continue`

Notice that blank spaces in the statements have no effect on the compiler. We place them there for clarity. Likewise, the placement of mathematically superfluous parentheses should cause compilers no problems. Compilers used to stumble over extra parentheses and were not smart enough to recognize invariant code, and so one had to define local variables outside of the *Do* loops rather than repeat the same calculations within. While this is still legal, it requires a larger number of stores and fetches from memory and takes more time to process than leaving the invariant code within the *Do* loop.

- Although it is faster to leave invariant code within your *Do* loops, it is faster to *factor out* calculations involving constant scalar operations:

Not factored (SLOW)	Factored (FAST)
`sum = 0.`	`sum = 0.`
`Do 10 i = 1,100`	`Do 10 i = 1, 100`
`10 sum = sum + fact * a(i)`	`10 sum = sum + a(i)`
	`sum = fact * sum`

- You can squeeze some more speed out of your program by avoiding elementary operations that take extra time. Try to avoid: number conversion, expressions which mix integers and floating point numbers, conversions from single to double precision, and divisions where multiplications can be used instead. As we see here, this usually means writing longer, less clear, and less elegant code:

SLOWER	FASTER
`c conversions needed`	`c no conversions`
	`c = 0.`
`do 10 i =1, 99`	`do 10 i =1, 99`
	`c = c + 1.`
`10 x(i) = x(i) * i`	`10 x(i) = x(i) * c`
`c divisions`	`c multiplications`
`y = x/2.`	`y = 0.5 * x`

11.7 Debugging Checklists

1. Use at least double precision (64-bit words) to avoid numerical problems, especially as the calculations take longer and longer.

2. Employ good programming style to find and prevent bugs:

      (a) meaningful and consistent variable names,

      (b) clear structures,

      (c) lots of useful comments,

      (d) small subroutines,

      (e) object-oriented programming (change variables only where expected).

3. Check each program part separately.

4. Compare with exact cases.

5. Start with running code and then make changes gradually. Check after each change that the code still reproduces standard cases.

Specific Checklist

1. Compare sizes of COMMONS in different program parts.

2. Check size of object files; too small or too big indicates problems.

3. Check cross-reference map for misspelled variables.

4. Check map for undefined variables.

5. Check that each variable is used, or else ask yourself why is it there?

6. Recompile often to be sure objects are current (or use *Makefiles*).

7. Recompile individual subroutines for their own map.

8. Check that you are running the most recent code revisions (or use*Makefiles*).

9. Maintain and use up-to-date source listings.

10. Examine lots of output including plots and printouts (turn on with D option).

11. Discontinuous physical variables indicate bugs (or chaos).

12. Compare results with known cases (analytic or published).

13. Many runs don't necessarily make a right program.

14. Keep in-code option for full printouts (use D option to turn on).

15. Save standard runs with full output (especially when porting code).

16. Don't trust code until all bugs (even small ones) are removed.

17. Use anyone as a consultant (you've been staring at the bug too long).

18. Don't look only at your bottom line (final answers).

19. Build in automatic checks and error messages (divide by 0, variable outside of physical range, etc.).

20. *Use Unix tools such as* **dbx, xdbx.**

11.8   Programming with Matrices

Models for physical systems often end up as large systems of linear equations. To make the structure of these systems more transparent or to approximate them, the linear equations are often converted to matrix form. This is good for us since the computer is just the right tool for matrix manipulations. On the one hand, these manipulations often perform a fairly standard and small set of instructions over and over again. This means the coding is fairly straightforward, easy to check, and if written with some generality, is applicable to many problems just by changing the input. On the other hand, we may tire of doing the same thing over and over and over again, but the computer does not. In fact, matrix manipulations have been a classical problem for computers, and much of what makes supercomputers "super" is their wired-in capability of doing bulk matrix operations (more about that in Chapters 12-14).

In this section, we discuss some points to keep in mind when dealing with matrices on computers. For information on numerical methods for matrices, we refer the reader to the books in the Bibliography and the subroutine libraries. We are assuming that realistic problems in research or development require large matrices, and not necessarily with the high symmetry often assumed in the elementary texts, so that you will need to use the various algorithms which maximize speed, minimize round-off error, and are applicable to wide classes of matrices.

Matrix Programming Pitfalls

Too many scientific programming problems arise from the improper use of arrays on computers.[8] We don't know whether this is because of the large amount of scientific programming that use matrices or because of the complexity of matrix representations; yet we know there are pitfalls out there. Here are a few:

Finite Size It is all too easy to forget that computers are finite. But such a memory lapse leads to difficulties when the number of indices in an array or the dimension of the array is large. Let us say, for example, that you represent some data set with a four-dimensional array DIMENSION A(100,100,100,100). Each index has a *physical dimension* of 100. This array occupies $(10^2)^4$ words $\approx 1000\text{MB} = 1\text{GB}$ of memory (if you even have that much).

Complex, Double Precision, Double Dimension Making a single precision matrix complex, or double precision, doubles the size of the matrix. Doubling the dimension of a matrix leads to a geometric increase in storage.

Processing Time It is a rule of thumb that a matrix operation such as inversion requires N^3 steps for a square matrix of dimension N. Thus doubling the dimensions of a 2D matrix (as happens when the number of integration steps or grid points are doubled) leads to an *eightfold* increase in processing time.

---

[8]Even a vector $V(N)$ is considered to be an array, only it is one-dimensional.

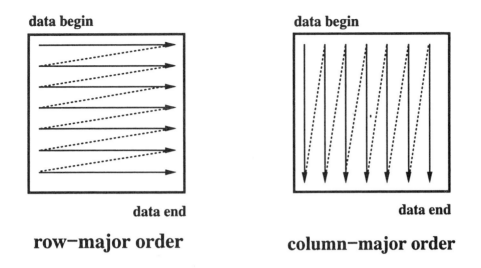

row–major order　　　　**column–major order**

Figure 11.6: Column-major order used for data storage in Fortran and row-major order used for storage in C and Pascal.

Paging Many computer systems have *virtual memory* in which disk space or some other *slow* memory is automatically used when a program requires more random access memory than is allocated to a particular user (discussed further in Chapters 12 and 13). When these *page faults* occurs, a *page* of memory is written back and forth between RAM and disk, a relatively slow process. Let's say you have a program which runs in time T and is near the memory limit at which paging occurs. By increasing the physical dimensions of some matrices in your program by even a small amount but enough to require paging, you will find a large increase in the time it takes your program to run, possibly up to $10T$.

Matrix Storage Although we think of matrices as multidimensional blocks of stored numbers, the computer stores them sequentially as a linear string of numbers. In the C language this means the matrix $a(i, j)$ is stored in *row-major order*, as shown in Figure 11.6. In Fortran this means *column-major order*, as also shown in Figure 11.6. For example, a matrix declared `dimension A(3,3)` in Fortran is stored as

$$a(1, 1)'a(2, 1)'a(3, 1)a(1, 2)'a(2, 2)'a(3, 2)a(1, 3)a(2, 3)a(3, 3) \qquad (11.1)$$

(We explain the primes soon.) This is often confusing and for good reason; the first index is varying more rapidly than the second one–which is backwards from the usual way of counting and a car's odometer. It is, nevertheless, important to keep this linear storage scheme in mind to avoid programming errors and to understand your output during debugging.

Physical and Logical Dimensions When you run a program you must tell the computer how much of its physical memory it should set aside in storage for the arrays you define. This is called *physical memory* and is usually large enough to handle all foreseeable cases. In Fortran you command the computer to reserve storage with a statement such as DIMENSION a(3,3). You write double a[3][3]; in C. Often you will run your program without the full complement of values possible to store in the matrices (perhaps because you are running small test cases or because you just like to declare all dimensions to be 10000 to impress your colleagues). The amount of memory you actually use to store numbers is the matrix's *logical size.*

As an example, let's say you have declared DIMENSION a(3,3) but only use a logical dimension of (2,2). That means only the primed values of the matrix in Equation (11.1) have been defined. Clearly they do not occupy sequential locations in memory and so an algorithm processing this matrix has to know which values to pick out of memory. Likewise, the subroutines you pull from a library often need to know *both* the physical and logical sizes of your arrays. For example, in the subroutine cmatin.f given on the floppy, ndim is the physical dimension while n is the logical dimension.

Passing Sizes to Subprograms As indicated above, passing sizes to subprograms causes many errors and requires constant vigilance. Not only must you pass the logical and physical dimensions separately, but you must also watch that the sizes of your matrices do not exceed the allowed bounds in some subprograms. This usually occurs without an error message, and most likely will give you the wrong answers.[9] If you have the source code of the subroutines you are calling, you should check the DIMENSION statements in them for limits and general storage schemes. You should build warning messages into them or into the calling program so you will be notified if the bounds are exceeded.

Too Many Sizes Since incompatibility in the sizes of arrays in different parts of your program causes errors, it is a good idea to build in some scheme which guarantees or at least checks for compatibility. A subroutine using a matrix passed to it as an argument does not check if your operations go beyond the dimensions of the matrix; it just takes the starting location for the matrix and works from there.

Program Main	In main program.
DIMENSION a(100), b(400)	
SUBROUTINE Sample(a)	In subroutine.
DIMENSION a(10)	Smaller dimension.
a(300) = 12	Way out of bounds, but no message.

If you go beyond the declared limits you may affect another variable in memory (in this case *b*), use a variable defined for a different purpose, or use an undefined variable. One way to provide size compatibility is to actually declare array sizes in only your main program and then to pass those sizes along to your subprograms as arguments.

Equivalencing Using an EQUIVALENCE statement to overlay several arrays in the same memory location saves memory. It also can ruin some of the matrices already stored in

---

[9]There will be error messages if you are running with a version of your program compiled with the *debugging option* which watches array bounds.

memory (especially if the equivalenced matrices are of different sizes) and makes vectorizing difficult. Use it judiciously and only when you run a program within limited computing resources or if the savings are too great to pass up (and do include comments).

Say What's Happening As you now see, keeping track of array indices is both important and at times complicated. You decrease errors and problems by using self-explanatory labels for your indices, for example, `Nre = 1, 2` for real and imaginary parts, `Ndim` for the physical dimension of index `N`, and the like. Furthermore, it is always helpful to make up comment tables describing the meaning of the variables passed and to be generous in including these comments in different parts of the program. What it all comes down to is this, when you finally figure out how to do it, write it down. This not only benefits other users but keeps you from making errors.

Clarity versus Efficiency When dealing with matrices you have to try to find a happy medium between beauty and practicality. We need to balance the clarity of the operations being performed against the efficiency with which the computer does them. For example, having one matrix with many indices such as $V(L, Nre, Nspin, k, kp, Z, A)$ may be neat packaging, but it may require the computer to jump through large blocks of memory to get to the particular values needed, that is, it requires very large *stride*. (You alleviate this somewhat by making the left-most index vary most rapidly.) What you may want to do is keep the program as simple as possible, especially during the building and debugging stages. Then, when it is correct and ready for production runs, produce another version for speed. By doing this you can check your answers with the easy-to-follow version and minimize the time you spend figuring out what the program does.

Subscript 0 Recent versions of Fortran compilers permit `DIMENSION a(0:99)` statements which start indexing the array at 0 (and end at 99). This is in contrast to the older Fortran `DIMENSION a(100)` statement which has the index run from 1 to 100. This new freedom is valuable because it permits you to program up subscripts in much the same way they are written in mathematical equations, and it makes the interfacing with C easier. Furthermore, since both schemes store the array in memory in exactly the same way, it is possible to mix the two notations in different parts of the same program. The pitfall is serious: the mathematical equations you use, such as these recursion relations

$$(l+1)P_{l+1} - (2l+1)xP_l + lP_{l-1} = 0, \quad l = 0, 1, \ldots \qquad (11.2)$$
$$iP_i - (2i-1)xP_{i-1} + (i-1)P_{i-2} = 0, \quad i(= l+1) = 1, 2, \ldots \qquad (11.3)$$

differ in the two schemes, and mixing the two leads to errors. This is particularly a concern if you use old style "dusty deck" subroutines and make new-style modifications.

Tests It is *always* a good idea to test subroutines before relying on them. This is particularly true with library routines where your logic and the programmer's may not coincide. To start with, declare the physical dimensions of your matrices to be realistic, but use matrices with small logical dimensions whose properties (inverses, eigenvalues, etc.) you work out on your own (some of these are in the test cases). If the problem scales correctly, you can move ahead because you know you are using the routines correctly. For your more realistic cases you'll want to check that your inverse works and that the eigenvalues and eigenvectors satisfy the eigenvalue equations, that is,

$$AA^{-1} = A^{-1}A = I \tag{11.4}$$
$$H\vec{\psi}_n = E_n\vec{\psi}_n \tag{11.5}$$

In addition, you may want to explore the limits of size or the precision of these operations and build checks and warnings into your programs.

11.9 Subroutine Libraries

For industrial- or research-strength computing, the computational scientist will probably *not* want to write their own matrix subroutines but get them instead from a subroutine library. Not only do the library routines work well, but they are often *optimized* for a particular machine's architecture. For example, by using locally optimized subroutine calls on a workstation and supercomputer, you may automatically tune some of the most numerically-intensive parts of your program to the RISC or vector architecture respectively.

Further descriptions of a number of libraries and the procedures for getting them off the electronic network are given in Chapter 4, *Computer-Computer Interactions*. Some standard libraries are:

IMSL International Mathematics Society Library ($)

ESSL Engineering and Scientific Subroutine Library (IBM) ($)

NAG Numerical Algorithm Group (from the laboratories and universities of the United Kingdom) ($)

CM LIB U.S. Department of Commerce (includes EISPACK)

SLATEC U.S. DOD, DOE, DOC

CERN European Center for Nuclear Research

LINPACK, LAPACK, EISPACK, CMLIB, and SLATEC are in the public domain, while ESSL, IMSL, and NAG are proprietary ($) (yet often available on a mainframe or an institution-wide site license).

Some general categories you might find are:

Single Precision 4-*byte* (32 *bit*) length words (64 on "big" machines).

Double Precision 8-*byte* (64 *bit*) length words (128 on "big" machines).

Complex Use complex numbers (either single or double precision).

Vector Use special hardware for arithmetical operations on an entire *vector* simultaneously.

Scalar Not for vector processing.

Parallel Use special hardware for a number of different arithmetical operations on different variables or vectors at one time.

Matrix Type Real, complex, symmetric, nonsymmetric, Hermitian, sparse, ...

In general, serious scientific calculations almost always require double precision sooner or later, and especially on 32-bit-word workstations or when dealing with large matrices where the round-off error accumulates. Although it may be hard to believe, many workstation Fortran compilers produce faster running code in double precision than single precision because the hardware intrinsically performs all calculations in double precision.

Using these libraries may require some effort. If the entire library has been previously compiled, you will need to call the desired routine in your source code, and during compilation link in (the *-l* option) the rest of the library. If only source code is available, you will need to extract the appropriate subroutine *and* all the sub-subroutines it calls.

Matrix Test Cases

1. Find the inverse of

$$A = \begin{bmatrix} 4 & -2 & 1 \\ 3 & 6 & -4 \\ 2 & 1 & 8 \end{bmatrix} \tag{11.6}$$

Check the result in both directions and verify that

$$A^{-1} = \frac{1}{263} \begin{bmatrix} 52 & 17 & 2 \\ -32 & 30 & 19 \\ -9 & -8 & 30 \end{bmatrix} \tag{11.7}$$

2. Again consider the matrix A. Find the solutions $\vec{x_1}, \vec{x_2}, \vec{x_3}$ of

$$A\vec{x_i} = \vec{b_i} \tag{11.8}$$

$$\vec{b_1} = \begin{bmatrix} 12 \\ -25 \\ 32 \end{bmatrix}, \quad \vec{b_2} = \begin{bmatrix} 4 \\ -10 \\ 22 \end{bmatrix}, \quad \vec{b_3} = \begin{bmatrix} 20 \\ -30 \\ 40 \end{bmatrix} \tag{11.9}$$

They should be

$$\vec{x_1} = \begin{bmatrix} 1 \\ -2 \\ 4 \end{bmatrix}, \quad \vec{x_2} = \begin{bmatrix} 0.312 \\ -0.038 \\ 2.677 \end{bmatrix}, \quad \vec{x_3} = \begin{bmatrix} 2.319 \\ -2.965 \\ 4.790 \end{bmatrix} \tag{11.10}$$

3. Consider the matrix

$$H = \begin{bmatrix} a & b \\ -b & a \end{bmatrix}, \quad (a, b) = arbitrary \tag{11.11}$$

Use the computer to show that the eigenvalues and eigenvectors are the complex conjugates

$$\vec{\psi_1} = \begin{bmatrix} 1 \\ -i \end{bmatrix}, \quad E_1 = a - ib \tag{11.12}$$

$$\vec{\psi_2} = \begin{bmatrix} 1. \\ +i \end{bmatrix}, \quad E_2 = a + ib \tag{11.13}$$

4. Verify that the eigenvalues for the matrix

$$A = \begin{bmatrix} -2 & 2 & -3 \\ 2 & 1 & -6 \\ -1 & -2 & 0 \end{bmatrix} \tag{11.14}$$

are $E_1 = 5$ and $E_2 = E_3 = -3$. The eigenvector for E_1 is

$$\vec{x_1} = \begin{bmatrix} 1 \\ 2 \\ -1 \end{bmatrix} \tag{11.15}$$

while two linearly independent eigenvectors with eigenvalue 5 are

$$\vec{x_2} = \begin{bmatrix} -2 \\ 1 \\ 0 \end{bmatrix}, \vec{x_3} = \begin{bmatrix} 3 \\ 0 \\ 1 \end{bmatrix} \tag{11.16}$$

CHAPTER 12

RISC AND SUPERCOMPUTER ARCHITECTURES

... there are no clocks to measure time
but the beating of our singing hearts.

—Harold Littlebird, Santo Domingo/Languna Pueblo

12.1 Definitions

In this chapter we discuss some features of the architecture or structure of high performance computers and how they impact the software you write and run. We explain the meanings of common terms and, for a change, concentrate on the hardware. Our order for presenting this material reflects the operational viewpoint of scientists and engineers who prefer to get a tool working before mastering it. In Chapter 13, *Programming RISC and Vector Machines*, we suggest some ways to take advantage of computer architecture in your programming, specific extensions to Fortran for incorporating vector processing, and examples of the kinds of program structures which can be vectorized. Although RISC and vector architectures are also used on parallel computers, we put parallel concerns off until Chapter 14.[1]

What Is a Supercomputer?

By definition, supercomputers comprise the class of fastest and most powerful computers available. They have always existed and will continue to exist as long as computers are around. Although we may sound like a pair of old fogies by observing that younger generations always seem astounded by what older ones considered to be supercomputers, this is reasonable since computer performance has increased by a factor of about 10 every seven years since 1950.

On a more technical level, supercomputers are machines with good balance among major elements, including:

---

[1] Some of the material in Chapters 12–14 originated in the lecture notes of A. Rossi.

- multi-staged (pipelined) functional units,

- multiple CPUs,

- fast central registers,

- very large and fast memories,

- very fast communication speed among functional units,

- vector or array processors (around since 1975), and

- software which uses all the above effectively.

True supercomputers get major computing jobs done quickly by having all their parts working together and by doing many things at one time.

Currently, supercomputing almost always refers to *vector* and *parallel* computers. While all of the supercomponents on a supercomputer may make your program run faster, it is the vector and parallel processing on a specific machine to which you personally tune your programs to provide the greatest speedup. In a vector computer there is integrated processing of a whole array of numbers. In a parallel computer there is simultaneous and independent processing of different programs or different segments of the same program in different central processing units (discussed further in Chapter 14, *Parallel Computing*).

What Is Vector Processing?

Often the most demanding part of a scientific computation involves a matrix operation. On a classical (von Neumann) scalar computer, the addition of two vectors of physical length 99 to form a third,

$$[A] + [B] = [C] \tag{12.1}$$

ultimately requires 99 sequential additions,

```
a(1)+b(1)=c(1)  a(2)+b(2)=c(2)  ...   a(99)+b(99)=c(99)
--->------->------ run time ----->------>----------
```

There is actually much behind-the-scene work here since each of these additions involves a *fetch* of the ith element of the array A from its storage location in memory, the *fetch* of the ith element of the array B from its storage location in memory, the addition of the numeric values of these two elements in a CPU register, and then the *storage* of the sum into the ith element of the array C in memory. While it is nice that the computer has to do the boring repetitions for all elements rather than you, this does slow the computer down quite a bit and is wasteful in the sense that much of the time is spent telling the computer again and again how and where to fetch, add, and store. Keeping this in mind makes it easier to appreciate that a good part of what makes supercomputers "super" is their built-in capability to perform integrated operations on an entire *section* of a matrix. For example, with our vector addition (12.1), the successive additions of the elements get grouped together and overlayed (we discuss pipelining soon):

a(1)+b(1)=c(1)	First add.
a(2)+b(2)=c(2)	Second add just a cycle behind.
a(3)+b(3)=c(3)	Third add just a cycle behind.
...	
a(Z)+b(Z)=c(Z)	Up to Z elements possible.
--- run time --->	

In spite of the fact that this "vector arithmetic" may speed up a program by a factor of 10, this is still considerably less than the section size Z of 256 on the IBM ES/9000, or 64 on Cray since in reality the computer does not process all Z elements in one cycle or step. The exact speedup depends on the details of your program, the overhead time spent moving data to and from memory, and the portion devoted to matrices; it is never as large as you hoped for.

Note that while we speak of "vector" processing, this hardware treats matrices (mathematical tensors) of multiple dimensions—but still remains "vector" in the computer sense of treating only one subscript at a time ("matrix processing" would handle both columns and rows). In the same way, when we refer to an "array" we mean any variable with subscripts, be it a one-dimensional vector or a multidimensional matrix.

What Is a Workstation?

Workstations are computers small enough in size and cost to be used by a small group or an individual at his or her own work location, yet powerful enough for large scale scientific and engineering applications. Typically workstations run a Unix operating system and have good graphics capability, although they may vary considerably in overall capabilities and types of processors. Yet what has happened to washing machines and irons has also happened to workstations. Over time, designs for any one type of product seem to have more and more in common. Modern workstations also have a lot in common with supercomputers, so much so that it makes sense to discuss them together. While vector and parallel processing is not available on all workstations, the concerns of a programmer with how data are stored in relation to the architectural elements of the computer is quite relevant to both.

12.2   Limits to Vector Performance

Several terms describe the steps in migration (that is the moving) of programs over to a supercomputer. The first is *enabling*, which is when you transfer your existing code to the new machine, compile it, study the error messages, and make (presumably minor) syntactical changes until your program executes with no errors. You could then begin *vectorization*, which is the process of adapting an enabled program so it can use the vector facilities. In many cases it is possible to use the automatic vectorization option of a complier for this purpose. Another part of the process is *profiling* or *hotspot analysis*. This is when you try to discover those often small parts of your code in which most of the computation time is spent. (A survival tool known as *common sense* dictates that this is where you should be spending your time vectorizing.) After you have profiled your program, you *vector tune* it by optimizing it for vector hardware. But before doing all of the above, you may also find some familiarity with the theory behind vector performance valuable.

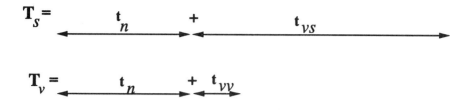

Figure 12.1: Decomposition of scalar and vector run times into nonvectorizable time t_n, potentially vectorizable time t_{vs}, and vectorized time t_{vv}.

As those of us who have kept a beloved family member waiting know, it is a fact of life that the slowest operation determines the rate of a sequential process. The rule of thumb is that most large scientific programs spend the majority of their time in 10–20% of the code, the slowest part. It is these parts which are worth the effort of streamlining. If these rate-determining parts involve arrays, you may be able to get some good speedup with vector hardware.

However, not every calculation—even if it utilizes subscripted variables—can be sped up by vector processing. Those which can are *vectorizable*, with the degree of vectorizability depending on the fraction of the program devoted to vector calculations as well as the specifics of the calculation. There are various ways in which the performance improvement expected from vectorization can be expressed, and here we look at a simple one known as *Amdahl's law*. As symbolized in Figure 12.1, assume that T_s, the total time it takes a program to run in *scalar* mode, consists of two components

$$T_s \; = \; t_n + t_{vs} \tag{12.2}$$
$$t_n \; = \; \text{nonvectorizable time} \tag{12.3}$$
$$t_{vs} \; = \; \text{vectorizable time} \tag{12.4}$$

where vectorizable time t_{vs} corresponds to time spent in those Do loops capable of using the vector hardware. We assume the nonvectorizable time t_n does not change when we run this same program with the vector hardware, while the time spent in the vectorizable Do loops decrease to t_{vv}. Accordingly, the total time to run the program with a vector machine is

$$T_v \; = \; t_n + t_{vv} \tag{12.5}$$
$$t_{vv} \; = \; \text{vectorized time} \tag{12.6}$$

The maximum speedup possible for a completely vectorizable program depends on the hardware characteristics of the individual computer. We measure this speedup by v, the ratio of times it takes to process the same vectorizable code on a scalar and vector machine,

$$v \; = \; \text{vector–scalar speedup ratio} \; = \; \frac{t_{vs}}{t_{vv}} \tag{12.7}$$

For the Cray $v \approx 10$, for the IBM $v \approx 5$. The *speedup* possible by using a vector machine for your particular piece of code (which is most likely not 100% vectorizable) is likewise defined as

$$S_v = \frac{t_n + t_{nv}}{t_n + t_{vv}} \tag{12.8}$$

The speedup your code attains is clearly a function of the fraction of your code which is vectorizable, which in turn is defined as

$$f = \text{fraction vectorizable} = \frac{t_{vs}}{t_n + t_{vs}} \tag{12.9}$$

If we put these pieces together, we obtain the speedup S_v as a function of the fraction of code vectorizable f and the elementary vector/scalar speedup v,

$$S_v = \frac{v}{v - f(v - 1)} \tag{12.10}$$

A plot of this function is shown in Figure 12.2. You can see that as the percent of vectorized code approaches 100, the program speedup S_v approaches the hardware limit v. Yet since we live in a world where we sometimes must wait for a loved one to get done first, we also see that unless the fraction of vectorized code is very close to 1 ($> 90\%$), even increasing the speedup s to a great extent will not speed the program up significantly (for $v = \infty, S_v = (1 - f)^{-1}$). Thus having a compiler which is able to vectorize a larger fraction of your program may well be more important than having hardware with a very large vector–scalar speed v.

Below is a typical profile of an application program. The profile has identified a "hotspot" which consumes 72 minutes in execution time while all other parts of the program consume only 28 minutes. Let us assume that the hotspot is vectorizable and that after vectorization the hotspot runs in 18 minutes. This means a performance improvement for the vectorizable part of the program of 4 : 1 is possible:

$$\text{vector-scalar speedup} = \frac{t_{vs}}{t_{vv}} = \frac{72}{18} = \frac{4}{1} \tag{12.11}$$

$$\text{percent vectorizable} = 100 \times \frac{t_{vs}}{t_n + t_{vs}} = 100 \frac{72}{100} = 72\%$$

The best *overall* improvement we can expect is accordingly about 2 : 1,

$$\text{program speedup} = \frac{T_s}{T_v} = \frac{28 + 72}{28 + 18} = 2.2 \tag{12.12}$$

If the actual speedup is less than this, it probably means the vector feature is not being utilized efficiently.

12.3 Memory Hierarchy

It is difficult to properly program a computer without understanding its hardware. And it is hard to understand the hardware without understanding the software for which the hardware was designed. It may be helpful, therefore, to keep in mind some pictures of the components of a high performance computer. The classical model of computer architecture is a CPU sequentially executing a stream of instructions which operates upon a continuous block of memory. This is basically the abstract *Turing machine* (a device with a finite

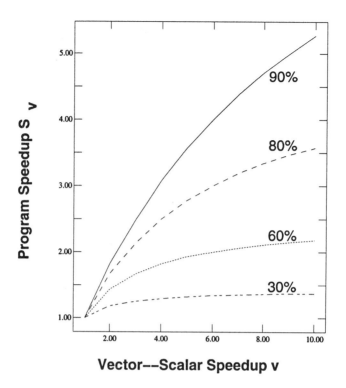

Figure 12.2: Amdahl's law for vector performance. The program speedup S_v versus vector–scalar speedup ratio v for various fractions of the code which can be vectorized.

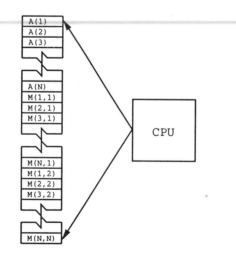

Figure 12.3: The logical arrangement of CPU and memory showing a Fortran array, $A(N)$, and matrix $M(N, N)$ loaded into memory.

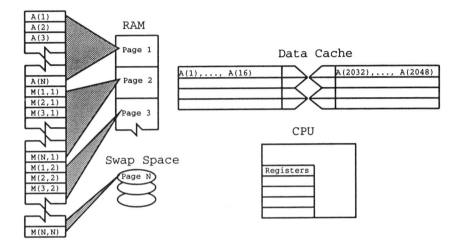

Figure 12.4: The elements of a computer's memory architecture.

number of internal states, using an infinite "tape" as input, output, and memory). In this example, a matrix would be stored in memory in a block just like we normally write it, Figure 12.3.

The real world is, unfortunately, more complicated. First, matrices are not stored in blocks, but rather in linear order. For example, in Fortran the leftmost subscript varies most rapidly (*column-major order*), so a matrix dimensioned m(3,3) is stored as

$$m(1, 1)\, m(2, 1)\, m(3, 1)\, m(1, 2)\, m(2, 2)\, m(3, 2)\, m(1, 3)\, m(2, 3)\, m(3, 3) \qquad (12.13)$$

In the C language, the numbering begins at 0 and is in row-major order,

$$m(0, 0)\, m(0, 1)\, m(0, 2)\, m(1, 0)\, m(1, 1)\, m(1, 2)\, m(2, 0)\, m(2, 1)\, m(2, 2) \qquad (12.14)$$

Secondly, as indicated in Figures 12.4 and 12.5, the values for the matrix elements may not even be stored all in one place.

You see in Figure 12.5 a schematic workstation or supercomputer which shows the complex memory architecture arising from an effort to balance speed and cost. This is a hierarchical arrangement with fast, expensive memory, supplemented by slow, less expensive memory. Although the numerical values are machine specific (and appear to change daily), the features are general. A high performance computer is a well coordinated whole, so a discussion of this memory hierarchy will draw us quickly into its other aspects, such as relative speed of the different units.

CPU Central Processor Unit. At the top of the pyramid you see the fastest part of the computer, the *execution* or *central processing unit*. This is the computing and controlling part of the computer which accepts and acts on instructions. In the good old days the CPU filled up basement rooms, but these days it is contained on a single chip or set of chips. The CPU actually consists of a number of *registers* which are

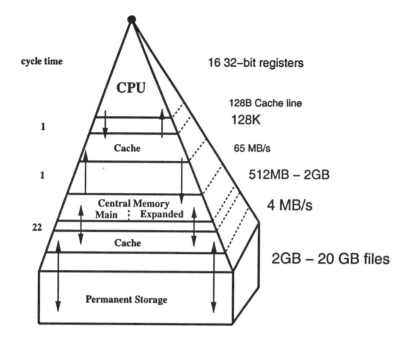

cycle time

CPU

16 32–bit registers

1

128B Cache line
128K

Cache

65 MB/s

1

512MB – 2GB

Central Memory
Main : Expanded

4 MB/s

22

Cache

2GB – 20 GB files

Permanent Storage

Figure 12.5: Typical memory hierarchy for single-processor high performance computer.

very high speed (and very expensive) memory units. It is in these registers where the basic ingredients of computation take place; that is, the *instructions* or orders to the hardware to do things like fetch, store, operate (add, subtract, multiply, ...) on data residing in specific parts of the computer. The group of instructions currently in use is called the *instruction stack*, and as the operations of your code are performed, the instruction stack changes like a window moving down your code. To accomplish all this processing, the CPU usually has separate registers for instructions, addresses, and *operands* (current data).

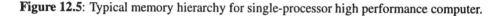

In addition to the CPU registers, there are other registers reserved for vector processing. The number of these registers, as well as the maximum number of independent

Table 12.1: Contents of Supercomputer Executive Units

COMPUTER	MAX #CPUs	VECTOR REGISTERS (max #)	STEP (elements)
IBM ES/9000	6	8 x 64-bit	256/128
Cray 1	1	8 x 64-bit	64
Cray 2	4	8 x 64-bit	64
Cray XMP	4	8 x 64-bit	64
Cray YMP	8	8 x 64-bit	64

Table 12.2: Central Storage for Several Supercomputers

COMPUTER	MAIN STORAGE	EXPANDED STORAGE
IBM ES/9000	2048 MB	8192/2 GB
Cray 1	256 MB	
Cray 2	256 Mwords	
Cray XMP	16 Mwords	
Cray YMP	32 Mwords	2 Gwords
Convex C240	128 MB	4.3 GB

CPUs possible for several different super computers, are given in Table 12.3. As you can see, the *partition* or *strip* of Z elements which can be processed at one time on vector hardware may be so large that it will not all fit into the CPU simultaneously. Accordingly, all Z elements are not processed in parallel.

FPU Floating Point (or Arithmetic) Unit. This is a piece of fast hardware designed for floating point arithmetic. It may be a separate unit called a *math co-processor* and is often on the same board or chip as the CPU.

Cache The next level down the pyramid in Figure 12.5 is the *high speed buffer* or *cache*. As processor speeds increased, computer designers found that normal RAM was no longer able to keep up with the processor's demands. Therefore the cache was introduced as a small, very fast bit of memory for holding instructions, addresses, and data in their passage between the very fast CPU registers and the slower main RAM memory. The main memory is dynamic RAM, called DRAM, while the cache is static RAM, or SRAM. If this intermediary storage cache is close to the CPU and used properly, it eliminates the need for the CPU to wait for data to be fetched from memory. While it is simpler to eliminate the cache by making all memory very fast (as on the Cray), this is usually a prohibitively expensive approach and may, at least indirectly, limit the programmer to smaller memory sizes.

Let us now can return to the question of why our original matrix is not stored all in one place. As you can see, portions of the matrix A in Figure 12.4 are stored in pages on the disk which are *swapped in* as needed. The cache holds a copy of the array A for fast access by the CPU, while inside the CPU a number of registers hold specific values of A needed to perform a calculation.

RAM Random Access Memory or central memory. On the next level down the pyramid in Figure 12.5 is *central storage*. It consists of *main* storage and (sometimes) a slower but larger *expanded storage*. RAM can be accessed directly, that is to say in random order, and it can be accessed quickly, that is to say without mechanical devices. It is where your program resides while it is being processed. Some typical amounts of this central storage for supercomputers are given in Table 12.3. Workstations can approach these same figures if your wallet permits (the X Window System by itself demands a minimum of 16 MB for good performance).

Pages Central memory is organized into *pages*, which are blocks of memory of fixed length. The operating system labels and organizes its memory pages much like we do the pages of books; they are numbered and kept track of with a *table of contents*.

Hard Disk Finally, at the bottom of the memory pyramid is the permanent storage on magnetic disks or optical devices. Although disks are very slow compared to RAM, they can store vast amounts of data and often partially compensate for their slower speeds by using a cache of their own, the *paging storage controller*. The hard disks that can be connected to workstations continue to get bigger, cheaper, and more robust. This is good because operating systems and applications also continue to get bigger, more interdependent, and more complex. For example, storing a complete Unix system itself now requires nearly 300 MB.

Virtual Memory Appropriate to its name, there is a part of memory which you will not find in our figures because it is *virtual* (it is also not visible because some computers, like the Crays, have no virtual memory). Virtual memory reflects an economic balance between fast, but expensive, memory and slow, but less expensive, memory. It offers a tremendous advantage to the computational scientist by permitting your program to use more pages of memory than will physically fit into RAM at one time. Pages not currently in use are stored in slower memory and brought into fast memory only when needed. The separate memory location for this switching is known as *swap space*, and that is shown in Figure 12.4. The effective size of memory is greatly extended, and it becomes possible to run programs on small computers which otherwise would require larger machines (or extensive reprogramming). You will pay a price for virtual memory with the considerable slowdown of your program's speed when it is actually invoked, but this may be cheap compared to the time you would need spend reprogramming (more about that later).

Displays Although we may not appreciate it until we have to pay for it, the high resolution output device or display also contains a large amount of memory. Displays are described in more detail in Chapter 6, *Introduction to Graphics and Visualization*.

Data Transfer

The arrows in the memory pyramid in Figure 12.5 represent data transfers between memory units. By looking carefully you will see that they do not always point in two directions. This is because high speed channels tend to be one-way-streets. While communication standards for supercomputers vary from manufacturer to manufacturer, there is some uniformity on workstations:

SCSI ("scuzzy") Bus A bus is a communication channel (bunch of wires) used for transmitting information quickly among different parts of a computer. The SCSI standard (or port on the computer's backside) is commonly used to attach hard disks and tape drives from various manufacturers. It can handle up to seven devices and transmits information at 2–5 MB per second.

I/O Bus The I/O bus is a communication channel used for attaching display adapters and other devices to the computer. It is not as standardized as the SCSI one used for attaching hard disks.

Although you cannot see it, the processing and data flow in Figure 12.5 are actually quantized:

Cycles It usually takes 1 cycle to transfer data into the CPU from cache.

Cache and Data Lines The data transferred to and from the cache or CPU are grouped into *cache lines* or *data lines*. For example, the cache line is 128 bytes long on an IBM. Furthermore, there is a *latency* here, that is, it takes time to bring data from memory into cache.

Multiple Channels The number of data channels connected to the registers is small (see the arrows in Figure 12.5); Cray XMP uses 1 for fetch and 1 for store, IBM ES/9000 uses 1 for fetch and 1 for store, Fujitsu uses 2 for fetch or store, and the NEC SX2 uses 2 for fetch and 2 for store.

Memory Banks On the Cray, NEC and Fujitsu, the main memory is divided into *memory banks* (8 on the Cray 1, 256 on the Y-MP) which are automatically accessed cyclically:

Bank:	**1**	**2**	**3**	**4**	**5**	**6**	**7**	**8**
subscript values	1	2	3	4	5	6	7	8
	9	10	11	12	13	14	15	16
	17	18	19	20	21	22	23	24
...								

Because successive elements of an array are stored in successive banks, in this example 8 words can be retrieved in one fell swoop—which is useful if your program requires adjacent words (*stride 1*), but not if your program requires every 9th word (*stride 9*). While the fetch takes 8 machine cycles, you get 8 words, and so the effective access time is reduced to 1 cycle/word (if you actually want those adjacent words). This scheme may obviously lead to *memory conflicts*, and thus additional waiting around, if your program does not access matrices with stride 1 or some simple integer multiple of the number of data banks.

Pages Data transfer to central memory from permanent memory occurs in *pages*. On a workstation the pages are usually 4096 bytes long, and we assume that length in our discussions. The transfer rate is $\approx$ 70 MB/s for a fast workstation and $\approx$ 1000 MB/s for the Cray YMP.

Page Faults If your program references a memory location on a page not present in central storage, the entire page must be copied from the lower level memory. To make room for the new page, the least recently used page in central memory is discarded (or copied to expanded storage if the data have changed). On some machines these are such slow processes that the computer may go on and do something else while the data are being transferred. These *page faults* cost overhead time and increase significantly the time you have to wait for your program to finish (*wall clock time*). This is the basic problem with virtual memory.

Clearly the processor time and real time needed to execute your program is decreased by minimizing transfers among different levels of memory. This can be done by making full use of memory pages and cache loads and by trying to have all the needed data in each phase of a computation fit into the allocated main or cache storage. The Fortran or C compiler will try to do this for you, but its success will be affected by your programming style. We discuss this style of programming in the next chapter.

Clock Speed, Cycles

We have been quoting the speed of computers in *cycles*, which is almost always the time it takes the processing unit to execute one instruction. Actually *the clock* is that part of the CPU which sets the basic speed for driving the entire system. For example, on the Cray 1 the time to execute one instruction is:

$$\tau = 12.5\,\text{ns} = 12.5 \times 10^{-9}\text{s} \qquad (12.15)$$

The corresponding number of instructions per second, or *speed*, is

$$1/\tau = 1/12.5 \times 10^{-9} = 80 \times 10^{6}\,\text{instructions/s} = 80\,\text{Mips} \qquad (12.16)$$

On the IBM ES/9000, $\tau = 8$ ns $\Rightarrow$ 125 Mips. On the Cray 2, $\tau = 4.1$ ns $\Rightarrow$ 244 Mips, but because it takes two cycles for each floating point operation on the Cray 2, the effective time is 8.2 ns (122 Mips). As a comparative workstation time, we note that the midline, IBM RS/6000/550 has $\tau = 24$ ns $\Rightarrow$ 42 Mips, essentially the same as a Cray 1.

While the cycle time measures the time required for the hardware to execute an elementary instruction, there are a good number of factors involved in determining the total time needed for a realistic calculation. A better measure of the speed in realistic calculations is *flops*, the number of *floating point operations per second,* or Megaflops, *mflop*. If the peak speed on a vector processor, for example, is about 150 Megaflop, an optimized library package such as ESSL may attain 120 mflop, a well-programmed application may run at 40–50 mflop, while a less carefully programmed application may run at 30 mflop. But even this is not a complete measure since a supercomputer can do many things at one time and so it is the total performance on some program which really counts; for that purpose you must experiment or get the manufacturer to produce a trial run for you.

The Central Processor

Now that our trip down memory lane has acquainted us with a supercomputer's major parts, we return to the central processing unit, and see how it gets to be so fast. The CPU is often *pipelined*, that is, has the ability to begin the steps necessary to execute the next instruction before the current instruction has finished. A simple analogy to pipelined architecture is an assembly line or a bucket brigade. In the latter, one person fills a bucket and passes it to the next person, who in turn passes it to the next, and so on until it reaches the person who throws the water on the fire. The person filling the buckets at the front end of the line does not have to wait for each bucket to get all the way to the fire at the end of the line before filling another bucket and passing it along.

In this same way, a processor fetches, reads, and decodes an instruction while another instruction is still executing. Consequently, even though it may take more than one cycle to perform some operations, it is possible for data to be entering and leaving the CPU on each cycle. The compiler's scheduling of the timing with pipelined architecture is critical since instructions can be issued each cycle, yet it takes several cycles to perform an operation (there are, for example, 4 cycles for an add), and there is little value in just having the units sitting around waiting.

Consider, for example, the operation $c = (a + b)/(d * f)$:

c = (a + b)/(d*f)	time
A1: `fetch a fetch b add`	t_1
A2: `fetch d fetch f mult`	t_1
A3: `divide`	t_2
——>—— pipeline flow ——>——	

Here the pipelined arithmetic units A1 and A2 are simultaneously doing their jobs (each of which is fetching operands while something else is going on), yet the third arithmetic unit A3 must wait for the first two to complete their tasks before it gets something to process.

To attain a further speedup, supercomputers usually permit *chaining* or *overlapping* of the vector units so that a second unit begins processing the output from the first even before the first unit has finished producing all its output. This leads to significant speedup as well as a new measure of time, *chime*, or time needed for a chained vector operation. In a related vein, supercomputers can get further speedup by *multiple memory access*. As an example, the Cray XMP can perform two memory reads and one store simultaneously.

12.4 CPU Design

RISC is an acronym for Reduced Instruction Set Computer. It is a CPU design developed for high performance computers and is used in all high performance workstations—at least in spirit—as well as many low end machines and supercomputers. In some sense RISC is a design philosophy, perhaps even an ideal. It is an approach to central computer architecture which increases the arithmetic speed of the CPU by decreasing the number of instructions the CPU must follow. As with many an ideal translated into reality (in this case silicon), compromises and adjustments occur. Yet this is okay with users since we are more concerned with getting our work done than whether a certain processor embodies a true ideal. RISC's original advocates claimed it was the best of three worlds: it could deliver high performance while also reducing manufacturing costs and design times. To a large extent RISC has lived up to its promises.

RISC versus CISC

We discuss RISC both as an interesting concept in CPU design and also to see what is necessary to optimize our codes for this type of computer. To understand RISC, we can contrast it to *CISC*, Complex Instruction Set Computers. In the late 1970s, processor designers began to take advantage of Very Large Scale Integration *VLSI* which allowed the placement of hundreds of thousands of devices on a single CPU chip. For example, the Motorola 68000 was introduced in 1979 and found favor among workstation designers who made it the heart of many Unix machines including the classic Suns and Apollos. Although those original Unix machines are quite obsolete, the chip is still ticking along today as the heart of many Apple Macintoshes.

A great deal of that Motorola 68000 chip is dedicated to *microcode*. This is an internal ROM on the chip containing machine language instructions programmed by the chip designer. These instructions operate on bytes, 16-bit or 32-bit words, and in some sense they set the operating characteristics of the computer. The address of the memory locations to be operated upon with this microcode is determined by any 1 of 14 addressing modes;

this adds up to over 1000 different instructions available to the microcode programmer. Although the basic instructions of the microcode were quite functional, they were not fast, a typical instruction on the 68000 taking more than 10 cycles. This was as expected because the goal of this complex machine language on a chip was to mimic the upper level languages already familiar to programmers. In fact, some designers began to discuss which language should become the standard microcode language, with Pascal and *Forth* as contenders for this primitive code.

The alternative to putting a high-level language in silicon is to rely on a high-level compiler to translate a high level language such as Fortran or C into efficient machine instructions. As compilers improved, developers relied upon them more rather than exploit the breadth of instructions available in CISC designs. Empirical studies bored out this improvement. A 1975 study by Alexander and Wortman of the *XLP* compiler on the IBM System/360 showed that 10 low-level machine instructions accounted for 80% of the instructions executed, while some 30 low-level instructions accounted for 99% of the use.

The RISC philosophy is to have the compiler utilize fully just these few instructions available at the chip level. The combination of a good optimizing compiler and a simple but efficient instruction set replaces the CISC design of a complex instruction set and microcode. The hope was that a simpler scheme would be cheaper to design and produce, that the processor would run at increased speeds, and that the space saved in the silicon by eliminating the large microcode could be used to attain greater arithmetic power.

The theory behind this philosophy for RISC design is the simple equation describing the execution time of a program

$$CPU\ time = \#\ instructions \times cycles/instruction \times cycle\ time \qquad (12.17)$$

Here $CPU time$ is the time required by a program, $\#\ instructions$ is the total number of machine-level instructions the program requires (sometimes called the *path length*); $cycles/instruction$ is the number of CPU clock cycles each instruction requires; and *cycle time* is the actual time it takes for 1 CPU cycle. Since the total CPU time is proportional to the first power of each variable on the right-hand side of (12.17), a fractional decrease in any one of them results in the same fractional decrease in *CPU time*, that is, improved performance.

As we view Equation (12.17) we can understand the CISC philosophy which tries to reduce *CPU time* by reducing the *# instructions*, as well as the RISC philosophy which tries to reduce *CPU time* by reducing the *cycles per instruction* (preferably to one). For RISC to achieve an increase in performance requires a greater decrease in cycle time and cycles/instruction than the increase in the number of instructions. For example, a CISC design may have a single `string-copy` instruction taking hundreds of long cycles to execute, while to accomplish the same task, a RISC design may need many repetitions of a whole series of instructions, yet with each instruction taking fewer short clock cycles.

An additional advantage of the RISC design, at least for arithmetic processing, results from the elimination of the space on the chip needed to store the large microcode. By using the space to increase the number of internal registers for the CPU to use, it is possible to obtain deeper or longer pipelines and thus a significantly lower probability of memory conflict. It is also possible to use this space for instruction-level parallelism.

Elements of RISC

Although the various RISC implementations all differ somewhat, we list here some of the specific attributes of a modern RISC system. Don't view this list as a recipe because it is in some sense redundant. The key to high performance is single-cycle execution. The remaining items are just ways to implement that.

Single-Cycle Execution Most machine-level instructions completed in a single clock cycle.

Small Instruction Set A set containing fewer than 100 instructions.

Register-Based Instructions Operations which are done on values contained in registers with memory access confined to load and store to and from registers.

Simple Instruction Format Fewer varieties of ways with which to deal with memory addresses and modes than the number of instruction formats found in CISC.

Many Registers More than 32 registers.

Pipelining Concurrent processing of several instructions or parts of instructions.

No Microcode Now provided by compiler and not on chip.

High Level Language The language compilers use to improve performance.

RISC Pioneers

The history of RISC shows a number of early, key contributors. The earliest effort to deliberately create a processor design using the above ideas was the 801 project at IBM's T. J. Watson Research Center under the direction of John Cocke.[2] The original work was done because the team was trying to design a large telephone switching network which required a very fast processor. The telephone switching project was canceled in 1975 without building a computer, but the design became an excellent basis for a general purpose processor and led eventually to the 801 machine.

The 801 was a single-instruction-per-cycle, register-based machine, designed in conjunction with an optimizing compiler. Its design was completed in 1978 and had some of its components—notably the instruction set—adopted as the basis for IBM's RT workstation. Unfortunately the RT's processor, the ROMP, had to be modified from the original 801 design in order to incorporate it into commercial VLSI circuits. The tradeoffs included a smaller number of registers and no memory caches.

Nevertheless, the 801 design team continued its work on a second design until 1985, at which time most of them began work on a second generation RISC processor dubbed "America." The America project included new design advances in floating point integration, compiler architectures, and instruction level parallelism. This design led to IBM's RISC System/6000, which we describe more completely in a later section as a *superscalar* design.

At about the same time as the early work at IBM, Seymour Cray was exploiting elements of what would eventually become RISC in his mainframe designs of both the

---

[2]The 801 got its name from the building which housed the design team. The group responsible for this work has now moved to a new site and changed their name from the 801 group to the RISC group.

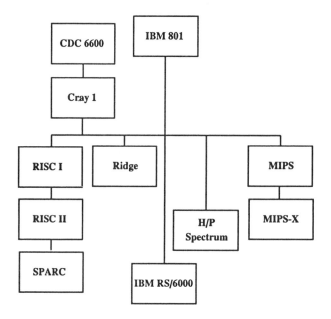

Figure 12.6: Possible family tree of RISC architecture.

Control Data Corporation's CDC 6600, and later, the Cray 1. Cray's designs emphasized the use of register-based operations, restricted memory access in load/store instructions, and pipelined execution.

Finally, in 1980, the actual term RISC was coined by David Patterson and David Ditzel in the RISC I and RISC II projects at Berkeley. These early designs were the basis for Sun's SPARC processors. Shortly after the RISC I project, the Stanford MIPS project began under the direction of John Hennessy. This led to the processor marketed by MIPS Computer Systems.

Numerous developmental projects and early RISC vendors dot the historical landscape. Figure 12.6 shows some of the genealogy of RISC. Ridge Computers was an early supplier of relatively high performance RISC machines which had a great impact on science. One of these early efforts was the Ridge 32C, whose processor had 16 general purpose registers and pipelining as well as a microcoded machine instruction set. Although the 32C did not attain the RISC ideal of 1 cycle per instruction, it did give both authors of this book their first experiences on RISC machines. In fact, a Ridge 32C still runs in one author's physics lab, at least on cool days.

RISC, Pipelining, and Floating Point Math

The RISC design is successful partly because of its frequent use of pipelining. Pipelining is not a new idea, having been used on mainframes and supercomputers for many years (and even in the MOS Technology's 6502, the processor used in Apple II computers). As already discussed, pipelining is the ability of the processor to begin the steps necessary to execute the next instruction before the current instruction has finished. Within the RISC design, pipelining is made simpler by having each instruction require the same sequence of steps: first fetching an instruction into the registers, then decoding it, then getting the operands from the registers, then executing the instruction, and finally placing the results into a register. The universality of this common sequence permits the hardware to be designed so that each step has its own hardware stage in a pipeline. While an individual step may take a full cycle or more, once the pipeline is fully loaded the processor is able to complete one instruction every cycle—just as the bucket brigade delivers a bucket of water every cycle even though an individual bucket has to travel through many hands.

While many RISC designs may provide extremely good performance for general computing, they also send some instructions to a CISC processor which is specialized for arithmetic with floating point numbers. The problem is that floating point arithmetic does not fit in well with the RISC scheme because floating point numbers are generally 64 bits and so they literally do not fit into the general purpose processor registers.[3] In addition, floating point operations take more that one clock cycle, and impede the pipeline.

To avoid incompatibility with floating point operations, some RISC systems have special design features to achieve good floating point performance. One such feature is parallel execution of multiple instructions. Another is the use of compilers which overlap operations, permitting the processor to continue useful work on one set of floating point operations while waiting for a second set of floating point operations to complete. For the floating point performance to actually match the performance of the rest of the processor, a custom floating point unit (FPU), which is an integral part of the processor's design, is required. For example, through the use of a heavily pipelined FPU with increased access to memory, the RISC System 6000 is capable of producing a floating point result every clock cycle.

Sun's SPARC

Sun's version of RISC is SPARC, Scalable Processor Architecture. It is based on the work done on the RISC projects at Berkeley and is the essence of simplicity, uniting the RISC advantage of reduced design time and costs with newly available semiconductor technologies. Furthermore, this design is *scalable*, that is, the same basic design is used for lower cost implementations running at tens of Mips as well as with the higher performance implementations running at hundreds of Mips.

The original SPARC processed a rather minimal 50 instructions, excluding floating point ones, with separate memory management and floating point units. The integer processing unit and floating point processing unit operated concurrently—but not in one integral design—with the integer unit extracting floating point instructions and placing them in a queue for the floating point unit. The unique feature of the SPARC design is the way in which it organizes the internal registers. In particular, the design is made scalable by having the number of registers vary in different implementations (initially up to a maximum of 120). In all implementations the registers are organized into sets of 24 registers called *windows*, supplemented by an additional eight *global* registers. The registers within each window are equally divided among *out* registers, *in* registers, and *local* registers. The register windows *rotate* providing the CPU with access to different windows and allowing the in and out registers from different windows to interact. This grouping of registers provides support for separate registers within different function calls which are designed

---

[3]Newer, 64-bit RISC architectures are now available.

for shared library support. Fortunately the compiler and not the user must deal with these complications.

IBM's Super Scalar Design

The IBM's RISC System/6000 is a second-generation design from the 801 project and is an interesting comparison to the SPARC design. The IBM design has 184 instructions (including 21 floating point ones)—which is triple the number of the SPARC design—and even includes a *string-move* operation which is surely not in the spirit of RISC. However, the RISC System/6000 was designed for an optimal balance between its particular compiler and machine instructions. The design team had access to several empirical studies of how applications consume CPU time and use instructions sets, and these studies showed that Unix and commercial applications used string-move operations for up to 30% of the total CPU usage. Adding hardware support for these types of applications is then in keeping with the RISC philosophy.

There are two major features distinguishing the RISC System/6000 design from other RISC processors: an instruction–level parallelism called *superscalar* and a high performance floating point processor integrated into the CPU design. The superscalar parallelism is achieved by separating the processor into three units which execute instructions separately: the integer unit, the floating point unit, and the branch unit. This design actually executes up to five operations per cycle: a branch instruction, an integer instruction, a conditional register instruction, and a floating point multiply–add instruction (which is counted as two operations). On the average (and when it works), it actually exceeds the RISC goal of one instruction per clock cycle.

The second major feature of the IBM design is the strong emphasis on floating point performance. The floating point unit is capable of completing an operation every clock cycle. Since these instructions include the multiply–add instruction, $D = A \times B + C$, the FPU actually achieves two floating point operations per clock cycle (a performance similar to a supercomputer's vector processor). To achieve this performance, the floating point unit is highly pipelined, as are vector processors. However, unlike a vector processor, the RISC System/6000 requires an average of only five clock cycles to fill the pipeline and produce the first result, while vector processors sometimes take more than a hundred cycles. To prevent an I/O bottle neck, the RS/6000 has two pipelines independently feeding the floating point unit, thus permitting the processor to complete a floating point load or store in one clock cycle. In addition, the FPU contains 32 floating point registers to hold constants or intermediate values.

12.5   Conclusion

We marvel at the complexity of memory and processing of supercomputers and workstations. Fortunately the operating system maps the physically fragmented pages of memory into a logically continuous *address space* for us. We only need to be aware that our program slows down drastically if it repeatedly has to access data which are paged to disk and it slows down considerably if it repeatedly refers to array elements not present in cache. Thus, while we are not forced to acquire any awareness of the architecture of our computer, as Backus said in Chapter 1, if we don't acquire some knowledge of it, we will likely get our noses rubbed in it.

PROGRAMMING FOR RISC AND VECTOR

We have seen in the preceding chapter that a high performance computer's memory has a number of key elements including cache, memory pages, and internal registers. Programming for optimized use of these elements is not difficult once you have a basic understanding of the memory architecture, of how programming constructs affect memory access and of the pitfalls to avoid. Of course as you optimize more for a specific piece of hardware with its special compiler features, you make your programs less portable.

Inasmuch as we encourage you to optimize your programs for your specific machine, we are obliged to tell you that this view is controversial within the computational science community. Those with a stronger belief in computer science than we may tell you that the compiler and not the scientist should do all the worrying about CPU and memory architecture since it generally may do a better job than you. Those experienced at running various large and complex scientific programs on a variety of machines often appear to have a somewhat differing view; if you want to get the most speed out of a significant scientific calculation, then you have to go into the program and adjust it by hand to the particular CPU and memory architecture of your machine. Because we have found speedup factors of three to five, the argument is not just academic. Our best advice at present is for you to decide whether the effort is worth it for the problem at hand. If your program will be run often and has a direct relation to your personal productivity, some experimentation may be worth the effort.

13.1 Virtual Memory

Virtual memory extends the effective size of a computer by making use of relatively plentiful (and cheap) hard disk space. More importantly, an application program *sees* a continuous span of memory addresses available for use which is greater than the size of the central memory within the machine. A combination of operating system and hardware *maps* this continuous span of memory into pages with typical lengths of 4 KB. As indicated in Figure 12.4, when the application accesses the memory location for m(i,j), the page of memory holding this address is found, and the virtual address is translated into a memory location within the 4KB memory page. A *page fault* occurs if the page resides on disk rather than in fast RAM. When a needed datum is on the disk, an entire 4K page containing this datum is read into memory while the least-recently used page in RAM is swapped onto the disk. This page swapping is the origin of the general programming rule pertaining to page space:

Avoid page faults.

Memory references should not be scattered throughout the entire address range. You should group together those data and program parts in memory which are used sequentially.

Virtual memory not only permits the computer to run *one* program which otherwise would be too big for memory, but also allows *multitasking*, a simultaneous loading into memory more programs than fit into physical RAM. Although the ensuing switching among applications uses up computing cycles by avoiding long waits while an application is loaded into memory, multitasking increases the total throughout and permits an improved computing environment for you. For example, it is multitasking which permits the X Windows System to provide us with the multiple windows we like so much because even though each X application uses a fair amount of memory, only the single application currently receiving input must actually reside in memory. The rest are *paged out* to disk. This explains why you may notice a slight delay when switching to an idle window as the page(s) for the now-active program is placed into RAM, and simultaneously the least-used application still in memory is paged out.

While paging makes little appear big, you pay a price because your program's run time increases with each page fault. Further, the Great American Dictum that competition is good does not apply to computer systems with paging. If virtual memory must be shared among multiple programs which run simultaneously, there will be memory access *conflicts* and the performance of all programs will suffer (the computer's version of sibling rivalry). In situations like these you will make more effective use of virtual memory by organizing your programs to successively perform their calculations on subsets of data, each completely fitting into RAM, and correspondingly lessening the need for paging.

Programming with Virtual Memory

The size of that piece of memory in which a program works is called its *working set size*. In general, good modular programming style and data organization decreases the working set size. It is common practice not to concern ourselves much with paging except when our program has outgrown its machine and we can't get a bigger machine on which to run. For those of you whose programs run out of space or are painfully slowed down by paging, here are some pointers on programming with virtual memory.

Reducing the *working set size* of an existing program requires *global optimization*. This is hard to demonstrate with the code fragments used in the examples, so our pointers are somewhat fragmented. The first specific rule is:

Worry about reducing the working set size only if your program is large.

You will know it is *large* if it is greater that the physical size of RAM, or if running it conflicts with fellow users on a machine in which the memory is shared. Smaller programs which keep all the data in central memory will not pose this concern. Rule two for working with virtual memory is:

Avoid simultaneous calculations in the same program.

Complete each major calculation before starting another to avoid competition for memory and consequent page faults. In the examples below, you may assume that the user's functions force12 and force21 are large subprograms that each have their own local and global variables—as well as—their own significant memory requirements. In the first example, two matrices are filled simultaneously, one for the elements of force12 and the other for the elements of force21:

BAD program, too simultaneous.	
| ```
Do j = 1, n
   Do i = 1,n
      f12(i,j) = force12(pion(i), pion(j))
      f21(i,j) = force21(pion(i), pion(j))
      ftot = f12(i,j) + f21(i,j)
   EndDo
EndDo
``` | Fill f12.<br>Fill f21, &<br>then ftot. |

You can see that each iteration of the Do loop requires the data and code for all the functions and access to all elements of the matrices and arrays. The working set size of this calculation is the sum of the sizes of the arrays f12(N,N), f21(N,N) and pion(N) plus the sums of the sizes of the functions force12 and force21. Here's how this calculation looks broken into separate components:

GOOD program, 2 loops.	
| ```
Do j = 1, n
   Do i = 1, n
      f12(i,j) = force12(pion(i), pion(j))
   EndDo
EndDo
``` | Fill just f12. |
| ```
Do j = 1, n
   Do i = 1, n
      f21(i,j) = force21(pion(i), pion(j))
   EndDo
EndDo
``` | 2nd nest.<br><br>Fill just f21. |
| ```
Do j = 1,n
   Do i = 1, n
      ftot = f12(i,j) + f21(i,j)
   EndDo
EndDo
``` | 3rd nest.<br><br>Compute ftot. |

In this example the separate calculations become independent and the working set size is reduced. The working set size of the first Do loop is the sum of the sizes of the arrays f12(N,N) and pion(N) and the function force12. This is approximately half the previous size. The size of the last Do loop is just the sum of the sizes for the two arrays. The working set size of the entire program is the larger of the working set sizes for the different Do loops.

You can estimate the actual amount of paging in these examples after assuming that either force function is too large to coexist in physical memory with the other force function. In the first example, calculating force12 requires that the data and code for this function be paged into memory. Calculating force21 requires that the data and code for force12 be paged out and that force21 be paged in. The total number of times you must page is approximately N^2, where N is the dimension of the arrays. (This neglects the sum of ftot since the data requirements for this addition are only for pages of matrices f12(N,N) and f21(N,N).) In the second example, you do all of the force12 calculations and *then* all of the force21 calculations and, consequently, you only have to page once!

The third rule in reducing working set size is to *group data elements close together in COMMON blocks if they are going to be used together in calculations*. The data structures are laid out in memory in the same order as declared which avoids jumping around and paging. As an example, consider the code:

`COMMON /pp/ zed, ylt(9), part(9), zpart1(49123)`	Zparts are
`*             , zpart2(49123), med2(9)`	tacked on.
`Do j = 1, n`	
`   ylt(j) = zed*part(j)/med2(9)`	Variables used.

Here the variables zed, ylt, and part are used in the same calculations and are adjacent in memory because the programmer grouped them together in COMMON. Later, when the programmer realized the array med2 was needed, it got tacked onto the end of COMMON. All the data comprising the variables zed, ylt, and part fit into one page, but the med2 variable is on a different page because the large array zpart2(49123) separates it from the other variables. In fact, the system may be forced to make the entire 4-KB page available in order to fetch the 72 bytes of data in med2. While it is difficult for the Fortran or C programmer to assure the placement of variables within page boundaries, you will improve your chances by grouping data elements together.

13.2 Programming with Data Cache and Registers

Data caches have grown in importance as high-performance workstations have become more prevalent. On systems that use a data cache—which include almost all high end workstations and many supercomputers—this may well be the single most important programming consideration. This is because continually referencing data that are not in the cache (*cache misses*) may lead to an order-of-magnitude increase in CPU time and a waste of valuable computing power. While it is important to make full use of the cache on smaller workstations that have a cache of a few kilobytes or less, with that small a cache only the basic optimizations of sequentially reading and writing data can be implemented. Even if you use a computer like a PC or a Cray which has no data cache, you'll find it worth your time to understand cache flow requirements if you ever want to port your programs.

As indicated in Figure 12.4, the data cache holds in its own fast RAM a copy of some of the data in memory. The basics are the same for all caches but the specifics are

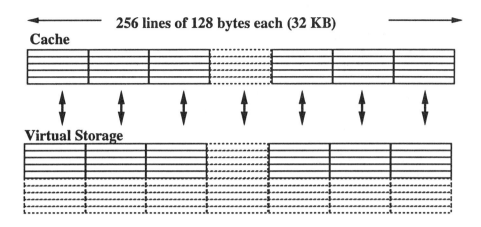

Figure 13.1: The cache manager's view of RAM. Each 128-byte cache line is read into one of four lines in cache.

manufacturer-dependent. We describe here the functioning of the *four-way associative cache* used by IBM RS/6000.[1] When the CPU tries to address a memory location, that is, tries to read (fetch) or write (store) data, the *cache manager* checks to see if the data are in cache. If they are not, the cache manager reads the data from memory into cache and then the CPU reads or writes the data directly from the cache. Just as virtual memory moves blocks of memory called pages, the cache moves blocks of memory called *lines*. In the example in Figure 13.1, the cache line or *bandwidth* is 128 bytes which translates to sixteen 64-bit double-precision floating point numbers.

There is another aspect of cache to consider. A number of cache lines are grouped in larger blocks called *sets*. In the example, 128-byte lines are organized into 16-KB sets, with the cache having four 16K sets (for a total 128KB cache). Furthermore, as is also indicated in Figure 13.1, the cache manager views RAM in 16KB sets of 128-byte lines. This means that any line of memory may be read into one of four lines in cache. When all four lines are full, the new line read in overwrites an existing line. If the data in the existing line have changed while in cache, the whole line is first written back into RAM, and then the new line is read in. This is why this cache arrangement is termed a *four-way associative cache.*

Working with a Data Cache

For high-performance computing we should write programs which keep in cache as much of the data we process as possible. While it is difficult to isolate the effects of cache from other elements of the computer's architecture, we estimate its importance by comparing the time it takes to step through matrix elements row by row to the time it takes to step through matrix elements column by column. As we have already emphasized in Chapter 11, *Scientific Programming Hints*, Fortran matrices are stored in memory in successive memory

---

[1]Other systems like those from HP use a *direct cache* which is less complex than the *four-way associative cache* but which requires a larger size to be as effective.

locations with the row index varying most rapidly (column-major order),

$$m(1, 1)\, m(2, 1)\, m(3, 1)\, m(1, 2)\, m(2, 2)\, m(3, 2)\, m(1, 3) \dots \qquad (13.1)$$

Let's say in your programming you refer to a matrix by columns,

`Do j = 1, 999`	A simple Do loop.
`    x(j) = m(1,j)`	Sequential column reference.

This makes large jumps through memory with the memory locations addressed not yet read into cache.

You can test the importance of cache flow on your machine by comparing the time it takes to run these two simple codes:

`      DIMENSION Vec(idim,jdim)`	Loop *A*.
`      Do 200 j = 1, jdim`	
`        Do 200 i=1, idim`	
`          Ans = Ans + Vec(i,j)*Vec(i,j)`	Stride 1 fetch.
`200 Continue`	
`      DIMENSION Vec(idim,jdim)`	Loop *B*.
`      Do 300 i = 1, idim`	
`        Do 300 j = 1, jdim`	
`          Ans = Ans + Vec(i,j)*Vec(i,j)`	Stride jdim fetch.
`300 Continue`	

Loop *A* steps through the matrix `Vec` in column order. Loop *B* goes in row order. By changing the size of the columns (the left index for Fortran) we change the size of the step (*stride*) we take through memory. Both loops take us through all elements of the matrix, but the stride is different. (You will recall that when data are read into cache, a definite number of elements, a line, are read in at once.) By increasing the stride and moving ahead faster, we use fewer elements in each cache line, but require additional swapping and loading of cache, and thereby slow down the whole process!

If you run the codes on your computer for increasing column size `idim` and compare the times for loop *A* versus those for loop *B*, you will get some estimate of the effect of cache on your particular computer. Figure 13.2 is a graph of the ratios of times for loop *A* and loop *B* for a number of computer architectures. As you can see, a machine with a very small cache, such as the Sun SPARC Station, is sensitive to stride.

In summary, the basic rule in programming for cache is *keep the stride low, preferably at 1*. In other words, *first vary the leftmost index on Fortran matrices, the rightmost on C matrices*.

Blocking or Strip Mining

Sometimes no matter how hard you try it is just not possible to make the references to a matrix stride one within some loop. What is a programmer to do? Well, an alternative is to *block* the loops into *strips* which fit exactly into the cache line. This *blocking* or

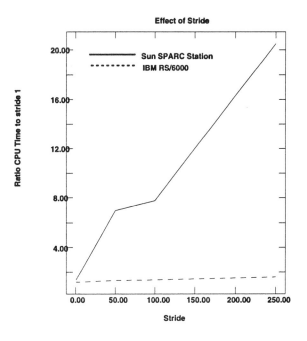

Figure 13.2: Increase in CPU times for various size strides compared to stride of one.

strip-mining is also used for better optimizing codes for vector processors, as discussed later in this chapter.

Blocking requires the strip to be the exact size of the cache line, and this varies from system to system, so specific examples must be architecture dependent. The technique is general, however, as is its failure for extremely small caches. For an IBM RISC System 6000, there is a cache size of 64 KB and a cache line of 128 bytes. If all of the floating point variables are double precision (8 bytes), this converts to 16 floating point matrix elements per cache line.

Consider these loops:

BAD cache use.	
` DIMENSION A(800,160),  B(160,800)`	
` DIMENSION C(800,160)`	
` Do 200 j = 1, 160`	Outer Do.
`    Do 200 i = 1, 800`	Inner Do.
`       C(i,j) = C(i,j) + A(i,j) * B(j,i)`	Note B reversal.
`200 Continue`	

Because the rightmost (column) index for matrix B varies most rapidly (not what we recommend), matrix B is accessed with stride 160. In the first iteration of the innermost i loop, a cache line is filled with 16 elements of the matrices A, B, and C. Specifically, A(1,1), A(2,1),... A(16,1) and B(1,1), B(2,1),... B(16,1) and C(1,1), C(2,1),

... C(16,1) are read into cache. All 16 elements of A and C are used in the following computations, but B(2,1) is not used until the inner loop is completed. By that time the cache line containing B(2,1) has been swapped out of the cache and replaced with a line containing elements that were needed in the inner loop.

A more optimal use of cache is:

GOOD cache use.	

``
      DIMENSION A(800,160), B(160,800)
      DIMENSION C(800,160)
      Do 200 jj = 1,160,16
        Do 200 i = 1,800
          Do 200 j = jj, jj+15
             C(i,j) = C(i,j) + A(i,j) * B(j,i)
  200 Continue
``
	
	For 16-element strip.
	Same as before.
	For each strip.
	Same as before.

You can see that by adding another loop so that 16 iterations of the j loop are completed with each iteration of the i loop, you will utilize all of the elements of B in the cache line. Of course, this requires that 16 more cache lines, or 256 more elements of A and C, be read into the cache, but we have the space to simultaneously hold all 256 elements of A and B so varying the outer index of these matrices on the blocking loop does not hurt performance. With each iteration of the i loop, 16 more cache lines of A and C and one cache line of B are read. These elements are not referenced again when each iteration is complete, thereby permitting them to be overwritten the next time through the loop.

We actually cheated somewhat in this example by assuming each matrix started on a cache line. In reality, the matrix may start anywhere in memory, so the first cache line containing a given matrix may also have other variables in it, and subsequent lines would not begin on multiples of 16. Such an offset means that the jj+15 blocking would force two lines of matrix B to be read in, which reduces the effectiveness of the method.

We have also found the necessity of worrying about details is not as high in practise as it may appear because coarser blocking sizes, say 50 rather than 16, works well with IBM's cache architecture. Experimentation with your particular system is required, but you need to remember to keep the blocking small enough so that all elements of the inner loop fit into cache.

Another way we tried to keep our example simple was that we intentionally picked the dimension to be 160, which is a multiple 16. If we had used a more realistic dimension, we would have had to add an extra loop to clean up the remaining elements which did not exactly fit into the last strip. Yet some balance here is of value; as we add in more special programming constructs, the code becomes less readable and more difficult to maintain.

Registers

Using the CPUs internal registers is common practice for C programmers but rarer among Fortran users. Modern CPUs have many internal registers, including floating point registers, index registers, and general purpose registers. Fortunately for those of you more interested in the results of computations than in computer architectures, modern compilers do a very good, if not an excellent, job at managing the register use for us, and (as discussed in

Chapter 11, *Scientific Programming Hints*) we only need to give the compiler some hints to make sure it does its job well.

Registers are used to hold interminate values during a calculation. The grouping of repeated calculations helps the compiler detect values that should be held in registers. For an example, examine the loop:

```Do i = 1, N F1(i) = S1(i) - E1*C(i)/(Etot(i) - Sqrt(Ovlp)) F2(i) = S2(i) - C(i)*E2/(Etot(i) - Sqrt(Ovlp)) EndDo```	*Ovlp* unchanged.

You will first notice that `Sqrt(Ovlp)` is not dependent on the loop index `i` and yet it is calculated twice for each iteration over `i`. The square root function is very time consuming and so our first optimization is to move this *section of invariant code* into a temporary variable outside the loop:

```tmp = Sqrt(Ovlp) Do I = 1, N F1(i) = S1(i) - E1*C(i)/(Etot(i) - tmp) F2(i) = S2(i) - E2*C(i)/(Etot(i) - tmp) EndDo```	Invariant code.

The compiler should now be able to place this value into an internal register where it is available during the loop calculations. This type of reconstruction is really something the optimizer should be able to do on its own, and some can.

You saw that the expression `C(i)/(Etot(i) - Sqrt(Ovlp))` is calculated twice in the loop. By adding parentheses to this expression, we clue the compiler that the same expressions appear on each line:

```tmp = Sqrt(Ovlp) Do I=1,N F1(i) = S1(i) - E1* (C(i)/(Etot(i) - tmp)) F2(i) = S2(i) - E2* (C(i)/(Etot(i) - tmp)) EndDo```	Added ( ). Added ( ).

The compiler should now be able to recognize the repeated use of the expression, evaluate it only once per iteration, and store the value in a register for repeated use. All compilers are able to detect repeated calculations, so this should be quicker than forcing the compiler to see the repetition by assigning to it a temporary variable (fewer stores and fetches):

```tmp = Sqrt(Ovlp) Do I=1,N tmp2 = C(i)/(Etot(i) - tmp) F1(i) = S1(i) - E1*tmp2 F2(i) = S2(i) - E2*tmp2 EndDo```	Slower. The force play. 1 fetch. 2nd fetch.

If your compiler does not recognize the repetition, then using the temporary variable tmp2 within the Do is still an improvement because the floating point division takes far more time than reading a value from memory.

Example: Matrix Multiplication

The penultimate example of memory usage is large matrix multiplication. This involves all of the concerns with stride, blocking, register use, and paging. Consider the matrix multiplication

$$[C] = [A] \times [B] \tag{13.2}$$

The natural way to code this is as a standard definition of multiplication:

$$c_{ij} = \sum_{k=1}^{N} a_{ik} \times b_{kj} \tag{13.3}$$

The sum is a column of A times a row of B. The Fortran code implementing this multiplication is

`Do 10 i = 1, N`	Row.
`  Do 10 j = 1, N`	Column.
`    c(i,j) = 0.0`	Initialize.
`    Do 10 k = 1, N`	
`      c(i,j) = c(i,j) + a(i,k)*b(k,j)`	Accumulate sum.
`10 Continue`	

The problem is that while the B has stride 1, the C has stride N. You can solve the problem by performing the initialization in another loop:

`Do 20 j = 1, N`	Initialization.
`  Do 10 i = 1, N`	
`    c(i,j) = 0.0`	
`10 Continue`	
`  Do 20 k = 1, N`	
`    Do 20 i = 1, N`	
`      c(i,j) = c(i,j) + a(i,k)*b(k,j)`	
`20 Continue`	

On a Sun SPARC Station the difference in CPU times for these two programs is a factor of 100. In many realistic applications, such a slowdown dominates the calculation.

In summary, you have seen how to use *blocking* to speed up matrix multiplication. You have also seen a more general solution by changing the programming. The lesson is the one we began with: despite the advances in compilers and hardware, for top performance you must still be aware of the computer architecture and know how to use it. In other sections we present specifics on how to tune such problems for RISC and vector machines.

13.3   Vectorizability and Program Analysis

While all of the supercomponents on a supercomputer may well make your program run faster, it is the vector processing for which you are most personally responsible and which can give you the greatest speedup. In the preceding chapter we examined some of the hardware components of a supercomputer in order to broaden our general education as well as to improve our ability to program them.

Now we will examine several software aspects of vectorization and focus on a few standard procedures for vectorizing some common program structures. In the process we give some specifics on how to use the compiler options to optimize your vectorization, to check that the compiler is doing it properly, and to direct the compiler to do it properly if it has decided not to.

You saw in Chapter 12's discussion of Amdahl's law that unless a large fraction of the computationally intensive part of your program is vectorized, the running time for your program will be limited by its scalar part. How, then, do you go about vectorizing a large fraction of your codes? The easiest path is to change nothing yourself and let the compiler do its job. The next easiest is to remove your own personal utility subroutines and use vectorized library routines (written by people who are paid to do that kind of stuff).

At this point, if you want to be serious, you start looking at your code and its use of subscripted variables in either vectors or matrices. However, not every calculation involving subscripted variables can take advantage of vector hardware. Those which can are called *vectorizable* with the degree of vectorizability depending on the fraction of your program devoted to vector calculations and the specifics of the calculation. The Do loop, specifically, is the basic unit of vectorization. Only those parts of your calculation involving Do loops are vectorizable, and then only if:

- calculations within the loop for one value of the loop index i have no implicit or explicit dependence on a previous value of i; and

- all calculations involving variables which depend on i can be performed simultaneously.

You may also notice that there are a number of software features on vector machines which will speed up parts of your program without requiring any particular effort on your part. For example, the Fortran compiler usually has access to *compound instructions*, that is, instructions which can simultaneously perform two vector arithmetical operations such as: multiply and add, multiply and subtract, and multiply and accumulate. Because compound instructions execute at double speed, that is, two *flops* per cycle (in contrast to most other vector instructions which execute at one flop per cycle) this effectively doubles the speed of the computation. (This is in addition to the vector speedup obtained from each computation being performed on a vector of section $Z \approx 100$ elements.) If you can write your Do loop to contain mainly compound instructions, your program will achieve a floating point operation rate which approaches the hardware limit.

13.4   Comparison of Scalar and Vector Arithmetic

To use vector hardware properly and efficiently requires an understanding of how the Fortran compiler turns your formulas and array references into machine code. Consider, for example, the addition of two vectors of physical dimension N:

$$C \; = \; A + B \tag{13.4}$$

$$\begin{bmatrix} c_1 \\ c_2 \\ c_3 \\ \vdots \\ c_N \end{bmatrix} = \begin{bmatrix} a_1 \\ a_2 \\ a_3 \\ \vdots \\ a_N \end{bmatrix} + \begin{bmatrix} b_1 \\ b_2 \\ b_3 \\ \vdots \\ b_N \end{bmatrix} \tag{13.5}$$

The matrix addition (13.4) may have a typical Fortran coding:

`Do 10 i = 1,N`	Repeat N times.
`    c(i) = a(i) + b(i)`	Add element by element.
`10 continue`	

This adds the matrices by independently adding each element of the matrices together.

Scalar Processing of Do Loop

The arithmetic on a computer is performed in the *registers* of the executive unit. In *scalar processing* these registers hold only one number (array element) at a time, and so matrix addition is accomplished by *sequentially* loading into the scalar registers each individual element of A and each individual element of B, adding them together in the registers, and then storing the sum in the corresponding single element in C. The elementary machine language pseudocode may look like this:

`LOAD  ELEMENT  COUNT`	Retrieve $N = A$'s dimension.
`LOAD  a(i)  INTO`	Load element $a(i)$ into register on each pass.
`ADD  b(i)  TO`	Adds $b(i)$ to number in scalar register.
`STORE  c(i)  FROM`	Copy value from scalar register into $c(i)$.
`DECREMENT  COUNT  BY  1`	Decrease loop index by 1.

Vector Processing of Do Loop

A computer with *vector processing* has registers which hold a number $Z \approx 100$ of elements at one time. As you will recall from our discussion of cache storage, the partitions of the arrays in your program of length Z are called *sections* or *strips*, and the partitioning of the arrays is called *strip mining*. If your program accesses data with *stride* 1 (for example: `x(1,1),x(2,1),x(3,1),x(1,2)` $\cdots$), these strips will be mined from adjacent data elements; if the stride is not 1 (for example the diagonal: `x(1,1),x(2,2),x(3,3),x(4,4)` $\cdots$), some prospecting through memory is mandatory before the mining gets done.

Returning now to our vector addition (13.4), the machine pseudocode for vector hardware looks similar to the scalar case, only now Z times more work gets done in each step:

LOAD ELEMENT COUNT	Retrieve $N = A$'s dimension.
LOAD a(i):a(i+Z) INTO	Load Z a's each pass through loop.
ADD b(i):b(i+Z) TO	Add Z b's to Z numbers in register.
STORE c(i):c(i+Z) FROM	Place Z values from register into C.
DECREMENT COUNT BY Z	Decrease loop index by Z.

Although the Fortran code you write is the same for scalar or vector processing, the compiler knows the computer's hardware can handle Z elements at one time and will produce different machine code. This is equivalent to your having written the following Fortran code (lines beginning with * are compiler-generated code):

`Do 10 i= 1, N, Z`	i 1: 500, steps of $Z=128$.
	(i.e., $i = 1,129,257,385$).
`*     Do 5 j = 0, min(127,N-i)`	$j=0{:}127, 0{:}127, 0{:}127, 0{:}115$.
`*5      c(i+j) = a(i+j) + b(i+j)`	Span space in steps:
	$a(1+0{:}127), a(129+0{:}127),$
	$a(257+0{:}127), a(385+0{:}115)$.
`10 continue`	

This shows how a full strip of length 128 as well as a *remnant* of length 116 are handled by the vector processor. On some compilers, the remnant strip is actually processed as if it were full length but with only 116 defined values stored. While this full processing is usually harmless, it is not if one of the undefined values happens to overflow.

13.5 Inner and Outer Loop Consideration

Now that you have an idea of how the compiler translates your Fortran code to take advantage of the vector facilities, you will want to consider how you should be writing Fortran in order to take advantage of the compiler's abilities. Only you are smart enough to know and think about what your program is actually meant to do.[2] This means that at some point, you should appreciate what the compiler is doing to guarantee that the vectorization is correct. For example, consider a simple set of nested Do loops which adds a vector b to each column of a matrix a and places the result in the next column over in a:

`DIMENSION a(500,501)`	
`Do 10 J = 1,N`	The outer J Do loop.
`  Do 20 I = 1,N`	The inner I Do loop.
`    a(I,J+1) = a(I,J) + b(I)`	Add $b(I)$ and shift.
`20   Continue`	End inner.
`10 Continue`	End outer.

Remember, for vector processing too you will want to keep in mind how the computer stores matrices. For example, in Fortran they are stored in *column-major* order, that is, as

---

[2]Searle (1990), Penrose (1990).

a linear string of elements with the *leftmost* index varying most rapidly (the opposite of an odometer):

$$a(1, 1), a(2, 1), \cdots, a(N, 1), a(1, 2), a(2, 2), \cdots, a(N, 2), \cdots, a(N, N)$$

Vector versus Scalar Nested Loops

If you want your *scalar program* to execute Do loop nests most rapidly, it is good practice to have:

- The leftmost subscript be the one which is varied by the innermost Do 20 loop. (As the inner loop gets repeated by the outer loops, this permits the computer to walk straight through memory with the least jumping around.)

- The order of the subscripts vary from left to right in matching order of motion from inner loop to outer loop (i = inner, j = outer), for the same reason as above.

- The dimension of arrays for the leftmost subscripts contain the largest values. (This produces the largest span of sequentially used elements physically close to each other in memory.)

While these rules of thumb are useful for all computations, there are additional rules which are important for vector processing of *nested vector Do loops*. Specifically, on machines using cache, it probably takes the same time to load to or store from a register as it does to execute a vector computation (one machine cycle), so you can save about 30% in running time if you avoid loading the cache more than necessary. Instead, try to reuse the data currently stored in the vector registers. This is done with techniques known as *outer loop vectorization* and *loop distribution*. To understand the benefit of outer loop vectorization, let's look at how nested loops are vectorized. Consider the preceding nested Do loops. They are converted by the compiler to the effective Fortran statements:

`      Do 10 j = 1,N`	Same as original.
`*        Do 20 ii = 1,N,Z`	Chunking loop begins here,
	ii=1,129,257,385.
`*           Do 21 i = 0, min(Z-1,N-ii)`	The vector load loop.
	0:127, 0:127
	0:127, 0:115
`*21       vr1(i) = b(ii+i)`	Place 1 *b* in temporary variable.
`*         Do 22 i = 0, min(Z-1,N-ii)`	0:127, 0:127, 0:127, 0:115.
`*22       vr2(i) = vr1(i) + a(ii+i,J)`	A vector add.
`*         Do 23 i = 0, min(Z-1,N-ii)`	0:127, 0:127, 0:127,0:115.
`*23          a(ii+i,J+1) = vr2(i)`	Same as before.
`20       Continue`	
`10 Continue`	

The asterisk indicates compiler-generated code. The inner loops represent single vector instructions, the dummy variables *vr*1 and *vr*2 symbolize vector registers, and the variable Z is the vector register section size ($Z = 128$ is assumed in the comments).

In the effective Fortran code, the 20 loop splits the vector a into chunks of length Z which fit exactly into the vector registers (except the last one, a remnant). This loop is called the *sectioning, blocking, stringing,* or *chunking* loop. The 21 loop within this is a *vector load*, the 22 loop is a *vector add*, with the a elements being fetched directly from storage (without passing through cache), and lastly the 23 loop places the vector register's load of elements back into storage.

Even though the original Fortran for these statements followed good scalar programming practice by having the leftmost index vary most rapidly, and the inner loop over the leftmost index, it does not produce optimal vector coding because the vector registers are not being reused. Each time the j loop gets repeated, the vector register (denoted by $vr1$) gets loaded with a *new* section of B. Because of this, Z different elements of B get loaded sequentially. The problem (also addressed in our discussion of cache) is that when a section of B is required again, it will no longer be in the registers. The calculation must wait for it to be reloaded.

Surprisingly, if the outer loop is chosen for vectorization (not possible with all compilers), then it is possible to reuse the vector register. To accomplish this, you change the original Fortran code so that i is the *outer* Do loop index:

```Do 10 i = 1,N```	Outer loop now vectorized.
``` Do 20 j = 1,N```	Inner J loop.
``` a(i,j+1) = a(i,j) + b(i)```	Add $b(i)$ to column and shift.
```20 Continue```	
```10 Continue```	

The computed answer will be the same, but the compiler gets there quite differently since the j loop can be run with $b(i)$ remaining in the vector registers. You'll see the difference in the effective Fortran code generated by the compiler:

```Do 10 ii=1,N,Z```	Vectorize chunking loop.
	$i=1, 129, 257, 385.$
```* Do 11 i = 0, min(Z-1,N-ii)```	Vector load into vr1.
	$0:127, 0:127, 0:127, 0:115.$
```*11 vr1(i) = b(ii+i)```	Temporary b store.
``` Do 20 j = 1,N```	Only 2 vector instructions.
```* Do 21 i = 0, min(Z-1,N-ii)```	$0:127, 0:127, 0:127, 0:115$
```*21 vr2(i) = vr1(i) + a(ii+i,j)```	Vector add, vr1 unchanged.
```* Do 22 i = 0, min(Z-1,N-ii)```	$0:127, 0:127, 0:127, 0:115.$
```*22 a(ii+i,j+1) = vr2(i)```	Store back into a.
```20 Continue```	
```10 Continue```	

By now using the chunking loop 10 for vectorization, the loop 11 gets loaded into vector register $vr1$. The inner loop 20 now contains only two vector instructions, so rather than being discarded after a single use, the elements in vector register $vr1$ are used N times (which can be 100's or 1000's) during the iteration of the j loop. This reduces machine time by about 30%.

Loop Unrolling

If your vector compiler does not permit vectorization of an outer loop, you can force it to reuse the vector registers by personally going through and *unrolling* the outer loop. In this exercise you will take what was a succinct piece of coding and replace the implicit iterations of a Do loop with an explicit sequence of statements which are usually less in number than the full count of the Do loop. With this now enlarged sequence of statements, the compiler has a better chance to exhibit its innate intelligence and recognize the repeated references to an operand, thereby avoiding reloading it. For example, here are the original, nested Fortran loops

`Do 10 j = 1, N`	The outer loop.
`    Do 20 i = 1, N`	The inner loop.
`        a(i,j+1) = a(i,j) + b(i)`	Add $b(i)$ and shift.
`20    Continue`	
`10 Continue`	

This code can have the j loop unrolled into:

`Do 10 j = 1, N/k*k, k`	Partial outer loop in chunks.
`    Do 20 i = 1, N`	The inner Do loop.
`        a(i,j+1) = a(i,j) + b(i)`	Add b and shift.
`        a(i,j+2) = a(i,j+1) + b(i)`	Add b and shift.
`        ...`	...
`20      a(i,j+k) = a(i,j+k-1)+b(i)`	Add b and shift.
`10 Continue`	
`    Do 30 j = N/k*k+1, N`	Remaining jvv values, no chunks.
`        Do 40 i = 1, N`	All i values.
`            a(i,j+1) = a(i,j) + b(i)`	Basic add and shift again.
`40      Continue`	
`30 Continue`	

In a later section, we will show you how to use a Fortran compiler to assist you in various stages of vectorization and how to solve some of the problems it uncovers.

Indirect Addressing

Indirect addressing is a reference to an array where the subscript argument itself is a variable. For example:

`Do 99 n = 1, nlim`	Loop over subscript index.
`99 c(nc(n)) = a(na(n)) + b(nb(n))`	Subscripts can be anything.

Because $na, nb,$ and nc are variables with no guarantee of being continuous or even monotonic, the arrays $a(na(n)), b(nb(n)),$ and $c(nc(n))$ may be scattered throughout memory, making retrieval slow. If possible, try to avoid the use of *indirect addressing* in your programs. It inhibits or prevents vectorization. Although vector computers sometimes contain a piece of hardware called *gather/scatter* that permit vectorization of programs with indirect addressing, it still slows down programs.

To understand the effect of indirect addressing, here is an example of a possible elementary pseudocode generated by the compiler as it translated the preceding two lines of Fortran (v0–v4 are vector registers):

`fetch na(1:128) to v0`	Get subscripts $na(1:128)$ for a.
`fetch nb(1:128) to v1`	Get subscripts $nb(1:128)$ for b.
`fetch a to v2 for addresses in v0`	Get values $a(na(1:128))$.
`fetch b to v3 for addresses in v1`	Get values $b(nb(1:128))$.
`add v2 to v3 and store in v4`	Add $a(na(1:128))$ to $b(nb(1:128))$.
`fetch nc(1:128) into v5`	Get subscripts $nc(1:128)$ for c.
`store v4 in c(v5)`	Update value for $c(nc(1:128))$.

The pseudocode shows that the vector processor may well run into data path or memory bank conflict because there is no way to guarantee that the subscripts given by the arrays $na(n), nb(n)$, and $nc(n)$ do not overlap themselves (e.g. $na(n) = 1, 2, 3, 1, 2, 3, 1, ...$). These conflicts make the processor wait around and ultimately increase processing time. Indirect addressing will, likewise, reduce the overlapping and chaining of instructions. Finally, then, it should be no surprise that it may be faster to process the statements in scalar than vector mode (something the compiler will decide for you).

Array Bounds

Although they may not complain to you about it, most compilers assume that your subscripts stay within the bounds declared in the DIMENSION statement. For example:

`REAL b(10,10)`	10 x 10 declared.
`Do 1 i = 1, 20`	First index beyond bounds.
`    b(i,2) = b(i,1)`	$b(20,2)$ reached.
`1 continue`	

While this may work in scalar processing, it is unlikely to give the correct answer with vector processing.

13.6   Vector Programming Hints

Now that you are familiar with how vector processing operates, we give some hints for programming with a vector processor. You may wish to consult Chapter 11, *Scientific Programming Hints*, and compare, since vector processing is different.

- The cache is used most effectively when vectors are accessed with a stride of 1. *Use the smallest stride possible especially for the most rapidly varying loop in a nest.*

- The compiler ordinarily vectorizes the leftmost index. This provides a stride of 1.

- Vectorizing on the leftmost Dimension at the innermost loop level provides the best storage reference patterns.

- However, it is advantageous to vectorize *outer* Do loops when:

    - vector loads can be removed from the inner loop,

    - arrays are referenced in different ways in a loop.

- For scalar code, the most rapidly varying loop is always the innermost loop, for vector code the vectorized loop will be the one which varies most rapidly regardless of its relative position (if permitted).

13.7   An Example of Vector Compiling

Most of the work required to convert your dusty-deck source code to run on a vector computer is done by the Fortran or C compiler. Even the reprogramming you personally may have to do is outlined or highlighted by the compiler. To give a better feel for the process and define some additional vector-programming constructs, we and the compiler now examine some code fragments. Although our examples are taken from an IBM machine, the technique is general. We conclude by giving in Appendix B a sample program running in different modes—an experiment you can try yourself with the copy of this program on the floppy.

When you run your dusty-deck program on a vector machine, the scalar parts of your code should compile with no unusual problems while the vector processor will automatically handle certain matrix operations—if you invoked that option. Even though most of this can be done with minimal input on your part, here are a few points to keep in mind so it seems less like black magic:

- The compiler automatically vectorizes eligible statements for Do loops but not for other types of operations.

- If your program has a nest of Do loops, only one can be vectorized. The compiler usually selects the one whose vectorization will lead to the fastest execution.

- The compiler issues a report showing the vectorization decisions it made. You may study this report and suggest alternatives.

- Vector versions of most intrinsic math functions are automatically used.

- Vectorization may not be possible with the lowest level(s) of optimization.

Compilation Commands and Options

To compile the program in file `progname`, issue the command:

```
FORTVS2 progname (VECtor(vector suboptions) other options
```

With IBM VS FORTRAN you get automatic vectorization by specifying the *VECTOR* compile-time option and specifying optimization level *OPTIMIZE(2)* or *OPTIMIZE(3)*.

The vector suboptions are (underline = default):

```
REPORT(TERM | LIST | XLIST | SLIST | STAT)|    NOREPORT
```

VS FORTRAN OPTIONS

TERM	Report given at terminal.
LIST	Short `LISTING` file.
XLIST	Cross-referenced `LISTING` file.
SLIST	Vector report similar to source listing.
STAT	Add vector statistics to `LISTING`.
INTRINSIC|NONINTRINSIC	Vectorize out-of-line intrinsic function.
IVA|NOIVA	Information file for interactive debug.
REDUCTION|NOREDUCTION	Vectorize reduction functions.
SIZE(ANY|LOCAL | n)	Specify section size of computer.

Stages of Vector Compilation

Before a Do loop is converted into instructions for the vector hardware, the compiler takes your program through four stages of qualification checks. It probes down to eight levels of nesting and then decides to vectorize a particular loop only if the vector mode will be faster than the scalar mode. The compiler indicates its thinking to you with symbols in brackets. The stages of vectorization are:

1. **Analysis:** a check to see if your program's logic is evident and if its operations are supported; if not, it is *unanalyzable* [UNAN].

2. **Recurrence detection:** analysis for vectorizable logic [RECR].

3. **Operation support:** a check for hardware support [UNSP].

4. **Vector selection:** compiler's choice for fastest execution is [SCAL/VECT/ELIG].

Stage 1: Analysis

A loop will be flagged as unanalyzable UNAN if it contains:

- Calls to external subroutines or nonintrinsic functions.

- Loops other than Do loops.

- Branches out of, around, or backwards within a loop.

- Input/output statements (these do not use fast hardware).

- ASSIGN, ENTRY, RETURN, PAUSE, or STOP statements.

- Assigned or computed GO TO statements.

- Non INTEGER*4 Do loop parameters.

- Do loop parameters in EQUIVALENCE statements.

- CHARACTER data.

Subroutine Calls The compiler cannot look into the subroutine to determine if it contains vectorizable code or analyze a Do loop if it calls a subprogram. This is for good reason, because your subroutine may completely rearrange the order and values of all matrices. If the part of your program containing the subroutine call is numerically intensive, as revealed by a *profile*, for example, then it may be worth the effort to recode. Unfortunately, the cure of bringing the subroutine *in line*, that is, transferring its code to the part of your program which called the subroutine, produces unattractive code (less modular and less readable by humans). For example, let's say you had the subroutine

Sub-subroutine call	
| ```
UNAN +---- Do 40 j = 1, n
     |         x(j) = y(j) - z(j)
     |         Call Sub(j,x(j),z(j))
Subroutine Sub (i, a, b)
COMMON y
y(i) = a + b
``` | The problem. |

You would change it to

Changed in-line subroutine	
| ```
VECT +---- Do 40 j = 1, n
     |         x(j) = y(j) - z(j)
     |         y(j) = x(j) + z(j)
     +---- 40 Continue
``` | Inlined Sub. |

Non Do Loops An example of a loop which is not a Do loop is:

Non Do Loop	
| ```
       i = 1
   25 continue
         If (i .Gt.  n) Go to 26
         b(i) = x(i)**a(i)  * c
         i = i + 1
         Go to 25
   26 Continue
``` | Loop control.<br><br>Increase index. |

Its equivalent Do loop (which can be vectorized) is:

A real Do loop.	
| ```
     Do 25 i = 1, n
          b(i) = x(i)**a(i)  * c
   25 Continue
``` | A real Do loop. |

If you program a *branch-out-of loop*, it will be unanalyzable and the compiler will mark it as UNAN. You correct this by *distributing* the loop. For example this loop is UNAN

A Branch-Out-of Loop	
| ```
UNAN +------Do 40 j = 1, n
     |        x(j) = y(j) - z(j)
     |        If (x(j) .Lt.  0.)  Go to 50
     |        root(j) = Sqrt ((x(j))
     +------40 Continue
 50      jlast = j - 1
``` | Compiler shows loop.<br><br>Branch out. |

You must recode this branch-out-of loop into several loops before the compiler can analyze it. Even though some of the new loops may be unanalyzable, you may get a speedup if the numerically intensive work is placed into loops which can be vectorized:

Branch-Out-of Loop Replacement	
| ```
VECT +--------- Do 41 j = 1, n
     |
     +--------- 41 tempx(j) = y(j) - z(j)
UNAN +------- Do 42 j = 1, n
     |
     +------- 42 If (tempx(j).lt.0) Goto 51
     51 jlast = j - 1
     If (jlast .eq.  0) Goto 52
VECT +------ Do 43 j = 1, jlast
     |          x(j) = tempx(j)
     +----- 43 root(j) = Sqrt (x(j))
        If (jlast .eq.  n) Goto 53
     52 x(jlast+1) = tempx(jlast+1)
     53 Continue
``` | Vectorizable.<br><br>Temporary variable.<br>Unanalyzable jump.<br><br><br><br>Vectorizable. |

I/O Statements　Input and output statements cannot be analyzed by the compiler for vectorization:

Unanalyzable	
| ```
UNAN +-------- Do 30 i = 1, n
     |            a(I) = c(I)**2
     |            b(I) = c(I)**0.5
     |            Write (6,*) a(i), b(i)
     +------ 30 Continue
``` | <br><br><br>The problem. |

They are best moved outside of your computing loop into an unanalyzable I/O loop:
```

Recoded to Partially Vectorizable	
| ```
VECT +------ Do 30 i = 1, n
      |           a(i) = c(i) ** 2
      |           b(i) = c(i) ** 0.5
     +---- 30 Continue
``` | No write here. |
| ```
UNAN +-------- Do 31 I = 1, n
      |             Write (6,*) a(I), b(I)
     +-------- 31 Continue
``` | Write loop. |

Stage 2: Recurrence Detection (Data Dependence)

A *data dependence* is when your code uses a storage location more than once, that is, when two statements use or define identical storage locations. For example:

| ```
S x = ...
T y = ...   x
``` | Use $x$ before redefined. |
|---|---|

Here the statement S must execute before the statement T since S defines a value which is used in T. This type of true data dependence occurs whenever two statements use identical storage locations (a store followed by a fetch from that same location). While you are not (necessarily) doing anything wrong when you construct a data dependence, it restricts vectorization.

A *recurrence* occurs when one or more statements form a cycle of dependences, specifically, when the processing of a statement at an earlier time affects its processing at a later time (we give an example soon). In terms of dependences, statements S and T form a recurrence if there is a dependence from S to T as well as a dependence from T to S. This kills vectorization.

An **anti-dependence** is a fetch from a memory, location followed by a store to that same location:

```
S y = ...   x
T x = ...
```

Here it's necessary to have statement S execute before statement T because S must reference x before T redefines it.

If your code is not directly vectorizable, the compiler will determine when it is safe to interchange loops, to distribute a loop into multiple loops, and to reorder statements within a loop. Sometimes it cannot proceed safely because a *recurrence* of some type occurs. For example,

| ```
RECR +--- Do 99 j = 1, 100
      |       a(j+1) = a(j) + b(j)
     +--- 99 Continue
``` | Latter $a$ depends on earlier $a$. |
|---|---|

We see the *recurrence* by looking at the explicit statements generated by this loop,

`a(2)  = a(1) + b(1)`
`a(3)  = a(2) + b(2)`
`.    .    .`
`a(101) = a(100) + b(100)`
	a(2) computed & stored.
	New *a*(2) fetched.

The recurrence is in a value for $a(2)$ being stored and then fetched at a later time. While this is fine for scalar operations, it is a problem in vector mode where we would have $a(3)$ computed with the old value of $a(2)$:

$$\begin{bmatrix} a(2) \\ a(3) \\ \vdots \\ a(101) \end{bmatrix} = \begin{bmatrix} a(1) \\ a(2) \\ \vdots \\ a(100) \end{bmatrix} + \begin{bmatrix} b(1) \\ b(2) \\ \vdots \\ b(100) \end{bmatrix} \tag{13.6}$$

Thus, in vector mode, with all 100 elements of A and B being fetched before the add, the value in $a(2)$ is being fetched before it is stored! This might give the wrong answer. A Do loop with a recurrence cannot be vectorized.

If your program's results are modified by moving an outer loop to the innermost level, vectorization is prohibited on the outer loop. This is called *loop interchange preventing dependence*. Here's an example:

`     Do 15 i = 1, n`
`       Do 15 j = 1, m`
`15     a(i-1,j+1) = a(i,j)`
	`     Do 15 j = 1, m`
	`       Do 15 i = 1, n`
	`15     a(i-1,j+1) = a(i,j)`

The execution of these loops in scalar mode would be

`a(0,2) = a(1,1)`
`a(0,3) = a(1,2)`
`a(1,2) = a(2,1)`
`a(1,3) = a(2,2)`
	`a(0,2) = a(1,1)`
	`a(1,2) = a(2,1)`
	`a(0,3) = a(1,2)`
	`a(1,3) = a(2,2)`

We see that the value in element $a(0, 3)$ depends on the order of the Do loop. Accordingly, the outer loop cannot be moved inwards and therefore cannot be vectorized.

An **anti-dependence** is a fetch from memory followed by a store to that same location. For example:

`S  y = ...    x` `T  x = ...`	Use x before redefined.

In this case it is necessary to have statement S execute before statement T because S must reference x before T redefines it. A single statement antidependence also is possible within a Do loop:

`a(j-1) = a(j) + b(j)`
produces machine pseudocode
`fetch a(0), a(1), ...  a(157)`
`store a(0) = a(1) + b(1)`
`store a(1) = a(2) + b(2)`
	Early depends on latter.

Single-statement anti-dependences *will* vectorize because the value of $a(j-1)$ will be computed with fetched values of $a(j)$ and $b(j)$ which are not changed by the computation. In a multiple-statement dependence, the compiler examines the order of fetches and stores in a Do loop, and determines whether it can safely vectorize the loop. For example, here is a loop with an anti-dependence on a:

`VECT +---- Do 30 j = 1, n` `	a(j) = b(j) + c(j)` `	e(j) = a(j+1)` ` +-- 30 Continue`	Antidependence on a.

The compiler will automatically reorder these two statements in order to preserve the order of fetches and store on A during vector operations. It is marked VECT.

Sometimes the compiler tries several different ways to vectorize your program, and if they all these fail, it marks the loop RECR and quits (we should all show such sense). Here is an example of a loop very similar to the preceding one, but by using b in the second statement, there now exists two anti-dependences:

`RECR +----Do 30 j = 1,n` `	a(j) = b(j) + c(j)` `	b(j) = a(j+1)` ` +--- 30 Continue`	Antidependence on a. b depends on a.

The effects of these differing orders is seen in the machine pseudocode:

Scalar Execution	
`a(1) = b(1) + c(1)`	Fetch $b(1)$ & store $a(1)$.
`b(1) = a(2)`	Fetch $a(2)$ & store $b(1)$.
`a(2) = b(2) + c(2)`	Fetch $b(2)$ & store $a(2)$.
`b(2) = a(3)`	Fetch $a(3)$ & store $b(2)$.

Yet the forward and backward anti-dependences form a nonvectorizable *cycle* of dependences.

Vectorization Attempt 1	
`a(1) = b(1) + c(1)`	Fetch $b(1)$ & store $a(1)$.
`a(2) = b(2) + c(2)`	Fetch $b(2)$ & store $a(2)$.
`b(1) = a(2)`	Order now different.
`b(2) = a(3)`	Order now different.
Vectorization Attempt 2	
`b(1) = a(2)`	Fetch $a(2)$ & store $b(1)$, OK.
`b(2) = a(3)`	Fetch $a(3)$ & store $b(2)$, OK.
`a(1) = b(1) + c(1)`	Order now different.
`a(2) = b(2) + c(2)`	Order now different.

Node Splitting

The recurrence formed by forward and backward anti-dependences can be *broken* by defining a temporary scalar variable. This technique, known as *node splitting*, permits the compiler to expand the scalar temporaries into vector temporaries. For example, we could recode the previous loop to the vectorizable form in which the order of the fetches and stores are preserved using the temporary scalar variable `temp`:

`VECT +---- Do 30 j = 1, n`	Same.
`	temp = b(j) + c(j)`	Scalar temporary.
`	b(j) = a(j+1)`	
`	a(j) = temp`	The split.
`      +---- 30 Continue`	
Vector Machine Code—with Node Splitting	
`t(1) = b(1) + c(1)`	Fetch $b(1)$.
`t(2) = b(2) + c(2)`	Fetch $b(2)$.
`. . .`	
`b(1) = a(2)`	Fetch $a(2)$ & store $b(1)$.
`b(2) = a(3)`	Fetch $a(3)$ & store $b(2)$.
`. . .`	
`a(1) = t(1)`	Store $a(1)$.
`a(2) = t(2)`	Store $a(2)$.

Partial Sums Reduction

It is a fact that many of the equations computational scientists deal with involve vector inner products, sums of squares, or sums of matrix elements. Nevertheless, the common scalar techniques used to perform these partial sums have inherent recurrences. For example, consider the standard accumulation of a sum (also called *reduction operation*)

```
          sum = 0.
VECT +---- Do 30 j = 1, n
     |          sum = sum + a(j)
     +--30 Continue
```

The variable sum carries a recurrence because on every iteration of the Do loop, sum must be fetched and then stored. Yet in vector mode, the stores occur only at the end of a Do loop, so the Do loop does not appear to be vectorizable. The solution to this dilemma lies in a piece of hardware called *partial sums* which holds onto the partial sums or *accumulators* without continuous stores and fetches. Unfortunately, integer sums are *not* vectorized; you have to change your integer accumulators to REAL ones.

There is an interesting fine point in dealing with *partial sums* which may trouble you if you are careful and check your results after each modification. As you will recall, due to finite word length, floating point addition is not an associative process on a computer. Now, since the order in which data elements are added when using partial sums is not the same as in scalar addition, the numerical results will be slightly different in scalar and vector mode even though the algebraic results are not. In fact, this difference is an empirical indicator of the round-off error in your calculation.

Scalar Expansion

A common procedure in scientific programming is to use a Do loop to sum a series. Although it takes fewer lines of code to store the accumulating sum in the element of an array which will ultimately contain the final sum, this leads to an unnecessary recurrence. *Scalar expansion* is the replacement of a vector variable $t(i, j)$, which does not really have to be an element of an array by a temporary scalar variable so the partial sum can be handled by the hardware. We have already done this in node splitting. For example, we would do some recoding

Unnecessary recurrence, need recode.	
| ```
RECR +----Do 15 i = 1, len
     |       Do 15 j = 1, len
     |          t(i,j) = 0.0
     |          Do 15 k = 1, len
     |             t(i,j) =t(i,j)+a(i,k)*b(k,j)
     +-15 Continue
``` | Initialize sum.<br><br>Build vector sum. |
| **Recode with scalar expansion.** | |
| ```
VECT +----- Do 15 i = 1, len
     |        Do 15 j = 1, len
     |          temp = 0.0
     |          Do 17 k = 1, len
     |             temp=temp+a(i,k)*b(k,j)
     | 17        Continue
     |          t(i,j) = temp
     +-- 15 Continue
``` | Recoded.<br><br>Initial sum.<br><br>Build scalar sum. |

In order for scalar expansion to work:

- temp must be local to the loop in which it is used .

- temp cannot be defined in terms of a variable defined before the loop.

- The first reference to `temp` must be a *store* (`temp = ...`).

- If `temp` is used again after the loop, it must be in another store.

- `temp` cannot be present in a COMMON or EQUIVALENCE statement.

Summary of Recurrence

- The compiler determines when it is safe to interchange loops, to distribute a loop into multiple loops, and to reorder statements within a loop.

- If an outer loop cannot be moved safely to the innermost loop level, then vectorization cannot occur on the outer loop.

- A single-statement *true dependence* of the type $a(j + 1) = ...a(j)$ is a *recurrence* preventing vectorization.

- A single-statement *anti-dependence* of the type $a(j - 1) = ...a(j)$ vectorizes.

- If the compiler flags a loop with multiple statements as a recurrence, you can try introducing *temporaries* to *break* that recurrence.

- The compiler often cannot analyze complicated array subscripts, EQUIVALENCEd arrays, or arrays using indirect addressing [$a(j) = b(ind(j))$]. You must reprogram these references if you want them vectorized.

- The compiler may flag a loop as a recurrence (and refuse to vectorize it) even though no recurrence occurs. These *fake* recurrences can be overridden with compiler directives—but you better be sure no recurrences really occur because a slow, correct answer is more desirable than a fast, wrong one.

Stage 3: Nonvectorizable Operations

Your particular model of vector hardware may not be able to vectorize some constructs which a different model can. In the operation support stage of compilation, loops are checked for hardware support of the operations you have coded. A loop containing an *unsupported* operation will not be vectorized.

Typical Unsupported Operations

1. Data types *Real*16, Complex*32, Logical*1*.

2. *Integer*2* variables governed by an `If` statement.

3. Relational expressions which need to be stored, e.g., `l = a.GE.b`

4. Intrinsic functions from the families *Dim, Mod, Sign, Nint, Anint, Btest*.

5. Noninductive subscripts governed by an `If` statement (see example).

6. Noninductive subscripts to an *Integer*2* array.

7. Mathematical operations *Integer** Integer, Integer/Integer, Real** Integer, Double** Integer, Complex** Integer, (Double Complex)** Integer, Complex** Complex, (Double Complex)** (Double Complex), Complex Divide, Double Complex Divide.* It is not illegal to use these, but they will be evaluated using scalar routines only.

8. Intrinsic functions *Acos, Asin, Cotan, Cosh, Sinh, Erf, Erfc, Gamma, Algamma, Tanh, Tan, Ccos, Csin, Cexp, Clog, CSqrt* and their double-precision counterparts.

Typical Supported Operations

1. Data types *Real*4, Real*8, Complex*8, Complex*16, Logical*4, Integer*4.*

2. Mathematical operations *Real** Real, Double** Double.*

3. Intrinsic functions *Amin1, Amax1, Sqrt, Exp, Alog, Sin, Cos, Atan, Cabs, Alog10, Atan2* and their double-precision counterparts.

As an example of the compiler's apology, here is an unsupported loop containing a noninductive subscript governed by an If statement and the compiler's response:

```
UNSP+----Do 20 j = 1, n
    |       If (b(j) .GT. xold) Then        Indirect addressing.
    |          b(j) = a(j) + p*c(j**2)
    |       End If
    +--20 Continue
UNSP   ARRAY C USED IN CONDITIONALLY EXECUTED
CODE, HAS NON--INDUCTIVE SUBSCRIPTS
```

The problem here is the indirect addressing. We can force the compiler to vectorize the code by defining a dummy vector ct(j):

```
VECT +----  Do 20 J = 1, N
     |         ct(j) = c(j**2)
     |         IF (b(j) .GT. xold) Then
     |            b(j) = a(j) + p*ct(j)
     |         End IF
     +--  20 Continue
```

Stage 4: Selecting a Best Buy

The compiler estimates the *cost* or number of cycles that will be expended to execute given sections of code. It then chooses which regions to vectorize (if any) based on its estimates of the total number of cycles required to execute all possible combinations of nested loops. The compiler will mark ELIG those loops which were found eligible for vectorization but which the compiler decided to run in the scalar mode since it appears faster.

While the cost estimates can get detailed, it is handy to keep some points in mind. There is an overhead cost to loop initialization in both the scalar and vector modes, with the vector cost being higher. More elements are involved. (And this is higher on the IBMs than the Crays because the IBMs have longer vector loads.) Each executed instruction adds to the cost. For example, it costs 30 cycles for a division in scalar mode and 15 cycles for a division in vector mode. Much of the cost on a computer with a cache is associated with loading and unloading the cache. There is a cost for fetching and storing operands which depends on the stride for each dimension.

Compiler Directives

By issuing *directives* you can personally override or at least influence some of the vectorization decisions made by the compiler. Three types of directives relevant to vector processing are:

VS FORTRAN DIRECTIVES

assume count	Tell compiler typical number of loop iterations.
ignore	Tell compiler to ignore recurrence it found.
prefer	Your preference for how to execute some loop.

It is generally not wise to micromanage the compiler and clutter your program with directives. Instead, profile your program and optimize those sections in which the program spends the most time. For example, `assume count` is preferable to `prefer` because it helps the compiler manage vectorization. And of course, double check before issuing `ignore`; better slow than wrong:

```
@PROCESS DIRECTIVE('*VDIR')                          The directive.
     Program Vec
     REAL a, b
     COMPLEX c, d
     PARAMETER (n = 600)
     DIMENSION a(n), b(n), c(n), d(n)
     Do 10 k = 1, n
         a(k) = Float(K)
         b(k) = a(k)/(1 + a(k))
         c(k) = Cmplx(a(k), b(k))
         d(k) = Cmplx(b(k),b(k))
  10 Continue
c complex vector divide slow, prefer scalar:        Directive.
C*VDIR PREFER SCALAR
     Do 11 k = 1, n
         d(k) = c(k)/d(k)
  11 Continue
     Do 12 k = 1, n
         a(k+1) = a(k) + b(k)
  12 Continue
```

Since we know that complex division is slow in vector mode, we have used PREFER to override the compiler's economic decision. If you do not trust your insight, you can actually time your code and then tell the compiler what's best.

You use the IGNORE RECRDEPS directive when your knowledge of how the program works guarantees no recurrence. For example, in the loop below there is no recurrence for odd $l < 50$ (and we know odd $l < 50$ is what we will read into the program):

```@PROCESS DIRECTIVE('*VDIR')``` ``` Program Vec2``` ``` . . .``` ``` Read (5, *) L``` ```c No recurrence since L always odd.``` ```C*VDIR IGNORE RECRDEPS``` ``` Do 13 k = 1, n, 2``` ``` a(k) = a(k-L) + b(k)``` ``` 13 Continue``` ```c No recurrence since n always < 50.``` ```C*VDIR IGNORE RECRDEPS``` ``` Do 15 j = 1, n``` ``` a(j+50) = a(j) + b(j)``` ``` 15 Continue```	Read in L. Recur if $n > 50$.

Likewise, the compiler assumes recurrences between EQUIVALENCEd variables or variables with unknown indirect addressing. If you know there are no recurrences you can direct the compiler to ignore the possibility. Use the directive IGNORE EQUDEPS to tell the compiler to ignore dependences arising from equivalence dependences:

``` REAL*4 a1(100), b1(100), c1(100)``` ``` REAL*4 a2(100), b2(100), c2(100)``` ``` EQUIVALENCE (a1(1), a2(1))``` ``` EQUIVALENCE (b1(1), b2(1))``` ``` EQUIVALENCE (c1(1), c2(1))``` ```C*VDIR IGNORE EQUDEPS(a1, a2, b1)``` ``` Do 10 i = 1,n``` ``` a1(i) = a2(i)``` ``` b1(i) = b2(i)``` ``` c1(i) = c2(i)``` ``` 10 Continue```	The problem. The problem. The problem. Ignore equivalence dependence. Ignore equivalence dependence. Equivalence dependence.

The assume count directive is used to tell the compiler an average or approximate number of times a Do loop is to be executed (the trip count). Telling the compiler this information is helpful if your programming does not make the actual trip count obvious or if the trip count depends on your input data. For example,

```@PROCESS DIRECTIVE('*VDIR')```	
``` PARAMETER (nlim = 300)```	
``` IF (n .LT. 20) Go to 30```	
```C*VDIR ASSUME COUNT (100)```	Assume $n = 100$.
``` Do 10 k = 1, n```	
``` 10 Continue```	
``` Go to 40```	
```C*VDIR ASSUME COUNT (5)```	Assume $n = 5$.
``` 30 Do 11 k = 1, n```	
``` 11 Continue```	
``` 40 Continue```	
```C*VDIR ASSUME COUNT (nlim)```	
``` Do 50 k = 1, n```	Assume $n = nlim$.
``` 50 Continue```	

In this case a symbolic constant has been used as the constant for the `assume count` directive.

The `on/off` keywords in the vector or compiler directive cause the directives to apply to more than one Do loop. For example,

```C*VDIR ASSUME COUNT(50) ON```	Set all counts to 50.
```C*VDIR ASSUME COUNT(I = 4, J = 200) ON```	Set count for i, j.
``` Do 10 i = 1, n1```	Assumed count is 4.
``` Do 10 j = 1, n2```	Assumed count is 200.
``` Do 10 k = 1, n3```	Assumed count is 50.
```C*VDIR ASSUME COUNT(500) ON```	Set all counts to 500.
``` Do 20 i = 1, n4```	Assumed count is 500.
``` Do 20 j = 1, n5```	Assumed count is 200.
``` Do 20 k = 1, n6```	Assumed count is 50.
```C*VDIR ASSUME COUNT OFF```	Set all counts to 500.
``` Do 30 i = 1, n7```	Assumed count is 65 (actual value).
``` Do 30 j = 1, n8```	Assumed count is 65 (actual value).
```C*VDIR PREFER SCALAR ON```	
``` Do 40 i = 1, 100```	Will not vectorize.
``` Do 40 j = 1, 100```	Will not vectorize.
```C*VDIR PREFER VECTOR```	
``` Do 50 i = 1, n3```	Will vectorize if eligible.
``` Do 50 j = 1, n4```	Will not vectorize.
```C*VDIR PREFER SCALAR OFF```	
``` Do 60 i = 1, n4```	Normal vector analysis.
``` Do 60 j = 1, n4```	Normal vector analysis.

Sample Fortran Runs

In Appendix B, *Profiling and Tuning for Hardware*, we provide actual examples of a Fortran program running in scalar mode and then in vector mode. Also indicated are the reports from the compiler as well as some of the changes made in order to run well in the vector mode. We recommend that you take these programs (the source codes are on the floppy and in the Appendix), and then, *in order*, study, compile, and compare your results with those given here. After you have the different versions running, feel free to experiment with different modifications or compiler options. Using a *makefile* or the *source code control system (SCCS)* may be helpful too.

## CHAPTER 14

PARALLEL COMPUTING

Gather ye rosebuds while ye may,
Old time is still a-flying;
And this same flower that smiles today
Tomorrow will be dying.

—Robert Herrick

14.1 Types of Parallel Systems

We have already seen that many of the tasks on a high performance computer occur in parallel as a consequence of internal structures such as pipelined and segmented CPUs, hierarchical memory, and independent I/O processors. While this processing is in parallel, in modern terminology *parallel computing* denotes a computing environment in which some number of identical processors are running asynchronously but communicating with each other to avoid conflicts or to exchange intermediate answers.

The motivation behind parallel computing is to get more computing done in a fixed amount of time by having the computer do several unrelated jobs at one time or by having it work on different pieces of the same job at one time. The theory behind parallel computing is that since there is a limit to the speed of a *serial* machine or since it gets very expensive when you try to make it run very fast, at some point it becomes more efficient to have a number of processors running for a shorter time in parallel than a single processor running for a longer time or at a higher speed. Even though parallel computing may decrease the elapsed time for a big job to get done, there may also be a decrease in efficiencies of the individual processors. In the serial processing of a big job, the one processor is kept busy; in parallel processing, the processors must spend some time communicating or waiting rather than crunching numbers.

Yet when a speedup is needed of up to a 1,000 or 10,000 (to the Teraflop regime), parallel processing seems inevitable. Possibly this explains why industry and the computer science community appear to have such high interest in *massively parallel* computing. The largest supercomputers in service today are massively parallel machines. As these

325

machines continue to acquire the full integration of hardware and software we associate with supercomputers, they are becoming the next generation of scientific workhorses.

In a broad sense, concurrent or parallel processing is the best approach for problems: 1) which otherwise would not be solved (for example a simulation to replace an expensive, dangerous, or forbidden experiment); 2) whose solutions we cannot afford to wait for; or 3) which use more memory then can be efficiently addressed by a single processor. While probably not the best approach to computing for daily computing chores, parallel processing may be the only viable approach for the grand challenges of computing. From a marketing point of view, it may also be inevitable as the price of components keeps decreasing.

For a computational scientist to effectively employ parallel computing requires knowledge of parallel programming, appropriate algorithms, architecture, and software tools. Considering the complexity, state of flux, and machine dependencies of these subjects, we present this chapter as an introduction which aims to make the jargon somewhat clearer and simultaneously clarify the main concepts. Some specific examples for few-processor systems are thrown in. To write and run programs on present-day parallel computers, we are afraid you will have to really study the manufacturer's manuals. However the future seems to be Fortran 90 and High Performance Fortran (HPF). These new versions of Fortran, with their parallel extensions, will allow users to write parallel codes with the same ease as current Fortran programs are written for vector machines. Currently, Fortran 90 is available for the Connection Machines.

Instruction and Data Streams

The processors in a concurrent processing computer are placed at the *nodes* of the internal communication network within the computer. For short, the processors themselves are often called nodes. One way of categorizing parallel systems is by how they handle instructions and data. From this viewpoint there are four types of machines:

Single Instruction, Single Data (SISD) These are the traditional (and least expensive) types of serial computers in which a single instruction is executed and acts upon a single data stream before the next instruction and next data stream are encountered.

Single Instruction, Multiple Data (SIMD) Here instructions are processed from a single stream, but they act concurrently on multiple pieces of data. Generally the nodes are very simple and relatively slow processors, but are very large in number.[1] The Thinking Machines CM-2 is one of the best examples of a successful commercial SIMD machine. The smallest CM-2 has 4096 one bit processors and the largest, 65,536.

Multiple Instruction, Multiple Data (MIMD) In this category each processor runs independently of the others with independent instructions and data. These are the type of machines that employ *message passing*. They can be a collection of workstations linked with a network or more sophisticated machines such as the Intel Paragon or Thinking Machine's CM-5 with over a thousand processors.

---

[1] Sometimes vector processors are considered a special instance of SIMD machines. Vector processors seldom perform operations in parallel, however. Instead they have long pipelines which allow the processors to complete one operation every clock cycle. The experimental IBM GF-11 is an exception.

It is possible for the multiple data streams to be extracted from a common memory and for the different central processors to be running completely independent programs. In fact, the running of independent programs is not very different from the multitasking feature familiar on mainframes, workstations, and some PCs. In multitasking (for example Unix) several independent programs reside in the computer's memory simultaneously and share the processing time in a round robin or priority order. In multiprocessing these jobs may all be running at the same time. Clearly, though, this gets more complicated if these separate processors are operating on different parts of the *same* program since then synchronization and load balance (keeping all processors equally busy) are a concern.

Computer Granularity

In addition to instruction and data streams, another way to categorize both the hardware and software in parallel computing is by *granularity*, a *grain* defined as a measure of the computational work to be done.[2]

Coarse Grain Parallel Here there are separate programs running on separate computer systems with the systems coupled via a conventional communication network. For example, three Sun SPARC Stations or six IBM RS/6000's sharing the same files across a network but with a different central memory system for each workstation. Each computer could be operating on a different and independent part of one problem at the same time.[3]

Medium Grain Parallel This is the most common system in use now. It has several processors executing (possibly different) programs simultaneously while accessing a common memory. The processors are usually placed on a common *bus* (communication channel) and communicate with each other through the memory system. Medium grain programs have different, independent, *parallel subroutines* running on different processors. Because the compilers often are not smart enough to figure out which parts of the program to run like that, the programmer must use multitasking routines like those we discuss later in this chapter.

Fine Grain Parallel As the granularity decreases and the number of nodes increases, there is an increased requirement for fast communication among the nodes. For this reason fine grain systems tend to be completely custom-designed machines. The communication may be via a central bus or shared memory for a small number of nodes (less than eight) or through some form of high speed network for massively parallel machines. In this latter case, the compiler divides the work among the processing nodes. For example, different Do loops of a program may be running on different nodes.

14.2   Overview of Machines

Now that we have some idea of the general structure of concurrent processing computers, we can look at some of the machines in existence. We've organized our view according to the number of processors:

---

[2]Sometimes defined more specifically as the ratio of computation work to communication work.
[3]Some experts define our medium as coarse, yet this fine point changes with time.

1. **Small numbers (2–8) of very powerful processors, shared memory.** Here each processor usually has a vector facility attached (so that all you learned in Chapters 12 and 13 is recyclable). These machines are the traditional supercomputers, and include the Cray 2 (4 CPUs), IBM ES/9000 (8 CPUs), and Convex C2xx (4 CPUs). The parallel processing in this class often serves to increase the throughput by working on different jobs, although when exceptional performance is needed, the software is there to have all processors work on the same job. These latter types of decisions, as well as the control of the processors, are usually made by the CPU *scheduler*. The scheduler tries to keep all processors busy, but if the work load is low, it will let them all work on one job.

2. **8–256 medium power processors, shared memory.** Machines in this group include the Alliant FX (28 CPUs), the BBN TC2000 Butterfly (256 CPUs), and the Sequent Balance (30 CPUs). These machines are challenging to program and come with some sophisticated software packages to assist code migration and development. They are not yet considered general purpose machines and will probably grow in number as some of the general purpose machines of the previous group move up in multiplicity.

3. **100's–1000 and more medium power processors, individual memory.** Machines in this class include the Hypercube, NCUBE (512-8194 CPUs), the Intel iPSC/2 (128 CPUs), and the Thinking Machines CM-5 with 16,000 processors. Because communication often limits the speedup in these machines, some have developed intricate interconnection schemes. Most new machines are of this class. The individual processors are often versions of general purpose CPUs found in workstations such as the SPARC nodes that comprise the CM-5. These are generally often MIMD machines employing a *message-passing* system.

4. **1000's low power processors, synchronous architecture.** Machines in this class include the Connection Machine CM-2 (4096-65,536 CPUs) and the MasPar (16,384 CPUs). These are SIMD machines and are relatively easy to program thanks to sophisticated SIMD compilers.

It has been argued that medium grain parallel computers are most likely to predominate in the future since this permits an amortization of processor cost. We have specifically discussed earlier in this book the high speed RISC workstations which compute at rates just recently reserved for supercomputers. As these start to be mass produced their price should fall to the point where hundreds or thousands of them will be used as processors. (This also means that the efficient use of cache and pipelines, so important to attain high processing rates on the workstations, will also be important on these parallel machines.) The difficulty in this type of parallelism is that the computation speed of the workstations is already some 100's of times faster than the communication speed. Therefore the *latency* due to communication limits the speedup. The communication bottleneck is handled by completing more of the computation at each node before having it communicate with another node; this implies a coarse grain system, distributed memory, and the optimal use of cache and pipelines at each node.

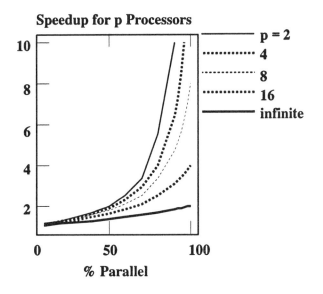

Figure 14.1: Speedup as a function of number of processors and percent parallel code.

14.3 Parallel Performance Equations

Although everyone working in a cafeteria line appears to be working hard and fast, the ketchup dispenser has an onion partially blocking its output and this slows the whole line down. This is an example of the slowest step in a complex process determining the overall rate. An analogous situation holds for parallel processing where the onion is often issuing the instructions (approximately one every 6 cycles). Since the computation cannot proceed without instructions, this one slow step may eliminate the advantage of multitasking over vector processing. We see this effect with the parallel version of Amdahl's law. Let

$$p \quad = \quad \text{number of processors} \tag{14.1}$$
$$T_1 \quad = \quad \text{1-processor time, } T_p = p\text{-processor time} \tag{14.2}$$

The theoretical limit for the speedup S_p attainable with concurrent processing is then

$$S_p = \frac{T_1}{T_p} \quad \rightarrow p \tag{14.3}$$

This limit is never met for a number of reasons: some of the program inevitably is serial, data and memory conflicts occur, communication and synchronization of the processors takes time, and it is rare to attain perfectly even load balance among all the processors. For the moment we will ignore these complications and concentrate on how the *serial* part of the code affects the total speedup, Figure 14.1. We define f to be the fraction of the program to be run on multiple processors,

$$f = p \frac{T_p}{T_1} \tag{14.4}$$

Table 14.1: Speedup S_p for p processors with $f\%$ of Parallel Code.

$f(\%)$	$p = 1$	$p = 2$	$p = 4$	$p = 8$	$p = 16$	$p = 32$	$p = 64$	$p = \infty$
20	1.00	1.11	1.18	1.21	1.23	1.24	1.25	1.25
60	1.00	1.43	1.82	2.11	2.29	2.39	2.44	2.50
94	1.00	1.89	3.39	5.63	8.42	11.19	13.39	16.67
100	1.00	2.00	4.00	8.00	16.00	32.00	64.00	∞

The time T_p spent on the p parallel processors is then related to T_s, the serial time, by

$$T_p = f\,\frac{T_1}{p}, \quad T_s = (1 - f)T_1 \tag{14.5}$$

Accordingly, the speedup S_p as a function of f and the number of processors is

$$S_p = \frac{T_1}{T_s + T_p} = \frac{1}{1 - f + f/p} \tag{14.6}$$

The theoretical speedups are given in Table 14.1 and Figure 14.1. Clearly the speedup will not be great unless most of the code is run in parallel. We see that even an infinite number of processors give a speedup of only 2 when half the code is parallelized or a speedup of only 2.5 if 60% of the code is parallelized.

Efficiency and Scaling

The preceding performance equations indicate the need for approximately 90% parallel code before concurrent processing really pays off. We emphasize this effect by normalizing the speedup by the number of processors to obtain the *efficiency* η. The fraction f in terms of η is then:

$$\eta \equiv \frac{S_p}{p} \Rightarrow f = 1 - \frac{1/\eta - 1}{p - 1} \tag{14.7}$$

We see from the right-hand side of (14.7) and Table 14.2, that as the number of processors p increases, the fraction of parallel code f decreases, and accordingly the efficiency η decreases. This reflects the physical fact that as a code keeps getting divided into smaller and smaller pieces, eventually some processors must wait. In practice this breakdown in scaling may not be as bad as it seems because it would normally be only the bigger and bigger problems that get placed on more and more processors (this is accounted for in parallel benchmarking).

Communication Overhead

Let us now assume that our code is all parallel so that the efficiency is 100% and the speedup is

$$S_p = \frac{T_1}{T_p} = p \tag{14.8}$$

Table 14.2: Efficiency η for p processors with $f\%$ Parallel Code.

$f(\%)$	$p = 1$	$p = 4$	$p = 64$
20	1.00	0.30	0.02
60	1.00	0.46	0.04
94	1.00	0.85	0.21
100	1.00	1.00	1.00

That is, we are assuming it took no time for the processors to communicate. In the presence of *communication time* or *latency* T_c, the speedup is decreased to approximately

$$S_p = \frac{T_1}{T_1/p + T_c} < p \tag{14.9}$$

We see in this case that in order to obtain a speedup unaffected by communication latency, we need:

$$\frac{T_1}{p} \gg T_c \;\;\Rightarrow p \ll \frac{T_1}{T_c} \tag{14.10}$$

This means that as you divide the problem up into smaller and smaller pieces in order to run on more and more processors, at some point the communication time T_c must slow down the computation. For example, if

$$T_1 \;\approx\; (10\,\text{Mflops})^{-1} = 10^{-7}\,\text{s} \tag{14.11}$$

$$T_c \;\approx\; 10\mu s = 10^{-5}s \tag{14.12}$$

Communication times are a factor of 100 *too high*, so p is not even equal to 1, and we are limited to coarse grain systems.[4] Adding more processors does not speed up the results but instead increases the time they have to wait around.

14.4 Multitasking Programming

It only makes sense to run the most numerically intensive codes on parallel machines, and these tend to be very large programs assembled over a number of years or decades. It should come as no surprise, then, that the programming languages for the parallel machines are primarily Fortran with explicit parallel extensions (Fortran 90) and, to a lesser extent, the C language. While the language may be familiar, parallel programming becomes more demanding as the number of processors increases, and it may be best to rewrite a code written for one CPU rather than to try convert it to parallel. Indeed, the development of algorithms and programs best suited to massively parallel architecture is a current area of research. We concentrate, instead, on parallel processing for machines with a small number of processors.

---

[4]A. Williams in Greenwell et al. (1992).

Parallelization Strategy

The key to parallel programming is to identify where your program will benefit from parallel execution. To do that, the programmer must understand the program's data structures at a level similar to that of vector processing, must know how to synchronize the results generated by different processors, and must assign tasks to the different processors of approximately equivalent numerical intensity (*balance the load*).

In one approach, the programmer breaks off pieces of the code into *parallel subroutines* which are independent enough to run simultaneously on separate processors. These can be loops, subroutines or whole sections of code. It is the programmer's responsibility to ensure that the breakup is valid and equivalent to the original program. For example, if the most intensive part of a program is the evaluation of a large Hamiltonian matrix whose elements are independent of each other, then one processor can evaluate the top half of the matrix while another processor simultaneously evaluates the bottom half (a process which may require you to modify your serial algorithm). This type of partitioning is called *macrotasking, high level, global* or *coarse grain parallelism* and, by breaking the program up into big pieces, it sometimes requires more memory than is available.

Alternatively, in *microtasking* or *fine grain parallelism*, the programmer avoids partitioning the code and instead marks off *processes* or *threads* at the loop and statement levels to run concurrently on multiple processors (real or virtual). The compiler then automatically generates parallel code that should be computationally equivalent to that of the serial program (if it's not, then the compiler's at fault). Fine grain parallelism usually does not require several copies of a big program. It requires only a slight increase in memory and minor program modification. In some ways, microtasking and the associated *AUTOTASKING* are similar to the vectorization we studied previously. While both macro- and microtasking are possible on the IBM ES/9000 and Cray 2, Y-MP, and X-MP, it is probably easier to start by examining microtasking.

Multitask Organization

A typical organization of a program for multitasking is given in the flow chart below. The operating system organizes the work into units called *tasks*, and the tasks then assign work to each processor. There is a main task to control the overall execution as well as subtasks that run parts of the program (called *parallel subroutines* or *subtasks*) independently of each other. These parallel subroutines can be distinctive subprograms or multiple copies of the same subprogram. The main task program does its own computations as well as actually calling and scheduling the parallel subroutines (the taskmaster can even do its processing while waiting for the parallel subroutines to be completed).

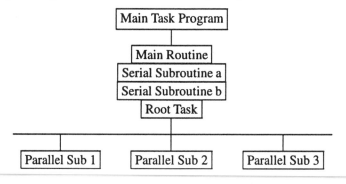

Since the objective of multiprocessing is to improve turn-around time, the programmer helps meet this objective by keeping all the processors busy all the time and by avoiding storage conflicts from different parallel subprograms. You divide your program into sub-tasks of approximately equal numerical intensity which will run simultaneously on different processors. The rule of thumb here is to make the task with the largest granularity (work load) dominant by forcing it to execute first and to keep all the processors busy by having the number of tasks be an integer multiple of the number of processors.

While the vector processors will often work on the innermost loop of your program, the parallel subroutines should be of broad scope—which usually means the outermost loop. For example, vectorizing an outer vector of length 3 would not produce much, if any, speedup. But if many floating point operations are needed to calculate the value of this vector in each dimension, then this may be a good choice for three-way parallel.

To avoid storage conflicts, design your program so that parallel subtasks use data that are independent of the data in the main task and in other parallel tasks. This means that these data should not be modified *or even examined* by different tasks simultaneously. In organizing these multiple tasks, some concern about *overhead costs* is appropriate. These costs tend to be high for fine-grain programming and to vary for different scheduling commands. For example, on the Cray 1:

COMMAND (name)	OVERHEAD COST (in cycles)
TSKSTART (first call)	15,000
TSKSTART (latter calls)	30–400
TSKWAIT	3–15
LOCK	3–15
EVENTS	3–15

14.5   An Example of Multitasking Fortran

Here we give a concrete example of the actual steps involved in designing and writing a parallel Fortran program on a machine with a few processors. This will clarify, we hope, the problem of *scaling* discussed earlier. We examine the simple summation of a series[5]

$$s = \sum_{i=1}^{8} a_i \qquad (14.13)$$

On a serial computer we would simply evaluate

s = a(1)+a(2)+a(3)+a(4)+a(5)+a(6)+a(7)+a(8)	Serial sum.

On a two-processor machine we divide the work up for both processors to handle and then, after calling a synchronization routine to make sure each processor has finished its partial sum, add the partial sums together on one processor:

---

[5]Gentzsch et al. (1988).

CPU 1	CPU 2
s1 = a(1)+a(2)+a(3)+a(4)	s2=a(5)+a(6)+a(7)+a(8)
synchronization	synchronization
s = s1 + s2	—

As you can see, if each addition takes one cycle and we start counting after the processors have been loaded, then it takes eight cycles for the serial sum and five for the parallel sum (including the additions in the partial sums but not the synchronization). If we are given four processors on which to divide up our run, we do get a speedup, but of only one more cycle:

CPU 1	CPU 2	CPU 3	CPU 4
s1=a(1)+a(2)	s2=a(3)+a(4)	s3=a(5)+a(6)	s4=a(7)+a(8)
synchro	synchro	synchro	synchro
s5=s1+s2	s6=s3+s4	—	—
synchro	synchro	synchro	synchro
s=s5+s6	—	—	—

Clearly, as the task gets broken up, there is less work for each processor (a decrease in granularity), an increase in the programming needed to set up the calculation, as well as an increase in the need for processors to wait for other processors to finish their assignments. Of course, ours is a small task so the overhead costs appear high, but it does demonstrate that only bigger problems are worth the effort.

To get some feel for the extensions needed in Fortran to accomplish parallel tasks, we examine the Multi Tasking Facility (MTF) on the IBM ES/9000. This is a set of user-accessible subroutines permitting a program to use all of the processors in a multiple processing environment. Once invoked, the MTF does the initialization as well as the scheduling and synchronization needed by the parallel subroutines.

Initialization of the multitasking facility is accomplished by Fortran calls in addition to the AUTOTASK subparameter on the EXEC statement. You personally create parallel tasks with the ORIGINATE statement (which itself may originate additional tasks).

Scheduling of a parallel subroutine is done by making a call to DSPTCH from within the main task. DSPTCH then assigns the subroutine to a subtask which may be executed in parallel with the main task, with other copies of itself or with other parallel subroutines. Once the tasks are *assigned*, the main task program *schedules* each for execution with another call to DSPTCH using the parallel subroutine's name and a different argument.

Synchronization is done from the main task program by calls to SYNCRO. This causes the main task program to wait for the completion of the subtasks (more details later).

Parallel Partial Sum Program

To see how it is actually done, here is a program which computes the sum in Equation (14.13) on two processors by creating two instances of the parallel subroutine paradd (the Parallel Fortran language extensions are indicated with uppercase letters):

| ```
      SUBROUTINE paradd(nfirst,nlast,k)
c
c subroutine called by tasks k=1 and k=2
c different instances share array A in common
c
      real a(9), sum(2)
      common/add/a,sum
      sum(k) = 0.
      do 4 i = nfirst, nlast
    4 sum(k) = sum(k) + a(i)
      return
      end
``` | **Parallel sub.** |

| ```
      program twosums
      real a(9), sum(2)
      integer*4 idtask(2), ii(2), nfirst(2),
    1 nlast(2)
      common /add/ a, sum
c this programmed for 2 processors
      NPROC =2
c now create nproc task
      do 1 I =1, nproc
    1 ORIGINATE ANY TASK idtask(i)
      do 2 i = 1, 9
    2 a(i) = 1.
       nfirst(1) = 1
       nlast(1) = 4
       nfirst(2) = 5
       nlast(2) = 9
c nproc tasks executed in parallel
      do 3 i = 1, nproc
         ii(i) = i
    3 DISPATCH TASK idtask(i),sharing(add),
     * CALLING paradd(nfirst(i),
     * nlast(i),ii(i))
      WAIT FOR ALL TASKS
c end of parallel section
      s = sum(1) + sum(2)
      stop
      end
``` | From Gentzsch et al. (1988).<br><br><br><br><br>Declared # of processors.<br>Could be >2.<br>Ordinary loop.<br>Originate parallel task. |

You see that the array *ii* is needed to pass the value of *i* because the subroutines may actually be dispatched at different times—in which case the the value of *i* will have changed.

Converting Programs to Multitasking

When converting your program to multitasking with a common shared memory system, we recommend you follow a number of steps:

1. **Start with running code.** Make sure your old scalar code runs on your old machine. Next get it running in scalar mode on the supercomputer. Then vectorize it, being careful to use the vector analysis to detect and clarify the data dependencies. Keep in mind that vectorization and parallelization will hamper each other if you reduce the vector length in your division of the program into tasks.

2. **Analyze the data dependencies** in order to see which parts are computationally independent, that is, which parts will not modify or examine the same data during simultaneous execution. The new parallel subroutines can be different parts of your code or even different iterations of the same Do loop. Confirming that life is not simple, good serial codes often do not make good parallel codes since parallel codes depend on sharing global information. In these cases, you may have to make the algorithms be more local in nature. You will be assisted in conversion by applying standard techniques (to be discussed later).

3. **Define "parallel subroutines"** from parts of your program (possibly collections of subroutines or iterations of Do loops) separate from the main task and coded as a Fortran subroutine. Be aware that there is no guarantee as to the order in which the subroutines are run. Consequently, you should not count on a definite order for data transfer among subroutines. Start by parallelizing only the most time-consuming parts of your program, and make sure the parallel tasks are numerically intensive enough (granular enough) to be worth the overhead associated with their creation, synchronization, and communication.

4. **Insert calls to parallel subroutines in your main program** by replacing those sections of code identified for parallel computation with `Call DSPTCH`. For cases in which the same subroutine runs a number of times with different data, the `Call` may be within a Do loop. While this schedules the subroutine for parallel computation in either case, if the program also requires that some or all previously scheduled tasks have completed execution before the present one, then a `Call SYNCRO` must also be inserted. Synchronization is mandatory because different subroutines will be of different granularity. Between the synchronization points the parallel tasks should be independent and able to proceed in any order.

5. **Data storage and transfer require care.** Data in COMMON storage are available to all subroutines. Any subroutine may change the data there even while another subroutine is using them. If your data transfer is via the arguments in subroutines, then you need to keep in mind that these arguments are not the true value of the data, but rather the location in memory at which to find the data. Consequently, one subroutine may be reading data which are being modified by a different routine. On some systems it is possible to define local or temporary variables which only one subroutine may access (for example, with the SAVE DATA statements on the Crays).

6. **Debug** your parallel code with an open mind because some conventional debugging techniques may no longer work. As an example, parallel subroutines may run in different orders, and therefore identical input may produce different output in different runs. For this reason you may want to add LOCKS and BARRIERS or NOPARALLEL to your program to help isolate errors as you eventually force the system to run with just one processor.

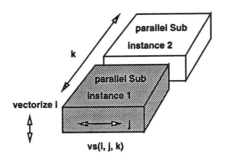

Figure 14.2: Multitasked outer (k) loop, vectorized inner (i) loop.

Sample Changes Made for Multitasking

Implementation of multitasking in a Fortran environment depends on the relation of operations in the different parts of the program. Three common classes for these operations are: unrelated, nested, and split vector.

Unrelated Operations

Unrelated and independent subroutines may be scheduled concurrently if they have different output (they can have the same input data). If these subroutines also have some vector content, then that too must be independent of the other concurrent subroutines.

Nested Operations

These are vector and scalar operations performed in a nested manner and programmed in Fortran as *vector (inner)* and *parallel (outer) Do loops*. If the operations are independent, the inner Do loop acts on a group of vector elements simultaneously using the vector processors, while the outer Do loop is divided into sections each of which is placed on a separate parallel processor. For example, consider this program which defines a three-dimensional array:

```
      Do 10 k =1,  km
         s(1,1,k)  = 0.
         Do 10 j = 2,jm
            Do 10 i = 2,im
               s(i,j,k)  = x(i,j,k)**2
               p(i,j,k)  = s(i-1,j-1,k)
10 Continue
```

Here each iteration of the outermost Do loop over k is independent of the other iterations and so is assigned for multitasking with each k iteration becoming a separate parallel subroutine. (This does mean that, in this example, the parallel subroutines are all the same—an affair called *multiple instances*.) Since each parallel processor also has vector capability, each parallel subroutine is sped up by vectorizing the inner loop over i; we show this symbolically in Figure 14.2.

The parallel version of the code which permits copies of Sub to be scheduled for multiple tasks is:

| ```
Subroutine Sub(klim1,klim2,x,s,p,im,jm)
Real x(50,99,50),p(50,99,50),s(50,99,50)
Do 10 k = klim1, klim2
   s(1,1,k) = 0.
   Do 10 j = 2,jm
      Do 10 i = 2,im
         s(i,j,k) = x(i,j,k)**2
         p(i,j,k) = s(i-1,j-1,k)
10 Continue
``` | Begin parallel.<br><br><br>Begin vector.<br><br><br>End, end. |

The programmer must ensure that the range of k values covered by the Do k (outer) loop is distributed over the processors. As an example, let's assume you have two processors for your use or that the program naturally breaks into two parts of about equal numerical intensity. Accordingly, we call DSPTCH twice in order to schedule the work load over two processors (two instances) and then use the subroutine SYNCHRO to make the program wait until both instances are finished. As explicitly programmed, each processor will then simultaneously take care of $km/2$ sets of $jm - 1$ vectors of length $im - 1$:

| ```
c Execute 2 instances of parallel
c      subroutine Sub
 kh = km/2
 kms = kh+1
 Call DSPTCH('Sub',1,kh,x,s,,p,im,jm)
 Call DSPTCH('Sub',kms,km,x,s,p,im,jm)
c Wait for Subs to complete execution
 Call SYNCHRO
``` | <br><br>Number of sets.<br><br>Schedule CPU1.<br>Schedule CPU2.<br><br>Wait. |

Split Vector Operations

Sometimes a program will contain vectors which are so long that they may be broken up into subvectors with each subvector placed on a different processor–and still permit each processor to use its vector hardware on the subvectors. This combination of vector and parallel processing is known as *split vector operations*. For example:

Long Vector Operation	Split Vector Operation	Split Vector Operation
Do 9 i = 1, 300 9 a(i) = b(i)+c(i)	Do 9 i =1,100 9 a(i) = b(i)+c(i)	Do 9 i = 101, 200 9 a(i) = b(i)+c(i)

Here each of the two Do loops over 9 is vectorized on a separate processor. Even if your program does not explicitly have long vectors, sometimes the speedup gained by

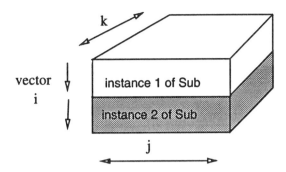

Figure 14.3: One parallel subroutine running in two instances.

constructing long vectors from other elements of your program is worth the effort. To do this, you map (collapse or combine) multidimensional arrays into one dimensional form.[6]

It is also possible to split vector operations up over several processors in the more complicated situation where there are several nested Do loops. For example:

CPU1	CPU2
`Do 1 k = 2, km`	`Do 1 k = 2, km`
`  Do 1 j = 2, jm`	`  Do 1 j = 2, jm`
`    Do 1 i = 1, im/2`	`    Do 1 i = im/2 +1, im`
`1 a(i,j,k) = a(i,j-1,k-1)/2`	`1 a(i,j,k) = a(i,j-1,k-1)/2`

You must take care in this instance (so what's new) if there are constraints imposed by recurrence relations. As seen here and in Figure 14.3, each of these Do loops is run in parallel.

Load Balancing

In order to balance the load among several parallel processors, you may have to form into parallel subroutines parts of your code which at first appear rather disjoint. An interesting numerical effect occurs with breaking up calculations in this way. It is known that round-off errors usually cause the forward and backwards summation of a series, as an example, to differ slightly. Likewise, there will be a slight numerical difference between the sum of partial sums and the single direct sum. If the precise value of the sum is critical in your program, this may cause some difficulty. For example, here two Do loop nests are separated by some scalar code:

---

[6]Because the creation of long vectors may well make your program much harder for the human mind to follow, it may be better not to do the rearrangement until after the program is debugged. Likewise, keep the mechanism or original code within your program so you have the option of going back to the original formulation as needed.

Original Serial Code	
| ```
     sum = 0.
     Do 90 k =1,  n
        Do 90 j = 1,  1
           Do 90 i =1,  n
              a(i,j,k)  = ...
 90 sum = sum + a(i,j,k)
c scalar code begin
     sum = sum/n**3
c scalar code end
     Do 99 k = 1,km
        Do 99 j = 1,  jm
           Do 99 i = 1,  im
 99 a(i,j,k) = ...
``` | Begin 1st nest.<br><br><br><br><br>End 1st nest.<br><br>Scalar code.<br><br>Begin 2nd nest.<br><br><br>End 2nd nest. |

The scalar *sum* is now expanded (the same technique used in vectorization) so that each of the four instances of the parallel subroutine computes a partial sum which then gets summed in the main program:

Rewritten Parallel Main Task	
| ```
     Dimension psum(4)
     nsect = 4
     ...
     Do 5 isect = 1, nsect
        Call DSPTCH('sub', klow(isect),
       * khi(isect),a, x, n, psum(isect))
  5 Continue
     sum = 0
     Do 10 isect = 1, nsect
 10 sum = sum + psum(isect)
     sum = sum/N**3
``` | <br>4 parallel sections.<br>Whatever else needed.<br><br>Schedule 4<br>instances.<br><br>Initialize.<br><br>Sum partial sums.<br>Same as before. |

Rewritten Parallel Subroutine	
| ```
     Subroutine Sub(klim1,klim2,a,x,n,ssum)
c parallel subroutine with 2 nested Do's
     DIMENSION a(n,n,*),  x(n,n,*)
     ssum = 0.
     Do 8 k = klim1, klim2
        Do 8 j =1, n
           Do 8 i = 1, n
              a(i,j,k) = ...
  8 ssum = ssum + a(i,j,k)
     Do 9 k = klim1, klim2
        Do 9 j = 1, n
           Do 9 i=1, n
  9 a(i,j,k) = a(i,j,k) + x(i,j,k)
     RETURN
     END
``` | |
```

14.6 MIMD and Message-Passing Programming

As the number of nodes in a parallel machine grows beyond six or eight, it becomes difficult for the processors to share a common memory. It remains possible to do it, but then any one processor often spends a significant amount of its time waiting for the other processors to complete their memory access before it gains access to the shared memory. An alternative, which has gained wide acceptance for coarse and medium grain systems, is *distributed memory*. In *distributed memory* computers, each processor has its own memory and the processors exchange data among themselves over a high speed network. The data exchanged or *passed* among processors have encoded forward and return addresses and are called *messages*.

For a messages-passing program to be successful, the data must be divided among nodes so that—at least for a while—each node has all the data it needs to run an independent subtask. As a program begins execution, data are sent to all nodes. When all nodes have completed their subtasks, they exchange data again in order for each node to have a complete new set of data to perform the next subtask. This repeated cycle of data exchange followed by processing continues until the full task is completed.

Message-passing MIMD programs are *Single Program Multiple Data*. This means the programmer writes a single program that is executed on all of the nodes. Often a separate host program, which starts the programs on the nodes, reads the input files and organizes the output.

Let's look at a sample problem, a finite-element calculation of a two-dimensional thin film under stress. We partition the problem by assigning a region of the film to each node. At each time step, the function calculated on each node depends on the values calculated on each of its nearest neighbors in the previous time step as well as the values calculated on the node itself. The nodes perform calculations like this:

Pass $f(t)$ to neighbor to the left.	
If first node in row, pass value to last node in row.	Make ring.
Read $f(t)$ from neighbor.	
Pass $f(t)$ to neighbor above.	
If first node in column, pass value to last node in column.	Make ring.
Read $f(t)$ from neighbor.	
Calculate $f(t + dt)$.	Do next step.
Repeat until system reaches a steady state.	

On the receiving node, every write is paired with a read. This groups the columns and rows into *rings*. The procedure is efficient if the nodes are on a communication mesh so that all nodes are passing messages to their neighbors simultaneously. If the nodes are connected by a traditional network, such as an ethernet, not only is the communication intrinsically slow, but worse, since only one message travels along the network at a time, there are $2N$ communication steps rather than just 2 for the mesh.[7]

Although MIMD systems are becoming very popular, a number of standards, such as a standard programming language, have yet to be adopted. Two popular systems are *Express*, a commercial product from ParaSoft Corporation, and *PVM*, a package developed

---

[7]See discussion in Chapter 4, *Computer–Computer Interactions*.

at Oak Ridge National Laboratory. Both hide the messy details of passing messages and synchronization, and are available for use on MIMD machines or for clusters of workstations.

The existence and utility of these packages mean that parallel systems do not have to consist of only a set of dedicated processors. They can also be a number of workstations from various manufactures scattered throughout a whole department. And while the top priority of these workstations will be the work of their owners, when there are no local demands on them, they will automatically switch over to helping someone else's big problem get done concurrently. The integrated sum is tremendous computing power which might otherwise go wasted.

14.7   Examples of Parallel Programs

An Express Fortran Example

The program pert was used as our example in the appendix *Profile and Tuning for Hardware*. Here it is rewritten for a parallel cluster of workstations using Parasoft's Express message passing system.

```
         PROGRAM PERTPAR
         PARAMETER (LDIM=2050)
         DOUBLE PRECISION HAM(LDIM,LDIM),COEF(LDIM),SIGMA(LDIM)
         DOUBLE PRECISION OVLP, ENER, ERR, STEP, OVLPSRT
         DOUBLE PRECISION CPU, CPU1, CPU0
         COMMON /XPRESS/ NOCARE, NORDER, NONODE, IHOST, IALNOD, IALPRC,
        & Isize(10), Istart(10), Iend(10)
         INTEGER NPROC, PROC, NSPLIT(2), TYPE, ADD
         INTEGER ENV(4), GLOBAL(2), LSIZE(2), LSTART(2)

         call KXINIT
         call KXPARA(ENV)
         TYPE = 123
         PROC=ENV(1)
         NPROC=ENV(2)
         GLOBAL(1)=LDIM
         GLOBAL(2)=LDIM
c We split the Hamiltonian by rows so it is a 1D split
         CALL KXGDSP(NPROC, 1, NSPLIT)
         CALL KXGDIN(1, NSPLIT)
         CALL KXGDSI(PROC, GLOBAL, LSIZE, LSTART)
c Now we create a globe list of the domain of each node
         CALL KXCONC(LSIZE(1), 4, Isize, 4, 0, IALNOD,  0, TYPE)
         CALL KXCONC(Nstart, 4, Istart, 4, 0, IALNOD,  0, TYPE)
         CALL KXCONC(N, 4, Iend, 4, 0, IALNOD,  0, TYPE)
         Nstart=LSTART(1) +1
         N=LSIZE(1) + LSTART(1)
*
* SET UP HAMILTONIAN AND STARTING VECTOR
c Hamiltonian is distributed by rows over the nodes.
c COEF is also distributed to all nodes.
         DO 100 I=Nstart,N
            DO 110 J=1,LDIM
               HAM(J,I)=0.3**ABS(J-I)
110         CONTINUE
            HAM(I,I)=I
```

```
100       CONTINUE
          DO 120 J=1,LDIM
             COEF(J)=0.0
120       CONTINUE
          COEF(1)=1.0D0
*
* START ITERATING TOWARDS THE SOLUTION
          CPU0 =MCLOCK ()
          ERR=1.0
          ITER=0
200       IF(ITER.LT.30 .AND. ERR.GT.1.0E-8) THEN
             ITER=ITER+1
*
* COMPUTE ENERGY AND NORM OF CURRENT APPROXIMATION, AND NORMALIZE
             ENER=0.0
             OVLP=0.0
             DO 210 I=Nstart,N
             call kmulti(6)
                OVLP=OVLP+COEF(I)*COEF(I)
                SIGMA(I)=0.0
                DO 211 J=1,LDIM
                   SIGMA(I)=SIGMA(I)+COEF(J)*HAM(J,I)
211          CONTINUE
                ENER=ENER+COEF(I)*SIGMA(I)
210       CONTINUE
4         format(1x, 'Proc:',i2,' ENER:',e8.3,' OVLP:',e8.3)
          call kflush(6)
          CALL KXCOMB(ENER, ADD, 8, 1, IALNOD,  0, TYPE)
          CALL KXCOMB(OVLP, ADD, 8, 1, IALNOD,  0, TYPE)
          ENER=ENER/OVLP
          OVLPSRT=1.0/SQRT(OVLP)
c Here COEF becomes distributed among the nodes
          DO 220 I=Nstart,N
             COEF(I)=COEF(I)*OVLPSRT
             SIGMA(I)=SIGMA(I)*OVLPSRT
220       CONTINUE
*
* COMPUTE UPDATE AND ERROR NORM
          ERR=0.0
          DO 230 I=Nstart,N
             IF(I.EQ.1) GO TO 230
             STEP=(SIGMA(I)-ENER*COEF(I))/(ENER-HAM(I,I))
             COEF(I)=COEF(I)+STEP
             ERR=ERR+STEP**2
230       CONTINUE
c      Distribute COEF on all nodes again
          DO 240 i=1,NPROC
             J = Isize(i) * 8
             call KXBROD(COEF(Istart(i)), i-1, J, IALNOD,  0, TYPE)
240       CONTINUE
          CALL KXCOMB(ERR, ADD, 8, 1, IALNOD,  0, TYPE)
          ERR=SQRT(ERR)
          call ksingl(6)
          WRITE(6,'(1X,I2,F10.5,E14.6,E14.6)') ITER,ENER,ERR,COEF(1)
          call kflush(6)
          GO TO 200
          END IF
          CPU1 =MCLOCK()
          CPU=1.0E-02*(CPU1-CPU0)
          call kmulti(6)
```

```
         WRITE(6,9) proc, CPU
         call kflush(6)
9        format(1x, 'Proc:',i2,' CPU time:',f10.6,' sec.')
         STOP
         END
c
c        ADD function
c
         Integer Function ADD(X,Y,SIZE)
c
         Real*8 X,Y
         Integer Size
         X = X + Y
         ADD = 0
         RETURN
         END
```

A Fortran 90 Example Program

Here is a simple example written in Thinking Machine's CMF Fortran. It solves Laplace's equation on a unit square. The boundary condition is $f = 1$ when $y = 1$, and $f = 2$ elsewhere. The initial condition is $F = 0$ in the interior of the square.

```
         program laplace
         implicit none
         integer N, i, j, k
         logical M
         parameter (N=32)
         double precision F, dF, Max
         dimension F(N,N), dF(N,N), M(N,N)

CMF$   layout F(:SERIAL,:NEWS), dF(:SERIAL,:NEWS)

         Max = 1.0
         k = 0
         F = 0.0
         M = .false.
         M(2:N:N-1,2:N:N-1) = .true.
         F(1:N:N-1,1:N) = 2.0
         F(1:N,1) = 2.0
         F(1:N,N) = 1.0
         dF = F
         do while ( Max > 0.003)

            where (M)
             dF = 0.25*(cshift(F,DIM=1,SHIFT=1) + cshift(F,DIM=1,SHIFT=-1)
     &              + cshift(F,DIM=2,SHIFT=1) + cshift(F,DIM=2,SHIFT=-1))
            end where
            Max = maxval(abs(F - df))
            F = dF
            k = k + 1
            if ( k == 20 ) then
               write(*,*) 'Max: ',Max
               k = 0
            end if
         end do

         end
```

CHAPTER 15

FUTURE SCIENTIFIC COMPUTING

> $\cdots$ *Gutenberg's invention, which so empowered Jefferson and his colleagues in their fight for democracy, seems to pale before the rise of electronic communications and innovations, from telegraph to television, to the microprocessor and the emergence of a new computerized world—an information age. As in the past, original thinking is required to develop a system that will enable our civilization to make the most sensible use of this potent technology.*
>
> —U.S. Senator Al Gore, 1991

Books and magazine articles are always being written on the future of computing and its effects on society. Indeed, university computer science departments and industrial research laboratories appear to have numerous people thinking and publishing seriously on just this topic. Our aim in this chapter is much narrower; namely, predicting the type of computing and computing tools scientists and engineers need now and may soon have for their technical work. Quite likely the technical work on which this book focuses, and the present desktop computing paradigm in which we now exist, will continue within the next paradigm, which is believed to be "networked computing". In the network paradigm, computers surround us all, be we in our offices, homes, or vehicles. Although that new paradigm may be convenient and satisfying, we hope the ubiquitous computer environment does not drown us in busy work such as electronic mail and conferences, thereby stifling rather than encouraging creativity and originality.

Obviously by producing a book of this sort, we (and the publishers) are betting that the future contains Unix and compiled languages like Fortran and C. In a broader view we see computers continuing to change the method by which scientists and engineers work as well as the nature of that work. We suspect the general trends we have noted in this book, such as blending different computers, distributed computing, and network computing, will continue into the future; they represent functioning and useful systems which have evolved from scientists and engineers trying to get their work done in efficient and productive ways.

Recall our discussion of supercomputers. You will remember that we defined them as computers having a good balance among all their parts. Analogously, future scientific computing will probably see a stronger balance and more standardization in all the major components of computing: numerical performance, operating systems, visualization, software, hardware, programming languages, computational algorithms, and computer–computer communications. After all, the point of all these systems is to solve otherwise insoluble problems and to access otherwise inaccessible knowledge. By serving human needs, the strong balance provided by a better integration of these major components should lead to a more productive working environment for our technical and creative needs. If all goes well, this technical computing environment may have such a strong impact as to dissolve into the fabric of science and engineering; that is, we will be using all this computing power without even thinking about it.[1]

15.1   Hardware

We have seen an approximate doubling of computer performance every five years. We have seen machines with the power of yesterday's supercomputer become today's desktop companion. That trend continues so rapidly that our present workstations are nearly on par with the scalar computers of the supercomputing centers; they are already more powerful than the machines used by entire universities just a few short years ago.

The present day RISC workstations with their very fast microprocessing chips, extensive pipelining, and highly optimizing compilers designed for their own specific central processing chip have given us this desktop performance. In the future we expect desktop vector and parallel workstations to be commonplace (refer to Chapters 12–14). Clearly vector processing is not a big jump in technology since it has been in existence for nearly two decades, and has worked well for many scientific and engineering problems. Having a vector processor on our desktops makes sense. A consequence of the doubling in performance of parallel computers within approximately a one-year period is that there is no question that future computing will be much more, but not necessarily universally, parallel.[2] However, as discussed in Chapter 14, the particular flavor of parallelism which will dominate (if any) is not clear. In any case, the system programming will be more complicated if a data flow or asynchronous architecture system is adopted; with processing dictated by the availability of data from various processors (and possibly over a network) rather than all processing marching to the system clock, there is less coordination and more worries for the programmer.

A specific vision of parallel computing in the near future is a system of multiple layers of computers, with some layers having differing degrees and styles of parallelism. The user will then assemble the best combination or plan of attack depending on the problem needing to be solved and the resources available. For example, if the problem is nearly solvable in reasonable time with the desktop facilities available or just needs more cases to be run, then the scientist needs only farm the problem out to a self-regulating network of workstations to use some of the unused cycles on them. At the other extreme, if the problem requires a thousandfold increase in computing power even to get just one case done, then the scientist may find it worth the programming and bureaucratic troubles of getting time, reprogramming, and running on a massively parallel machine to attain the requisite trillions of operations per second. The ease with which all this will be done depends on the training of personnel, intelligent and flexible software (to avoid reprogramming becoming a research project), and system compatibility and ability to scale (to permit easy transfers).

---

[1] Weiser (1991).

[2] Special purpose parallel computers such as those for image and sound recognition and processing will continue to overwhelm the capabilities of more general machines programmed in a portable language.

15.2 Systems and Software

One of the big selling points in computer applications designed for business needs is the ability of large companies such as IBM and DEC to provide the entire bundle of hardware pieces, software tools, systems, and personnel which are designed to work well together and to meet the actual needs of business. Unfortunately while the authors have yet to find such golden bundles to meet their scientific and engineering needs, Unix, as described in this book, has given us the means to assemble a valuable collection of tools. Fortunately, the trend towards standardization and open architecture is continuing (we wish the Open Software Foundation the best of luck), and a number of standard tools are emerging.

We already can see developing a transparent computing environment in which all users have essentially the same multiple-window interface and tools to use within these windows. This includes Unix as the operating system, Fortran and C as the programming language, X Windows as the windowing environment, TCP/IP, ISO, *telnet*, and *ftp* for communications, Phigs+ as graphic primitive tools (and *PEX* as the combination *Phigs+ + X*), LATEX for document preparation and manuscript communication, postscript printers for hard copies, *vi* and Gnu *Emacs* for editing, *Xgraph* for quick plots, *Gnuplot* and *ACE/gr* for publication plotting, *NCAR Graphics* and *NCSA XImage* for color visualization and data analysis, *Mathematica, Maple, Reduce*, and similar programs for symbolic manipulation, and numerical spreadsheet programs for data manipulation and processing.

15.3 Programming

The future should continue to see the development, dissemination, and support of a good number of standard scientific and engineering codes which form a backbone for computational science. This is both a great time saver as well as recognition of the valuable work done by our predecessors. However, we hope the future contains better systems for training and rewarding the personnel who design and run these codes. It harms the progress of science and leads to unreliable engineering to have different groups obtain significantly different results and conclusions after performing what should be the same calculations (or, worse yet, after running the same code).

Chapter 4 on *Computer–Computer Interactions* indicated that as more and more data become available to us, and manipulating those data become part of our work, object-oriented programming with its ease of handling visual objects will become more essential. Further, the software may be able to produce finished drawings and appropriate mathematical equations from our sketches, or from our limited data or even from our vocal descriptions. Continuing a good thing, just as the Unix *talk* utility already permits two users to communicate simultaneously over a network, with *groupware* we should be able to have a bunch of collaborators work on some 3D (or more) models simultaneously, even though they may be all over the world and talking in different languages at the same time.

In line with the recognition of the value in using, maintaining, and extending existing programs, the future should see codes which can be used more easily by others than just their developers. This means a continued emphasis on structuring, documentation, and publication as well as following the techniques of structured and *object-oriented programming*. Presumably new codes should be written in an object-oriented language, be it $C++$, a Fortran extension, or a blend of both.

The effort to institutionalize computational science and its associated scientific programming as a discipline is not simple. Much of computational science is interdisciplinary in nature: a fusion of computer science, mathematics, and specific disciplines such as physics, molecular biology, or chemistry. Unfortunately our academic institutions are not interdisciplinary in nature and so changes come slowly. *It has been said that the only comparable thing to changing a university's curriculum is moving a cemetery.*

In terms of specific trends in future programming, there will by necessity be developments to improve algorithms for RISC, vector, and parallel architectures as well as reformulation of the equations of science and engineering to make them more compatible with solutions by computers. A big part of this improvement is needed in the tools for code development and debugging. As the problems solved get more realistic and complicated, so will the codes, and then their debugging will become even more of a grand challenge. Further, since the future will see computer simulations used more and more as laboratory replacements, the need for more reliable numerical predictions will increase. Possibly we will see *expert systems* applied to program development, algorithm optimization, and the debugging and interpretation of results from complex technical programs. To check results requires codes which both run efficiently, so others can afford to check, as well as codes which are portable so others can run the programs.

15.4   Visualization

Although we have just barely touched on the subject of visualization in this book, we expect visualization to continue to grow in importance in the future. On the one hand, since it's the interactions with humans which ultimately make computers useful, and since a large fraction of the human nervous system is dedicated to visual processing, visual output is inevitably the most effective way for a computer to interact with humans. On the other hand, the technologies needed to make this interaction work—fast computers, high resolution color displays, video and laser recording, and fast mass storage—continue to be improved and to get less expensive. Future displays probably will be more interactive, will be integrated with large databases and servers, and will incorporate video technology. And as indicated previously, the standardization of tools, such as *X Windows, Unix,* and *Graphigs + PEX,* is the glue holding these advances together.

Two-dimensional visualizations and three-dimensional perspective renderings will continue to grow in importance. Yet as the amount and complexity of information and data grow, so, too, will the sophistication of the techniques we need to examine them. For example, with more widespread computing power we should all have available a *virtual reality* in which data and output can be examined in three- (or more) dimensional space using our hands, eyes, and feet to help manipulate the information. While the trend for the general population may be ubiquitous computing which does not separate the user from the world outside, the technical reality for a scientist or engineer may well be the virtual one inside a cell, inside a proton, or sitting on the wing of a supersonic jet.

15.5   Networking

If you recall the table in *Introduction,* Chapter 1, it indicated that the four decades from the 1960s to the 1990s have witnessed four paradigms of computing: batch, timesharing, desktop, and networking. The near future promises to bring tremendous advances in networked computing. This includes connecting various machines together into a hypercomputer as well as having universal and exceedingly fast access to a geographically far-removed computer. For instance, while presently the NSFNET in the United States has achieved data transmission rates of approximately 45 megabits/second, the broadband integrated services digital networks now being planned will transmit approximately 150 megabits/second. The National Research and Education Network in the United States will be fiber optics, and when available in the latter 1990s, should achieve 1000 megabits/second.[3]

It is easy to foresee that these high speed networks can change the way we shop and the way we communicate with each other, but there must be appropriate advances in application technology before more than a small fraction of the information from the information age will be useful to scientists and engineers. There already is, for example, the equivalent of warehouses full of information being collected by scientific satellites. And most of it is not being studied. In the future we need to have application software that is easy to use, and easy to use over a network, that has the artificial intelligence to search through warehouses full of data for just the information or effect which interest us. While it seems impossible for a computer to develop the intuition and originality of a human assistant, a machine could be excellent at recognizing repetitive patterns and at keeping a diary of what has transpired and what your plans are for the future. We may well need supercomputers to do this, but we do need to be able to get the work done.

In terms of the practical details presented in the network paradigm for computing (the last column of the table in Chapter 1), the information base may be in the form of an ultra large hypermedia net. The appropriate programming will be more objected oriented than word or number oriented, with advances in technology permitting script, voice, sketch, or formula input. Since the network will be rather universal, computing can be done most anywhere, with groups of people located anywhere within the span of the network working together. Of course, the previous computer paradigms will not necessarily die out, so we can still get our calculations and modeling done within the previous paradigms of this book.

My meadow lies green,
And my corn is unshorn,
My barn is to build,
And my babe is unborn.

—Child, No 210

---

[3]Dertouzos (1991), Gore (1991), Tesler (1991).

SAMPLE DOT FILES

A.1 Sample .cshrc (csh)

```
#
# .cshrc    -- sourced by the C-shell each time it runs
#
# don't allow '>' to overwrite files
set noclobber
# Only run following if interactive shell, not a shell script
#
if ({$}?prompt) then
    set prompt="$HOST\% "
#   use file completion
    set filec
#   save last 50 commands
    set history=50
    set savehist=50
#   notify when new mail comes in
    if ( {$}?MAIL ) then
        set mail = (0 /usr/spool/mail/your_name)
    endif

    alias ll ls -lC
    alias ls ls -F
    alias l ls -Fx
#   try this under AIX
    alias tree 'li -R -Obcd'
    alias j jobs -l
    alias h history
    alias hh 'history |less'
    alias mv mv -i
    alias cp cp -i
    alias rm    '/bin/rm -i'
    alias   cd 'cd !*;echo " ";pwd;echo " ";ls'
    alias   cd..    'cd ..'
    alias   print   'pr -l63 -n -f !* | lp'
#   use for fortran print outs
    alias   prtf    'pr -e3 -l66 -w80 -o4 -f !* | lp'
```

A.2   Sample .login (csh)

```
#
# .login    -- Commands executed by csh only when logging in
#
# Your PATH maybe already set for you.
# To create your own you must know the location of all of the
# executable directories on your system.
# set path (/bin /usr/bin /etc /usr/ucb /usr/bin/X11)
#
# Add to PATH by adding our bin and curent directories to front of path
# the set path = (. $home/bin \$path)

# Handy definition
setenv  HOST `hostname`
# don't let control-d logout
set ignoreeof

# This will prompt you for a terminal type
# If the system does not know it
set noglob
set term = (`tset -m ansi:ansi -m :?ansi -r -S -Q`)
if ( $status == 0 ) then
    setenv TERM "$term"
endif
unset term noglob
# This is the way to determine what port you are on in csh.
set tty = `tty`
switch ( $tty:t )
    case console:
    # start up X
    xinit 2> /dev/null
    # or
    # startx 2> /dev/null
    exit
        breaksw
    case hft/*:
        # Under AIX this is the console
        breaksw
    case tty[1-9]?:
        # Under SCO this would be the name of the console
        breaksw
    case ttyp[1-9:
        # a remote login or xterm
        breaksw
endsw
```

A.3   Sample .logout (csh)

```
#
# .logout -- this is run when you logoff
#
# clear the screen
clear
#end with wisecrack
/usr/games/fortune -wa
```

A.4 Sample .kshrc (sh, ksh)

```
# .kshrc    -- Commands executed by the Korn shell at startup
#
# Only interactive shells run .kshrc, stty commands good here.
# This makes intr be \^{}c so System V acts like BSD stty intr '^{}c'
# Or this would make BSD act like SysV    stty intr '\^{}?'

# Set environmental variables#
# Set the command line editor to be vi like.
export VISUAL="vi"

# Now we set our aliases
# All the ls stuff
alias l='/bin/ls -CF'
alias ll='/bin/ls -l'
alias ls='/bin/ls -CF'
alias lt='/bin/ls -CFt'
alias dir='ls -lF'
# change ps behavior
alias ps='/bin/ps -af'
alias pse='/bin/ps -eaf'
#  -i makes commands ask before over writing existing files
alias cp='cp -i'
alias mv='mv -i'
alias rm='rm -i'
alias cd..='cd ..'
alias who='who -u'
alias his=history
alias open='chmod go r'
alias shut='chmod go-r'
# Here make aliases so can use BSD style printing commands
alias lpq='lpstat -o'
alias lpr='cancel'
```

A.5 Sample .profile (sh, ksh)

```
#
# .profile    -- Commands executed by a login using ksh or sh
#
# Your PATH maybe already set for you.
# To create your own you must know the location of all of the
# executable directories on your system.
# PATH=/bin:/usr/bin:/etc:/usr/ucb:/usr/bin/X11
# Here we add to the PATH by adding our bin directory and
# the current directory to the front of the path
# Footnote about path
PATH=.:$HOME/bin:\$PATH
export PATH

# Set the environmental variable LOGNAME
    LOGNAME=$(logname)
    export LOGNAME
# This is handy variable to have
    HOST=$(hostname)
    export HOST

# Set the MAIL environmental variable so shell inform us of new mail
```

```
MAIL=/usr/spool/mail/$LOGNAME
export MAIL
# If there is a .kshrc then use it. It may be .envfile or .kshenv,
# the name is determined here so call it what you want.
# The complicated expression says only read .kshrc if
# the shell is interactive, not a shell script.
FILE=$HOME/.kshrc
ENV='$\{FILE[(\_\$-=0)+(\_=1)-\_\$\{-\%\%*i*\}]\}'
export ENV

# Set file  permissions default umask. Makes new files readable by
# everyone, writable only by the owner.
umask 022

# For systems with tset this line will check if your terminal type
# is xterm. If not it will prompt you to enter a terminal type.
eval `tset -m xterm:xterm -m $TERM:?\$\{TERM:-xterm\} -r -s -Q`

#Don't let \^{}d logout
set -o ignoreeof

# Set a prompt with the hostname in it.
case $LOGNAME in
    root)    PS1="$(HOST)\# " ;;
    *)       PS1="$(HOST)\$ " ;;
esac
export PS1

# This is a nice way to determine what port you are on and start X
# from console. The tty command returns your port name. Match with
# name of your console port. We strip off  "/dev/" with sed.
tty=$(tty | sed 's;/dev/;;')
case $tty in
    console )
        # start up X
         xinit 2> /dev/null
        # or
        # startx 2> /dev/null
        exit
        ;;
    hft/*)
        # Under AIX this is the console
        ;;
    tty[1-9]? )
        # Under SCO this would be the name of the console
        ;;
    ttyp[1-9] )
        # on a remote login or xterm
        ;;
esac
```

A.6   Sample .emacs File (Emacs editor)

```
(setq compile-command "make")
(display-time)
(global-set-key "." 'buffer-menu)
(global-set-key "," 'compile)
(global-set-key "" 'shell)
```

```
(setq mh-progs "/usr/bin/")
(setq mh-lib "/usr/lib/mh")
(setq mh-summary-height 10)
(setq dired-listing-switches "-alt")
(setq list-directory-verbose-switches "-alt")
(setq auto-save-default)
(setq default-major-mode 'latex-mode)
(setq-default case-fold-search nil)
(setq text-mode-hook '(lambda () (auto-fill-mode 1)))
(setq backup-by-copying nil)
(setq backup-by-copying-when-linked t)
;; A protection against Trojan Horses via environment variables
(setq inhibit-local-variables t)
(setq kept-new-versions 3)
(setq kept-old-versions 0)
(setq list-matching-lins-default-context-lines 2)
(setq require-final-newline 1)
(setq version-control t)
(setq mail-archive-file-name "~/Mail/out")
(setq display-time-day-and-date t)
;;Since .emacspfkeys pertains to terminal types, load it from
;;/usr/lib/gnuemacs/lisp/term/{term name} (load-file "~/.emacspfkeys")
(setq shell-pushd-regexp "pu")
(setq shell-popd-regexp "po")
;; Following line locates for emacs local functions for load-file
(setq load-path (list "/usr/local/lib/emacs/lisp"))
(put 'narrow-to-page 'disabled nil)
```

A.7 Sample .xinitrc (X windows)

```
#!/bin/sh
#
# Executed when you start X; can add clients.
# Prior to X11R5, .Xdefaults used, now .Xresources (either OK).
if [ -f $HOME/.Xdefaults ]; then
    xrdb -merge $HOME/.Xdefaults
fi
if [ -f $HOME/.Xresources ]; then
    xrdb -merge $HOME/.Xresources
fi
# Set the background color
if [ -f /usr/bin/X11/xsetroot ]; then
xsetroot -solid steelblue
fi
# Everybody needs to know what time it is
if [ -f /usr/bin/X11/xclock ]; then
xclock -geometry 80x80 &
fi
# Tone down the bell
xset b 5 500 200
# Speed up the mouse
xset m 4 2
# The window manager
mwm  &
# Add your clients here
# If we exit from this xterm X will close.
xterm -T Exit_Here
exit
```

A.8   Sample .Xdefaults for mwm (X windows)

```
!
xterm*Font: -adobe-courier-bold-r-normal--12-*
xterm*background: White
xterm*vt100.geometry: 80x45+0+0
xterm*foreground:    Black
xterm.titleBar: true
xterm.titleFont: Rom14
xterm*cursorColor:   Red
xterm*fullCursor:    true
xterm*scrollBar:     true
xterm*saveLines:     1000
xterm*loginShell:    true
xterm*fontMenu*font1*Label: Unreadable
xterm*VT100*font1:          nil2
! You may also want to try:
! xterm*VT100*font1:          -adobe-courier-bold-r-normal--8-*
xterm*fontMenu*font2*Label: Small
xterm*VT100*font2:          -adobe-courier-bold-r-normal--12-*
xterm*fontMenu*font3*Label: Medium
xterm*VT100*font3:          -adobe-courier-bold-r-normal--14-*
xterm*fontMenu*font4*Label: Large
xterm*VT100*font4:          -adobe-courier-bold-r-normal--18-*
! The X11R5 xterm has 6 fonts lines but X11R4 has only 4.
! xterm*fontMenu*font5*Label: Large
! xterm*VT100*font5:          9x15
! xterm*fontMenu*font6*Label: Huge
! xterm*VT100*font6:          10x20
! Useful if your on a Sun
!xterm.ttyModes:  dec

emacs*geometry: 80x50+10+100
emacs*background: white
emacs*useBitmap: true
emacs*foreground: Black
emacs*cursorColor: Red
emacs*pointerColor: Cyan
emacs*font:  -adobe-courier-bold-r-normal--14-*
emacs*title:

xclock*mode: analog
xclock*update: 1
xclock*foreground: grey20
xclock*background: grey87
xclock*geometry: 120x120-10+80


! The editor option only works in the later version of Xmh
xmh.EditorCommand: emacs %s
!or if you use vi: xmh.EditorCommand: /usr/local/X11R5/bin/xterm -e vi %s
xmh*printcommand: lpr $*
xmh*font: -adobe-courier-bold-r-normal--14-*
xmh*foreground: Black
xmh*background:   #d0d0d0
xmh.Geometry:          750x875+200+75
xmh.TocGeometry:         750x500
xmh.CompGeometry: 580x475+250+50

Xmh*viewButtons.append.Translations:#override\n\
   <Btn1Down>,<Btn1Up>: XmhAppendView()unset()\n
```

```
Xmh*CommandButtonCount:     8
Xmh*commandBox.button1.label: inc
Xmh*commandBox.button1.translations: #override\
    <Btn1Down>,<Btn1Up>: XmhIncorporateNewMail()
Xmh*commandBox.button2.label: compose
Xmh*commandBox.button2.translations: #override\
    <Btn1Down>,<Btn1Up>: XmhComposeMessage()
Xmh*commandBox.button3.label: next
Xmh*commandBox.button3.translations: #override\
    <Btn1Down>,<Btn1Up>: XmhViewNextMessage()
Xmh*commandBox.button4.label: prev
Xmh*commandBox.button4.translations: #override\
    <Btn1Down>,<Btn1Up>: XmhViewPreviousMessage()
Xmh*commandBox.button5.label: commit
Xmh*commandBox.button5.translations: #override\
    <Btn1Down>,<Btn1Up>: XmhCommitChanges()
Xmh*commandBox.button6.label: delete
Xmh*commandBox.button6.translations: #override\
    <Btn1Down>,<Btn1Up>: XmhMarkDelete()
Xmh*commandBox.button7.label: move
Xmh*commandBox.button7.translations: #override\
    <Btn1Down>,<Btn1Up>: XmhMarkMove()
Xmh*commandBox.button8.label: reply to viewed msg
Xmh*commandBox.button8.translations: #override\
    <Btn1Down>,<Btn1Up>: XmhViewReply()
xbiff*geometry:        50x50-10+90

! You will need to put your userid here
xbiff*file:    /usr/spool/mail/fink
xbiff*foreground: grey60
xbiff*background: white
xbiff*update:     10
xbiff*title:
xrn.geometry: =750x880+0+0
! start up as icon
xrn*iconic: true
xrn*editorCommand:   xterm -fn '-adobe-courier-bold-r-normal--12-*' -e vi %s
! Useful to cut down on the noise
xrn.leaveHeaders: newsgroups,subject,from,date
xrn*background:       gray35
xrn*foreground:       black
xrn*font:     -adobe-courier-bold-r-normal--12-*
xrn*border:          LightGray
xrn*Text*background:   #c0c0df
xrn*Text*foreground:   black
xrn*Text*font:    -adobe-courier-bold-r-normal--14-*
! Focus policy
!Mwm*keyboardFocusPolicy: explicit
! Or
Mwm*keyboardFocusPolicy: pointer
! And select auto raise True or False
Mwm*focusAutoRaise:      True
!Mwm*focusAutoRaise:      False
!Mwm*buttonBindings:DefaultButtonBindings
!Mwm*fontList: -adobe-courier-bold-r-normal--14-*
!Mwm*menu*font:          -adobe-courier-bold-r-normal--14-*
Mwm*useIconBox:     False
Mwm*xclock*clientDecoration: border
Mwm*xbiff*clientDecoration: border
Mwm*iconImageMinimum:    50x50
```

A.9   Sample .mailrc (mail)

```
# Preset variables,      same as available with online set command
set ask
set askcc #asks if CC: wanted
set autoinclude
set autosign=~/.signature #use signature in .signature file
set cwd=/u/rubin/Mail
set mbox=/u/rubin/Mail/mbox     #where to put mail
set print_cmd=lp             #local print command
set prompt="Message #%m: "     #prompt
set record=Mail/.outmail      #for copies of outgoing mail
set visual=/usr/bin/vi        #your choice of editor
#                                          aliases
alias group       <ghe> <tim> <lu> <rubin> <victor> # number of people
alias loren       <doof@milton.u.washington.edu>    # full address
```

A.10   Sample .signature (mail)

```
--------------------------------------------------------------------
   Professor I. M. Tweed                        iam@ivy.tower.edu
   Department of Physics                          212-555-1152
   Cascadia State College                    fax: 503-555-1212
--------------------------------------------------------------------
```

APPENDIX B

PROFILING AND TUNING FOR HARDWARE

In this appendix we go about profiling and tuning a Fortran program named *pert*. The tuning differs from the usual optimization in that we tune the program for the vector and superscalar architectures found on specific computers. For all machines and tunings, the program returns the same answers but runs for different lengths of time. The run times, or more precisely speedups, are presented in Table B.1. To set the scale properly, we normalize the times *relative* to the CPU time consumed by the base program on each machine. The base program has no optimizations or modifications. While we will discuss these results in turn, we recommend that you get the different versions of *pert* running on your computer (the source codes are on the floppy) and compare your results with those in Table B.1.

Note, that while *pert* is shorter than any program normally worth the effort of tuning, it does solve an eigenvalue problem and so has some realism. Nevertheless, a large program is made up of small subroutines and requires the same profiling to reveal the "hot spots" in the code where the CPU spends much of its time.

Table B.1: Effect of Tuning on Platforms with Different Architectures.

	base	pert	pert1	pert2	pert3	pert4
	(no opt)	(-O)	(Sqrt)	(Vector)	(index)	(unroll)
Sun SparcStation I	1	1.7	1.8	2.1	2.5	2.8
IBM RS/6000	1	8.0	8.1	0.9	8.1	10.5
IBM 3090 vector $ldim=2^n$	1	2.3	2.3	18.0	5.1 14.4	5.4 16.8
Ardent Stellar $ldim=2^n$	1	3.8	3.9	2.7	3.5 3.8	4.0 4.3

B.1   Nonoptimized Code Listing: pert

```
c       pert: a Fortran example program.
c
        Program pert
        Parameter (ldim = 2050)
        Implicit Double Precision (a-h,o-z)
        Dimension ham(ldim,ldim),coef(ldim),sigma(ldim)
c
c       set up Hamiltonian and starting vector
        Do 10 i = 1,ldim
           Do 11 j = 1,ldim
              If( Abs(j-i) .gt. 10) Then
                 ham(j,i) = 0.0
              Else
                 ham(j,i) = 0.3**Abs(j-i)
              EndIf
  11       Continue
           ham(i,i) = i
           coef(i) = 0.0
  10    Continue
        coef(1) = 1.0
c
c       start iterating towards the solution
        err = 1.0
           iter = 0
  20    If (iter .lt.15 .and. err. gt. 1.0e-6) Then
              iter = iter + 1
c
c       compute current energy \& norm, \& normalize
        ener = 0.0
        ovlp = 0.0
        Do 21   i = 1,ldim
           ovlp = ovlp+coef(i)*coef(i)
           sigma(i) = 0.0
           Do 30   j = 1,ldim
              sigma(i) = sigma(i) + coef(j)*ham(j,i)
  30       Continue
           ener = ener + coef(i)*sigma(i)
  21    Continue
        ener = ener/ovlp
        Do 22   I = 1,ldim
           coef(i) = coef(i)/Sqrt(ovlp)
           sigma(i) = sigma(i)/Sqrt(ovlp)
  22    Continue
c compute update and error norm
c
        err = 0.0
        Do 23 i = 1,ldim
           If (i.eq.1) GoTo 23
           step = (sigma(i) - ener*coef(i))/(ener-ham(i,i))
           coef(i) = coef(i) + step
           err = err + step**2
  23    Continue
        err = Sqrt(err)
        Write(*,'(1x,i2,7f10.5)') iter,ener,err,coef(1)
        GoTo 20
        EndIf
        Stop
        End
```

B.2 The Nontuned Program: pert

The *pert* program computes ener, the lowest eigenvalue, and coef, the corresponding eigenvector of a predominantly diagonal Hamiltonian matrix ham. As indicated in Table B.1, we use this program with no optimization as the standard on each platform to set the unit of speed for that platform. The eigenvector c has elements coef(i) and norm ovlp, the latter used in an intermediate normalization of the eigenvector. The diagonalization algorithm is an iterative perturbation expansion which is effectively a modification of the power or Davidson method:

$$H\vec{c} = E\vec{c} \tag{B.1}$$

$$c(k) \simeq c(k) + \frac{H - E}{E - H(k,k)}c(k) \tag{B.2}$$

$$E \simeq \frac{\langle \vec{c}|H|\vec{c}\rangle}{\langle \vec{c}|\vec{c}\rangle} \tag{B.3}$$

B.3 Profiling

Here we use the profiler **gprof** on *pert* on a Sun SPARC Station to determine the time spent in different parts of the program, as well as the number of times all functions and subroutines are called:

```
%   f77 -O -pg -o pert1 pert1.f        Compile with profiling option.
%   pert1                              Run and produce gmon.out
%   gprof pert | more                  Do profile.
```

In spite of *pert* being rather simple for a profile, the analysis is interesting, for example, here's what it tells us about the function sqrt:

				called/total	parents	
index	%time self	descendants		called+self	name	index
				called/total	children	
	0.02	0.00	23111/23111	_MAIN_ [3]	
[11]	0.1 0.02	0.00	23111	_sqrt [11]	

This says the sqrt function is called some 23,111 times by *pert*—which may be somewhat of a concern since sqrt is usually a rather slow function. Yet we also see that only 10% of the code's time is spend evaluating that function, so it's by no means a hot spot for this code. Nevertheless, we invoke our pedagogical license and tune for the sqrt function as if it were worthy of the effort.

B.4   With Basic Optimization: pert1

```
c       pert1: a Fortran example program, basic optimization.
c
      Program pert1
      PARAMETER (ldim = 2050)
      Implicit Double Precision (a-h,o-z)
      Dimension ham(ldim,ldim),coef(ldim),sigma(ldim)
c
c       set up Hamiltonian and starting vector
c
      Do 10 i = 1,ldim
         Do 11 j = 1,ldim
            If( Abs(j-i) .gt. 10) Then
               ham(j,i) = 0.0
            Else
               ham(j,i) = 0.3**Abs(j-i)
            EndIf
  11     Continue
         ham(i,i) = i
         coef(i) = 0.0
  10  Continue
      coef(1) = 1.0
c
c       start iterating towards the solution
      err = 1.0
      iter = 0
  20    if(iter.lt.15 .and. err.gt.1.0e-6) Then
           iter = iter+1
c       compute energy, norm of current approximation,\&  normalize
c
      ener = 0.0
      ovlp = 0.0
      Do 21   i = 1,ldim
         ovlp = ovlp+coef(i)*coef(i)
         sigma(i) = 0.0
         Do 30   j = 1,ldim
            sigma(i) = sigma(i)+coef(j)*ham(j,i)
  30     Continue
         ener = ener+coef(i)*sigma(i)
  21     Continue
      ener = ener/ovlp
      fact  = 1.0/Sqrt(ovlp)
      coef(1)  =   fact*coef(1)
      err  =   0.0
      Do 22   i = 2,ldim
         t          =    fact*coef(i)
         u          =    fact*sigma(i) - ener*t
         step       =    u/(ener - ham(i,i))
         coef(i)    =    t + step
         err        =    err + step*step
  22 Continue
      err = Sqrt(err)
      Write(*,'(1x,i2,7f10.5)') iter,ener,err,coef(1)
      GoTo 20
      EndIf
      Stop
      End
```

Now that we have used **gprof** to look through the listing, we apply some basic optimizations and produce *pert1*. We notice immediately that sqrt(ovlp) is called twice in the main Do loop, which is clearly a waste of time since the overlap ovlp and correspondingly sqrt(ovlp) are constant throughout the loop. Consequently, we speed up the code by calculating sqrt(ovlp) only once in the loop. Next we convert the division by sqrt(ovlp) into a multiplication by 1/Sqrt(ovlp) since most computers multiply faster than divide.

We now notice that fact*coef(i) is unnecessarily repeated in the loop. We substitute a local scalar variable t for it and thereby calculate it only once. This should speed up the code somewhat since the compiler now can store the scalar variable in a register for fast access, whereas before it had to go into ROM to retrieve the array element.

Really, we shouldn't have to do this since an optimizing compiler should recognize repeated expressions within a loop, calculate them only once, and hold the value in a register. We were being conservative. Problems do sometimes arise when the repeated expression is *not* written exactly the same each time:

Exactly repeated expressions.	Will recognize.
H(i) = sin(phi) + alpha*scale + offset E(i) = cos(phi) + alpha*scale + offset	Repeat last 3 variables.
Not exactly repeated expressions.	Won't recognize.
H(i) = sin(phi) + offset + scale*alpha E(i) = cos(phi) + alpha*scale + offset	Repeated, yet mixed.

As discussed in the Chapter 11, you can improve the compiler's ability to recognize repeated expressions and make the code clearer by using parentheses to group expressions.

In our example you may be left wondering why the compiler is smart enough to recognize repetitions of fact*coef(i) but not of sqrt(ovlp). The reason is that sqrt is a function and not just an expression to evaluate; calling a subprogram may have side effects beyond just returning a value, and the compiler knows it does not know those possible side effects. Consequently compilers seldom will move a function outside of a loop even if it is an intrinsic function. There are preprocessors which rewrite source code for you and will move intrinsic functions; unfortunately they may also leave you with a hard-to-read code.

Now that we have done some tuning, we run **gprof** on our revised code pert1. The part of the profile analyzing sqrt() is

```
                              called/total      parents
index %time self descendants called+self  name         index
                              called/total      children
-----------------------------------------------------------
            0.00        0.00      22/22         _MAIN_ [2]
[153]  0.0 0.00        0.00      22            _Sqrt [153]
-----------------------------------------------------------
```

Notice there are now only 22 calls to sqrt where previously there were 23,111, and that the program spends 0.0% doing it (yet it never spent much time there in the first place).

The overall savings would be greater in a realistic case with large matrices or where the tuned code is the inner loop of a large program. The lesson is twofold: writing clean code saves CPU time, but dramatic savings requires you to spend your efforts where the program spends most of its time.

For the next step in tuning we remove the If(i.eq.1) GoTo 23 condition from the loop. Whereas some compilers do permit If statements inside vector loops, If statements do slow the program down ("are not free"). As a general practice we remove all If statements, I/O calls, and user-written subroutine calls from loops to be vectorized.

The final change made was to replace err = err + step**2 by err = err + step*step since multiplication is faster than exponentiation. Once again, while this optimization is handled automatically by some compilers, we also want to ensure that the expression has the form of add + multiply since this form is often handled as one floating point calculation on vector and advanced RISC machines, an important feature to keep in mind.[1] As we see from the *pert1* column in Table B.1, these modifications lead to a relatively small speedup.

B.5   Tuned for Vector Processing: pert2

```
c      pert2: a Fortran example program, vector tuned.
c
       Program pert2
       PARAMETER (ldim = 2050)
       Implicit Double Precision (a-h,o-z)
       Dimension  ham(ldim,ldim),coef(ldim),sigma(ldim),diag(ldim)
c
c    set up Hamiltonian and starting vector
c
       Do 10 i = 1,ldim
          Do 11 j = 1,ldim
             If( Abs(j-i) .gt. 10) Then
                ham(j,i) = 0.0
             Else
                ham(j,i) = 0.3**Abs(j-i)
             EndIf
 11       Continue
       ham(i,i) = i
       coef(i) = 0.0
 10    Continue
       coef(1) = 1.0
c
c    start iterating towards the solution
c
       Do 15 i = 1,ldim
          diag(i) = ham(i,i)
 15    Continue
       err = 1.0
       iter = 0
 20    If (iter.lt.15 .and. err.gt.1.0e-6) Then
             iter = iter+1
c
c    compute energy, norm of current approximation,\&  normalize
c
```

---

[1] The careful reader will notice that the definition $coef(i) = coef(i) + step$ can accordingly be sped up if written as a scalar add + multiply from $coef(i) = t + step$.

```
      ener = 0.0
      ovlp = 0.0
      Do 21   i = 1,ldim
         ovlp = ovlp+coef(i)*coef(i)
         t = 0.0
         Do 30   j = 1,ldim
            t = t + coef(j)*ham(i,j)
30       Continue
         sigma(i) = t
         ener = ener + coef(i)*t
21    Continue
      ener = ener/ovlp
      fact  = 1.0/Sqrt(ovlp)
      coef(1)  =  fact*coef(1)
      err  =  0.0
      Do 22   i = 2,ldim
         t          =    fact*coef(i)
         u          =    fact*sigma(i) - ener*t
         step       =    u/(ener - diag(i))
         coef(i)    =    t + step
         err        =    err + step*step
22 Continue
      err = Sqrt(err)
      Write(*,'(1x,i2,7f10.5)') iter,ener,err,coef(1)
      GoTo 20
      EndIf
      Stop
      End
```

In this version of `pert` we optimize the code for vector processing and for the intermediate memory cache found on the IBM 3090 (ES/9000). The techniques are useful on any vector machine with an associative cache. We are concerned about *cache misses*, that is, retrieving the variables from memory needed in a calculational step but not having all the variables fitting into cache. This slows down processing considerably. We note that the definition of `step` uses only the diagonal values of the matrix `ham`, that is, `ham(i,i)`. Accordingly there is a very large *stride* for accessing the matrix, and to speed up the processing we created an array `diag` to hold the diagonal elements. The data are then stride 1.

We also tried to speed up the code by *strip mining* or *blocking* the major loop for the vectors. Rather than spilt the loop into separate pieces, we simply interchanged the index on the `ham` matrix so that the vector processor may grab a full stride at one time. As we see from Table B.1 under *pert2*, this speeds up the calculation by a factor of 9 on the 3090 but slows it down on almost all other machines!

B.6   Running Vector-Tuned Code on RISC: pert3

As we see from Table B.1, the modifications `pert2` for vector hardware work very well on the IBM 3090 but slow the code down on RISC workstations. To pinpoint the reason for this, we create `pert3`, in which we change the matrix indices back. As we see from the table, this removes most of the speedup attained on the 3090 but also removes most of the slowdown for the other platforms.

```fortran
c       pert3: a Fortran example program, RISC tuned.
c
      Program pert3
      PARAMETER (ldim = 2050)
      Implicit Double Precision (a-h,o-z)
      Dimension ham(ldim,ldim),coef(ldim),sigma(ldim),diag(ldim)
c
c       set up Hamiltonian and starting vector
      Do 10  i = 1,ldim
         Do 10 j = 1,ldim
            If( Abs(j-i) .gt. 10) Then
               ham(j,i) = 0.0
            Else
               ham(j,i) = 0.3**Abs(j-i)
            EndIf
 10   Continue
c
c       start iterating towards the solution
      Do 15 i = 1,ldim
         ham(i,i) = i
         coef(i) = 0.0
         diag(i) = ham(i,i)
 15   Continue
      coef(1) = 1.0
      err = 1.0
      iter = 0
 20   If(iter.lt.15 .and. err.gt.1.0e-6) Then
            iter = iter+1
c      compute energy, norm of current approximation,\&  normalize
c
      ener = 0.0
      ovlp = 0.0
      Do 21  i = 1,ldim
         ovlp = ovlp+coef(i)*coef(i)
         t = 0.0
         Do 30   j = 1,ldim
            t = t + coef(j)*ham(j,i)
 30      Continue
         sigma(i) = t
         ener = ener + coef(i)*t
 21   Continue
      ener = ener/ovlp
      fact  = 1.0/Sqrt(ovlp)
      coef(1)  =  fact*coef(1)
      err  =  0.0
      Do 22  i = 2,ldim
         t          =   fact*coef(i)
         u          =   fact*sigma(i) - ener*t
         step       =   u/(ener - diag(i))
         coef(i)    =   t + step
         err        =   err + step*step
 22 Continue
      err = Sqrt(err)
      Write(*,'(1x,i2,7f10.5)') iter,ener,err,coef(1)
      GoTo 20
      EndIf
      Stop
      End
```

B.7 Tuned for Superscalar: pert4

```
      Program pert4
      PARAMETER (ldim = 2050)
      Implicit Double Precision (a-h,o-z)
      Dimension ham(ldim,ldim),coef(ldim),sigma(ldim),diag(ldim)
c     set up Hamiltonian and starting vector
      Do 10 i = 1,ldim
         Do 10 j = 1,ldim
            If( Abs(j-i) .gt. 10) Then
               ham(j,i) = 0.0
            Else
               ham(j,i) = 0.3**Abs(j-i)
            EndIf
 10   Continue
c     start iterating towards the solution
      Do 15 i = 1,ldim
         ham(i,i) = i
         coef(i)  = 0.0
         diag(i)  = ham(i,i)
 15   Continue
      coef(1) = 1.0
      err = 1.0
      iter = 0
 20   If(iter.lt.15 .and. err.gt.1.0e-6) Then
         iter = iter+1
      ener = 0.0
      ovlp1 = 0.0
      ovlp2 = 0.0
      Do 21   i = 1,ldim-1,2
         ovlp1 = ovlp1+coef(i)*coef(i)
         ovlp2 = ovlp2+coef(i+1)*coef(i+1)
         t1    = 0.0
         t2    = 0.0
         Do 30   j = 1,ldim
            t1 = t1 + coef(j)*ham(j,i)
            t2 = t2 + coef(j)*ham(j,i+1)
 30      Continue
      sigma(i)   = t1
      sigma(i+1) = t2
      ener       = ener + coef(i)*t1 + coef(i)*t2
 21   Continue
      ovlp = ovlp1 + ovlp2
      ener = ener/ovlp
      fact  = 1.0/Sqrt(ovlp)
      coef(1)  = fact*coef(1)
      err  =  0.0
      Do 22   i = 2,ldim
         t           =    fact*coef(i)
         u           =    fact*sigma(i) - ener*t
         step        =    u/(ener - diag(i))
         coef(i)     =    t + step
         err         =    err + step*step
 22   Continue
      err = Sqrt(err)
      Write(*,'(1x,i2,7f10.5)') iter,ener,err,coef(1)
      GoTo 20
      EndIf
      Stop
      End
```

Once again we optimize the program for a particular machine. This time we unroll the Do loops in order to ensure that the superscalar floating point arithmetic unit on the IBM RISC System 6000 is not idle for too long. We are conservative in our changes and only go two levels down in unrolling the loops. Greater unrolling and blocking would produce better results at the expense of less clear code. We see a 25% speedup on the RS/6000 for *pert4*, and a somewhat smaller increase on other machines.

B.8   Discussion

The results presented in Table B.1 show four versions of `pert` compared to the orignal version compiled with no optimizations and no programming assistance to vectorization. In order to remove the effect of the differing speeds of the various machines, the speedups are measured relative to the speed of the nontuned, nonoptimized program on each machine. All of the *pert* versions were compiled with the same options on the respective machines, namely, full compiler optimization and vectorization.

First we notice that compiler optimization helps significantly in all cases (*nontuned versus pert*). The improvement is greatest (≈ 8) on the RS6000 and the least (≈ 2) on the Sun (about the same as on the IBM mainframe 3090). Next, as expected, we notice that the simple improvements to the `sqrt` made in *pert1* produced very little speedup since **gprof** shows that the program spends little time with `sqrt`.

Next we note that *pert2* optimized for the 3090 vector processing produced a factor-of-8 speedup (and that's a factor of 18 over nonoptimized code). However, the program now runs slower on all the workstations except for the Sun. So when we produced *pert3* by removing one of the vector changes, namely, switching the matrix indexes, this version eliminates much of the speedup on the vector 3090, but restored the performance on the workstations. This shows that the improvement in stride provided by using an array to hold diagonal elements of the large matrix was important on the vector 3090 and the Sun (which has a small direct cache).

The *pert3* column of Table B.1 shows the effect of setting the dimensions of the matrix and arrays to an exact power of 2 with the aim of improving the cache flow. This has a dramatic effect on the 3090 (factor of 3) and somewhat improved the Ardent (both machines have cache and vectors). Finally we note that unrolling the loops in *pert4* led to a marked improvement on the RS6000—as we had hoped. It also improved the Sun and the vector machines, particularly for the case when the matrix size was set to a power of 2.

The examples given here demonstrate some techniques for optimizing programs and how to attain increased performance by tuning to a particular machine. Unfortunately, tuning for the architecture on one machine reduces the portability of the code, and we must take care to be able to convert our programs to other architectures as we move them around. For this latter purpose, the Unix tools of Chapter 10 are valuable.

GLOSSARY

address The numerical designation of a location in memory.

algorithm A set of rules for solving a problem independently of the software or hardware.

analog The mapping of numbers to continuous values of some physical observable, for example, speed and a car's speedometer.

architecture The overall design of a computer in terms of its major components: memory, processing, I/O, and communication.

argument A parameter passed from one program part to another or to a command.

arpanet A wide area network originally developed by the U.S. Army and now extended into the internet.

array (matrix) A bunch of numbers stored together which can be referenced by one or more subscripts. Single-indexed arrays represent mathematical vectors, double- and higher- indexed arrays represent tensors. Each number in an array is an **array element**.

bit Contraction of "binary digit"; the digits 0 or 1 used in a binary representation of numbers. Usually 8 bits are combined to form a byte and 32 bits are combined to form a single precision, floating point number.

basic machine language Instructions telling the hardware to do basic operations like store or add binary numbers.

box The electronics making up a computer, as in a "fast box."

boot up Loading the system into memory from disk.

byte 8 bits of storage, the amount needed for a single character.

bus A communication channel (bunch of wires) used for transmitting information quickly among computer parts.

cache   A small, very fast part of memory used as temporary storage between the very fast CPU registers and the fast main memory.

central processing unit (CPU)   The part of a computer which accepts and acts on instructions; where calculations are done and communications controlled. Also used generically for the computer's electronics (not terminals and I/O devices).

chime   Chained vector time. A chime begins each time a resource gets reused in a Do loop.

column-major order   The method used by Fortran to store matrices in which the leftmost subscript varies most rapidly and attains its maximum value before the subscript to the right is incremented.

compiler   A program which translates source code from a high level computer language to machine language or object code.

compiler directive   A nonexecutable statement supplying the compiler with directions for its operation but which does not get translated directly into executable code.

concurrent processing   Same as parallel processing; simultaneous execution of several, related instructions.

cycle time (clock cycle)   The time it takes the central processing unit (CPU) to execute the simplest instruction.

data   Information stored in numerical form; plural of datum.

data dependence   Two statements using or defining identical storage locations.

dependence   A relation among program statements in which the results depend upon the order in which the statements are executed. May prevent vectorization.

digital   Representation of numbers in a discrete form (decimal, octal, or binary) but not in analog form (meter reading).

dimension of array   The maximum value of each subscript of an array. The **logical dimension** is the largest value actually used by the program, the **physical dimension** is the value declared in a DIMENSION statement.

ethernet   A high speed local area network (LAN) composed of specific cable technology and communication protocols.

executable program   A set of instructions which can be loaded into the computer's memory and executed.

executable statement   A statement causing the computer to act, as for example, to add numbers. A data or continue statement is not executable.

environmental variables   Used by the system to pass information to programs and customize their behavior.

indirect addressing   The use of an array element as the subscript (index) for yet a different array. For example, $a(j(i))$.

induction variable (subscript) An integer variable which is changed by a fixed amount as an operation is performed. The index of a Do loop is an example.

floating point The representation of numbers in terms of mantissa and base raised to some power so that the decimal point floats during calculations; scientific notation.

flops Floating point operations per second. Also measured in Megaflops mflops (10^6 flops), Gigaflops gflops (10^9 flops), and Teraflops tflops (10^{12} flops).

Fortran An acronym for **fo**rmula **tran**slation.

gflops Gigaflops, 10^9 floating point operations per second.

instructions Orders to the hardware to do basic things like fetch, store, and add.

instruction stack Group of instructions currently in use; like a window moving down your code as operations are performed.

kernel The inner or central part of a large program or of an operating system which does not get modified (much) when run on different computers.

linker A program which combines a number of programs to form a complete set of instructions which can be *loaded* into the computer's memory and followed by the computer.

loop A set of instructions executed repeatedly as long as some condition is met.

machine language The set of instructions understood by elementary processors.

machine precision The maximum positive number which can be added to the number stored as 1 without changing the number stored as 1.

mainframe A large computer, usually at a central location, which serves many users and is capable of turning out much work.

main program A part of a program which calls subprograms but cannot be called by them.

main storage The fast, electronic memory; physical memory.

massively parallel Simultaneous processing on a very large number of central processing units.

Megaflop (mflop) Millions of floating point operations per second.

mips Millions of instructions per second.

multi-processors Computers with more than one processor.

multi-tasking The system by which several jobs reside in a computer's memory simultaneously. On non parallel computers each jobs receives CPU time in turn.

object program (code) A program in basic machine language produced by compiling a high level language.

operating system   The program that controls the computer and decides when to run applications, process I/O, and shells.

optimizer   A program (or programmer) that modifies a program to make it run more quickly.

parallel (concurrent) processing   Simultaneous and essentially independent processing in different central processing units. If the number of separate multi processors gets very large, it is **massively parallel**.

parallelization   Rewriting an existing program to run on a computer with multiple processing units.

physical memory   Fast, electronic memory of a computer; main memory; physical memory stands in contrast to *virtual memory*.

pipeline (segmented) arithmetic units   Assembly line approach to central processing in which parts of the CPU simultaneously gather, store, and process data.

PostScript   A standard language for sending text and graphics to printers.

program   Set of actions or instructions that a machine is capable of interpreting and executing or the act of creating a program.

RAM   The random access or central memory which can be reached directly.

recurrence   A statement or variable in a loop which uses the value of some variable computed in a previous iteration. May affect vectorization.

registers   Very high speed memory used by the central processing unit.

RISC   Reduced Instruction Set Computer; a CPU design which increases arithmetic speed by decreasing the number of instructions the CPU must follow.

scalar   A data value (number); for example, element a_4 of an array or the value of π.

scalar processing   Calculations in which numbers are processed in sequence. Also, processing units (hardware) which process machine code in sequence. Different from vector and parallel processing.

section size (strip)   The number of elements which can be executed with one command on vector hardware. Breaking up an array into strips is **strip mining**.

segmented arithmetic units   See pipelined arithmetic units.

shell   The command line interpreter; the part of the operating system with which the user interacts.

source code   Program in high level language needing compilation to run.

stride   Number of array elements which gets stepped through as an operation repeats.

subprogram   The part of a program invoked by another program unit.

supercomputer   The class of fastest and most powerful computers available.

superscalar A second generation RISC designed for an optimal balance between compiler and machine instructions.

telnet The protocol suite for the TCP/IP internet network which permits a terminal on one host computer to seem as if directly connected to another computer on the network. Also the name of a terminal emulator program written by NCSA for using PCs on the internet.

Teraflop (tflop) 10^{12} floating point operations per second.

vector A group of N numbers in memory arranged in one-dimensional order.

vectorization Reorganization of a program so the compiler can utilize vector hardware.

vector processing Calculations in which an entire vector of numbers is processed with one operation.

virtual memory Memory which resides on the slow, hard disk and not in the fast electronics.

visualization The production of two and three dimensional pictures or graphs of the numerical results of computations.

workstations A class of computers small enough in size and cost to be used by a small group or an individual in their own work location yet powerful enough for large-scale scientific and engineering applications. Typically with a Unix operating system and good graphics.

word A unit of main storage, usually 1, 2, 4, 6, or 8 bytes.

CONTENTS OF FLOPPY DISKETTE

- File README.TXT (Description of floppy contents and instructions.)

- File get.sh (Script to copy floppy to workstation.)

- Directory area (Sample source files which run.):

  ```
  area.c   area.f
  ```

- Directory c_fort (Sample Fortran–C language calls.):

  ```
  Makefile
  c_fort.c   area_f.f   (Calling Fortran from C.)
  fort_c.f   area_c.c   (Calling C from Fortran.)
  ```

- Directory dotfiles (Sample setup files, dotfiles without the .):

  ```
  Xdefaults   emacs    login     mwmrc    xinitrc    cshrc
  kshrc       logout   profile   mailrc   signature
  ```

- Directory graphics (Data for graphics examples.):

  ```
  2.dat      data.graph   gnu3d.data   kp.points
  3.dat      demo.xg      kp.data      pictures.c
  ImT.dat    exp.data     kp.param     xwindow\
  ```

- Subdirectory xwindow (Producing window dumps from within X.):

  ```
  mkxwd            (Script for creating dump; -help for directions.)
  window.print     (Script to create postscript file of window.)
  xpr.man          (Man pages for xpr (print).)
  xwd.man          (Man pages for xwd (window dump).)
  ```

- Directory matrices (Sample matrix manipulation subroutines.):

  ```
  cmatin.f    (Complex matrix inversion.)
  eigenc.f    (Complex eigenvalue search.)
  ```

- Directory `parallel`:

`pertpar.f`	(An Express message-passing example.)
`laplace.fcm`	(A Connection Machine example.)

- Directory `pert` (Source code for various levels of tuning.):

  `pert.f`   `pert1.f`   `pert2.f`   `pert3.f`   `pert4.f`

- Directory `scripts` (Sample shell scripts.):

Makefile	(Sample makefile.)
ex1.sh	(A first script.)
ex2.sh	(Run a program.)
ex3.sh	(Using the case statement.)
ex4.sh	(Run a program with different inputs.)
ex5.sh	(A simple **dosread**.)
ex6.sh	(Improved **dosread**.)
ex7.sh	(Run a program with different inputs and outputs.)
bell	(Ring the bell.)

- Directory `latex` (LATEXformats used for this book.):

`README.txt`	`local.tex`	`wbk10.sty`	`title.tex`
`wpsfont.sty`	`wbook.sty`	`wtimes.sty`	

REFERENCES

Unix Books

ARTHUR, L. J. (1986), *Unix Shell Programming*, John Wiley & Sons, New York.

BACH, M. J. (1986), *The Design of the Unix Operating System* Prentice-Hall, Englewood Cliffs.

BOLSKY, M. I. AND D. G. KORN (1989), *The Korn Shell*, Prentice-Hall, Englewood Cliffs.

CHRISTIAN, K. C. (1988), *The Unix Operating System*, 2nd Ed., John Wiley & Sons, New York.

CHRISTIAN, K. C. (1988), *Unix Command Reference Guide*, John Wiley & Sons, New York.

HUNTER, H. H. AND K. B. HUNTER (1991), *Unix Systems, Advanced Administration and Management Handbook*, Macmillan, New York.

KERNIGHAN, B. W. AND S. P. MORGAN (1982), The UNIX Operating System: A Model for Software Design, *Science*, **215**, 779.

LEFFLER, S., M. MCKUSICK, M. KARELS, AND J. QUARTERMAN (1989), *The Design and Implementation of the 4.3 BSD Unix Operating System*, Addison-Wesley, Reading.

LOUKIDES, M. (1990), *Unix for Fortran Programmers*, O'Reilly & Associates, Sebastopol.

LOUKIDES, M. (1990), *System Performance Tuning*, O'Reilly & Associates, Sebastopol.

MCGILTON H. AND R. MORGAN (1983), *Introducing the Unix System*, McGraw-Hill, New York.

MORGAN, R. AND H. MCGILTON (1987), *Introducing Unix System V*, McGraw-Hill, New York.

PEEK, J. (1990), *MH & xmh, E-mail for Users & Programmers*, O'Reilly & Associates, Sebastopol.

SOBELL, M. G. (1984), *A Practical Guide to the Unix System*, Benjamin-Cummings, Menlo Park.

SOBELL, M. G. (1985), *A Practical Guide to Unix System V*, Benjamin-Cummings, Menlo Park.

TALBOT, S. (1990), *Managing Projects with Make*, O'Reilly & Associates, Sebastopol.

WAITE, M. ED. (1987), *Unix Papers for Unix Developers and Power Users*, Howard W. Sams, Indianapolis.

Programming and Languages

ANGUS, I., G. FOX, J. KIM, AND D. WALKER (1990), *Solving Problems on Concurrent Processors*, Vols. I & II, Prentice-Hall, Englewood Cliffs.

ANSI (1989), *American National Standard for Information Systems – Programming Language C*, ANSI X3.159–1989.

AT&T (1985), *The C Programmer's Handbook*, Prentice-Hall, Englewood Cliffs.

BAKER, L. (1989), *C Tools for Scientists and Engineers*, McGraw-Hill, New York.

BELL, R. (1990), *IBM RISC System/6000 Performance Tuning for Numerically Intensive FORTRAN and C Programs*, IBM Document No. GG24-3611.

DEC (1991), *DEC Fortran^{TM} for ULTRIX^{TM} RISC Systems, User Manual*, AA-PE1CA--TE, Digital Equipment Corporation, Maynard.

HP (1989), *HP FORTRAN 77/HP-UX Programmer's Guide*, Second Edition, E0889.

IBM (1988), *IBM Engineering and Scientific Subroutine Library, Guide and Reference*, Release 3, SC23-0184-3, Armonk.

IBM (1990), *IBM VS FORTRAN Version 2, Programming Guide for CMS and MVS*, Release 5, SC26-4222-5, Armonk.

IBM (1991), *IBM AIX XL FORTRAN User's Guide*, SC09-1268, Armonk.

IBM (1991), *IBM AIX XL FORTRAN Reference Manual*, SC09-1267, Armonk.

KELLEY, A. AND I. POHL (1989), *A Book on C*, 2nd Ed., Benjamin-Cummings, Redwood City.

KERNIGHAN, B. W. AND D. M. RITCHIE (1978), *The C Programming Language*, Prentice-Hall, Englewood Cliffs.

MOSES, G. A. (1988), *Engineering Applications Software Development Using Fortran 77*, John Wiley & Sons, New York.

NBSIR (1984), *Guide to Available Mathematical Software*, NBSIR 84-2824, U.S. Department of Commerce, National Bureau of Standards.

NESC (1984), Abstract 820, Slatec 2.0, 9/84.

NYHOFF, L. AND S. LEESTMA (1988), *FORTRAN 77 for Engineers and Scientists*, 2nd Ed., MacMillan, New York.

PINSON L. J. AND R. S. WIENER (1991), *Objective-C Object-Oriented Programming Techniques*, Addison-Wesley, Reading.

POLLACK, S. V. (1982), *Structured Fortran 77 Programming*, Boyd & Fraser, San Francisco.

SMITH, D. N. (1991), *Concepts of Object-Oriented Programming*, McGraw-Hill, New York.

STALLMAN, R. (1991), *GNU Emacs Manual*, 6th Ed., Emacs Version 18, Richard M. Stallman.

STROUTSTRUP, B. (1986), *The C++ Programming Language*, Addison-Wesley, Reading.

SUN (1990), *Sun Floating Point Programmers Guide*, Sun Microsystems Inc., Mountain View.

SUN (1990), *Sun Programming Utilities and Libraries*, Sun Microsystems Inc., Mountain View.

WANG, H. H. (1986), *Introduction to Vectorization Techniques on the IBM 3090 Vector Facility*, IBM Palo Alto Scientific Center, G320-3489.

WEXELBLAT, R. L. (1981), *History of Programming Languages*, Academic Press, New York.

Communications

DERTOUZOS, M. L. (1991), Communications, Computers and Networks, *Scientific American* **265**, 62.

DONGARRA, J. J. AND E. GROSSE (1987), Distribution of Mathematical Software Via Electronic Mail, *Comm. ACM*, **30**, 403.

FREY, D. AND R. ADAMS (1989), *!%@:: A Directory of Electronic Mail Addressing and Networks*, O'Reilly & Associates, Sebastopol.

HANCOCK, B. (1988), *Designing and Implementing Ethernet Networks*, QED Information Sciences, Wellesley.

TESLER, L. G. (1991), Networked Computing in the 1990s, *Scientific American* **265**, 86.

Supercomputing

CRAY (1990), *Cray Y-MP Computer Systems Functional Description Manual* HR-04001-0C, Cray Research, Mendota Heights.

DOERR, H. AND F. VERDIER (1989), *Introduction to Vectorization*, Cornell National Supercomputing Facility, Ithaca.

DUBRULLE, A. A., R. G. SCARBOROUGH, AND H.G. KOLSKY (1985), *How to Write Good Vectorizable Fortran*, IBM Palo Alto Scientific Center, G320-3478.

FICHERA, R. M (1990), An Introduction to Superchips, Parallel Processors and Supercomputing, *Supercomputing Review*, San Diego.

FLYNN, M. J. (1966), Very High-Speed Computing Systems, *Proc. IEEE* **54**.

GENTZSH W., F. SZELÉNYI, AND V. ZECCA (1988), *Use of Parallel FORTRAN for some Engineering Problems on the IBM 3090 VF Multiprocessor*, IBM European Center for Scientific and Engineering Computing, Rome (Italy).

GENTZSCH, W. (1989), *Proceedings, Supercomputing '89*, Fourth International Conference on Supercomputing, Santa Clara, L. P. Kartashev and S. I. Kartashev, Eds, Intl. Supercomputing Institute, St. Petersburg.

HENNESSY, J. AND D. PATTERSON (1990), *Computer Architecture, A Quantitative Approach*, Morgan Kaufmann, San Mateo.

IBM (1986), *Designing and Writing FORTRAN Programs for Vector and Parallel Processing, IBM SC23-03337-00*, 1st Ed., Armonk.

LEVESQUE, J. M. AND J. W. WILLIAMSON (1989), *A Guidebook to Fortran on Supercomputers*, Academic Press, San Diego.

ROSSI, A. (1988), *REREP Course*, IBM T.J. Watson Research Center, Yorktown Heights.

STONE, H. (1990), *High-Performance Computer Architecture*, Addison-Wesley, Reading.

The X Windows Systems

IBM (1988), *IBM AIX X-Windows Programmer's Reference*, SC23-2118-1.

IBM (1988), *IBM AIX X-Windows User's Guide*, SBOF-1868-0.

QUERCIA, V. AND T. O'REILLY (1990), *X Window System User's Guide*, Vol. 3, O'Reilly & Associates, Sebastopol.

Numerical Analysis

ACTON, F. S. (1970), *Numerical Methods That Work*, Harper & Row, New York.

DONGARRA, J. J. AND S. C. EISENSTAT (1984), Squeezing the Most Out of an Algorithm in Cray Fortran, *ACM Trans. Mathematical Software*, 219.

FRÖBERG, C-E (1985), *Numerical Mathematics, Theory and Computer Applications*, Benjamin-Cummings, Menlo Park.

HILDEBRAND, F. B. (1956), *Introduction to Numerical Analysis*, McGraw-Hill, New York.

PRESS, W.H., B. P. FLANNERY, S. A. TEUKOLSKY, AND W. T. VETTERING (1986), *Numerical Recipes, the Art of Scientific Computing*, Cambridge University Press, Cambridge.

THOMPSON, W. J. (1992), *Computing for Scientists and Engineers: A Workbook for Analysis, Numerics and Applications*, John Wiley & Sons, New York.

WILKINSON, J. H. (1965), *The Algebraic Eigenvalue Problem*, Clarendon, Oxford.

WILKINSON, J. H. AND C. REINSCH (1971), *Handbook for Automatic Computation*, Vol. II, *Linear Algebar*, Springer-Verlag, New York.

Miscellaneous

ABRAMS, M. H., ED. (1962), *The Norton Anthology of English Literature*, W.W. Norton & Co, New York.

BRANDENBURG, J. (1991), The Land They Knew, *National Geographic* **180**, 35.

BRANDON, M. AND K. K. CURTIS (1983), *A National Computing Environment for Academic Research*, NSF Working Group on Computers for Research, NSF 83-84.

CHRISTENSEN, S. M., ED. (1984), *Supermicrocomputers*, Proceedings of Workshop on the Applications of Supermicrocomputer Workstations in Physics and Astronomy, NSF, Chapel Hill.

CHURCHLAND, P. M., AND P. S. CHURCHLAND (1990), Could a Machine Think?, *Scientific American* **262**, 32.

DEWDNEY, A. K. (1986), Computer Recreations, *Scientific American* **255**, 14.

DOHERTY, W. J. AND W. G. POPE (1986), Computing As A Tool For Human Augmentation, *IBM Systems Journal* **25**, 306.

GORE, A. (1991), Infrastructure for the Global Village, *Scientific American* **265**, 150.

GREENWELL, D. L., R. K. KALIA, P. VASHISTA, AND H. W. MYRON EDS. (1992), *Workshop Report on Undergraduate and Graduate Education in Computational Sciences*, Louisiana State University.

JANSEN, H. (1989), *Computational Physics Notes*, Oregon State University.

LANDAU, R. H. (1992), *Computational Physics Notes*, Oregon State University.

LAX, P. D. (1982), Chairman, *Report of the Panel on Large Scale Computing in Science and Engineering*, National Science Foundation 83-13.

POTOK, C. (1975), *In the Beginning*, Ballantine, Fawcett Crest, New York.

PRESS, W. H. (1981), *Prospectus for Computational Physics*, Report by the Subcommittee on Computational Facilities for Theoretical Research.

RHEINGOLD, E. (1981), *Tools for Thought*, Academic Press, New York.

SEARLE, J. R. (1990), Is the Brain's Mind a Computer Program? *Scientific American* **262**, 26.

SPENCER, H, W. E. HOUGHTON, AND H. BARROWS, (1964), *British Literature*, D.C. Heath & Co., Boston.

THOMPSON, W. J. (1984), *Computing in Applied Science*, John Wiley & Sons, New York.

WEISER, M. (1991), The Computer for the 21st Century, *Scientific American* **265**, 94.

WRIGHT, K. (1990), The Road to the Global Village, *Scientific American* .

INDEX